The History of the Birds of Britain

The forty-eight colour plates in this book were originally commissioned from David Reid-Henry by the publishers H.F. and G. Witherby Ltd for a guide to the birds of Britain. For various reasons that guide never came to fruition.

In this book, with the cooperation of Witherbys, the publishers Collins have used Reid-Henry's superb paintings, with the addition of much of his sketchbook material, mainly pencil drawings (often unfinished), to illustrate Dr Colin Harrison's informative text, which traces the background to Britain's bird populations and assesses their present and future status.

The author explains the way in which each species fits into today's environment, and how the problems and opportunities it faces shape its behaviour, life style and choice of habitat.

THE HISTORY

OF

THE BIRDS

OF

BRITAIN

Colour plates and drawings by

DAVID REID-HENRY

Text by

COLIN HARRISON

COLLINS

8 GRAFTON STREET, LONDON

in association with

H. F. AND G. WITHERBY

First published in Great Britain in 1988 by
William Collins Sons & Co. Ltd
London · Glasgow · Sydney · Auckland · Toronto · Johannesburg

Colour illustrations copyright © 1988 H.F. & G. Witherby Ltd
Black-and-white illustrations copyright © 1988 Louise Reid-Henry
Text copyright © 1988 Colin J.O. Harrison

ISBN 0 00 219794 4

Colour Reproduction by Bright Arts (HK) Ltd, Hong Kong
Typeset by Servis Filmsetting Ltd, Manchester
Made and printed in Singapore by CS Graphics Pte Ltd

Contents

Foreword

David Reid-Henry was perhaps the greatest delineator of birds of prey who ever lived. Ask any falconer. Certainly he will be ranked with Thorburn, Lodge, Fuertes, Sutton, and Tunnicliffe as one of the twentieth century's foremost painters of bird life. In the great tradition of British bird painting, we can now place him in perspective as the successor to George Lodge in the depiction of birds of prey and game birds.

In fact, as a young man he was much influenced by George Lodge. During the war, while David was at Sandhurst, he learned that Lodge lived nearby in Camberley. Later, David wrote me with deep feeling about his relationship with Lodge.

'I rang him up and, reminding him of his having met my father twenty years previously, asked if I could come and see him. He received me with the most genial hospitality and from that time on all my spare time was spent at his house. He became one of the greatest friends I shall ever hope to know. When I first went into his studio, it was entering the gates of Heaven. Never had I seen such glorious paintings of birds on the grand style. There were huge canvases of gyr falcons, golden eagles and everything in which I could take a delight. He was a brilliant taxidermist and the studio was full of the most wonderful mounts of gyrs, peregrines, goshawks and all types of sporting birds.

' You may not know his work well but you must not judge him by the plates in Bannerman's Birds of the British Isles. Many people do, and it is not generally known that nearly all those plates were done when he was well past eighty and some as lately as his ninety-second year when he only had one eye! He was in fact painting on the afternoon before his death.

' I lived beneath the shadow of George Lodge from the time I first met him until he died. He worshipped old Joseph Wolf and used to say that there would never be a greater draughtsman of birds than Wolf. But on the other hand, Wolf certainly did not know raptorial birds as well as Lodge, who for over sixty-five years had known all the great falconers of the Old Hawking Club and had been with The Field when some of the greatest falconry of all time was practised. He was a mine of knowledge and very ready to pass on what he knew. But he never had any pupils. In fact all I learnt from him came as a result of our conversations. He would never demonstrate anything. However, I promise you I learned plenty out of those talks with him!'

After the war, Reid-Henry began a distinguished career as an ornithological illustrator. One of the first books he illustrated was Cave and MacDonald's Birds of the Sudan. Those illustrations remain among the finest ever done of African birds. He went on to illustrate many books and contributed several plates to the journal Avicultural Magazine.

David never copied photos nor took short cuts; he drew from life, often spending months in the field to become acquainted with habitat as well as bird. In order to study birds of prey, he became a falconer. Amazingly, he caught and trained to the glove a huge African Crowned Eagle which he kept for more than 10 years. His painting technique was time consuming and precise – he did not dash on quick washes in watercolour. His skill as an artist was a direct result of the profound knowledge of birds gleaned from first-hand experience and painstaking technique in painting. Yet he was criticised by some for taking too much time to complete a plate. His feelings on this, his Christian philosophy, and his increasing frustration with illustrating bird books are best put in his own words:

'To me there is only pleasure in drawing from life! Anything short of that is a bore. That is why I so hate illustrating books on birds I have never seen. I know they are bound to be wrong no matter how hard I may try to get them right. This is terribly frustrating. I feel my integrity is at stake, and that hits me where it hurts most. You see, when I decided to make bird painting my career, I determined that to be in faith with my Christian profession I would never do a shoddy job. With this in mind I have frequently destroyed work that I could easily sell because if it was not good enough for my judgement, it was certainly no good for my Lord.

'Much that I did in earlier days I can now fault, but when I did it, it was done to the very best of my ability; and so I have never had to be ashamed of anything in my work, although in the light of more experience I could now improve on that early work.'

Finally, the desire to create art, rather than book illustration, was overpowering. David threw off the chains and vowed to do no more books, but to paint the pictures he saw in his mind's eye. He wrote to me in 1967,

'Believe me, there have been many occasions when I have been flat broke. I have spent a month on a book-plate, and got only £20 for it! I have now decided to paint no more illustrations, but only things I want to do. Since making up my mind about this, I have begun to make something of a living where I never could before.

'You have no idea of the relief, the sheer joyous exuberance I felt when I made the decision to have done with deadlines and commissions. It was as though I had suddenly come out of prison with a whole new world of opportunity before me. Well I am now 47 and I am certainly going to use my new freedom.'

God granted him only ten years to use this creative freedom. In the time left to him, he moved to Rhodesia and used this enormous creative energy to produce truly great works of art devoted mainly to the bird and animal life of Rhodesia and Southern Africa. Many of these will stand for all time as among the finest pieces of wildlife art ever done.

ALBERT EARL GILBERT
President, Society of Animal Artists (USA), March 1984

Preface

In writing this book I have tried to put the birds of Britain into their long-term context. All too often we look at them as though they were a mainly twentieth-century invention, with a few honoured by a passing mention in our written history. In fact, although we only see them within our own brief span of time, they are an assemblage of species that in slightly varying combinations has existed within a continuity stretching back at least a couple of million years.

For the great majority of species it is not yet possible to produce a continuous history. People who study our birds at present tend to see them as an avifauna with a known past that probably extends back no further than the latter part of the last century, and in some instances for less time than that. At the other extreme I have been trying to piece together some of their very early history based on buried bones; and that tends to tail away around the Roman period, or in many instances at the end of the last Ice Age. We are left with a gap in between, covering most of the last two thousand years, and only scattered scraps of information to fill it. This may be ideal for authors of historical romances, but it is highly frustrating for the inquisitive biologist.

There is still a need for these two millennia of the historic period to be looked at more closely from the birds' point of view – a need to assess the importance of the stages and changes in environment, climate, flora, hunting, farming, fishing, building and settlements, and more particularly in human attitudes. Even when this is achieved we will probably find that we only know about those areas where humans were most active, and can only guess what was happening in the extensive regions that were beyond the margins of regular human activity.

For the moment we are left snatching at trifles, trying to guess what species our early ancestors thought that they were looking at, and wishing that Keats had rhapsodised a little less about his Nightingale and had been a little more specific about the Tomtit that he shot on Hampstead Heath. Nor does it help, when trying to discover what happened to a species in Britain over the last ten thousand years, to find that no-one noticed its existence until about a hundred and fifty years ago.

In preparing the text I have been acutely aware of the fact that a work of this kind can only be undertaken by reference to many sources and research in many areas. Anyone who writes books based on factual information is aware that, regardless of the size of his own contribution, the new level of knowledge is gained to a considerable degree by climbing on the shoulders of other, earlier workers; and that the next pair of boots are likely to be planted on him in turn.

Where possible I have mentioned when species are thought to have first occurred in the British Isles. This can be useful, if only to correct the slightly misleading impression given when some species is welcomed as occurring or nesting for the first time with us; it may in fact have been moving in and out of the British Isles as climate dictated over many millennia. In doing so I have been helped considerably by the prior work done on the subject by James Fisher, some of which was published in the *Shell Bird Book*. Unfortunately he did not have time to do more than assemble published data, and when I seem to have ignored his references to Ice Age occurrences, it may mean that certain specimens have proved on re-examination to belong to different species.

At the other end of the period, for recent decades, one must increasingly turn to the work of the British Trust for Ornithology. For many species population fluctuations appear hardly to have existed prior to the BTO's Common Bird censuses; and the Atlases of Breeding and Wintering Birds are likely to become the latter-day Domesday Books of British ornithology.

In addition to difficulties raised by past time, problems can also be caused by place. Names and boundaries change over long periods. Our last changes of county boundaries, in addition to producing new smallish urban entities, also amalgamated some of the larger units of the past where human populations were small. In some instances I have retained such names in the text where they seemed to give a more precise picture of distributional change, hoping that it will not make the reader's task more difficult.

I have included a brief bibliography of some publications which are either useful sources or seem to have something of interest to say on the subject. There is not space to list them all. I hope that I will not have aggrieved people because of the omission of many, often more specific but less readily referable, sources that may also have played a part in this final work. I can only conclude by thanking all those whose past work has helped and inspired me, and by hoping that others will, in turn, find my work of use.

COLIN HARRISON

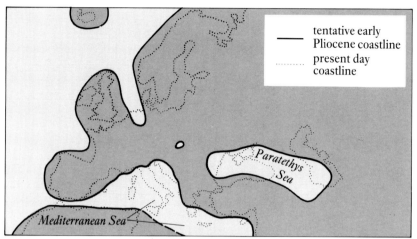

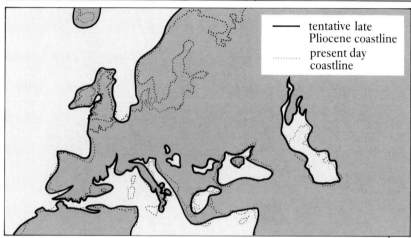

Britain and Europe
in the Pliocene period

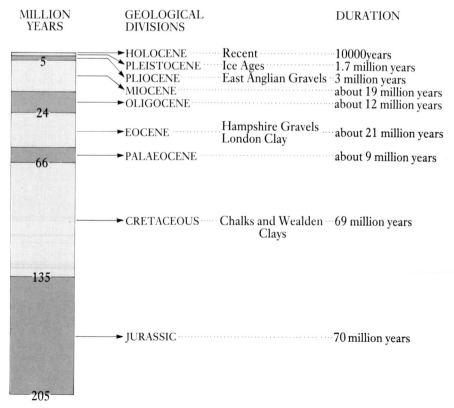

The past geological periods
during which birds were
present

MILLION YEARS	GEOLOGICAL DIVISIONS		DURATION
	HOLOCENE	Recent	10000years
5	PLEISTOCENE	Ice Ages	1.7 million years
	PLIOCENE	East Anglian Gravels	3 million years
	MIOCENE		about 19 million years
24	OLIGOCENE		about 12 million years
	EOCENE	Hampshire Gravels London Clay	about 21 million years
66	PALAEOCENE		about 9 million years
	CRETACEOUS	Chalks and Wealden Clays	69 million years
135			
	JURASSIC		70 million years
205			

8

The History of British Birds

The Earliest History

Birds in Britain have a very long history, but one whose evidence is so sparse and fragmented over time that it does not form a coherent picture. The earlier period is so far separated in time and conditions that it tells us little about our present-day birds.

The Jurassic period deposits of Britain have, so far, yielded no evidence of birds; although the earliest-known and much-debated species of the class Aves, *Archaeopteryx*, occurs during this period in the swamps of Germany. In the long Cretaceous period that followed from about 136 to 65 million years ago, and which laid down the wealden sands and clays and the great chalk layer that gave us our downlands, only a few bones have been found.

An early Cretaceous bone from the Weald establishes the occurrence of a small bird, *Wyleyia valdensis*, possibly a sea-bird of a very early group long extinct. Another two species from a single genus also occurred in the early Cretaceous although their remains were found reworked into the late Cretaceous deposits of Cambridgeshire. These belong to the genus *Enaliornis* and were toothed, diver-like sea-birds adapted for underwater swimming and related to the later and better-known *Hesperornis* of the Late Cretaceous of North America.

It is from the next stage, the Tertiary period, that fossils begin to provide valuable information about British birds. At the beginning of this period, in the Eocene and earliest Oligocene from about 55 to 35 million years ago, when the clays, sands and gravels of the London and Hampshire Basins were being laid down in shallow seas off the south-east shores of an earlier Britain, bird bones became more plentiful, relatively speaking. They provide evidence of a large, complex avifauna, lacking the large adaptive radiation of the small song-birds that provides about half the species in our present faunas, but otherwise showing a range of forms comparable with that occurring at the present day, and with a few others besides.

However, the continuity of evolutionary evidence is broken, as far as Britain is concerned, by a long period from the earliest Oligocene to the late Pliocene for which any evidence has long been eroded away. This gap lasts from about 36 to about 2 million years ago, and for us the modern British avifauna begins after this, in the last two million years or so.

The Pliocene Epoch covers the period from about 5 million to 1.6 million years BP (before present). Britain was then the western extremity of a continuous Eurasian landmass. It was mountainous in the north and west, the high ground of northern Scotland joining that of northern Ireland, while the present Irish Sea must have been broad lowlands with rivers draining southwards along it. Similarly the Channel between southern England and France was a valley area drained westwards by the Seine and southern English rivers. There may have been higher land bridges at the eastern end, in the wealden and downland regions. On the eastern side a large marine inlet existed around the position of the present North Sea, but the Baltic Sea did not exist.

For most of the time the Pliocene was a warmer period than at present, with less variation in annual climate and temperature. However, in the latter part it became cooler, with periodic still colder fluctuations of climate and an increasing ice-cap at the pole. From the material deposited near the coast of the proto-North Sea in the south, on what are now the coastal part of East Anglia and the Belgium lowlands, we find some scanty evidence of birds that were present in the early Pliocene. It indicates the presence in the proto-North Sea of large auks, differing from but possibly related to the Razorbill and Great Auk; and a tropic-bird resembling in some respects the Red-billed Tropic-bird *Phaethon aethereus* that now comes no further north in the Atlantic region than the Cape Verde Islands and the Caribbean.

The only British bird recorded from the Pliocene at present is also a sea-bird, the now-extinct North Atlantic Albatross *Diomedea anglica* found in the Coralline Crag deposits. It was a moderate-sized albatross, and from its bones the nearest living relative would appear to be the Short-tailed Albatross *D. albatrus* of the North Pacific. It is possible that both were derived from a parental stock that moved northwards from the typical albatross habitats of the southern oceans, and that the two populations became isolated and different in their respective oceans. The Short-tailed Albatross still survives, although brought to the verge of extinction by Japanese feather hunters and by a tendency to nest on actively volcanic islands.

The North Atlantic Albatross has its earliest known occurrence in the early Pliocene of Florida; then from East Anglia in the latter part of the Pliocene, and into the earliest Pleistocene. We know nothing about it, but suspect from the two well-separated countries of occurrence that it may have been widespread, and its disappearance seems to be linked with the worsening northern climate that ushered in the alternating glacial and milder periods of the ice ages, the Pleistocene.

The Pleistocene

Although the Pleistocene is sometimes called the Ice Age it is, in fact, a period of repeated ice ages. Over more than a million and a half years, cold winters and cool summers combined to permit the formation of extensive ice-caps, which in turn influenced climate elsewhere. Periods of more intensive cold were interspersed with warm intervals that were usually shorter in duration. At its most extreme extent an ice-cap covered the whole of northern Europe, and forest zones were pushed south and compressed into a narrow region bordering the

Mediterranean. Unexpectedly, deserts such as the Sahara were more, not less, extensive during such periods.

Any advance of glaciers or ice-caps tends to obliterate or scrape away earlier evidence, and hence there has always been a problem in working out the sequence of changes. Studies centred mainly on the alpine regions of Europe, examining glacial geology and the evidence of fossil mammals, resulted in the recognition of four major periods of glaciation, separated by warmer interglacial periods with climates at times warmer than those of the present day.

Subsequently two earlier periods were added, and until recently six glacials and interglacials were thought to have constituted the Pleistocene of Europe. It has been suggested, however, that the Recent (or Holocene) period since the end of the last glaciation, the one in which we are now, is probably just another interglacial. It is sometimes referred to as the Flandrian interglacial, the names for these periods tending to vary from one country to another and usually based on places in which evidence for them was found.

The major divisions recognised in Britain are as follows, with the most recent at the top

INTERGLACIALS	GLACIATIONS
13 Flandrian (present-day)	
	12 Devensian
11 Ipswichian	
	10 Wolstonian
9 Hoxnian	
	8 Anglian
7 Cromerian	
	6 Beestonian
5 Pastonian	
	4 Bavantian
3 Antian	
	2 Thurnian
1 Ludhamian	

But evidence has begun to accumulate that indicated a past pattern more complicated than this. Warmer interstadials have been recognised within individual glacial periods, and colder stages within the warmer interglacials. We are now faced with a need to superimpose a new pattern on this older list. In addition to studying the disturbed and damaged features of the land surface, and the fossils embedded in them, scientists have begun to look at sites where successive layers could accumulate over a long period of time and remain undisturbed. For this kind of evidence, two important sources have been deep and undisturbed peat deposits in southern Europe, and the sediments of the ocean beds.

These have given us a new picture. We now have a European Pleistocene period with some seventeen successive stages, each with a glacial period and a warmer interglacial. Each stage tended to last about a hundred thousand years, and for the latter part of the Pleistocene at least, the warmer periods are usually little more than a tenth of each stage, separated by long cold periods.

It has not yet been possible to correlate our old idea of the sequence of events with this new pattern, and a lot of re-adjustment may be necessary. For the moment we avoid undue confusion by using the older series of names listed above, but recognise that most of them should now be regarded as encompassing a series of climatic fluctuations.

During the longer cold periods of the Pleistocene snow accumulated on higher ground to form permanent ice-caps. These often increased in size, spread out, and gradually coalesced to form larger masses. In Europe the largest of these, usually assigned to the Wolstonian, covered most of the northern half of Europe. It extended right across the North Sea region and covered most of the British Isles except for a narrow southern zone south of a line from the northern side of the Thames Valley to the Bristol Channel. In the coldest part of the last glaciation, the Devensian, the ice again extended across the North Sea to the east coast as far south as the Wash, over most of Scotland, across northern England, north and central Wales, and the northern four-fifths of Ireland.

It is these massive ice-caps that most people associate with the colder Ice Age periods. Yet for long periods, possibly most of the time, and in some areas all of the time, the land was not wholly obscured by ice. It carried a flora and fauna – on ice edge, tundra, shrub tundra or cold steppe. The plants and animals that moved into Britain during these periods were those of the arctic regions of the present day, adapting to the varying factors of coldness, moisture and land surface. And like the modern Arctic, Britain may have been extensively used by migrant birds for breeding.

Migration in the past is difficult to establish. But when a group of bird species found at one site at one period consists of species typical of conditions that obtained there then, together with a few that normally breed under much colder conditions, it is almost certain that migration is occurring.

There is some evidence from Olduvai in East Africa in the Pliocene about two million years ago, when Bar-tailed Godwit and Corncrake occur with local species. In addition in at least two interglacial deposits in the Pleistocene of south-eastern England arctic-breeding waterfowl occur in warmer periods together with species of warmer habitats. In general the picture suggests that the annual migrations that we know today were already occurring, although probably over different ranges and to different destinations, from the Late Pliocene through to the present, modified as necessary during periods of climatic change.

During the coldest periods sea-levels fell by up to one hundred metres, creating extensive areas of dry lowland. Most of the North Sea area would have been dry, and the coastline might have included the Inner Hebrides and extended out and around Ireland and across to western Brittany. There would have been large rivers and estuaries in the Irish Sea and English Channel; but in the main this enormous additional extent of land would have been dry, and vegetated to some degree, possibly even forested in places. It must have provided support for a large population of the birds that utilise such habitats.

The increase in lowland would have been offset by the sterility of the high ground. Very low temperatures, and the likelihood of long-term snow and ice cover, would have made most of it uninhabitable. The slow movements of ice would strip off soils and softer sediments, restricting the areas of vegetative cover. The

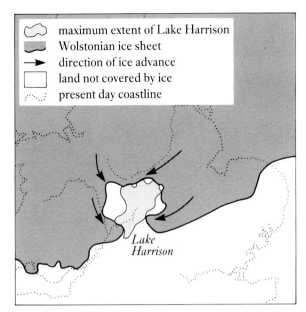

maximum extent of Lake Harrison
Wolstonian ice sheet
direction of ice advance
land not covered by ice
present day coastline

Lake Harrison

One of the temporary lakes formed by
spreading or melting ice-sheets
during the glaciations.

Britain in the Wolstonian glaciation.

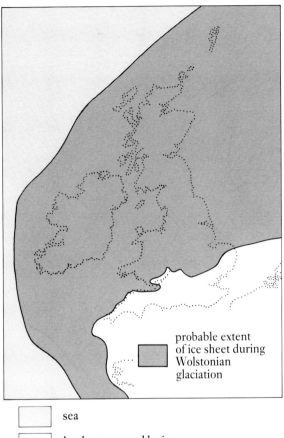

probable extent
of ice sheet during
Wolstonian
glaciation

sea

land not covered by ice

present day coastline

Britain in the Devensian glaciation.
The small area in Scotland represents
the Loch Lomond glacial readvance.

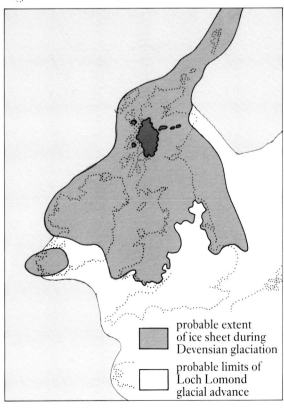

probable extent
of ice sheet during
Devensian glaciation

probable limits of
Loch Lomond
glacial advance

pressure of ice-caps and glaciers eroded mountain-tops,
and widened and gouged out valleys.

During warmer periods the sea-level rose again, and
the lower land exposed during glaciations was drowned.
Higher ground would have become inhabitable again,
and vegetated, save where ice might have removed soil
permanently. Oddly enough, although we can envisage
arctic conditions, we have very little concept of how the
land would have appeared at the warmest periods.

The transition from glacial periods to warmer interglacial, and back again, may often have been gradual,
but certainly not smooth; and it is in these intervening
periods of change that major alterations in land-form
can occur. For example, when an ice-cap melts, large
quantities of water are released. If an outlet is dammed,
large inland lakes may form and persist for a time, and
these may also occur during periods of cooling when ice
accumulates. In the Pleistocene such lakes occurred in
the Midlands, in Yorkshire, and in Scotland.

Flowing water may cut new channels and will deepen others; and blocked outlets may change the course of rivers or reverse the flow in valleys and cause significant permanent changes. The lower reaches and outlet of the Thames appear to have undergone several southward shifts during this period; and this appears to have been caused by obstruction from debris dumped by ice.

Indeed the movement, and later deposition, of huge amounts of material carried by ice on and in glaciers was of major significance during periods of glacial change. Stones and gravels, and sometimes great rocks, were caught up in the ice and often carried for considerable distances. They can sometimes be recognised by the smoothing and rounding caused by abrasion during this process. Some Scandinavian rock fragments were carried right across what is now the North Sea, and deposited in eastern England.

In some areas rounded stones were deposited in moraine ridges across the land. Much more often great sheets of gravels, sands and clays were deposited, and these are spread over most of the lowland areas of Britain. They may be of considerable thickness: the cliffs of north Norfolk are the edge of a deep layer of such material that overlies the chalk platform in northern East Anglia.

Where ice accumulated in the ground, its melting left small lakes and swamps, in some areas many in close proximity; in the British Isles there is some evidence of this in parts of Scotland and Ireland.

Events such as these considerably altered surface structure and drainage in Britain, and these would in turn affect the bird populations. Even if they did not affect the broad, overall range of a species during a particular period, they must have drastically altered the distribution and size of populations. Their effect would have been equally great on the vegetation, which for the Pleistocene as a whole must be seen as being as dynamic and fluid as the bird populations in its responses to changing conditions.

The basic, characteristic plant covering of the European region consists of belts of fairly uniform plant associations controlled by climate, and replacing each other from north to south. Much of the north is occupied by the cool boreal forest, mainly conifers with some birch and poplar; and then typical broadleaf temperate forest over mainland Europe, where humans have not destroyed it; and the more evergreen, warm, mediterranean to subtropical forest in the south. Where rainfall is low, or is made less available because of physiological effects such as cold, the forest tends to be replaced by thin scrub or grassland. The northern subarctic tundra is an example of this; and in eastern regions steppe-grassland may replace forest.

This pattern would be perfect on a uniform, level landscape; but changes in soil and rock and hills and valleys enable patches of vegetation to persist north or south of their normal range, and to create a more varied pattern.

To us with our relatively short-term view, these zones appear relatively permanent; but during periods of climatic change, such as the Pleistocene, the distribution of vegetation changed with the climate. The greatest distance from north to south in Europe is about 4,000km. During the changes from cold to warm climates and back again, the main shift of vegetation would involve considerably less distance than this. An advance of the wind-borne seeds of a tree, establishing seedlings a kilometre further each year could traverse most of the distance required in less than two thousand years – and there are at least ten thousand years involved in most of the shorter Pleistocene periods. In taking our present long-term view and discussing a series of such periods, we see this process as greatly accelerated. It becomes possible to see plant zones as moving belts, ebbing and flowing like liquid tides; and as these plant zones move, so the associated animal life moves with them.

In studying these changes and in trying to assess their impact on the bird life of the period, and discovering what that bird life was like, we have to seek out and identify the scanty, scattered evidence left lying in the ground.

Like the evidence available for other geological periods, the material providing information on Pleistocene birds is scrappy, and sporadic in occurrence. Much of it has only become available in recent years. It is based on bird bones that are usually single, and often broken or damaged; and in the past such objects proved difficult to identify. More comprehensive collections of comparative material help us to make a better job of it, though still with occasional doubts. In trying to assemble an overall picture of the British avifauna, it has been necessary to re-check earlier identifications which have not always been correct; and the evidence of error has made it advisable for the present to ignore sources where there may be some measure of doubt.

The material itself originates from two main sources. The bodies of birds which are killed or die in the open tend to be wholly destroyed by predators and scavengers; but where bodies end up in rivers, streams, lakes or swamps, the bones, although separated, may survive intact. They are found in later periods in the sands, gravels or clays left as residual deposits by such waters. Single species or small groups of birds identified from bones preserved in this way have been found, usually by excavation for other reasons, or during natural erosion, mostly in lowland and coastal areas of eastern Britain, and more particularly in south-east England.

Other bird remains occur in caves, and these are mostly in the more hilly regions of the west and north. The remains are usually embedded in the thin layers of soil and debris that accumulate on cave floors. Specimens are often well-preserved, but are very vulnerable to any kind of disturbance, including unskilled collecting, which can inadvertently shift a specimen through several hundred thousand years of history in a single small move.

The problem with birds is that few of them go into caves of their own accord. Some owls, Rock Doves, Swifts, Swallows, Starlings, Jackdaws and Choughs might nest in caves; but anything else is likely to have been carried in by a predator. The sample of species present is therefore skewed heavily in favour of the prey

Studies of Eagle Owl

most easily caught, and by the identity and preferences of the predator.

There is one very obvious example of this bias in evidence. There is every reason to suppose that the Snowy Owl *Nyctea scandiaca* occurred frequently over most of Britain during the glacial periods. However, it is a large predatory bird, preferring very open places; and the only evidence of the species from the whole southern half of Britain during the Pleistocene is a single leg-bone in a Devon cave.

The mammalian predators are likely to have been foxes, wolves or hyaenas, and these tend to crunch fragile bird bones to fragments, leaving only the harder ends of limb-bones of larger birds.

The avian predators included owls. Few owl species normally use caves, and some whose remains are found in caves were probably the prey of a larger hunter still, such as an Eagle Owl *Bubo bubo*. This and the Barn Owl are the two likely cave haunters. Owls tend to swallow their prey whole when possible, but the bones, complete or broken, are usually cast up, neatly cleaned, in a pellet of indigestible material. Barn Owl prey will be mostly small mammals, together with birds up to thrush size, but usually smaller. The Eagle Owl, which seems to have been present in Britain throughout the Pleistocene, takes a larger range of prey, from divers and large ducks and geese down to tiny birds; where it has done so, it probably provides the best sample of the local avifauna.

Diurnal birds of prey were other possible predators; but, since they do not usually enter caves, their activities are likely to have been restricted to the more shallow cave-shelters or around entrances to deeper caves. Where their presence is suspected, the possible species are White-tailed Eagle, Kestrel and possibly Peregrine Falcon at times. They are capable of swallowing and digesting bird bones, and those that they regurgitate in pellets may in the process have suffered some surface erosion. However, when feeding they tend to strip meat from a carcase, and the heavier parts of the skeleton and bonier parts of limbs may be discarded, and occur as undamaged remains.

The bones found in such sites are identified by comparison with those of more recent bird skeletons. In doing this we are fortunate in one respect: in birds, size is usually consistent among individuals of the same species. Other vertebrate groups tend to have longer periods of growth, producing age/size categories. Most birds have a very short growth period, and the skeleton often reaches its finite size in a few weeks. Bone size is therefore a useful criterion in species identification.

There is sometimes a problem where pairs of closely related species, that may be quite easily recognised by plumage colour or pattern, are virtually indistinguishable as skeletons, or can only be recognised from certain bones. One such pair is Blackbird and Ring Ousel. In such an instance this is unfortunate if one had hoped to derive clues to the site's former habitat conditions from the species present. (The one is likely to be linked with scrub or woodland, the other with open rocky places.) Conversely, however, it might be possible to guess at the more likely species if the conditions at the time are known from other evidence. Other species pairs causing similar problems are Common/Rough-legged Buzzard. Stonechat/Whinchat, and Carrion Crow/Rook.

The size problem is particularly relevant during ice ages, since one response of animals to increasing cold is to adapt by becoming larger. (The larger a body is, the smaller its surface-area in proportion to its mass, and thus the lower the heat-loss.) This is apparent with groups such as mammals which, when faced with problems of climatic fluctuation, must often adapt or become extinct. (This may also involve morphological characters other than mere size.) However, birds can just move away when conditions become unsuitable, provided that they have not become wholly sedentary; and they may then return when things improve. As a result there has been relatively little need for birds to adapt in order to cope with Britain's ice ages, and as a general rule their skeletons appear to have remained virtually unchanged from the late Pliocene to the present day.

One apparent exception in this matter of size consistency is the Eagle Owl. A leg bone found in the early Pastonian interglacial in Norfolk is finer and much more slender than those of the typical, large northern form, and resembles instead those of the smaller Eagle Owls of the saharo-sindian regions, which are currently regarded as a desert form of the species. By the next, Hoxnian, major interglacial a bone from Kent is as large as those of present-day, northern European Eagle Owls. It suggests a possibility that the smaller bird now occurring in deserts is closer to the ancestral form of the species; and that an ability to shelter in caves and to utilise a large range of animal prey of any climatic regime made it worthwhile for this owl to remain where it was in colder, glacial periods, and to adapt by increasing its size.

The bones of young birds, when they are growing, are partly cartilaginous. Very exceptionally, when a number of bones of a species are found at a site, a few may show evidence of this incomplete ossification, which indicates that breeding has occurred at that place or nearby. This is important evidence, for in most instances breeding can only be inferred from the presence of bones of adult birds that might have been expected to breed in the conditions believed to have existed at the time.

We are fortunate in two of the very scarce examples which have been found recently. Bones from caves on the south coast of Wales show that in the warmer part of the last, Ipswichian, interglacial Razorbills bred, seemingly in the caves. In the warmest period they were apparently replaced by breeding Cory's Shearwaters *Calonectris diomedea*. At present this large shearwater, which will use caves for nesting, does not breed further north than the Canary Islands and the Mediterranean: we therefore have one of the few good examples provided by birds of a northwards shift in a warm interglacial.

The other example, also from the South Wales coast, is the converse of this. Evidence from a cave indicates the presence in the last, Devensian, glaciation of a breeding colony of Barnacle Geese. This species, which now winters in Scotland and northern England, and around northern parts of Ireland, is an arctic-breeder in East Greenland, Spitzbergen and Novaya Zemlya. In order to escape predators such as the arctic fox it nests on rocky islands, but also inland on the ledges of rocky escarpments and gorges. In a glacial period with low sea-levels the Welsh coast cliffs would have been an escarpment-like outcrop, well inland, and resembling these present-day breeding sites. With this information, evidence of the presence of this species at two other inland sites during the Devensian glaciation, both of them with rocky gorges, suggests that it may have been a more widespread breeder during that period.

There is some other evidence of cold-period birds, such as the presence of Ptarmigan on the higher ground of Devon and Somerset during the Devensian. A cave near Dartmoor has a poorly-dated avifauna from the latter period and after, which nevertheless includes Shorelark, Snow Bunting and Lapland Bunting. If they bred then, the area might have had a more typical arctic-type avifauna.

Based on the total information at present available, the avifaunal variation between colder and warmer periods is in general less clearcut than might have been expected. One might attempt to explain this as a sampling of conditions over a longer period than was supposed, with a more changing climate. But similar comments have been made by botanists regarding the mixture of cold- and warm-indicating plant species in the colder Pleistocene periods. It is possible that the climatic fluctuations of this period, extreme as they may appear, did not result in the changes in flora and fauna that one might have predicted from modern studies of areas of the world such as Arctic and tropics where such climatic conditions are typical and more permanent.

Comments on some of our native species that are also known from the Pleistocene will be included in the text for that species, but there are some others relevant to this period which require discussion here. Some of them are species now extinct.

The earliest Pleistocene deposit yielding bird bones is the Red Crag of Suffolk. This dates back to the earliest Pleistocene, but also contains relics from many earlier eras, eroded from their geological resting places and re-incorporated in this layer. There are two birds from the Red Crag, both of them sea-birds. The first is the North Atlantic Albatross, mentioned earlier as a Pleistocene bird, and the Red Crag provides the last known evidence of its existence. The other is a species of black guillemot, Storer's Guillemot *Cepphus storeri*. Three species of the genus are extant. Our own Black Guillemot *C. grylle* occurs in the North Atlantic and Arctic Oceans, replaced in the North Pacific by the very similar Pigeon Guillemot *C. columba*; a larger bird, the Spectacled or Dusky Guillemot *C. carbo* is present in the north Pacific region from Japan to the Sea of Okhotsk and Kamchatka, partly overlapping the range of the last species. Storer's Guillemot, known only from this East Anglian site, is as large as the Spectacled Guillemot, and may have been its counterpart in the North Atlantic, although we have no information at present concerning the existence of any of the extant species at this earlier period.

The long subsequent Icenian Crag deposition period from about the Thurnian glaciation to the Pastonian interglacial produces only a single unexceptional Long-tailed Duck. The interglacial following this, the Cromerian, has more to offer; and the Forest Beds of north Norfolk during this period give us an interesting avifauna of some 600,000 years ago.

It was a period probably a little warmer than our present one. From pollen and faunal evidence there appears to have been fresh water, both fen and river, and the sea nearby. There were open grassy areas, and some temperate mixed oak-woodland. Presumably linked with this woodland were a group of song-birds; Blackbird or Ring Ousel (with the former more likely in this instance), Song Thrush or Redwing, Nuthatch, Starling and Jay. These species, and Jay and Nuthatch in particular, might be found in any mixed oak-wood today.

A more unexpected species that might have used these habitats, and to which some of the bones from the Forest Beds appear assignable, is the Mandarin Duck *Aix galericulata*. The present natural occurrence of the species is the wetter oak-wood habitats of China, although it has been introduced elsewhere. The related Wood Duck *A. sponsa* occurs on temperate forest waters in North America. In the early Pleistocene, Europe and western Eurasia appear to have shared with eastern Eurasia and North America a richer and more varied

Male Shorelark in breeding plumage

Male Lapland Bunting

temperate forest. With successive glaciations, during the ebb and flow of shifting vegetational zones, the east-to-west mountain masses and the seas of southern Europe, Mediterranean and Middle East appear to have presented increasing barriers. Re-colonisation in warmer periods seems to have been less successful, leading to impoverishment of the flora, and with it an impoverishment of the fauna. The Mandarin appears to be part of what we have lost.

There is a possible zoogeographic parallel in a quite unrelated species, the Azure-winged Magpie *Cyanopica cyanea*. In the colder glacial periods, species requiring warmer conditions were forced southwards and, because of the discontinuous areas of land, they tended to become isolated in a discontinuous chain of refuge areas extending from the Canary Islands, across the Mediterranean region and over to southern China. It was in such refuges that isolated populations might become separate subspecies or species.

One subspecies of the Azure-winged Magpie is found in southern China and Japan. Another isolate subspecies is near the opposite end of the chain in Spain and Portugal. Presumably any intervening populations failed to survive. Had the Iberian population not existed it would almost certainly be argued that this magpie had evolved only in the Far East. The occurrence of Mandarin Duck in western European temperate woodland in the past is at least as likely as the distribution pattern apparent in the magpie.

The Forest Beds have a fine range of ducks – dabblers, divers and sawbills – covering most of our modern fauna. One addition is based on a limb-bone of a diving duck, most like our Common Eider. However, it is far more stoutly built, and the proportions most nearly resemble those of the leg-bones of an Australian Musk Duck *Biziura lobata* (a species so adapted for diving and underwater feeding that the early settlers believed it to be flightless, until individuals began to crash-land at night on the shiny corrugated iron roofs of outback buildings, under the impression that they were water-holes). The Forest Bed bird has been separated as the Thick-legged Eider *Somateria gravipes*.

Another duck occurring at this period is the Red-crested Pochard *Netta rufina*. It is now an occasional visitor to Britain, but normally a bird of the warmer regions of southern Eurasia; its presence at this period might indicate reasonably deep, open water, and help confirm a warmer climate.

The next major period yields another extinct bird which raises more interesting questions concerning the early patterns of European bird distribution. It is a jungle fowl, *Gallus* species. At present there are four *Gallus* species in the oriental region, the most northerly being the Red Jungle Fowl *Gallus gallus* of northern India. This is the bird which gave rise to typical domestic fowl. It is thought that the earliest domestication took place about four thousand years ago, followed by dispersal westwards with human movement, domestic birds reaching Britain in about Roman times. By that time the bones found show evidence of both large and bantam domestic forms.

The bones from Pleistocene Britain are comparable in size to those of the wild Red Jungle Fowl. There is a bone from Ostend, Norfolk in what appears to have been an interstadial or unrecognised interglacial within the Anglian glacial period, and another bone in the last, Ipswichian, interglacial from Swanscombe in Kent. Neither appears to be associated with any human activity. The Ostend bone shows small differences from those of typical Red Jungle Fowl, and on this and the zoogeographical implications the bird has been separated as an extinct species, the European Jungle Fowl *G. europaeus*.

Other extinct jungle fowl species are known from the Pliocene of south-eastern Europe. The Pleistocene distribution pattern for this genus might have resembled that found in other game-birds such as quail or *Perdix* partridges. The repeated glaciations split populations to produce, in some instances, trios of similar species – one in Europe east to the Pamirs, another in China or south-east Asia, and a third in the Indian region south of the Himalayas. The pattern occurs in a number of bird genera.

In the case of the jungle fowl we would have had a north-west European species, now extinct, and the Red Jungle Fowl in India. It is not clear what happens in China, but there is now evidence from an eight thousand year old Stone Age pastoral community in the extreme north of China of jungle fowl bones. Since this region is well separated from the range of the Indian birds, and appears to antedate the latter's domestication by some four thousand years, the bones would appear to be of independent origin and to complete a predicted distribution pattern.

The occurrence of the European Jungle Fowl is interesting in that it raises doubts about the origins of very early wild-type jungle fowl remains from this region. We do not know the fate of the species. If it did not die out in the last glaciation there is just a possibility that the large array of domestic varieties of the fowl may include three different genotypes concealed among them. Although isolation during glaciations starts a process of increasing genetic isolation through sub-speciation to speciation, it may be incomplete. Separate recognisable entities may not be genetically separated, and if geographical barriers are overcome interbreeding between apparent species may occur; as we seem to be seeing at present in the Red-legged Partridge *Alectoris rufa* and the Chukar *A. chukar*.

Another extinct species showing the same type of distribution problem as the jungle fowl is the European Crane *Grus primigenia*. It was a big crane, about the size of the present-day Sarus Crane *Grus antigone*. The first evidence of its presence is from the London Basin in the

Ipswichian Interglacial. It was also present in the subsequent Devensian Glaciation, and is known from West Germany and north France. It occurs in Scotland in the Bronze Age, south-west England in the Iron Age, and our last record is from Romano-British times. It appears to have been a crane of north-west Europe, possibly migrating to the western Mediterranean.

On the large land areas of the northern hemisphere there are usually two breeding crane species. In North America the smaller bird is the grey Sandhill Crane G. canadensis, and across Europe the grey Common Crane G. grus. In North America the larger species is the mainly white Whooping Crane G. americana. In eastern Eurasia there is the larger and mainly white Manchurian or Japanese Crane G. japonica, in India the larger grey Sarus Crane occurs where the smaller species winters, but it does not breed, and in Central Eurasia, the large, mainly white Siberian crane G. leucogeranus. The pattern now has a gap in western Eurasia which would have been filled in the past by the European Crane. By extrapolation I suspect that it, too, would have had a mainly white plumage.

The last of these extinct birds comes from a cave in Devon where it occurs in a cold phase at the termination of the next-to-last, Wolstonian, glaciation, at a time when conditions were improving. It is a small Alectoris partridge, a little smaller than the Red-legged Partridge which is now the smallest member of the genus. The latter is only known from Britain as an introduced bird. The Devon bird was smaller still and, from the stratum in which it was found, would appear to be a cold-tolerant bird, unlike its close relatives. It has been given a separate identity as the Western Partridge A. sutcliffei.

Some species that are now stray visitors to Britain also occurred during the Pleistocene. The Ruddy Shelduck Tadorna ferruginea has been found at the same Devon site as the partridge in the Ipswichian interglacial, and at Pin Hole Cave in Derbyshire during the last glaciation. In Devon it appears as an odd bird out among the more frequent remains of the Common Shelduck. The Ruddy Shelduck is a species of drier regions, with shallow fresh or saline inland waters, and is sometimes referred to as a 'steppe' species. Although it is often claimed that during cooler Pleistocene periods Britain was a part of an extensive steppe zone across Europe, and although there is some evidence of this from studies of pollen, there is relatively little evidence of what might be regarded as a steppe-type avifauna.

The Red-breasted Goose Branta ruficollis occurs in the Ipswichian Interglacial in the London Basin. At present it has a small breeding range on the Siberian tundra and tends to move south-west in winter in eastern Hungary and the Balkans, with accidental strays further west. However, in the past it may well have had a more extensive range, and occurred further west, especially when glacial conditions changed the distribution of tundra. There are Pleistocene records of it from Crete and Italy.

Apart from these exceptions the bird life of Pleistocene Britain appears remarkably unexceptional, and not as varied as one might have hoped. It certainly cannot be compared with the mammals in this respect, lacking the equivalents of the bears, beavers, hyaenas, lions, hippopotami and elephants that made that fauna more exciting. This is probably one reason why it has hitherto received rather limited attention.

The Recent Period

THE CLIMATIC FACTOR

In looking at the birds of the Pleistocene ice ages, extending over a period of a million and a half years, and with sparse and fragmentary evidence, it is necessary to think in terms of fairly broad generalisations and conjecture. One would hope for more detailed information on the time that followed, the Recent or Holocene period in which we also live. It is a mere ten to twelve thousand years with which we are concerned. Geologists tend to take a gloomily disinterested view of it, and see it as just another interglacial. If this is so, then in another thousand years or so we may slide into another glacial period, assuming that the predicted warming of the world through man's tinkering with the carbon cycle does not counteract it.

It is during this period – the Recent, Holocene, or the Flandrian Interglacial – that we move into the avifauna that we know today, through stages of gradual modifications of climate and habitat. The changes begin a little before the end of the last, Devensian, glaciation.

The Devensian Glaciation is usually reckoned to have finished about 10,000 years ago. Before this occurred there was an interlude of warmer climate, the Windermere Interstadial, lasting from about 12,500 to 10,800 years before the present (BP not BC). Trees moved in – birch, juniper, hazel and alder – and there were general signs of amelioration; but at about the middle of the period it appears to have become more arid across Eurasia, trees giving way to grasses and

herbaceous plants – to a spread of steppe conditions. A shorter cold period occurred, lasting until about 10,250 BP and marking the final stage of the glaciation. It involved the accumulation of a 100km-long ice-cap on mountains in western Scotland, and is sometimes referred to as the Loch Lomond glacial readvance.

Following this last spasm of the ice ages, the climate began to warm more steadily. Trees re-invaded and began to form forests in suitable areas. As before, birch was the dominant tree at first, followed by pine and hazel. With conditions warming and drying, pine must have been dominant for a while; but except in the extreme north it was gradually replaced by broadleaf trees – elm, oak and lime.

During this period, with melting ice and warming seas, sea-levels rose, but not as suddenly as one might suppose. At about 9,000 BP what is now the southern North Sea was still dry land, and oak forest grew on the Dogger Bank. It was not until about a thousand years later that this was wholly submerged, and the rising sea joined that of the southern coast to complete the English Channel and isolate the British Isles.

About this time the severance with Ireland must also have occurred. There has always been a problem in calculating when this happened, complicated by post-glacial land levels rising during the later period. A number of elements of British wildlife, including some mammals, birds, reptiles, amphibians and plants for

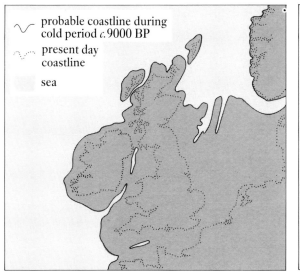
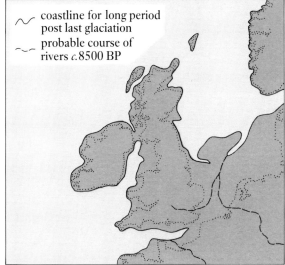

probable coastline during cold period *c.*9000 BP

present day coastline

sea

coastline for long period post last glaciation

probable course of rivers *c.*8500 BP

The changing coastline as sea-level rose after the last glaciation.

Changes during the last 12,000 years.

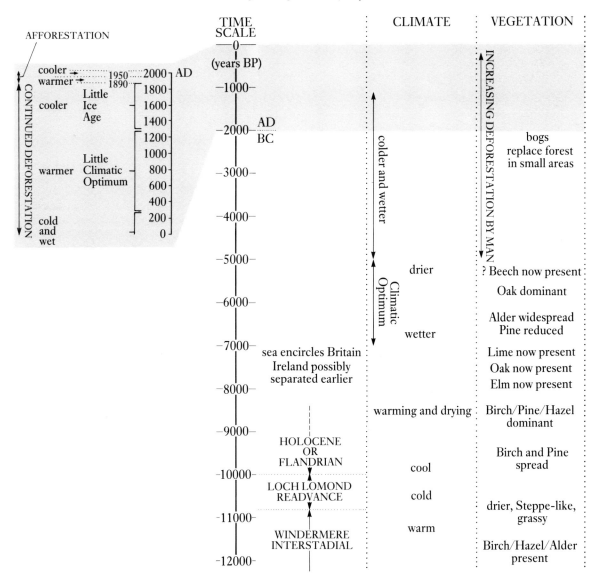

AFFORESTATION

CONTINUED DEFORESTATION

cooler → 1950 2000 AD
warmer → 1890 1800
cooler Little Ice Age 1600
1400
1200
warmer Little Climatic Optimum 1000
800
600
400
200
cold and wet 0

TIME SCALE
—0—
(years BP)
—1000—
—2000— AD / BC
—3000—
—4000—
—5000—
—6000—
—7000—
—8000—
—9000—
—10000—
—11000—
—12000—

sea encircles Britain
Ireland possibly separated earlier

HOLOCENE OR FLANDRIAN

LOCH LOMOND READVANCE

WINDERMERE INTERSTADIAL

CLIMATE

colder and wetter

Climatic Optimum

drier

wetter

warming and drying

cool

cold

warm

VEGETATION

INCREASING DEFORESTATION BY MAN

bogs replace forest in small areas

? Beech now present

Oak dominant

Alder widespread
Pine reduced

Lime now present
Oak now present
Elm now present

Birch/Pine/Hazel dominant

Birch and Pine spread

drier, Steppe-like, grassy

Birch/Hazel/Alder present

17

example, appear to have reached Britain before it was isolated, but do not occur in Ireland. From this it has been inferred that Ireland must have been separated from Britain before the English Channel was formed. However, the final connections between Ireland and Britain seem to have been in the extreme north-west of England and in south-west Scotland. Species which had invaded the south and east of England might have taken quite a time to colonise the more northerly parts from which they might have invaded Ireland. So a significant time-lapse in the separation of these islands does not seem to have been clearly established.

The post-glacial climatic amelioration reached a peak in the Climatic Optimum of about 7,000–5,000 BP, when temperatures generally averaged 2°–3°C warmer than today. It was a period of more rapidly rising sea-levels, reaching their highest point after the glaciations. It was the period when the great freshwater lake of the Baltic, that had formed south of the Scandinavian ice-cap, finally joined the eastern North Sea. The period was not only warmer, but also wetter. It may have been then that the last of the species needing a continental-type hot dry summer finally disappeared. Increasing rainfall and humidity brought about podsolation of soils and extension of marshes. In some regions extensive blanket-bogs were formed; but some similar bog formation also occurred in later wet periods.

Following this, there was a long gradual swing back to cooler conditions. This extended from about 3,000 to 2,300 BP. It was both colder and wet. It was during this period, from about 4,500 BP onwards, that man's activities in the form of deforestation and cultivation became generally apparent, from Neolithic cultures onwards. This period covers Bronze Age and Iron Age cultures and the Roman occupation.

For a shorter period, in early Medieval times about 1,000 to 600 BP, there was another warmer climatic fluctuation with summers about 1°C warmer than present on average, but less warm than those of the Climatic Optimum. This period is sometimes referred to as the Little Climatic Optimum. But the weather subsequently worsened again and history moves into the Little Ice Age: from the fourteenth to the nineteenth century our climate was again colder than in the past, and at its coldest for this period in the seventeenth century. The climate tended to be of a more continental type, the cold winters sometimes combined with short but hot summers.

By the 1880s there was evidence of climatic amelioration again. A warmer and more equable climate occurred from about 1880–1950, most marked in the 1920s and 1930s. Because this was a time during which long-term climatic studies were established, it was treated as a norm against which other climatic variations could be measured. But it was of fairly short duration and, since the early 1950s there has been a reversion to a colder cycle with more frequent extremes of weather: possibly the inception of another Little Ice Age.

RECENT BIRDS

It is only possible to make a brief, cursory survey here of some of the effects of those climatic flutuations over the last 10,000 years, mentioning some species and aspects which may not re-occur in the species discussions, where more detailed comments can be made. It is not the kind of time-span in which striking adaptations occur; and would mainly have involved a return to Britain of many species as conditions became more favourable, and some diminution or loss of those which were more closely adapted to cold conditions. In addition to this major resurgence, there would have been variations of a more minor nature, in response to the more recent short-term changes. Such variations might at times only be obvious in those species on the northern or southern extremes of their ranges. Even these may be difficult to evaluate because, by this time, man's activities had considerably modified many landscapes and habitats within the British Isles.

While one assumes that, with a fairly steady climatic warming after the last glaciation, an increase will be seen in the avifauna as bird species move back, probably following the plants and insects, there is in fact very little solid evidence for this. From what is found in caves it appears that there was an initial large increase of species at the end of the glacial period; but subsequently, without the time for a slow accumulation of separate layers of debris, the cave material becomes sparse and mixed; later bones of domestic goose, fowl and turkey help to confuse the picture. Later evidence is mostly from middens, and the range of species tends to be those eaten, or slaughtered for sport or spite.

It is usually more difficult, particularly with small samples, to establish what is absent from a fauna as opposed to what is present. However, our total evidence does highlight some losses.

At some period, and seemingly early on in the initial climatic warming-up, the Hazelhen *Tetrastes bonasia* disappeared from the British Isles. This is a small woodland grouse that is present through much of northern Europe, and occurred in southern England in the interglacials. Its loss was probably linked with a change in our seasonal climate. In Europe it is absent from the western end: the distribution suggests an intolerance of the north-western oceanic climate with its warmer, moist winters and cooler, moist summers, and a preference for a continental climate with a colder winter but hotter and drier summer.

Our evidence suggests that in the transitional periods at the ends of glaciations the climate was of a continental type. When this changed, we are likely to have lost the Hazelhen. It is difficult to establish this affinity of

Crested Lark

White Stork

European birds with climatic types; but other animals show it better. For example, the European terrapin or pond tortoise was present in Britain in periods of continental climate in the Pleistocene. It can hibernate through winter cold, but buries its eggs in earth to incubate, and a hot summer is needed to hatch them. When our summers became cooler and wetter, we lost it.

Two other bird species, which have been identified from bones in caves dated at about the end of the last glaciation, do not now occur as natives. One is the Crested Lark *Galerida cristata*. This species prefers drier and warmer conditions than does the Skylark. It now occurs as far north in Europe as the Channel coast of France, but seems to make no serious attempt to colonise further. The other species is the Pine Grosbeak *Pinicola enucleator*. In Europe it now has a continental-type distribution, but it is more northerly in general distribution and it might have been a preference for a cooler climate which drove it out as the British climate warmed towards the Climatic Optimum.

In general, the period up to the rising of sea-levels resulting in the opening-up of the English Channel must have been one in which colonising species from warmer regions moved in from the south. In theory, the Channel is such a minor barrier that it should have had little effect on a flying bird; and yet a number of species appear to have failed to cross it and settle as breeding species. Most of these are forest birds. In the last glaciation the main forest refuge, into which such birds were forced, seems to have been in eastern Eurasia, with relatively tiny ones in southern Europe. In the subsequent postglacial period, many of the forest species recolonising Europe appear to have come from the east, moving westwards. They may have arrived too late for a dry Channel crossing and, as forest species, some could have been reluctant to essay the crossing; but for others it may be necessary to adduce some other reason, not obvious at present, to explain why this has subsequently been a barrier.

The list appears to include at least the Little Bittern *Ixobrychus minutus*, Black Kite *Milvus migrans*, Pygmy Owl *Glaucidium passerinum*, Tengmalm's Owl *Aegolius funereus*, Black Woodpecker *Dryocopus martius*, Middle Spotted Woodpecker *Dendrocopos medius*, Grey-headed Woodpecker *Picus canus*, Great Reed Warbler *Acrocephalus arundinaceus*, Icterine Warbler *Hippolais icterina* and Melodious Warbler *H. polyglotta*. Although odd pairs of Little Bitterns have now nested, and two nests of eggs collected at the end of the last century and beginning of the present one are those of one or other of the last two warblers, none of these has successfully established a past foothold. Another species, the Great Grey Shrike *Lanius excubitor* is a regular, although scarce, winter visitor that might have been expected to have nested here in view of its extensive circum-holarctic range.

The problem of interpreting the effect of an apparent water barrier is demonstrated more strikingly in the case of the gap between Britain and Ireland. The separation of the two in the north is so small that it could hardly deter birds for long. In fact, there is a recent record of a Golden Eagle pair nesting by the Scottish coast and bringing prey to the nest from Ireland. Yet there are some sixty-six bird species nesting in Britain that do not do so in Ireland. For some, specialist requirements or limited distribution might provide a possible answer. For the rest, the reason may be less obvious, but can hardly be explained in terms of an isolating water barrier. Climatic difference would not seem significant, since Ireland has a rainfall average similar to that of western Britain, a milder winter, and a summer no cooler than mid and north Britain.

The White Stork *Ciconia ciconia* is a species that has failed to nest this far west in recent times, although it has reached the eastern shores of the North Sea. Evidence of its presence here is sporadic. It occurred in the cooler end of the warming period following the next-to-last, Wolstonian, glaciation in Devon, where it might have been nesting. Bones from Scotland in the Bronze Age, and from southern England in Roman times, might have been of stray birds; but there is an odd record of a pair appearing and nesting on St Giles Cathedral in Edinburgh in 1416. The last is believable as one of those unexpected divergences from typical behaviour to which birds are prone on rare occasions. Otherwise, the apparent absence of this species is probably confirmed by its omission from native folklore. It may share with the Hazelhen a need for hotter and drier summers.

A species that appears to have been lost so early that it has left no record, but for which loss there appears to be no obvious explanation, is the Eagle Owl *Bubo bubo*. There is evidence of its presence through most of the Ice Ages and possibly just afterwards. It is a widespread and ecologically adaptable bird, and it is difficult to account for its subsequent absence. If it did persist well into the Holocene, then the likeliest explanation is that it was exterminated early on by man. If this were so then it is surprising that it was achieved so effectively when other more conspicuous raptorial species survived, and equally surprising that no tales or legends of it lingered on afterwards.

Man-modified Britain

Since the Climatic Optimum Britain has for the last 6,000 years been an island on which the most widely distributed habitat was forest. In the south it was mainly broadleaf, with oak as the dominant tree in favourable areas. Further north, and on higher ground, ash and birch tended to predominate, with conifers in Scotland. Writers sometimes give the impression that in the early period the whole land surface was covered with trees, like some vast woolly blanket, but at best they probably covered no more than 60–70% of the country. There were areas too cold, too wet, with too thin a soil or too exposed a site. In such areas other habitats occurred to varying degrees, and helped to maintain the diversity of the bird population.

Evidence of early human activity is most apparent when it occurred as forest clearing. It began in Neolithic times when stone axes must have been used, possibly helped by fire. Stone axes were in time replaced by bronze axes, and these in turn by iron axes. James Fisher tried to assess the rate of disappearance of forest cover. Over England, Wales, and Scotland he estimated an original woodland of some 57 million acres.

He suggested that this was reduced to 40 million in Neolithic times, 30 to 35 by the end of the Bronze Age, 25 by the end of the Iron Age and less than 20 million by the end of the Roman occupation. There were about 10 million acres at the time of the Norman invasion, and a low of about 2 million in the mid eighteenth century. He suggested a total of about $2\frac{1}{2}$ million acres by the mid twentieth century. Eric Simms has suggested a final figure of about $3\frac{1}{2}$ million acres, presumably depending on how you define woodland; but in either case a reduction of forest cover to a sixteenth or a twentieth of its original extent is a drastic change in the availability of a key bird habitat due to man's activity.

The major replacement habitat over most of this cleared region, and for most of the period involved, was farmland in one form or another. In the intervening stages the clearing activity aided habitat diversity. Even in areas of clearance, loss of woodland was likely to be only partial. Unless clearing was continually maintained, the early stages of re-afforestation would rapidly return in the form of scrub and scattered trees. This process might be retarded by partial cutting and rough grazing; on poorer soils this tended to produce rough grassland, heathland and moorland as transient or potentially persistent stages.

Cutting of young growth for poles or firewood could lead to coppicing, in which areas are cut over at intervals and characterised by young tree growth springing from old stumps. As a form of woodland exploitation it appears to have been used for several thousand years. Another factor which also occurred during the cooler, wetter parts of this early period, inhibiting forest spread and in some areas destroying it, was the spread of blanket-bog, in particular in the north and west.

Early farming often appears to have utilised deliberate or inadvertent rotations, with fallows in some years, allowing land to grow a natural crop of weeds, possibly subjected to some grazing. This must have provided areas in which annual plants could flourish and would have been valuable for seed-eating birds.

Neolithic and Bronze Age cultures mostly concentrated their activities on the thinner woodlands and the more easily cultivated soils of southern chalk and sandy areas, mainly on uplands. The surroundings of lowland lakes, rivers and marshes, with their more luxuriant vegetation, seem to have been little affected at first; but these areas were used in the subsequent Iron Age when some settlements were built on piles in shallow lakes and marshes.

For such settlements the relatively abundant bird life was an obvious source of food. When hunting for food with a limited supply of weapons, the largest return for a single shot is the most desirable. There was therefore likely to be a bias towards the largest birds available, and this is reflected to some extent in the remains from some sites such as the lake villages of the Glastonbury levels in Somerset.

Here the birds taken included a good range of the predictable prey – swans, geese and ducks. In addition they ranged from herons, Bitterns, Cormorants, divers and Coots, right down to Moorhens and Dabchicks. One wonders whether some of these may not have been trapped by other methods, such as nets, rather than killed with arrows or spears. However, the prize quarry here were presumably cranes and pelicans. In addition to the Common Crane, which may have bred close by, the larger European Crane was also present. This has already been mentioned as a Pleistocene species, and this is one of the last sites where there is evidence of it. The likelihood that the larger bird would have been preferential prey may have helped to hasten its end.

The pelican was the Dalmatian Pelican *Pelecanus crispus*. It bred in the great swamps of the Somerset levels at that time, and also in the fenlands of eastern England, and perhaps elsewhere. We have no evidence of its presence in the warmer interglacials, but in the postglacial period it must have extended across Europe. It would have been difficult to exterminate a fenland species by early hunting, and it has been suggested that a minor climatic change may have led to its withdrawal from the north-western extremity of its range.

However it had another important vulnerability. All pelican species choose isolated areas for nesting, usually in large colonies. They are over-reactive to disturbance by possible predators, to which their response tends to be mass desertion, even when there are partly-grown young in the nests. The increasing intrusion and spread of humans could have caused great harm in this context, and it is probably this that has, in the course of history, rolled back their distribution from western England to the present one in the extreme south-east of Europe. What is certain is that we had it as a breeding species, and lost it fairly early on.

In the main the relationship of man with birds during this period, and for most of the subsequent centuries, involved unremitting slaughter. To set against this, there is only the evidence of limited domestication and some early introductions. Domesticated birds, unless selected for some attribute other than edibility, tend to develop larger and heavier bodies than do wild ones. This is reflected in their skeletons, and it seems likely that the Greylag Goose and Mallard became domesticated in the Iron Age. The ease with which the young of these species can become attached to human beings

Studies of Mallard (left) and Teal.

would have made the establishment of a domesticated flock around a marsh-dweller's homestead a relatively easy matter.

At this period of prehistory the chicken problem still persists. The European Jungle Fowl, also mentioned earlier, was based on bones from two interglacial periods where they did not appear to be associated with human activity. In the early Holocene, a bone occurs in a coastal cave of South Wales, among material dated from prior to the major rise in sea-level and with no evidence of accompanying human presence. In addition there are bones of the size of wild-type jungle fowl from the Glastonbury Iron Age settlement, possibly 250 years before the Roman invasion.

The last, Devensian, glaciation would have been a tidy time for the European Jungle Fowl to disappear, but there is here a hint of continuity that could have brought it into contact with the domesticated fowl of the Roman period, assuming the latter to have been imports. The Romans had breeds of various sizes, most of them larger and heavier than the wild-type speci-mens. From the Roman invasion onwards it is always assumed that the fowl that turn up so frequently in archaeological sites are domestic birds of eastern origin; prior to that it is still an open question.

Through the Dark Ages, the Anglo-Saxon period, and the Norman occupation there is little information on the British avifauna and no real evidence of further loss or gain. Human spread and occupation continued. Forest was reduced, and land was cultivated. The main farming method of medieval times involved large open fields divided into cultivated strips, part of the land lying fallow each year, and with areas of common land carrying a more natural vegetation but used as a source of plant and mineral material, and heavily grazed. The latter may have attracted some small birds of heath or rough grassland; but all that the arable land is likely to have offered, to those birds that could dodge the juvenile bird-scarers, were the insects and seeds of turned soil, and the crop plants and weeds of strips and fallows.

An addition at about this time was the Common Pheasant. The bones of this species and those of smaller individuals of the domestic fowl are so similar that there have been constant problems of misidentification, and a confusion of records. The Pheasant was kept by the Romans and some may have been brought to Britain as captive individuals; but the introduction to the country would appear to have been at or slightly before Norman times. It does not seem then to have had the importance attached to it later as a game-bird: Wild Boar and deer were the socially prestigious prey. The 'forests' set aside for these animals were simply large areas reserved for hunting; although woodland was the likeliest form of natural vegetation, it was not implicit in the earlier use of the name.

The colder period of the Little Ice Age beginning in the fourteenth century must have ushered in changes of bird distribution, with greater likelihood of loss than of gain of species. It is difficult to find evidence of this. One of the few apparent changes concerns the Golden Oriole, which up to the fourteenth century was listed among the commoner song-birds, and subsequently seems to have been scarce or absent until the present century, to a point where it was not commonly known.

One would have expected other temperature-sensi-tive species to have been affected, such as the Woodlark perhaps? One factor which makes such conjectures a little more difficult is that many of our native birds are summer visitors. For them it would be the summer temperature, rather than the acute cold of winter, which would be the relevant factor controlling presence or absence.

There were two major man-made changes in historic times that must have enormously affected numbers and distribution of birds in Britain. In the fourteenth century the gradual enclosure of open and common land commenced. In consolidating these smaller and permanently defined parcels of land, the new owners began to border their holdings with hedgerows. Hedgerows had been in existence a long time prior to this, but they appear only to have been used for small areas such as gardens, orchards or similar areas from which cattle needed to be excluded.

The great final planting of hedgerows seems to have been in the eighteenth century. At the beginning of that century about half the farmland was enclosed with hedgerows; and by the end of it virtually all was surrounded. Britain had acquired that widespread, reticulate pattern of hedgerows and trees that we regarded, at least until very recent times, as the typical character of most farmland.

Many of the hedgerows that we see today have become large and overgrown through lack of labour to keep them cut, except where they have been battered beyond recognition by mechanical flails. In the past they were likely to have been much lower and tighter structures. Single trees were often allowed to grow at intervals along them, providing shade and shelter for stock. The whole provided a rather limited but widespread habitat: long attenuated strips of something between woodland edge, and the edge where scrub meets herbage. For birds this is important, since the majority of species seem to prefer to inhabit edge situations where more than one type of habitat is available, and where interaction may provide additional features.

The other big change which was mainly initiated in the seventeenth century was the large-scale draining of low-lying marshy land. Methods devised by the Dutch were introduced into the great fen regions of East Anglia at this period, and began to reduce the marshland stronghold that extended from the Wash over much of Cambridgeshire and eastern Lincolnshire. It was a change that gradually spread to all those low-lying areas of extensive reed-beds, marsh and fresh water scattered around Britain. It is difficult to assess the changes that occurred in the bird life of an ecological region that was little known and poorly documented. It seems certain that about this time we lost the Common Crane as a breeding bird, and our breeding colonies of Spoonbills in various parts were last recorded in the sixteenth and seventeenth centuries. We can only guess at what else may have gone.

The eighteenth century, in consolidating the farmland pattern with the Acts of Enclosure, triggered off the early nineteenth-century urbanisation of the population. The towns became a significant, if forbidding, habitat, and the countryside was increasingly seen as a source of socially desirable 'sporting' amusements. The underlying attitude of the times has been well summarised in one of our folk-songs –

'There was a farmer's son, he went up on a hill,
he took his little gun for to see what he could kill, . . .'

Shooting birds for food and amusement had always been an activity of people throughout the country. The nineteenth century brought greatly improved guns and the possibility of much larger kills. Social fashion added a demand for a more ritualised setting. The objective was a maximum number of targets at limited sites, and this called for the management of the species concerned in an effort to produce the largest possible number at one time.

This resulted to a large extent in a shift away from traditional prey such as waterfowl and waders, although these were still included in the general slaughter, and towards the more easily controlled game-birds. Three species in particular were now involved. The Common Partridge was a grassland bird that thrived reasonably well in the hay-meadows, rough grazing and arable of the farmland of the period. On relatively unproductive open uplands the Red Grouse was capable of reproducing in large numbers where careful management maintained short heather moorland.

Male (left) and female Common Pheasant

The most important of the three was the Common Pheasant. Properly controlled, it was highly prolific and as manageable as the domestic fowl. It could be produced in large numbers. To maintain a semi-natural background against which to slaughter it, 'pheasant coverts' came into being. Although in its natural habitat it appears to be a bird of the dry, overgrown borders of reed-beds and marshes, in Britain it was traditionally regarded as a woodland species, and so the coverts were small areas of woodland or scrub with low shrubby ground cover. It has been argued with some truth that the widespread modification of small areas scattered through farmland, to create cover for pheasants, was of enormous benefit to birds such as small passerines, providing them with safe cover and suitable breeding sites. What is always omitted from such arguments is the other ecological cost of pheasant-rearing, and of gamekeeping generally.

Linked to the nineteenth-century vogue for game-bird shooting was a systematic and long-term attempt to exterminate everything that might remotely be suspected of being a potential predator of pheasants, however infrequently. There was a devastating slaughter of birds of prey, with thousands butchered – shot, trapped or poisoned. A telling example is the Red Kite, which began the period widespread and relatively common over most of Britain, and by the early part of the twentieth century was reduced to a few pairs in the remoter parts of Wales. The Hen Harrier was wiped out on mainland Scotland, the White-tailed Eagle reduced to extinction. We had the Goshawk as a breeding bird prior to this period.

It was not only the diurnal birds of prey that suffered. Owls were killed, and so were all the crows with the possible exception of the Chough. The spread of some crows that has so excited some people recently is probably a return to their more normal status.

Freshwater fish were also preserved for sport, particularly salmon and trout, and here again birds suffered. The Osprey was a major victim, ultimately lost as a breeding bird for over forty years. The fish-eating ducks such as Goosander and Red-breasted Merganser were killed, as were Cormorant and grebes; and, on suspicion of taking fish-fry and eggs, the killing included Kingfishers and Dippers.

At the same time there was shooting for shooting's sake, when anything might be a target. Sea-birds were shot at their nesting colonies, often for amusement, but sometimes for plumage to be used to decorate hats or clothing. The gulls which at this period began to visit towns in hard winters encountered the same reception. This was also the great period of collecting as a socially acceptable pastime. Collections of stuffed birds were used to ornament domestic and country-house interiors. Any rare bird was shot on sight; and individuals of most species other than the common birds had a price on their heads at a time of widespread rural and urban poverty. Egg-collecting helped to make matters worse.

The nineteenth century was a time when invention and engineering also took its toll of wilder habitats. New and more efficient methods of drainage began to complete what had been started some three hundred years before. Loss of habitat, combined with collecting and shooting, took its toll of marsh birds. We tend to forget that for about forty years we lost the Bittern as a regular breeder, and Black-tailed Godwit and Ruff have only recently begun to re-colonise.

On farmland the beginning of mechanisation started the process that would threaten the survival of a multitude of animals and plants in the next century; its initial and most conspicuous achievement was the change in hay-making that would relegate the Corncrake to the western fringes of Scotland.

The Twentieth Century

The twentieth century inherited a devastated, but still varied, bird fauna, and the beginnings of ideas of protection and conservation.

The countryside remained essentially a mosaic of varied habitats, but almost all of these were in an uneasy equilibrium maintained by human activities, largely centred around mixed farming. The forest had been reduced to an irregular patchwork of scattered fragments, most of them altered to some degree by selective human activity. Drainage and reclamation had removed most of the extensive marshland of low-lying areas. The large areas of fairly infertile upland in the west and north had been considerably modified, mainly as sheep walks but in some areas as grouse moors or deer forest. On poor acidic soils elsewhere a combination of grazing and fire helped maintain areas of heathland.

Farming in some form was the principal land use over some 80% of the country. Habitats varied in farmland, apart from by crop rotation. There was still an extensive acreage of permanent pastures, hay-meadows and open sheep-downs, and these carried their own rich flora and fauna.

The twentieth century is interesting for its climate. In spite of all that has been said up to now, one real problem in understanding the changes in bird distribution and populations in the past lies in the general lack of real data. Information is subjective, sparse and scattered; and all that we know, or can guess about, refers to the more obvious and striking changes. However, in looking at such changes in the present century we become aware of the finer details of climatic fluctuation which for the most part had passed unnoticed in earlier times.

During the first half of the present century, up to about the 1940s, Britain and northern Europe experienced a gradual warming-up of average temperatures, and a more moderate climate with milder winters. There were a few minor upsets, but in the main extreme conditions did not occur. From a long-term viewpoint this period was probably wholly atypical, and it is a little ironic that it was assumed to be the norm against which other climates could be measured.

It had been preceded by the Little Ice Age, centuries of colder and wetter weather. Birds began to respond to the new change with a northward and westward shift of ranges. Species respond to different degrees of change, and in some the first response to this climatic amelioration was already apparent in the latter part of the nineteenth century. In Britain it became more noticeable in the 1920s and peaked by about the mid 1940s. Some aspects of it were summarised by James Fisher in his *History of Birds* (1954).

It appeared to have affected not just Britain but the whole of Eurasia and North America, being more particularly apparent in the temperate to subarctic zones. It was probably best documented in northern Europe and the north-east Atlantic region. Southern species moved into the Faeroes, Iceland and even Greenland; while arctic species such as the Long-tailed Duck and Little Auk shifted the southern borders of their ranges further north. There was also evidence of a northerly range shift in species pairs that tended to replace each other latitudinally. Brambling gave way to Chaffinch, and Arctic Tern to Common Tern, in the zones where they encountered each other as breeding species.

Scandinavia as a whole showed impressive evidence of invasion and increase. Among the species involved there were some eighteen that moved in from the south, and a larger number from the south-east and east. The last included such species as Yellow-breasted Bunting *Emberiza aureola*, Red-breasted Flycatcher *Ficedula parva*, Greenish Warbler *Philloscopus trochiloides*, Arctic Warbler *Phylloscopus borealis*, Red-flanked Bluetail *Tarsiger cyanurus* and Scarlet Grosbeak *Carpodacus erythrinus*.

This invasion from the east may have had a slightly different basis from that of the movement back to northern regions in the recent warmer phase, and might have been part of a slow movement of much older origin. We recognise that our European avifauna may be regarded as ecologically impoverished. Refuges around the Mediterranean during the later glacial periods may have been small and inadequate, and southern barriers such as mountain ranges made it difficult to re-invade after the ice ages. Many species seem to have moved in from the east via Siberia. This was particularly true of forest species, since the major forest refuges in the latter part of the Pleistocene would appear to have been in eastern Eurasia.

Colonisation proceeds at different speeds in different species, and it is possible that because of various delaying factors, such as colder periods in historic times, some of these range extensions are still incomplete. The westward movement of a number of species into Scandinavia in the present century might be evidence of the resumption of a slow invasion that was triggered off after the glaciations ended. If so, then the final stages of this westward movement may yet reach Britain in the future.

In comparison with other parts of north-west Europe, the climate of Britain benefits from the stabilising influence of the warm North Atlantic Drift Current, which modifies extremes. Because of it, changes in our bird fauna resulting from climatic changes, such as that of the first half of the twentieth century, are less dramatic. They tend to result in population increase or decrease, and in local changes of range, rather than gain or loss of species. However, although other factors are often cited, this was the period when we gained such diverse species as Black-necked Grebe, Little Ringed Plover and Black Redstart. It was also a time when many birds extended their ranges into northern England and Scotland.

In the early 1950s there was evidence of an opposing swing in the climatic pattern, ushering in a period of colder, wetter weather that has continued until the present. There seems to be a reluctance to acknowledge the presence and effects of this, as though by adducing some instance which does not accord with it one could somehow prevent it happening.

Again its effects were wider than in Britain alone. At one moment, a single issue of a Norwegian bird journal mentioned the disappearance of the Woodlark from southern Norway, the discovery of the Three-toed Woodpecker *Picoides tridactylus* further south than previously recorded, and the discovery of Brünnich's Guillemots *Uria lomvia* in a number of coastal colonies of the Common Guillemot. Something was obviously happening.

In Britain, as in the earlier warm period, changes were small; and some species that had established new bridgeheads in the earlier period continued to hold them. There was some southward shift of distribution boundaries in various species, occasionally well-marked, as in the case of the Cirl Bunting.

The most striking thing, however, was the way in which the breeding species to find which at the beginning of the 1950s one might expect to travel to central Norway, were increasingly appearing, if only briefly, in northern Scotland and the northern islands. The list includes Great Northern Diver, Gyrfalcon, Goldeneye, Temminck's Stint, Wood Sandpiper, Snowy Owl, Shorelark, Bluethroat, Redwing, Fieldfare, Brambling and Lapland Bunting. The pres-

Gyrfalcon

ence of Wryneck in Scotland, and Red-backed Shrike on Orkney in 1970, at a time when both species were disappearing in south-east England was thought to be due to a westerly influx of bird originally breeding in Scandinavia. The same has been suggested for Scottish records of the Lesser Spotted Woodpecker. At the same time Snow Buntings increased as nesting birds in Scotland, and Redpolls and Siskins spread southwards.

There may be some debate concerning the species involved; but what is clear is that, in a period of some sixty years of the immediate past, two trends had been detectable in the presence and ranges of birds in Britain: a warming northward trend in the first half, and a colder southward one in the second half. It is impossible to believe that similar changes, although probably of differing degrees, had not been occurring through most of the past. It does help to emphasise that, in spite of what we know of the past history of our birds, it cannot represent more than a very general overview of all that must have occurred.

24

Final Comment

In introducing the twentieth century I briefly commented on the land-use situation at the beginning of the period. In the time up to the Second World War, agriculture in Britain was on the decline. During the war, and afterwards, agriculture and forestry have had a free hand in utilising the land for maximum productivity and profit. It was obviously not perceived at first that this might be harmful. In fact, the immediate post-war legislation was drafted with the assumption that the countryside would retain its mosaic of habitats provided that it was shielded from the dangers of urbanisation.

In this period we have now seen the destruction of woodland, removal of hedgerows and creation of huge fields. Rotation and mixed farming has disappeared to be replaced by repeated growth of cash crops: a monoculture maintained by artificial fertilizers and drenched with poison sprays. The run-off of chemicals has damaged marshland and fresh waters. The marginal land – rough grazing, heathland, grouse moor and deer forest – is being replaced by dense plantation of conifers.

What this means in terms of habitat loss over the last forty years has been investigated and summarised by the Nature Conservancy Council.

Grasslands have suffered. Of the species-rich hay-meadows 95% have lost most of their variety, and only 3% are undamaged. Of the open lowland grassed sheep walks we have lost 80%, most of it going to arable or 'improved' grass. Upland grasslands, heath and bog have lost 30% through damage, conifer planting or 'reclamation'; lowland heaths have decreased by 40%.

Fens and marshes have decreased by 60%, and lowland broadleaf woodland by 30–50%.

The hedgerows lost would encircle the equator five times!

Further damage and loss has affected habitats ranging from lakes and rivers to mudflats, saltings, beaches and dunes, and up to the high tops of mountains.

This is an appalling catalogue of habitat loss, especially in so short a time and with no guarantee that it has been slowed down or arrested. Looking at it from the narrowest point of view, we might argue that we have not as yet lost any bird species because of it, but there will have been few that have not been seriously affected by it. By considerable expenditure of money and effort we have managed to hold onto remnants of our full range of bird life; but this is not enough.

We value our birds as an integral part of our environment. If that means anything at all, it means that we want them as a natural part of our lives, not just something that we might briefly glimpse on a holiday after a long journey. The underlying motivation of much of the effort made by so many people has been to try to encourage and maintain in people generally the enthusiasm for preserving the variety of wildlife, and the feeling that this is a part of our natural heritage.

If we are forced to limit that wildlife to very small and scattered reserves where, simply to prevent undue disturbance, access must be limited, then we have problems. Things which are rightly or wrongly seen to be available only to a privileged minority are hardly likely to be regarded as the birthright of the population as a whole. This has been a background cause of social unrest and reaction in this country ever since the creation of the medieval hunting forests and the later pheasant coverts. People have conserved things for their own enjoyment, and not in order to maintain theories of ecological balance.

Another problem that arises from the decimation and fragmentation of so many types of habitat is the concomitant effect on the birds within them. We find ourselves trying to maintain small, relict reserves in widely scattered localities, and tacitly assume that local conditions are unlikely to alter. The whole theme of what I have already said is that change is inherent, and predictable in the long term. If slow change or sudden disaster, such as a very cold winter or hot and dry summer, were to alter conditions drastically, then a reserve might lose the components within it that ensured the survival of a species.

When this happens, if the species is a bird, we assume that it can move elsewhere and perhaps return, or that a population of the same species existing elsewhere will re-colonise if and when suitable conditions are restored. But we are not alone in the decimation of our varied habitats. If we and other countries continue to whittle down many habitat reserves into tiny sample refuges, then we are rapidly approaching the point where a bird that is forced to move by changing conditions will have nowhere to go to, and nowhere from which to return.

If these trends are not reversed, then the birds of Britain will continue to have a history – but no future.

Red Kite

Climatic Zones

A series of broad climatic zones occur in a sequence from north to south. They are determined by a temperature gradient, but are more often recognised in practice by the landscape produced by its secondary effects. Although the terms listed below are widely used, the definitions are hazy and sometimes vary; and they are in any case theoretical divisions which in practice merge into each other along ill-defined lines. They should be regarded as generalised divisions intended to help clarify the overall picture of distribution, rather than hard and fast definitions. The temperatures referred to in places are mean temperatures, and the extremes may vary considerably on either side of these.

ARCTIC ZONE
Winter temperature well below freezing, summer mean below 15°C. Ground frozen with permafrost, thawing at the surface in summer. Where not permanent snow or rock, usually tundra; moss or lichen tundra grading into shrub tundra.

ALPINE ZONE
This often has tundra-like vegetation on cold, high mountain areas, and may attract similar bird species. It appears to be an altitudinal equivalent of the Arctic zone and the two are often linked as the Arctic/Alpine zone; but the Alpine zone has a climate modified to some extent by that of the lower-altitude areas around it.

SUBARCTIC ZONE
A slightly milder zone, usually with low birch and willow shrub tundra grading into birch scrub and forest tundra on the borders of the Boreal zone.

BOREAL ZONE
Winter mean −3°C, summer mean above 15°C. A zone with cold winters and cool summers with more rain in summer. Recognisable as the broad northern zone of conifer forest.

TEMPERATE ZONE
Winter mean above −3°C, summer mean below 21°C. In western Europe lss than six months with mean temperature below 6°C, but with longer and colder winters further east. Rainfall more evenly spread in the west, mainly in summer in the east. A zone of generally milder winters and warmer summers, characterised over most of Europe by broad-leaf forest.

WARM TEMPERATE ZONE
Winter mean above 4°C, summer mean 21–27°C. A zone of mild, wet winters and dry, hot summers. Evergreen broad-leaf forest is typical of some of the zone, which may otherwise be characterised by dry areas with sparse vegetation.

SUBTROPICAL ZONE
Winter mean above 10°C, summer mean above 27°C. Within our range this is mainly an arid zone of high temperatures and little rainfall.

TROPICAL ZONE
Winter and summer means above 21°C. A zone of consistently high temperature and high rainfall, characterised by tropical forest.

Classification and Sequence

The sequence of orders and families in this book differs in some respects from the one most frequently in current use. Minor modifications of sequence have been necessary in order to fit the grouping of birds on the plates. This is less a departure from the orthodox than it might at first appear. Although at any particular period considerations that are more often editorial than scientific may make it appear that a currently used sequence is a final and inflexible arrangement, such arrangements are both subjective and subject to intermittent replacement, as anyone who has used a series of bird books published over the last thirty or forty years will be aware.

A taxonomic classification of species should be a logical and hierarchical arrangement that allows one to comprehend the relationships involved. However, the relationships within a large and evolutionarily divergent assembly of species can only adequately be envisaged as something resembling a three-dimensional branching tree on which the species existing at any given moment would be the groups of twigs present at one level. In order to use this in written form it is necessary to transform it into a single linear sequence. This transforms it into an artificial, arbitrary arrangement, involving choices of possible alternatives. A further complication is added by differences of opinion and new discoveries concerning relationships, which lead to changes in the accepted sequence.

I began my interest in birds when the standard work was Witherby's five-volume *Handbook*. This used a sequence produced early in the century by Ernst Hartert. It began with the passerines and ended with the game-birds. In 1930 Alexander Wetmore proposed another classification. He had worked on fossil birds, and using the rather scanty information about them known at the time he created a new sequence. It began with those orders and families which appeared to show evidence of early origin, and ended with those that he considered to be the most derived and specialised. In some respects it was virtually the reverse of Hartert's sequence, but with a divergence of views on passerine evolution.

By analogy with human development, Hartert regarded as the height of evolution that which showed evidence of greatest intelligence and adaptability. Believing that the crows were the birds in which this had been developed to the highest degree he put them at the beginning. Wetmore used morphological specialisation as his criterion. In his classification he gave the crows a low rating near the beginning of his passerines, his sequence being the reverse of Hartert's, and put the seed-eating finches and buntings at the end as his evolutionary climax.

The fifteen volumes of Peters's *Checklist of the Birds of the World* followed Wetmore, but changed in later volumes to use the reversed Hartert sequence, giving the crows as the last passerine family. There was considerable debate for a time on these alternatives. Later studies of varying aspects of ornithology indicated possible needs for further changes in parts of these sequences. The characters used varied from jaw musculature and syrinx structure to behaviour. In 1977 Karel Voous produced a list of birds of the Holarctic based mainly on Wetmore but using some of the later ideas. It was intended to be a flexible, tentative list, but was pounced on with a sigh of relief by the editors of some journals and pronounced to be the unquestionable orthodox sequence, effectively destroying its flexibility.

Meanwhile in the 1960s Charles Sibley had proposed the use of electrophoresis of egg-white protein as evidence of relationship, and had produced a comprehensive review of avian taxonomy. However he has now discarded it in favour of relationships revealed by DNA-DNA hybridisation, which he examined in association with Jon Ahlquist. The results, which are not yet fully available, are interesting. They appear to provide a more satisfactory arrangement in many instances, but would involve some drastic re-arrangement, particularly among the passerine families. It is argued that since DNA is the basic genetic unit within the body cells, the results must provide the final objective evidence of affinity. This may be true, but since similar claims were made for the egg-white protein studies there is likely to be some caution in accepting them wholly. What is certain is that we have yet another potential taxonomic sequence for birds.

Anyone faced with this series of changes in what is sometimes regarded as *the* official or acceptable sequence, must inevitably develop a more flexible approach to the subject; and small divergences from proposed sequences may no longer appear as some kind of scientific heresy.

The original paintings used in this book were probably based on the Witherby *Handbook* order, with one or two compromises for reasons of space. In order that species could be found in the text by those more accustomed to later arrangements, they have been re-arranged. However, there are problems in using the Voous arrangement currently widely used; and the best compromise appeared to be the modified Wetmore used during most of the late sixties and seventies.

There are still one or two peculiarities. The shearwaters come first, before the divers and grebes, coincidentally closer to recent views on the relationship of the first two taxa. The Cuckoo occurs later than it should, next to the woodpeckers as in the *Handbook*. The artist chose to put the Golden Oriole well out of sequence, with some of the more striking of the perching non-passerines on plate 32, and it is therefore far from its text which I have put with those species on plate 44.

Sequence and plate numbers are:

Tube-Noses

PROCELLARIIFORMES

The 'tube-noses' or procellariiform seabirds are the birds least tied to any country in their general way of life, yet forced to home to a small colony-site on island or coast where the need to land and nest appears to be just an unfortunate necessity. They are designed to survive at sea, travelling long distances in search of food. The bill is equipped with a sharp hooked tip to seize their prey, and the nostrils are characteristically shielded by short projecting tubes. Evolutionarily they appear to have originated in the southern oceans. The continuous circumpolar seas of the southern hemisphere, more sea than land, represented an ideal area for evolution, radiation and specialisation in these oceanic birds, and were available from very early times. There are suggestions that the movements of sea-birds between the Indian and Atlantic, and Pacific and Atlantic Oceans, with subsequent subspeciation or speciation, could have taken place around present-day Arabia and Central America in the Miocene and Pliocene epochs of the past; but in view of the ability of these birds to traverse huge areas of ocean a similar effect might have been achieved by direct invasions from the south in all these oceans.

Fulmars and shearwaters
Procellariidae

These are the typical sea-birds of this group, with long, stiff and narrow wings designed for gliding. They catch the small uplift of air from the edges of waves, which allows them to travel long distances with minimum expenditure of energy; but they are poorly designed for manoeuvring in landing or take-off. The legs and webbed feet are set well back for propulsion in swimming, but this makes it difficult to walk on land, where the legs offer poor support. Birds tend to shuffle along on bent legs, resting on the belly when they stop. This vulnerability on land is such that most shearwaters and petrels wait until it is dark before coming to the nest site. With little use of visual signals, and a need to locate a mate in darkness, the voice is well-developed instead. This is least so in the purring calls of petrels, but the Manx Shearwater has a raucous crowing.

Their food is fish or other small sea creatures taken at the surface or by diving. It may involve long searching; and the single egg and subsequent downy young one are adapted to periods of neglect as a safety device, since adults may be absent from a nest for several days, travelling long distances for food.

There are two species of the family nesting in Britain, both with close relatives in southern subantarctic seas, so similar that they have at times been regarded as conspecific. The more heavily-built Fulmar nests on open coastal cliff ledges. It is a subarctic species and we are on its southern limit. The more slender Manx Shearwater nests in colonies of burrows at island sites scattered along the western coasts from the Scillies to Shetland. It has closely-related species around New Zealand and in the Pacific, and a race in the Mediterranean, but is otherwise a North Atlantic bird that appears to have invaded from the south.

Fulmar *Fulmarus glacialis*
At first sight gull-like but with greyer wing-tips, it is a stouter-bodied, rounder-headed bird, white with a grey back, and with darker grey individuals in Arctic areas, known as 'Blue' Fulmars. The stout, stubby bill has a hooked upper mandible. The flight is a typical glide on stiff, straight wings, superbly controlled in rough weather, and with an occasional few short wing-beats in calm air. It takes small creatures and offal from the sea surface, and occasionally makes brief dives.

It nests on coasts and although it ranges a little further after breeding, birds in British waters do not travel far from the nest-sites, the young ones straying furthest. The nest-site is simply a reasonably broad ledge of some kind on a cliff or outcrop, occasionally a little way inland. It is sited so that a gliding bird can land and take off with minimal manoeuvring, but birds are often troubled by cliff-face updraughts. The site is bare of material and the single egg is tended by both parents, who indulge in noisy cackling displays. On such a site, with its strong bill and ability to vomit up and spew out quantities of oil in its defence, the Fulmar breeds successfully and has spread dramatically. It matures at nine years and has a potential life-expectancy of about thirty-five years.

It has been suggested that, beginning with the slender-billed Antarctic Fulmar *F. glacialoides*, moving north to give rise to the slender-billed Aleutian race of the northern Fulmar, the Atlantic bird could have come via the Bering Straits and Arctic Ocean. However, both oceans could have been colonised from the south.

In the North Atlantic the Fulmar is an arctic to subarctic species, breeding north to Spitzbergen; and a few centuries ago its southernmost colonies appear to have been on Greenland, Jan Mayen, just north of Iceland and on St Kilda. Its spread began two centuries

Studies of Fulmars

Manx Shearwater

Fulmar

Leach's Petrel

British Storm Petrel

Fulmar

D.M.H.

ago and, although changes in fishing and food availability have been suggested as the reason, it appears more closely linked to a slow warming of sea temperatures affecting the breeding group associated with the warmer North Atlantic Drift current in the area from Iceland to Britain. It spread around Iceland in the eighteenth century, to the Faeroes in the nineteenth, and to Shetland in 1878; and in a little over a century it has changed from being a British species of one remote island off Scotland to one of our most numerous sea-birds, now breeding right around the coasts of Britain. It has colonised all the coastal cliffs of the British Isles in a century, and also occupied a few crags and dunes near the coasts. It still appears to be increasing, with an estimate of over 300,000 pairs in the British Isles, of which about 90% are in north-west Scotland and the northern and western Isles.

Visiting Shearwaters

In addition to our breeding species there are other shearwaters that pass close offshore at times. While not a part of our breeding fauna – or in some instances no longer a part of it, and in others possibly not yet a part – they nevertheless help us to understand how our breeding birds might have first reached us. Like Fulmars, the shearwaters economise on energy while travelling long distances to hunt food. They glide, using the rising air currents from the edges of waves, and in doing so travel with the wind or at slight angles to it. The winds and currents of the world tend to move around the ocean basins, clockwise in the north, anti-clockwise in the south; and when not breeding the shearwaters may make extensive journeys on these.

The Little Shearwater *Puffinus assimilis*, like a small black-and-white Manx Shearwater with a more wing-beating and undulating flight, breeds in the Azores, Madeira and the Canary Islands. In addition to passing off south-west Britain when not breeding, individuals have recently occurred in Manx Shearwater colonies off South Wales as though prospecting an extension in range.

Cory's Shearwater *Calonectris diomedea* is a large, pale-coloured bird. It nests at sites in the Mediterranean, and on Atlantic islands from the Azores to the Cape Verdes. After breeding it moves north in the Atlantic, up to and sometimes around Britain. It is this species that nested in South Wales in the Ipswichian interglacial and possibly other warm Pleistocene periods.

Two other big species visit from much further south, appearing to follow the full possible figure-8 track through the south and north Atlantic, passing Britain at the northern end of the loops. The Great Shearwater *Puffinus gravis*, with a darkish cap, breeds on south Atlantic islands and visits us in its non-breeding winter period, our summer. The dark-plumaged Sooty Shearwater *P. griseus* nests in New Zealand and on sub-antarctic islands, and must spend most of its non-breeding period on this great circum-ocean trek. With journeys such as these, the northern oceans could have been colonised fairly easily by sea-birds originating in the southern hemisphere.

Manx Shearwater *Puffinus puffinus*

A slender, sea-skimming bird, black above and white below. It has the typical low-level flight, tilting from side to side, and with a few quick wing-beats at intervals. Seen singly or in small parties at sea, it may gather just off the breeding colony in large flocks over or on the sea, waiting for darkness before coming ashore. The bill is slender and hook-tipped and the food mainly small fish, snatched at the surface or in shallow dives.

The nests are in burrows or rock crevices, in a close colony on an island, usually near the sea edge, but sometimes on a high ridge further inland. Having a weak shuffling walk and needing a mound or rock to take off from, it is vulnerable to predators such as large gulls, and visits the nest only at night, preferably in dark moonless conditions. Activity is marked by a wild clamour of high, strangled crowing and cackling calls, birds in burrows calling to flying mates. The single egg sometimes rests on pulled-in plant material. The downy chick, fed like all procellariiform young on regurgitated food, becomes very large, and is deserted before it leaves the nest.

After breeding, they migrate south and west to wintering grounds off the east coast of South America, performing some or perhaps all of the big figure-8 loop around the North and South Atlantic. On return they pass near North America. Using the winds they may travel about 5,000 miles in two and a half weeks on their outward journey. Young birds return to prospect sites after two years, and begin breeding at five years old.

Very closely related forms, possibly not the same species, occur on islands around New Zealand and Hawaii, and off California. Our own bird breeds in the North Atlantic from Iceland south to the Salvage Islands; and another race or species breeds in the eastern Mediterranean. The Balearic Shearwater *P. mauritanicus* of the Western Mediterranean appears to be a separate species.

The Manx Shearwater seems to have few enemies other than man, and to be controlled by food and weather. Its British form certainly evolved in the North Atlantic although our fossil evidence only goes back to the early Holocene of Wales. Population variation around Britain seems to be purely local; but in recent decades the species has established a colony off the

Manx Shearwater

north-east coast of the USA. Perhaps this should be regarded as a re-colonisation of the western Atlantic: it was exterminated on Bermuda in historic times.

Colonies are scattered, mainly on islands, but with a few on coastal promontories, extending down the west coast from Shetland to the Scillies, and around Ireland. Populations fluctuate considerably, and nocturnal burrowing birds are hard to count. 1970 estimates were of 175,000–300,000 pairs.

Storm-petrels
Hydrobatidae

These small birds have bodies no bigger than large finches'. They have proportionally bigger tails than shearwaters, shorter wings, small bills and long legs, and they look more like migrant passerines, fluttering or swooping over the surface of the sea. In spite of this they are oceanic birds when not breeding, usually seen on the wing, and feeding by snatching small creatures from the surface. Occasionally, more particularly with Leach's Petrel, persistent westerly gales may force them onto a lee shore, and exhausted birds are driven inland, usually to disaster, in so-called 'wrecks'. The small storm-petrels occur world-wide, with our two species, the British Storm-petrel and Leach's Petrel extending furthest north. The stronger-flying Leach's Petrel occurs through the warmer oceans of the western hemisphere, but the smaller storm-petrels speciate round smaller groups of islands. Both nest in burrows and, like shearwaters, are night visitors to their nest-sites.

British Storm-petrel *Hydrobates pelagicus*
Usually seen as a tiny bird with fluttering flight, it skims and skitters along the surface in the troughs of waves with dangling legs, or apparently runs tip-toe on the surface. It appears sooty-black, with a bold white rump and square-ended tail; a faint pale line borders the wing-coverts. The flight appears deceptively weak for a bird that winters at sea. It comes to land on small islands, breeding in holes in rock screes, storm beaches, crevices or burrows. Compared with the larger petrel species it is silent, save for the purring calls at night from unmated birds in burrows, and sharper calls and churrs in the nocturnal flights around the nest-sites. The adults take turns of several days at the nest while the partner is away feeding.

It nests from Iceland, Faeroes and western British Isles to the Canaries and into the western Mediterranean; with evidence of some interchange of birds among colonies. After breeding it becomes an oceanic bird, occasionally seen following in the wake of ships. It moves southwards through the eastern North Atlantic, and occurs in winter at sea off the western coast of Africa. There is little evidence about its past; and what information there is has been confused by lack of certain knowledge about breeding sites and numbers. There was some decrease in the Scillies at the end of the last century, and more recently in Scotland, Ireland and south-west England; but its occurrence in the Lofoten Islands off western Norway may be of recent origin.

The island colonies vary from just a few pairs to around 10,000–20,000 in some sites off County Kerry, and on St Kilda, Priest Island and Foula. They occur from Shetland to the Hebrides, down the west side of Ireland, and on the Calf of Man, Bardsey, islands off Pembrokeshire, Gullard Rocks in Cornwall, and on the Scillies. Population guesses range from 50,000–150,000 pairs.

Leach's Petrel *Oceanodroma leucorhoa*
Compared with the British Storm-petrel this is bigger, with longer and more tapering wings, and an erratic, buoyant flight. The forked tail and grey centre-line on the white rump are less conspicuous than the pale band on the wing, as points of identity. The flight is faster and stronger, and food is picked up while hovering over the water's surface. It may be mainly a night feeder. It is a more oceanic species than the British Storm-petrel, with breeding colonies on just a few north-western islands. Like the latter it visits the nests at night. It is noisier at its nest-sites, with birds chasing in aerial display flights, and calling with a variably-pitched harsh staccato call. Purring song and screaming calls are used by birds in burrows. After breeding the birds disperse out to sea, some remaining long enough in northern waters for the occasional autumn 'wreck' to occur. In general they move into tropical waters and beyond into the South Atlantic.

The main breeding distribution of the species is across the North Pacific from Japan to California, and on the north-east seaboard of North America. The Atlantic colonies on the Westmann Islands, the Faeroes and western Scotland represent eastern outliers and might indicate a postglacial eastward extension of range, possibly encouraged by the North Atlantic Drift Current which reaches that area. At present Leach's Petrel only appears to nest on St Kilda, the Flannan Islands, North Rona and Sule Sgeir, all off the north-west of Scotland, and on Foula and Ramna Stacks on Shetland. It is not certain, however, that all colonies are known, and it may nest in the Shetlands, on Sule Skerry and some of the Outer Hebrides. There are past records and recent odd sightings from the west of Ireland as well. The total British population might be in the order of 5,000–10,000 pairs.

Divers or Loons

GAVIIFORMES

Gaviidae

This small and highly specialised quartet of species is too specialised for their relationship to other orders of birds to be apparent; but they are generally similar to others that show a high degree of adaptation to aquatic life.

For most people they are elusive birds, except at their breeding grounds in high latitudes. Seen on the water, typically with head up, bill a little raised and tail end almost awash, they have an uptilted appearance; and the smooth, tight feathering gives them an odd snaky-headed look. Under water and in the air they are bottle-shaped; an elongated and rounded body with a narrower elongated neck. At the front the head tapers to a narrow, sharp bill; and for propulsion in water the shortish stout legs are right at the rear, with strong webbed toes. The wings are somewhat small and narrow, easily tucked away and curved against the body, and the tail is barely apparent. In flight the line of head and neck sag slightly below that of the body, to give a very characteristic hunched silhouette.

The whole body is shaped for rapid underwater progress in pursuit of fish. In such swimming the legs are rotated to project outwards at the sides so that the main backward thrust is delivered laterally; and the tarsus of the leg is strongly laterally flattened to reduce resistance when the legs are pulled forwards. The wings may also be used to help in underwater swimming. Birds swimming on the surface frequently lower the head so that bill and eyes are just below the surface, looking for fish before they dive. Dives average about a minute in length and may go down to about 9 metres in depth.

As with other birds that have followed this evolutionary path, progress on land becomes difficult. The divers can only stagger a short way, and so the nest is built at the water's edge. Manoeuvrability in flight is also reduced, and the larger divers make a long take-off in clearing the surface. The breeding plumage shows bold striping on the neck and white chequering on the back, but with the pattern restricted to the head and neck in the Red-throated Diver. The voices are far-carrying, and the calls include unforgettable weird and eerie wailing, normally only heard from breeding birds. They breed on waters of the boreal to arctic zones, and spend the winter in ice-free coastal waters.

There are only four species in all, in size comparable to large ducks or geese, but differing in proportions. The smallest, the Red-throated Diver, occurs near coasts and larger waters in subarctic to boreal areas, sometimes at higher altitudes. Unlike the others it breeds on small, sometimes tiny waters, flying to the coast or lakes to feed. It is circumpolar in distribution.

The other three species resemble each other more closely and are probably of later common origin, with a distribution pattern that may be of Ice Age origin. There could have been an early separation on the two continents with the slightly smaller Black-throated Diver becoming a mainly boreal species, preferring larger lakes to those used by the Red-throated Diver. In North America a now larger form appears to have had its range split by the Pleistocene ice-cap. South of it, in habitats similar to those of the Black-throated Diver, a population produced the Great Northern Diver; while north-west of it in the Bering Strait refuge another population produced the slightly larger and heavier-billed White-billed Diver.

In some subsequent warmer period or periods the Black-throated Diver extended its range into north-western North America as a slightly smaller form that now overlaps in general range with the Great Northern Diver. The Great Northern Diver moved north and, later, possibly in the early Holocene, extended north-east across the Atlantic to southern Greenland and Iceland. The White-billed Diver spread along the coasts of the Arctic Ocean to occur from northern Russia to Hudson's Bay.

Red-throated Diver *Gavia stellata*
The smallest and palest of the four. On winter seas it looks ashy-grey, with a lot of white on face and neck, and upperparts grey with fine white speckling. At close range the finer, pointed bill, with the cut-away lower mandible tip giving it an uptilted appearance, is heightened by the bird's tendency to carry it slightly raised. In breeding plumage the head and neck are grey; the slender shape, uniform colour and dense, smooth plumage give it a slightly unbirdlike appearance. There is fine black-and-white striping down the back of the neck from the crown, and a narrow, dark, dull red neck-patch.

Its breeding requirements give it a limited distribution in Britain. It is mainly in Scotland west of a line from Arran to the Spey Valley, and north to Shetland, with a tiny population in the north of Ireland. It nests in scattered pairs, preferring tiny hill lochans and peat-pools of blanket-bog and moorland areas. It is a more agile and faster flyer than the other divers; and it needs to be, since it will fly to the coast or larger waters to feed, and must carry fish back to the young.

The calls include a mewing wail, a gobbling cooing call, a goose-like cackle in flight, and a crow-like warning bark. The elaborate displays of the breeding period involve ritualised postures, often with the two birds swimming side by side. In one display they tilt forwards with half-sunk bodies and extended necks, calling with down-pointed bills, in another they are almost upright, head, neck and bill extended upwards while they rush along side by side in this posture, the submerged legs wildly paddling the water.

The nest is usually a low heap of plant material on a slightly raised bank at the water's edge. The two long eggs produce downy grey chicks able to swim after the first day. They are fed on fish brought by the parents, squabbling for precedence; frequently only one survives. Fledging takes about six weeks. After breeding they disperse to coastal seas, sometimes visiting inland waters in passing. They may occur in loose groups or

Red-throated Diver

SUMMER

WINTER

Black-throated Diver

SUMMER

WINTER

Great Northern Diver

WINTER

SUMMER

D.M.HENRY

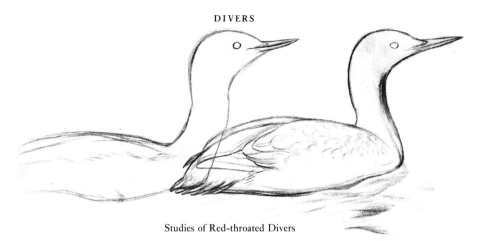

Studies of Red-throated Divers

small flocks. They prefer shallow waters and may occur offshore around most of Britain in winter.

Breeding as it does, it is very vulnerable to human disturbance, faced with which the adults may fly from the pool and leave the nest open to predators. This may be a reason for the limitations to its distribution. It may have been much more numerous in the Pleistocene, when there was more extensive tundra at times. It has one of the earlier British records, being present in North Norfolk five to six hundred thousand years ago. In recent times change has been slight, and it is difficult to be sure to what extent human interference may have been involved. It decreased in the last century, and has increased in the present one, the small Irish colony beginning about 1884. There was some south-westerly and south-easterly extension in Scotland, and large increases in island populations from Shetland to the Hebrides. It is still increasing, and now estimated at 1,000–2,000 pairs. In winter it is present around the coasts on inshore waters, breeding birds moving south and west, and joined by others from the Faeroes, Iceland, Greenland and Scandinavia. Winter populations have been estimated at about 12,000–15,000 birds.

Black-throated Diver *Gavia arctica*
A diver with an oddly dapper breeding dress suggesting an urbanity that accords neither with its wild setting nor its wilder calls. The sleekly grey head sets off a purple-black throat patch bordered by elongated black and white striping, and patches of white chequering orna-ment a black back. It is larger and heavier than the Red-throated Diver, with a more evenly-tapering bill. In winter it is more solitary, and with darker upperparts appears more black-and-white at a distance.

It winters in coastal waters, but at this period shows a rather discontinuous distribution around Britain. It tends to be absent from the waters of the Caithness region, Yorkshire to the Wash, and Devon to Galloway, but with some local likelihood around Pembrokeshire and the Wirral region. There is evidence of a probably wintering bird from South Wales in the early Holocene.

For breeding it requires the deeper and larger clear inland lakes and lochs, expecting to find fish close at hand; and it is more tolerant than the Red-throated Diver of waters within forests and with more heavily vegetated margins. There is usually one pair to a lake. It rises less easily from the water than does the Red-throated Diver and is more aquatic in its general behaviour. It too breeds only in the western half of Scotland, but tends to use more inland sites, and is absent from Orkney and Shetland.

It has similar ritualised and mutual displays to those of the Red-throated Diver. The calls are more striking, with plaintive rhythmic wails, almost curlew-like in rhythm and with some hint of the yodelling more marked in the Great Northern Diver; and strange, pulsing, hollow 'coraks' are used by disturbed birds. Postures are less stiffly upright, with head and neck held in a more easy S-curve; and when a number are together a 'circle dance' may occur with birds manoeuvring to show off the black neck-patch. Quarrelling may evoke an upright posture, treading water with arched neck and lowered bill, the posture heightened by plumage pattern.

The nest is a heap of plant material near the water's edge, where possible on a small island in the lake, away from predators. Food for the young is found nearby. Such nest-sites are vulnerable to changes in water-level, especially flooding, being nearer the water than those of other divers; and while this may seem a natural risk it appears to have caused significant loss in the recent past, possibly linked with use of lakes and reservoirs for water storage.

Black-throated Diver

It is also sensitive to human disturbance, and on larger lakes is liable to be affected by boating and similar activities. As a result it is scarce and dispersed as a British breeding bird, and breeding success has been very low in recent years. In general its total British population has probably been more affected by human activity in the long term than by climatic events. Numbers fell in the earlier part of the century, and there has been some contraction in the eastern part of its

34

range. However, there appears to have been some westward spread into the Scottish islands at this earlier period; and since the 1950s it has spread a little southwestwards, as far south as Galloway. Total numbers have fallen, with a current estimate of 100 breeding pairs or less, and very low breeding success. Some Scandinavian birds join native ones in winter, and birds are present in small numbers on inshore waters, mainly around Scotland and on the east and south coasts of England. Winter numbers are of about 1,300 birds, decreasing in a later winter moult migration to around Brittany.

Great Northern Diver *Gavia immer*

In northern North America this species is comfortably accepted as the Common Loon, but in western Europe its rarity, and the haunting wild wails and odd echoing laughter-like cries heard in the remote breeding setting, have given it a rather special status. It is the biggest of our regular divers, with heavy, tapering bill. It is better known as a winter visitor, with the typical pattern of dark above and white below, but it is slightly paler-bodied and thicker-necked than the similar Black-throated Diver.

Its breeding plumage, black, with a green-glossed neck patched with thin vertical striping in places as though showing through holes torn in a uniform dark covering, and white chequering and spotting all over the back, make it a conspicuous bird. Even more conspicuous is the voice. The calls are loud and far-carrying. Best known are the long, wolf-like, yodelling howls, and the rapid tremulo calls that rise to a sound like high-pitched crazy laughter. There are variants on these, some building to a crescendo from shorter, low-pitched notes, and also low moans and briefer calls.

Its ritual posturings in the breeding season are very like those of the Black-throated Diver, but perhaps a little more subdued and less elaborate. The conspicuous calls seem to play a greater part in territorial displays and advertisement than in the other species.

Its status as a British breeding species has a slender basis. It has long been suspected of breeding along the western coasts or islands of Scotland where individuals are often present in summer. There was a single observation of birds with young in 1970. For breeding it prefers large and reasonably deep lakes, and breeds in both boreal forest zones and more open tundra. Like the Black-throated diver it needs a large territory in which food will be present, islets for nesting; and it appears to feel safer in large open spaces.

The nest is a low mound of vegetation by the water's edge, preferably by water deep enough to allow an instant dive. As with other birds whose downy young swim with them soon after hatching, the young may be carried on the swimming parent's back which provides a convenient mobile resting place.

Migration from Greenland and Iceland would seem to be towards the south-west, birds usually migrating singly. It has a slower and stronger flight than the smaller divers, the wing-beat tempo more like that of a goose. In winter it occurs in coastal waters around the British Isles, though less frequently on the east coast of England. Non-breeding birds spend the summer around Shetland and down the western coasts of Scotland and Ireland. Its pattern of general distribution as a species suggests that it may have moved north-eastwards to colonise Iceland in the recent past. The occurrence of summering birds around western Britain suggests that a capacity for eastward expansion still continues. If like other northern species it has been affected by colder weather patterns since the 1950s, the apparent attempt to start breeding in Scotland might indicate a continuing tendency to spread, combined with a south-east shift.

The wintering population is estimated at about 3,500–4,500 birds.

White-billed Diver *Gavia adamsi*
NOT ILLUSTRATED

Once regarded as a form of the Great Northern Diver, this is an infrequent visitor to Britain. It is similar to the latter in appearance but the heavy, ivory-coloured bill has the underside of the lower mandible cut away towards the tip to give the bill an uptilted appearance, closer to the shape of the Red-throated Diver. Its breeding distribution is around the shores of the Arctic Sea. It has bred as far west as northern Finland, and birds from the western end of the range winter in coastal seas around northern and north-west Norway, and stray down into the North Sea. It is presumably the last movement from which we receive our visitors.

Grebes

PODICIPEDIFORMES

Podicipedidae

Although unrelated, grebes are the smaller exploiters of the divers' niche, chasing fish in fresh water and, by virtue of a smaller size, taking other small creatures such as water insects as well. The dense plumage of the virtually tail-less body may be fluffed out when they are on the surface to give a rather dumpy appearance, surmounted by a slender neck and narrow, sharp-billed head. Under water, like the divers, they are sleek and streamlined, with legs set back towards the rear of the body. The big feet lack webs but the toes are big flattened lobes that can overlap to form a single flat surface to impart a strong forward thrust. In the air they look all neck and wings, the body humped and the big lobed feet projecting behind. The wings show white patches in most species.

The breeding season ornamentation involves a change of neck colour; and fine slender feathering on the head can be erected to form striking ruffs and tufts, but quickly sleeked away to present no problem in under-water streamlining.

The position of the legs towards the rear of the body creates the usual problem in walking on land, and the grebes do so very awkwardly, semi-erect and staggering a little, and only moving short distances. They solve the problem when nesting by building in shallow water, making heaps of floating weed onto which they can climb more easily and return to the water rapidly. The otherwise conspicuous white eggs are quickly covered with nest material when the bird leaves them, becoming stained buff or brown. The downy young have a bold striped pattern. They are fed by both parents and when small may be carried on the backs of swimming adults, between the wings.

Britain has five species, two of them regular breeders – the largest and the smallest, two that are less certain breeders, and one winter visitor. The winter visitor is the Red-necked Grebe, large, but slightly smaller than the Great Crested Grebe. It has a discontinuous Holarctic distribution, in suitable areas up into the boreal zone. The Great Crested Grebe has a more southerly distribution, also extending to Africa and Australia, but extensively overlaps with the Red-necked in Russia and eastern Europe. There is separation by habitat preference, the Red-necked preferring smaller, shallower waters with more emergent vegetation and eating more insects. In view of their ranges it is difficult to guess at past distribution, but if they were potential competitors the Red-necked might have originated in North America where the Great Crested does not occur.

The smaller species form a more obvious pair, similar in size, and more strikingly identified by distinctive head plumes. The Slavonian is the more northerly species, extending across Eurasia and North America in the boreal zone. In Eurasia the Black-necked Grebe breeds through the temperate zone, south of the Slavonian and with only a slight overlap. Its range is broken by the Asiatic deserts. In North America it is absent in the east, and in the centre its range overlaps

extensively with that of the Slavonian Grebe; but the two have slightly differing habitat requirements.

The Black-necked Grebe also occurs in east Africa. As a species of more southerly, warmer and drier habitats it appears much more vulnerable to seasonal aridity and changes in the availability of water, resulting in shifts of range.

The smallest bird, the Dabchick, is an Old World species of temperate to tropical zones from Britain to Japan and south to southern Africa, Indonesia and the Papuan region.

Grest Crested Grebe *Podiceps cristatus*
This is the largest of our grebes. On the water it is the slenderness of the neck, the thin head and slim dagger bill, and the conspicuous whiteness of the breast, foreneck and face that first strike one; but when breeding it has a dandified elegance. The narrow black cap ends in a pair of shaggy black tufts; and from nape to chin, on either side, a chestnut ruff tipped with black can be raised and fanned to border the white cheeks like some Elizabethan extravagance. The dull and dark body is barely noticeable in all this; but the wings have a broad band bordering the secondaries and a wedge of white on the fore-edge. These come into sight when the wings are lifted and partly spread in display and are conspicuous in flight; and the crouching and mantling in display may enhance the frontal patterns of displayed head-plumes.

The similar sexes both display in striking and varied ways. They often face each other with ruffs and tippets erected in shock-headed display, sometimes holding trails of waterweeds and solemnly shaking their heads from side to side; or one may dive and then rise, silent and upright from beneath the water, with bowed head. The calls are an odd collection of abrupt low barkings and growls, and more subdued twanging and clinking notes.

The nest is in shallow water, usually hidden among growing vegetation. Although normally in scattered pairs they may exceptionally nest in loose colonies at some sites. The young are fed on fish and insects, and older young divided between the adults for care.

The Great Crested Grebe prefers deeper and more open waters than other species, without marked changes in level, and with aquatic vegetation. For breeding it uses lakes, freshwater lagoons and very slow-moving parts or rivers, and man-made waters such as reservoirs and gravel-pits. In general these are widespread enough for it to find sites over most of the British Isles. It tends to be absent from hilly areas of Devon and Cornwall, South Wales, and the Scottish Highland and islands, and from the south and south-east of Ireland. In winter it is normally absent from Scotland, Wales, northern England and parts of Ireland, with other more extensive movements if waters freeze. In winter it will also move to estuaries and shallow, sheltered coasts.

Grebes seem to be absent from Ice Age sites; but the Great Crested Grebe occurs later at Bronze Age and

Great Crested Grebe

WINTER

SUMMER

Red-necked Grebe

WINTER

Black-necked Grebe

SUMMER

Slavonian Grebe

WINTER

SUMMER

D.M.H.

Iron Age sites in eastern England, although seemingly not in the west. During the Little Ice Age of earlier centuries numbers seem to have become low. With climatic amelioration in the nineteenth century the population began to increase, but there was another problem.

With their wariness and rapid diving they may have been able to escape early hunters, but the increasing perfection of firearms made them much more vulnerable to shooting. In the last century it became fashionable to use the skin of the underside, with its dense white feathering, known to the trade as 'grebe fur', for making muffs and trimming garments. There was considerable slaughter and a drastic reduction in numbers. By 1860 there were only about 40 pairs in Britain, mainly in Cheshire and Norfolk, with a few elsewhere in northern England and East Anglia. These were mostly on protected private waters.

From 1870 onwards protective legislation began, and this may have helped to turn the tide, but in spite of the persecution there had already begun to be some overall increase, accompanied by a northward shift. This appeared to be linked with climatic improvement and, in conjunction with protection and the availability of new nest-sites, aided a build-up in population. The first nesting in Scotland occurred in 1877, and in Wales a few years later; but by 1931 there were about 1,200 pairs in Britain, and about 4,600 by 1965.

Recent increases have been aided by the increasing number of reservoirs and water-filled gravel-pits, which tend to provide suitable waters and may be rapidly colonised. However, the usefulness of reservoirs to this species (and grebes generally) is greatly reduced by the tendency for water-levels to fluctuate considerably in some summers and leave nests high and dry. On both types of waters the birds are likely to be vulnerable to the increasing popularity of inland waters for recreational purposes.

Red-necked Grebe *Podiceps grisegena*
A stocky, more aggressive-looking grebe, this is a size smaller than the Great Crested Grebe. It is a little stouter, with thicker neck and heavier head and bill. In winter its plumage is in shades of grey, but in summer the pale grey cheeks contrast with a chestnut neck and black cap.

Migratory over most of its range, it is a winter visitor to Britain. Its usual inland habitat requirements differ a little from those of the Great Crested Grebe. It prefers smaller, shallower waters with a more extensive and rich growth of plants standing in water, often at sites closely surrounded by trees. It feeds less on fish, and more on other creatures such as insects. Its general breeding range is within temperate to boreal, often within forested areas.

It is difficult to see why the westward extension of its European range should be in northern mainland Europe no further than Denmark. The present distribution suggests that for breeding it may need the warmer summers of the eastern continental-style climate.

Within Europe it appears to have shown an increase and spread in the late nineteenth century. There is no evidence at present of its occurrence in Britain in the past other than as a migrant or winter visitor. Its main post-breeding migration is westwards in Europe, and it winters mainly in the south-west Baltic and around the

Red-necked Grebe

North Sea. Outside the breeding season it tends to be rather solitary and silent, in ones and twos and more rarely in small groups.

At such times it occurs mainly in shallow tidal waters of coasts and estuaries. In Britain its more regular occurrences are on the east coast of England, and occasionally but infrequently on inland waters and reservoirs.

Slavonian Grebe *Podiceps auritus*
This is one of the smaller grebes; squat, round-bodied and stubby-billed. In winter it is very black and white, with white face and narrow dark cap. In summer flanks and neck are chestnut, and the head greenish-black with an upswept pair of lateral golden-orange tufts that give it the American name of 'Horned Grebe'. The feathers of the dark cheeks of the summer plumage are elongated like the ear-tufts, and can be spread to form a ruff, producing an erectile head ornamentation like that of the Great Crested Grebe.

It has a similar repertoire of displays, performed by both sexes, but in the weed-carrying performance they rise upright, treading water, and parade rapidly side by side. The calls are variants on trills, mostly harsher and lower-pitched than the calls of a Dabchick, but reminiscent of them. The nest is like that of other grebes, and often well-concealed among sedges or similar plant growth in water, with open water nearby. It appears to prefer shallow pools and smaller lakes with rich vegetation, but it can adapt to much more open conditions, on waters with bare surroundings and a thinner plant growth. When nesting on very small pools it will fly to larger ones nearby to feed.

It is a migrant and has a circumpolar breeding distribution in the boreal zone, also occurring in Iceland. On current evidence it appears to be a late invader as a breeding species in Britain. In winter most birds move to inshore coastal waters, with the majority of European breeders heading westwards to winter from Brittany to coastal Norway, and around the British Isles.

In Scotland it nests on more open waters than those preferred by the Black-necked Grebe; and the nests may be conspicuously anchored among sparse vegetation. It is limited to the extreme north-east and the first British nest was not recorded until 1908. The subsequent increase has been slow, with about 50–60 pairs in all in recent times, but in the 1980s, the total has been closer to 80 pairs at up to 44 sites, with about two-thirds confirmed as breeding. Their typical habitat and climatic choices may have limited them to this northern area during the warmer early part of this century, and the southward extension into Morayshire and Perthshire has taken place during the more recent cool climatic cycle.

The Scottish breeding birds appear to be a part of a northern population breeding also in northern Norway and Iceland, and wintering from the Faeroes through western Scotland to Ireland in the northern North Sea. Other wintering birds around the south and east coasts and England and in Wales seem to originate further east in Europe. There is an estimated total of about 450 birds, occurring on sheltered coastal water.

Black-necked Grebe *Podiceps nigricollis*

Similar in general size to the Slavonian Grebe, this species has a cut-away underside to the tip of the lower mandible that gives it a slender and pertly uptilted bill on a rounded, high-crowned head. In winter it also differs from the last species in having more extensively dark-smudged cheeks. In breeding plumage the flanks are chestnut, but neck and head are black, with an arching tuft of golden plumes across the face behind the eye.

Like those of the Slavonian Grebe, the bright head-plumes can be spread to form a larger patch, and the crown feathers erected in a high, peaked and flat-fronted black crest. The elaborate rituals of display posturing are similar to those of the last species, but the rearing up and parallel parading display lacks any weed-carrying. The voice is like that of the Slavonian Grebe, but less harsh and rather more subdued. The nest, in shallow water, is usually well-concealed in beds of emergent vegetation such as sedges and reeds. Unlike other grebes it typically nests in colonies, sometimes large and with the nests only about one metre apart. It prefers pools with a lush growth of plants around the margins, plenty of submerged and floating vegetation, and not necessarily very much open water. The greater part of the food is insects.

Although it has an extensive range through temperate Eurasia and North America it resembles the Slavonian Grebe in being a late invader of the British Isles as a breeding bird, in small numbers and at scattered sites; and its regular occurrence is now limited to two sites in Scotland. It is a migrant, like the Slavonian Grebe, but with more southerly movements; the northern limits are a little further south in the southern North Sea. Unlike that species it winters extensively on unfrozen lakes and reservoirs, with much smaller numbers in coastal waters; and it differs also in that in winter, as in summer, it is sociable and often occurs in flocks.

Breeding in the British Isles was first recorded in Wales in 1904 and Ireland in 1915, although in both countries it may have been present earlier. Breeding began in England in 1918 and Scotland in 1930. There was an extensive westward colonisation in Europe in 1918–20 and 1929–32, thought to have been initiated by the drying of steppe-lakes in the Caspian region; but a northward shift in North America as well suggests that the overall movements of the earlier part of this century were also a response to the warming climate of the period.

In Ireland a colony was established that increased to some 250 pairs by 1930 but was later lost through drainage and desiccation. Because it responds rapidly to variable water-levels by changing its breeding sites it may occur sporadically or exceptionally in a number of places, sometimes only for one season. In Britain this usually involves single scattered pairs, with only the two Scottish sites used regularly. The British breeding population was down to 11 pairs in the mid 1970s, but had risen in the 1980s to about 30 pairs at 15 localities, with about half confirmed as breeding. About 120 birds, mainly from western Europe, winter on scattered sheltered coasts and open inland waters.

Dabchick *Tachybaptus ruficollis*

The smallest of our grebes. Resting with feathers fluffed it looks little more than a powder-puff floating on the water, and the shortish neck and stubby bill make it look smaller still. Its surface appearance belies its underwater ability, where as a slim tapering shape propelled by large feet it can move almost as fast as a running person.

In winter it is drab brown with a pale throat, and in summer is only a little brighter. It is darker then, with dark chestnut cheeks and throat and a white patch at the base of the bill. It lacks the ornate plumes of other grebe species. It also lacks a white patch on the wings. Pairs have the complex repertoire of displays like other grebes, but in the absence of elaborate head-feathering the postures are less conspicuous, and also likely to occur in the concealment of water vegetation. The calls are mainly moderately high-pitched twittering trills. With the strong tendency for concealment in emergent vegetation and relative lack of conspicuous plumage, the calls may have a more important function in advertisement, and it is a relatively noisy species.

The nest is among emergent vegetation in water, usually well-concealed. It uses a considerable range of waters of all kinds, sometimes very small ponds, and often less than 1 m deep. When it is present on larger waters such as lakes it mainly uses the irregular and overgrown verges. It also occurs on slow-moving rivers and streams, canals and waterlogged marshlands. It is resident through much of its range, although moving if water freezes, and in winter occurs on almost all types of waters including ditches, estuaries and calmer coasts.

Its need appears to be for an abundance of vegetation in the water, both emergent and submerged, and it seems to prefer muddy-bottomed waters. It is widely dispersed over the British Isles, absent only from the drier and hilly areas where suitable waters are scarce. It is a little more thinly spread than the Great Crested Grebe in some areas, and possibly unable to compete with the latter if facilities are restricted. Over the British Isles as a whole it is resident and pairs tend to remain together. It migrates from the northern parts of its total range, and there is evidence of small winter movements both into and out of Britain, in addition to local shifts when water freezes.

Its general distribution is in the Old World temperate to tropical zones, and its past distribution is likely to have been affected by cold weather. It was certainly present on the Somerset Levels at the time of the Iron Age lake villages. Its numbers were probably smaller in the colder fourteenth to nineteenth centuries, and there was a definite increase in the latter part of the nineteenth and early twentieth century. However, its tendency to remain in its breeding areas as long as possible make it vulnerable to hard winters, particularly when there are sudden drops in temperature. There is therefore a fluctuation in population level in response to winter conditions, although a long breeding season may help it re-establish numbers. There is also a slight indication of a fall in numbers coinciding with the cooler climatic cycle since the early 1950s.

The breeding population in the mid 1970s was about 9,000–18,000 pairs spread over the British Isles. The winter total is nearer 11,000, lower than might be expected, and largely confined to lowlands.

Pelicans, Cormorants and Gannets

PELECANIFORMES

This order consists of moderate to large fish-eating birds. Among other characters in common, they have webbed feet on which the web also extends to the hind-toe, unlike those of other webbed-footed birds. They include species which pursue fish under water, and others that hunt by plunge-diving; and they tend to have an elastic throat-pouch to aid the swallowing of large prey. They mostly build nests on raised sites, rocks or trees, and the young, naked at first and downy later, take food directly from the parent's gullet. They appear to be forms which have been around, with relatively little change, for tens of millions of years, and their past history is a little difficult to unravel.

Three families were represented in Britain, one of which we have now lost. The Pelicans, Pelecanidae, were represented by the Dalmatian Pelican *Pelecanus crispus*. It now breeds in scattered sites from Greece to China. In Britain it was present in the early Holocene, into historic times. It may have been a summer visitor, but certainly bred in the then extensive marshlands of Somerset and East Anglia. The Romans recorded it nesting in the big river estuaries of Belgium, Netherlands and north-west Germany. In the Introduction, I suggested that human disturbance at nesting colonies may have led to its disappearance here, and the present distribution would fit this hypothesis.

The two extant families are the cormorants and shags, Phalacrocoracidae, and the gannets, Sulidae. Both have a wide general distribution, cosmopolitan but a little patchy.

Cormorants and Shags

Phalacrocoracidae

These dark-plumaged water birds are, by virtue of the posteriorly-placed legs, upright and auk-like on land, and identified by the thin snaky neck and narrow hook-tipped bill. Although walking with an awkward waddle, they can perch on branches and twigs. They are agile under water and when they surface may stay part-submerged, when the raised and uptilted head puts one in mind of the divers. In flight they are more goose-like

ADULT

Great Cormorant

JUVENILE

Shag

ADULT

JUVENILE

WINTER

Dabchick

SUMMER

D.M.HENRY

Great Cormorant (above) and Shag

than diver-like, flying with head and neck extended, tail spread, and with steady, shallow beats of long wings. They often fly in chevron formation or single file.

The plumage is not too well adapted for shedding water and in spite of some controversy their habit of perching for long periods with wings extended and half-spread, producing the very typical silhouette, really does seem to be for drying feathers. The young are drab brown with pale breasts, and the dark plumage of the adults is only ornamented in the breeding season by some finer feathers on the head, and a thigh-patch on the larger species.

They are adept underwater hunters, with long bodies propelled by the large feet. They can ingest large fish and their apparent skill in feeding has earned them the hatred of human fishermen, and many exaggerations concerning their total consumption of fish.

Of the two species the Great Cormorant, or Common Cormorant, is a species of both fresh and salt water. Its total range extends discontinuously from Eurasia to southern Africa and New Zealand, and into Greenland and north-eastern North America. The smaller Shag is a purely coastal species, ranging only from Iceland and Finland to Morocco, and through the Mediterranean and the Black Sea. It appears to be the westernmost representative of a series of five species replacing each other along the southern side of the palaearctic regions.

Where the two occur together on the coasts of the British Isles, the Shag appears to prefer to fish in deeper waters and a little further out than the Cormorant, reducing the likelihood of competition. For both the food is mainly or entirely fish. Because it feeds in shallow water most of the Cormorant's prey is bottom-living, but for this and the Shag most prey is brought to the surface to be dealt with and swallowed.

Great Cormorant *Phalacrocorax carbo*

A big black bird, sometimes seen as little more than a head and neck above the water, at others moving in level flapping flight, or again perched on a rock or buoy, with wings spread like an inverted 'W'. It shows a tapering bill, and a yellow patch of bare skin on the throat. The lighter brown young are pale on throat and belly.

In breeding plumage the black feathers are purple-glossed, the bare throat a brighter yellow, bordered by white cheeks and hind-throat. There is variable fine white streaking on the back of head and nape, and a white thigh-patch. The sexes are alike, and display occurs at a nest-site, involving the lifting of closed wings, uptilted tail, and head at times extended with open bill to show a yellow gape, or thrown back until the bill points at the tail.

Greeting postures are used, and nest material brought by the male is added to the nest with a ritualised mutual bowing ceremony. Additions to the nest in this manner go on through most of the breeding period. The main calls of nesting birds in a generally silent species are deep throaty growls, grunts and more vibrant, loud 'roaring' calls.

It is a sociable species at all times, and usually breeds in groups of pairs or larger colonies. Open sites are preferred with a number of pairs nesting on broad cliff ledges, flat tops of rock stacks or low islands, or even on the ground on low island sites. In low-lying areas without rock outcrops, such as inland lakes and marshes, it will nest in trees. The nests are heaps of coarse material, with some finer lining, and often close together. Although sites are often re-used, colonies may move, presumably because of disturbance of some kind.

The Great Cormorant has a long history in Britain with evidence of its presence in the warmer interglacials of the Ice Age as far back as the Middle Pleistocene, and associated with remains of waterfowl of fresh waters in some instances. In more recent times its main enemy appears to have been human. In the last century, and in the present one up until the 1960s, they were systematically shot at inland sites by those interested in fishing. Water Boards paid bounties for them. Such activities are almost certainly responsible for their general absence from inland river and lake habitats. Coastal colonies were subject to less systematic raids by fishermen.

In spite of this the Great Cormorant appears to have held its own over the centuries, and the shooting which has prevented colonisation of more inland sites seems to have had a less marked effect elsewhere. Although the information is inadequate, a small but steady decrease overall seems to have occurred in this century; but there have been local increases in areas where previous killing has ceased, and there is some indication that the fall in population has been reversed during the last few decades.

Its distribution in the British Isles is mainly coastal. Colonies occur on cliffs and islands from the Isle of Wight west and north to Caithness, sporadically in eastern Scotland and north-east England, on a few small sites on Kent and Sussex cliffs, and around most of Ireland. It is absent from most low-lying coasts as a breeder, but non-breeding birds occur in small numbers around most coasts and estuaries, and adults will move to such areas in winter.

There is a sprinkling of inland colonies in Lakeland, the central Highlands and western Ireland, usually at lakes or reservoirs with islands or nearby crags; and an Essex reservoir has been recently colonised. Nesting in trees, not uncommon elsewhere, no longer occurs except in inland Irish colonies, but might take place elsewhere in Britain in the absence of persecution. There is some evidence of nesting intentions in birds using gravel-pits and reservoirs in the London area.

In winter, birds tend to disperse rather than migrate, but there is evidence of a south-easterly and southerly shift, during which some birds cross the Channel. Wintering birds also use inland lakes, reservoirs and larger rivers.

There are about 8,000 breeding birds in the British Isles, giving a wintering population of 20,000–25,000 birds.

Shag *Phalacrocorax aristotelis*

A slim greenish-black cormorant of rocky coasts. A slightly smaller bird, it appears more snaky-necked, rounder-headed and more slender-billed than the Great Cormorant, with just a little yellow at the base of the bill. Young birds are drab brown with pale throats.

Although numbers may gather where there are large fish shoals, it is more solitary than the Great Cormorant, but may rest and roost in large groups. Its general habits are similar to the latter's, but it prefers deeper waters, although these may be in sheltered bays and inlets, and it tends to rest on rocks and cliff bases.

Breeding season adults are a dark glossy green, against which the vivid yellow of throat and gape is displayed in startling contrast in some displays. The plumage ornamentation is a small forward-curling tuft on top of the head. At the beginning of the season it is long enough to curl down over the forehead, but wears rapidly and is soon a short upright tuft. As in the Great Cormorant, pairing and display depend on the possession of a nest-site. Displays involve neck-extending and gaping, tail-cocking, and bowing and throwing-back of the head. Usually silent, it has a limited vocabulary at the nest, consisting mainly of a harsh 'ark' call and an odd clicking in the throat. Material is brought and added to the nest with solemn ceremony throughout the breeding period.

It tends to use small, sheltered cliff-sites for nesting, and these result in a loose scattered colony in most places. The nests are on sheltered ledges, or in corners, crevices and caves, and sometimes under boulders. The need for such sites limits its range as a breeding species to coasts with cliffs.

Its earlier history in Britain is probably similar to that of the Great Cormorant, but its more marine habitat has left us with hardly any evidence of it. In the main it may have escaped the persecution that the Great Cormorant suffered, simply because it was more difficult to get at. However, numbers decreased and colonies disappeared in the nineteenth century in north-east England and Dorset. In the present century it began to increase again and in some areas numbers rose rapidly from the late 1930s onwards. The increase has been particularly marked in the north-east of England and south-east of Scotland, restoring earlier losses rapidly.

The increase does not show a pattern typical of birds responding to a change in climatic conditions. The British Isles is at about the middle of its present latitudinal range and not a point at which such changes would be likely to be apparent. Apart from re-establishment of numbers where pressure from persecution ceased, some other factor or factors seem likely. The most probable is a change in the availability of fish stocks in the seas around the British Isles and more particularly in the North Sea. Such a change might be an indirect effect of climatic fluctuation.

It is present around most of Scotland including the islands, and north to Shetland, and around Ireland, but in eastern England has only two sites between Northumberland and the Isle of Wight, and is absent from around the Severn Estuary and much of the Lancashire coast area. Its winter dispersal is limited, and chiefly involves immature birds, some of which may visit rivers and inland waters. The population was estimated at about 31,600 pairs in 1970, with about 100,000–150,000 wintering birds.

Gannets and Boobies

Sulidae

This is a family specialised for a marine existence as plunge-divers. The wings are long and narrow, tapering and designed for using rising air currents from the waves, economising in energy. The eyes, under slightly bulging brows, have binocular vision for accurate aim, focussing beyond the bill-tip and from a front view giving the bird a slightly insane look that it shares with the heron family.

The bill itself is stout and tapering, and to aid in plunge-diving head first the nostrils are closed and breathing takes place through small flaps at the base of the bill. They hunt by flying above the sea, often at about 15–20m, and plunge head first after their prey, the wings half-closed, and extending back as the bird hits the water to disappear briefly and re-appear swallowing a fish.

Relatively sociable, they usually nest in colonies. The dense plumage lacks a brood-patch and the one or two eggs are incubated with warmth from the webs of the feet placed over them.

The smaller boobies occur in more tropical waters. The gannets, sometimes separated in the genus *Morus*, are birds of cooler waters. There are three separate species – North Atlantic, South African and Australian – sufficiently similar for some people to regard them as forms of a single species.

Gannet *Sula bassana*

With its 2m wing-span this is our largest sea-bird (if allowance is made for an occasional stray albatross). Usually seen flying out at sea, its white plumage with black-ended wings, and long body tapering to bill and tail, help to identify it. A sight of its powerful headlong dives leaves no doubt. Flight is slow and dignified, with long glides. Newly fledged young are blackish-brown heavily flecked with white, changing to adult plumage gradually over four years' moults.

It is a marine bird, coming to land only to breed. Display is linked with possession of a nest-site, re-used in successive years. It involves head-bowing and rearing, and bill-scissoring and mutual preening with its mate. Its loud harsh 'urrah' call-note is used at the nest and when gathering at a fish shoal, and softer groaning and croaking notes are also used at the nest. Nest colonies are often on the tops of rock stacks or small islands, less often on broad ledges of high, sheer cliffs. The birds are sociable but spiteful, and in the larger colonies on slopes or flatter ground the nests are set out with beautiful regularity, a double billstab apart.

The breeding range of the Gannet is from Brittany and the Channel Islands, north to northern Norway and Iceland, and on the western side of the Atlantic around Newfoundland and the Gulf of St Lawrence. The overall range is across the North Atlantic between these colonies, south to West Africa and the western Mediterranean in the east, and to the Caribbean in the west, but tending to keep within the shallower seas of the continental shelf.

There are seventeen colonies in the British Isles, two being in the Channel Islands, and they hold nearly three-quarters of the species's population. The easternmost sites, one at Bempton in Yorkshire (the only English site) and two on the Shetlands, are on cliffs. The island ones include the Bass Rock in the Firth of Forth; Fair Isle; four off north-west Scotland, including St Kilda, the largest colony; two off south-west Scotland; Grassholm, off south-west Wales, and opposite it Great Saltee off south-east Ireland; two off south-west Ireland; and two on Alderney.

Although long present around Britain, the Gannet's main problem was probably annual raids in which nestlings were taken for food by man. These may have been occurring from the Iron Age onwards, and may have kept the colonies at a level a little below their full potential. In the nineteenth century there was a more systematically destructive exploitation for eggs, and for adult plumage. It has been suggested that the overall decline may only have been about 20%, but small colonies suffered more, and at least one, on Lundy, disappeared by 1909. The Grassholm colony appears to have been founded in the early nineteenth century.

In the present century there has been both a recovery, and an increase. The population is estimated to have started the century at around 48,000 pairs, increasing to over 138,000 by 1970. The increase was in the order of 13% from 1900–39, $17\frac{1}{2}$% from 1939–49 and 115% from 1949–70. New colonies were established both around Britain and abroad. The Shetlands were colonised in 1914–17, Great Saltee in 1929, Bempton in 1937, Alderney in 1940, the Flannan Isles in 1969, and Fair Isle in 1974.

The population appears to be around a record high point. As with the Shag, this increase does not appear to be linked with climate, but rather with availability of food, in the case of the Gannet probably surface-shoaling fish such as the mackerel.

Herons, Storks and Spoonbills

CICONIIFORMES

An order of long-legged wading birds with considerable variation in bill structure. They feed on other creatures, particularly fish; tend to build large untidy nests, often on a raised site; and feed their young by regurgitating food for the young to take from their throats.

The ones which occur in Britain with any regularity are the herons, Ardeidae, and, much more sporadically and individually, the Spoonbill, in the Threskiornithidae. The White Stork in the Ciconiidae has turned up infrequently. It is one of those species that we might have expected to have occurred in the past but seems never to have established itself (see p. 19).

Eurasian Bittern

Grey Heron

Eurasian Spoonbill

Gannet

ADULT

FIRST-YEAR

D.M.HENRY

Herons and Bitterns

Ardeidae

This is a family of skinny, long-legged and long-necked birds. Their big broad wings and attenuated height gives a false impression of size, and make their bodies appear almost emaciated. The bill is long, slender and dagger-like, with the eyes close-set at its base. Legs and toes are long and thin. The long thin neck is angled, with a kink which enables it to straighten suddenly for a quick stabbing movement of the head. Broad wings provide lift rather than power, and the head is tucked back on the shoulders in flight, the neck folded below like a keel.

The food is mainly fish, but also includes any small creatures that come within range. The display plumage consists of long slender feathers on head, neck, breast or back.

There are three species that rank as British, although others visit at times. They are the Grey Heron, the Eurasian Bittern and the Little Bittern.

Grey Heron *Ardea cinerea*

A grey bird, over a metre tall, thin and erect when alert, squat and hunched when resting. In flight, with hunched head, and feet projecting behind, its big dark wings make it seem larger still. It flies with slow flaps and glides, seemingly laboured but capable of carrying it high and for long distances. When nesting it may travel up to 30km to feed. It defends individual feeding territories, but may rest and roost sociably.

Mainly grey and white it is ornamented with black eye-stripes that join in long plumes on the nape and can be erected in a spiky crest, and black-and-white streaked plumes on neck and breast. When it breeds, bill and feet briefly turn red. Display takes place on the nest, involving rigid postures, mostly with extended neck and head, and breast-plumes raised, accompanied by bill-snapping and rattling. At the nest it uses a range of croaks and 'squarks', but is otherwise rather silent, except for occasional loud, harsh 'fraank' calls.

The nests are large, untidy structures, usually in colonies in trees, more rarely in reed-beds or on rocks. Although pairs may shift annually, sites may be of long standing, a few having been in use for centuries. Its feeding habitat includes the margins of almost any kind of water, from lakes and rivers to ditches and marshes; it prefers fresh water but also occurs on estuaries and sometimes rocky shores. It mainly hunts by slow deliberate wading in shallow water.

Its general range is in temperate to tropical climates, from Eurasia south to Malaya, Sri Lanka and South Africa, but it is absent from drier regions. It is a migrant in cooler northern regions; but in Britain it is resident, with a fairly even overall distribution of breeding colonies. Winter movements are only local, with a small number of visitors from abroad.

The Grey Heron is not apparent in the Ice Ages until the latter part of the last glaciation, but occurs subsequently, and the extensive marshes prior to drainage must have supported a considerable population. As a conspicuous, vulnerable species it is surprising that it survived so well, but it was preserved as 'game' for centuries, and as a quarry species for falconry, which certainly afforded it some legal protection at heronries.

It has been censused in the present century, when numbers in England and Wales were found to be fairly stable at around 4,000–5,000 pairs; falling steeply to about 2,000 after some severe winters, but rapidly recovering. There was a decrease in numbers in the 1920s to 1950s in south and south-west Scotland, and more recently a fall in numbers in north-east England which was suspected to be linked with pesticide residues in food. However, there is still a fairly wide breeding distribution, and the total population in the British Isles appears to be rising. The number of pairs in England, Scotland, Wales and Northern Ireland was recently calculated at about 7,000–9,000 pairs.

Eurasian Bittern *Botaurus stellaris*

This is a reed-bed heron, its plumage mottled in the buff and blackish-brown of dead reeds. It tends to move half-hunched, with head low; although three-quarters the size of the Grey Heron, it looks much smaller. It is a skulker of large reed-beds in which it can clamber as well as creep, and unless disturbed when fishing at the reeds' edge is only seen very briefly, flapping low on big rounded wings like a huge owl. Breeding males may make occasional advertisement flights, circling low; but they are more usually heard than seen. A male in territory makes a deep, soft, far-carrying boom, like the sound made by blowing across a bottle mouth, to advertise its presence. It is polygamous and may have several females nesting in a territory. Females incubate and rear young on their own.

Distribution is limited by the availability of reed-beds, by or in water, and large enough to sustain resident birds. Generally distributed as a summer visitor across temperate Eurasia, it is resident in southern and western Europe. In Britain it is now limited to a few lowland areas. It breeds mainly in East Anglia in near-coastal sites, with one further inland; in east Kent and Humberside. There are isolated sites in Somerset, south Wales and north Lancashire. In winter it occurs more widely through eastern England from the Humber southwards, and more restricted areas of the south-west, north Lancashire and eastern Ireland. It suffers badly in severe winters. There are a small number of winter visitors from mainland Europe.

Its earliest evidence in Britain is in Neolithic to Bronze Age periods when it occurred in the swamps and fens that were then widespread. Its subsequent history is bound up with that of fen and wetlands, retreating as drainage occurred. It once bred as far north as southern Scotland, and in Ireland. It was still widespread in the early nineteenth century, but like other marsh birds was hard-hit by the extensive drainage that occurred until the mid-nineteenth century, with shooting and egg-collection as coup-de-grâces.

It last bred in Ireland about 1840, and in Britain had mainly disappeared by about 1850, with the last breeding occurring in Norfolk in 1868. A pair appears to have nested in 1886, but booming was not noted again until 1900 in Norfolk, and breeding was not proven to begin until 1911. Re-colonisation was centred on the Norfolk Broads, and with protection birds had increased to about 25 pairs in 1928; it bred in Suffolk in 1926. Leighton Moss in north Lancashire was not colonised until the early 1940s, and other sites soon after that.

Most of this spread took place in the warming climate up to the 1950s. After that a decrease was apparent. A booming male count of about 50 in Norfolk in 1954 was halved by 1970. Cooler climate and some particularly severe winters were probably mainly responsible, although reed-cutting, coypus and pollution have also been blamed. Currently the population has been estimated at about 80 pairs in Britain, about 50 of them in East Anglia.

Little Bittern *Ixobrychus minutus*
NOT IN THE COLOUR PLATE

If the large Eurasian Bittern is difficult to see and study, this teal-sized skulker of reed-beds and swamp thickets is even less likely to be noticed. The male is black, with a pale buff face, neck and underside, and pale, pinkish-buff wing-coverts forming a conspicuous patch. The female is similar but more sandy and brown-tinted, with streaked breast. It flies with quick wing-beats for short distances, diving into cover, clambers among reeds and bushes, and is mainly crepuscular. It has short croaking and throaty calls, and the nest is hidden in thick vegetation. It haunts reed-beds or swamps overgrown with tall plants, bushes and trees. It is easily overlooked, and breeding has not been proven in Britain.

There is suitable habitat, and it is difficult to see why it has not occurred more often, nor colonised, since it nests through most of Europe north to the south Baltic shore. Except as a vagrant it does not seem to have a history in Britain, and was first recorded in 1666. It is thought to have bred in East Anglia in the last century, in Suffolk and Norfolk in the early part of the present century, and in south-east England on possibly four occasions in the 1940s and 1950s. A calling male was heard in that area in 1970. Its first breeding was in Yorkshire in 1984. Apart from this it is a rarely-seen summer visitor.

Studies of Little Bittern

Spoonbills and ibises
Threskiornithidae

These are long-legged wading birds with bills specialised for probing mud in ibises, and broad lateral sweeping through water in spoonbills. They fly with necks extended. They are sociable, and colonial nesters.

Eurasian Spoonbill *Platalea leucorodia*
This is tall, white and heron- or stork-like, with a crested nape, and a widened and flattened end to the long bill. Young are distinguished by black-tipped wings. Distinctive in flight, it shows neck and bill extended forwards, and legs projecting behind. It feeds by wading forward with vigorous strides, half-rotating and swinging the bill from side to side through the water, taking any small creatures. For feeding it requires extensive shallow water with few plants but plenty of small animal life. It nests in colonies in dense reeds or trees, and is highly intolerant of disturbance at the nest-site. Like the Grey Heron it will fly some distance to feed. Display occurs at the nest-site with crest-raising, mutual preening, and grunting or groaning calls. Away from the nest it is silent.

Its general range is across the warmer southern Palaearctic and into India and the Red Sea area. On the Atlantic coasts it has bred as far north as Denmark. Specialised needs, draining of areas, taking of adults, eggs and young, and dislike of disturbance all contributed to past loss. It has decreased or disappeared in many parts of western Europe, where it now breeds only in the Netherlands and the Spanish Coto Doñana.

Its present status in Britain is that of an annual visitor in small numbers to the south-east coasts and marshes. It was present and presumably breeding in earlier centuries, although there is no very early evidence of it, and it mainly occurs in lists of birds eaten at banquets. Problems arise because its old name of 'shoveler' confuses it with the duck which now bears that name. The Spoonbill was breeding by the Thames at Fulham in London in 1523, in trees together with herons. It was recorded breeding in Sussex in 1570, in Pembroke in Wales in 1602, and in trees in Norfolk and Suffolk in the mid-seventeenth century. It has not bred since.

Waterfowl

ANSERIFORMES

This order contains a small, obscure family and a very large one. The three species of screamers, Anhimidae, are confined to South America; but the waterfowl family, Anatidae, is the large, cosmopolitan assemblage of swans, geese and ducks.

Swans, Geese and Ducks

Anatidae

This is the large family of webbed-footed, stubby-billed birds adapted to spending most of their time on water. They have a well-waterproofed plumage with a thick under-layer of down, and a layer of fat under the skin, to provide insulation. Typically they have rather short legs, with strong feet for propulsion when swimming on or under water.

Swans have long necks with which to reach down for underwater vegetation. Geese have proportionally longer legs and move more easily on land, where they spend much of their time, grazing and grubbing for plants and roots. Ducks have, in general, both short legs and short necks and must feed at or near the surface, or must dive for food.

They are strong-winged, and many species are migrant. Some take advantage of the wet tundra and marshy areas available in the north in summer. Display and mating usually take place on the water. The nest is in a hollow or cavity, lined only with material in immediate reach, but usually with an inner lining of down pulled from the parent's body. The young are downy, and able to run and feed soon after hatching, being guarded and brooded by the adults.

Swans

Cygnus species

Broad-bodied, and rather clumsy on land, these have strong bills for cropping vegetation and long necks for reaching down to pull up waterweed in shallow waters, up-ending at times in order to do so. They will also crop the herbage growing by water. The birds usually pair for life, and there is relatively little conspicuous display. The nests are large heaps of material at the water's edge or in shallow water, pulled in by both birds. The downy cygnets are grey, and when small are sometimes carried on the swimming parent's back. They feed themselves, but take advantage of plants dredged up by adults. Larger young are brown-feathered, and these remain in a family party until the next spring, moving and migrating with the parents.

There are three European species, more or less zoned by climate. Of the two bugling, loud-voiced swans the smaller Bewick's Swan breeds on arctic tundra, the larger Whooper Swan on boreal lakes and rivers, and both migrate south and south-west in winter. The Mute Swan replaces them in temperate regions, often resident and widely domesticated for centuries.

Mute Swan *Cygnus olor*

With high, knobbed forehead, gracefully curved neck, and wings arched when angry, this is the typical swan. In flight the wing-beats produce a deep, musical, rhythmic sound in place of the bugling calls of other species. Although called mute it has a range of snoring, grunting, hissing, and subdued trumpeting calls.

It is resident, and the species is probably best known for the aggressive threat posture of the territorial male, with head laid back between arched wings and breast thrust forwards. Territory is strongly defended, although young and unpaired birds, and some pairs, form non-breeding flocks. Exceptionally, in a few places as at Abbotsbury in Dorset, they nest in colonies.

Like other swans it feeds in shallow water by reaching down, up-ending at times, to reach plants and roots, and also grazes emergent water plants and grass and herbage growing by water. With these simple needs it occurs on all types of waters: lakes, rivers, pools, man-made reservoirs, gravel-pits and canals, and also on estuaries. However, it is slightly restricted by needing a long take-off into flight, pattering along the surface. Being bold and tame through semi-domestication it nests openly, and is able to breed over almost all of Britain and Ireland. It is absent from some unsuitable mountain areas, from some north-west Scottish islands and from the Shetlands. Outside Britain it is a species of the temperate zone of Eurasia, but with a very patchy distribution.

Although the British birds are mainly resident and territorial, some individuals, especially young ones, move around, and there is some interchange with mainland Europe in winter and hard weather.

Unlike the two migrant species from further north, its history in Britain does not appear to extend back very far, with earliest evidence in the Bronze and Iron Ages, when it was a bird of East Anglia and Somerset. It is not difficult to tame if taken when young, and became semi-domesticated. In medieval times it was a large and important food item, and was protected for this purpose. Domestication began in England before 1186. From the thirteenth to the eighteenth centuries swans were the property of the crown, assigned to others by licence and marked by cuts on bill or foot-webs, but not necessarily confined. Although subsequently the custom died out it has still afforded them some protection in England. Birds in Wales, Scotland and Ireland were

Mute Swan

Canada Goose

Barnacle Goose

Whooper Swan

Bewick's Swan

D.M.HENRY

not semi-domesticated, but may have been derived from such stocks.

Numbers have been assumed to be fairly constant over a long period but counts showed some 26,000 in the British Isles in 1955–56, and this was high: numbers on the Thames since 1823 revealed that the population had doubled. There was a rapid, continuing increase in the next five years, to a high in 1960–61, followed by a sudden drop in British numbers back to 1955 levels within a year.

From 1961 onwards there was a drop of about 8–15%, and the decline has continued. It is most evident in the areas of highest density, in south-east and midland England, where non-breeding flocks have diminished or disappeared, and breeding pairs have been reduced. It was found to be mainly due to lead-poisoning from swallowing fishing-line weights, with three to four thousand birds dying each year. In some areas there was a 50% loss between 1955 and 1978. The loss had been partly masked in statistics by increases elsewhere, in places linked with increasing availability of suitable gravel-pits; and there were increases in northern Scotland and North Wales. It is hoped that new legislation banning lead weights may help reverse the losses.

Whooper Swan *Cygnus cygnus*
The largest of our swans, this is long-bodied, straight-necked and with the forehead sloping down to the stout-based black-and-yellow bill. It is less aggressive, and wilder and more nervously alert than the Mute Swan, which it resembles in its general habits. Its flight is strong, lacking the musical wing-beats of the Mute Swan but usually accompanied by loud, resonant, bugling calls. It is a migrant, sociable when not breeding, with family parties remaining together until the following spring. It is suspicious of humans, and intolerant of disturbance when breeding. Its habitat preferences are similar to those of the Mute Swan, but it tolerates cooler climates, breeding in Iceland and across Eurasia in the boreal conifer-forest zone, using the larger and more open waters with shallows and under-water vegetation.

The British Isles appear to provide the winter quarters for migrants from Iceland, with some continental birds using southern Britain. Winter counts in Britain have totalled some 6,500 but since Iceland has about 10,000 some may have been missed. They occur mainly in Ireland and Scotland, on inland and coastal waters; and in Scotland have shown some shift from the Western Isles to more widespread inland sites. They tend to occur in small flocks and groups, well scattered, and small numbers are also found in England and Wales, becoming scarcer as one goes south. There are larger numbers in Northumberland, and around the Humber, Fens, East Anglia and on Anglesey.

A few birds usually summer in scattered localities in Scotland, but there is rarely breeding. It occurs on average about once in twenty years, in recent times on Benbecula in 1947, Tiree in 1978 and 1979, with subsequent breedings on Loch Lomond in 1979–82 and in East Anglia in 1983 involving one or both adults being of feral origin.

It has a long history as a British bird, being present in the Ice Ages from the Cromerian Interglacial of the Middle Pleistocene onwards, occurring in both colder and warmer periods and probably breeding at times. However, it is impossible to separate summer and winter visitors in most of the data. It seems to have been hunted for food by man from the Stone Ages onwards, presumably a winter visitor in the south, but apparently breeding on Orkney until the eighteenth century, and almost certainly a more regular breeder in Scotland until human activity drove it out.

Bewick's Swan *Cygnus bewickii*
Resembling a smaller version of the Whooper Swan, this has a shorter neck, higher-pitched voice and less yellow on the bill. It breeds further north than the latter, on the tundra from northern Russia to the Bering Straits. The population west of the Taymyr Peninsula migrates westwards to the countries around the southern North Sea, following well-defined routes. About a third of this European wintering population comes to the British Isles, with about a half to a third of this continuing to Ireland and the remainder staying in scattered lowland areas of England and sparsely in southern Scotland. Local flocks are often larger than those of the Whooper Swan, and are composed of family parties, the young sometimes accompanying the adults for two successive winters.

It has been visiting Britain for a long time. Its earliest recorded occurrence is in the Pastonian Glaciation of the Middle Pleistocene, and it was present later, in the Devensian Glaciation. Its presence in these colder periods might be evidence of breeding when tundra conditions were present here; its presence in the Neolithic/Bronze Age period in the Fens was probably as a winter visitor.

Since it was not identified and separated from the Whooper Swan by Yarrell in 1824 in England, there is little historical record. Sudden changes in winter range make it difficult to assess population changes. In the nineteenth century and the earlier part of this century it was relatively common in Scotland, mainly in the Western Isles where birds were on passage to Ireland, the main winter area. In the 1930s numbers decreased in Scotland and rose in England. There were influxes of several hundreds in the winters of 1938–39, and 1955–56 in England. These built up in the next fifteen years to about 1,500 with corresponding losses in Ireland where numbers fell to about half. British numbers rose to about 3,000 in 1966–67 and about 5,000 in 1982–83.

In addition to shifting their wintering areas they have also shown a tendency to feed more on cultivated areas. The provision of grain at some sites has led to regular visits and a build-up of numbers at Wexford in southern Ireland, Caerlaverock in Scotland, and Slimbridge and Welney in England. At the last site numbers in recent years rose to over a thousand birds.

Geese

Branta and Anser species

These are basically land-feeding birds, shorter-necked than swans but longer-necked than ducks. The legs are longer and stronger and they walk and run easily. They also swim, and mate on water. The bills are stouter; deep, narrow and short, with a strong tip, and designed for cropping grass and herbage and for shallow digging and tearing at roots, bulbs and tubers. The voice consists mainly of a variety of honking calls and a threat hiss. They usually pair for life, and display is largely limited to mutually congratulatory triumph ceremonies with outstretched necks. The young remain with the adults until the following spring, forming family parties within the migrating flocks. They are sociable, usually occurring in flocks when not breeding. Flight is strong and often in the typical chevron formations. The grey geese, *Anser* species, have wide ranges usually through open grassy habitats, while the *Branta* species tend to have more specialised niches.

Branta species

These are geese with a generally darker and more boldly-marked plumage, and with some black-and-white pattern on head and neck. There are three British species, one of them introduced. The Brent Goose is the smallest British goose, a circumpolar breeder on tundra, wintering on coasts where it feeds mainly in the intertidal zone. The Barnacle Goose is another arctic breeder, but in limited areas from East Greenland to Novaya Zemlya, wintering on coastal and island grassland of Britain, the Netherlands and West Germany. The introduced species is the Canada Goose which is adapted to breeding in more forested areas; by exploiting sites not usually used by grey geese, and as a partially tame species, it has established itself in Britain and Scandinavia.

Canada Goose *Branta canadensis*

This species is unmistakable: the largest goose, with black head and neck, and white cheeks and chinstrap. It has a deep honking voice. Because it was introduced and tame, little notice was taken of it as a British species, and information is sparse. It found an under-used niche in that it was a goose adapted to waters in semi-forested areas, prepared to nest among trees. Among grey geese the only potential competitor, the Bean Goose, nests further north and east.

It was known as a domesticated bird in Britain by 1678, and was breeding in parklands and grounds of some large estates in England in the eighteenth century. Feral flocks were present by the mid nineteenth century, and by the end of it birds were present in northern England. There is little information from Scotland, other than that there were over 2,000 on private waters in the 1930s that almost disappeared during the 1939-45 war. By the early 1950s there were again about 2,600 to 3,600 birds present in Britain.

Although the American populations are mainly migratory, the British birds do not usually move far, feeding and breeding in a limited area. There is some local movement in winter; and birds in north and midland England have begun to show a summer moult migration north to Beauly Firth in Inverness-shire. Surplus birds in local flocks have been extensively translocated by hopeful wildfowlers, unaware that these feral birds fail to behave as good targets.

In the last twenty years the population has trebled and is generally still rising, but in Norfolk numbers halved in the late 1960s. They have spread to rivers, reservoirs, gravel-pits and marshes. The main groupings are concentrated in south-east England, East Anglia, Derbyshire, west Midlands, Yorkshire, Lakeland, south Devon and Anglesey, with scattered sites elsewhere in England, Wales and Scotland. They are present on Strangford Lough and in north-west Ireland. There were about 30,000 in the mid 1980s.

Barnacle Goose *Branta leucopsis*

This is the most boldly patterned species in a soberly-coloured group. Its principal call is a penetrating and nagging yap, with softer conversation notes at times. It is a high arctic breeder, nesting in east Greenland, Spitzbergen and Novaya Zemlya. It nests by preference on sheer rock outcrops or cliffs, or small rocky islands, and downy young may have to drop from considerable heights to leave some of the nest sites. It is highly sociable, usually remaining in flocks on migration and in winter quarters. It spends the winter mainly grazing on coastal marshes and grasslands, moving away to sandbanks or open estuary waters to roost.

Each population migrates to separate wintering areas, and the British Isles holds two of these. East Greenland birds migrate via Iceland to the coastal areas and islands of north-western Scotland and Ireland. Spitzbergen birds winter on the Solway Firth of the western Scottish-English border, arriving via Norway; and the Siberian birds move down to the Netherlands.

Some of these populations may have occupied Britain to breed at times in the Pleistocene. There is evidence of this species breeding on the South Wales coast in the colder part of the final, Devensian, glaciation when the cliffs would have formed an inland escarpment. Other evidence of its presence during this cold period comes from the Cheddar Gorge in Somerset, Creswell Crags in Derbyshire, and from Jersey, all areas with steep rock outcrops, which at that period might have provided nesting-sites with tundra surface-water nearby. Early Holocene and Iron Age occurrences in the south-west suggest that in postglacial times the wintering areas may have extended further south-west than they do at present. Although it is relatively conservative in its wintering sites there is evidence from the continent of some shifts in recent times.

As a species it appears to have decreased in numbers in the late nineteenth century and the first half of this century. From the 1950s onwards numbers have trebled, with some differences between populations. The main winter haunt of Greenland birds is on the island of Islay which had about three-quarters of them (24,000) in the late 1970s. This led to claims of damage to crops and grassland, and the resultant shooting reduced the population by about a quarter and Islay's birds by over a third. Spitzbergen birds on the Solway dropped from several thousand in the 1930s to less than 400 in the late 1940s following shooting and wartime disturbance, but by the mid 1980s had risen again to reach 10,500. At present Britain offers winter refuge to about a third of the total population of this species.

Brent Goose *Branta bernicla*

This small dark goose is a sea-shore species, in its winter quarters as much a bird of the mudflats as a shelduck. It is stocky, with a short neck and smallish head, rather un-gooselike in its fast-flying, often irregularly bunched flocks, and its short, low-pitched calls. The dark-bellied form is illustrated, mainly black and grey, with a few pale markings apart from a white tail-end that is most conspicuous when it swims, riding high in the water. It breeds in arctic Siberia west of the Taymyr Peninsula; an even darker form, the Black Brant, breeds from the Taymyr Peninsula east to western arctic Canada. There is a pale-bellied form, with body and wings a lighter grey, and with paler edges to the flanks, which breeds from Franz Josef Land and Spitzbergen west to eastern arctic Canada.

Birds from three areas visit the British Isles in winter. Pale-bellied from Greenland (and some from arctic Canada) come to Ireland via Iceland, and those from Spitzbergen and Franz Josef Land reach Northumberland via Scandinavia. Dark-bellied birds from Siberia come to south-east England via the Baltic.

The Brent Goose breeds on low, level, wet or grassy tundra. In winter it feeds on eel-grass and also seaweeds on salt mudflats, and on saltmarsh plants; it has also learned to take young shoots of grain and other cultivated crops. It roosts on the sea. It stays in close flocks, families keeping together, and has low-pitched, abrupt honking or metallic notes.

There are a few records of it from the cooler parts of the last glaciation and into the early Holocene. Like the Barnacle Goose it might have bred here during the coldest periods. There is little historical information, and this may be due in part to its habit of feeding in the intertidal zone and resting on the sea, which would not have made it an easy prey. Numbers appear to fluctuate with both food-supply and breeding success in the Arctic, where conditions may be unsuitable at times.

Casual references suggest that its population was higher in the past, but in the 1920s and 1930s there was a drastic decrease of the eel-grass due to disease, and during this period the goose population also declined dramatically. On the Solway Firth, where several thousand birds were wintering even in the 1930s, barely any occur now. Since that crash in all populations, light-bellied birds wintering in Ireland have increased to about 12,000, and in Northumberland to about 2,000. However, the dark-bellied birds wintering in south-east England have rapidly increased to around, and possibly beyond, their earlier numbers: to about 16,000 in the 1950s and about 90,000 in the mid 1980s. This may have helped to encourage them to turn to agricultural crops late in the winter when eel-grass and seaweeds become scarce, and they show an increasing use of such food sources. Even with larger numbers the variation in breeding success from year to year is apparent as marked fluctuations in the numbers present.

Grey Geese

Anser species

This is a genus of rather similar-looking brownish-grey geese, with darker heads and necks, and variation in bill and leg colour. There are four regular British species, and one rare visitor. They tend to replace each other in general breeding distribution, overlapping more in winter.

The dark-necked Bean Goose is a tundra edge and northern boreal forest breeder, across Eurasia, migrating to Europe, China and Japan. The Pink-footed Goose is closely related, a little smaller and shorter-necked, and replaces it to the west in Greenland, Iceland and Spitzbergen, migrating in winter to around the North Sea. The Greylag Goose, the largest and palest species, is a temperate zone bird, breeding from Iceland and Britain, through Europe and Eurasia, and wintering in Western Europe, and from North Africa to China. The smaller, more heavily-patterned, White-fronted Goose breeds on circumpolar arctic tundra, and winters in the British Isles, on the western European coast and across warm-temperate Eurasia. The rare species is the Lesser White-fronted Goose, breeding in a more restricted zone of montane tundra, migrating to eastern Europe and warm-temperate Asia, but occasionally straying to Britain.

Bean Goose *Anser fabalis*

Slightly smaller than the Greylag Goose, this has a longish neck and longish bill, emphasised by an upright carriage, and a deep brown head and neck. Less noisy than most geese, its voice is sharper than the Greylag's

with sharp, disyllabic notes deeper than those of the Pink-footed Goose.

It breeds across northern Eurasia, mainly on tundra, but also extending into birch-and conifer-forest, mainly near water. Several subspecific forms are recognised and birds that visit Britain and other North Sea coasts appear to nest in Scandinavia. Possibly because of its forest habitat it is more agile on the wing than other large grey geese, rising more steeply.

Eastern Eurasia birds winter in China and Japan, but western birds move to open, low-lying grasslands between the southern Baltic and Belgium, and sporadically through Europe. The small numbers that reach Britain occur mainly in late winter and may represent a secondary dispersal from Denmark.

Our earliest records of the species is in South Wales in the last, Ipswichian, interglacial; and it is otherwise rarely recorded. It seems to have been more numerous in past centuries, being regarded as common and numerous in Scotland and northern England in the last century, but having declined steadily and disappeared from most of Scotland in the present century. This might be linked with declines in the breeding populations of Scandinavia due to changes in forest habitat and increased killing by man during the same period.

The decline seems to have continued until the 1970s, after which there has been a slight increase. About 200 occur regularly in the Yare Valley in East Anglia, and at another regular site in the Scottish Dee Valley there are usually 20–30 pairs, although there were about 200 birds in the 1950s. Small parties may occur at other

Bean Goose

Pink-footed Goose

Greylag Goose

White-fronted Goose

Brent Goose
DARK-BELLIED RACE

D.M.H.

scattered localities. However, there are larger influxes in hard winters, and since the British birds are part of a much larger North Sea wintering population it is difficult to judge the importance of these fluctuations.

Pink-footed Goose *Anser brachyrhynchus*
A more squat and stubby version of the Bean Goose, with pink on bill and legs, and sufficiently like it to have been sometimes regarded as a subspecies of it. Its shorter neck makes it look stouter, and is apparent in flight. The voice is higher-pitched and more musical than those of Bean or Greylag Goose. It has a restricted breeding range, breeding in Spitzbergen, east Greenland and Iceland. The birds wintering in Britain come from the last two areas, the smaller Greenland population migrating via Iceland. It nests in groups on restricted, annually-used sites, on mounds and ridges where predators are absent, but on ledges of gorges or rock outcrops in areas of greater vulnerability. It moves easily on land, and may cover long distances when the young are still flightless.

The migration is direct to eastern Scotland, birds later moving south as food-supplies decrease or hard weather dictates. Wintering birds are highly gregarious. They are particularly alert and suspicious, preferring to feed in large open areas. Flocks may gather at a large roost, dispersing to feed during the day. Roosts are typically on estuarine sandbanks and mudflats but, probably due to vulnerability to shooting at such sites, they have increasingly begun to roost on protected inland water. They may fly long distances to feed, typically on low-lying farmland, on grassland, stubbles or potato fields, and later on young sprouting crops. They may also feed on saltmarsh.

One might have expected that the Pink-footed Goose, like the Barnacle Goose, could have nested in Britain during the colder glacial periods of the Pleistocene. There are a number of records from Pin Hole Cave in Derbyshire, in the last glaciation, as well as from Jersey where the Barnacle Goose was also recorded, but otherwise little information.

Its numbers, at least of those that winter in Britain, may have been smaller in the past, since the population was showing a significant increase in Britain in the earlier part of the century. Flocks were mainly concentrated in eastern and midland Scotland, around the Solway Firth and Morecambe Bay, on the Lancashire coast and in the Fens. The increase continued with about 30,000 in 1950 and 101,000 in 1983. In the 1950s and 1960s they had decreased in parts of the winter range, particularly in eastern England, apparently due to an increased food supply in Scotland, with fewer birds moving south. With the still larger recent increase in numbers, also possibly linked to good winter food-supplies in Britain, they have spread back to around the Wash and north Norfolk, but are still in very small numbers on the Humber estuary.

Greylag Goose *Anser anser*
The largest and greyest of these geese, and our only native breeding goose. Although of slimmer and less sagging build, this is the ancestor of our domestic goose. When the wild bird is seen in strong flight, with the contrast of pale blue-grey wing coverts and dark flight feathers, its affinities seem even less obvious. However, it has the deep honking calls and raucous cries familiar

in the farmyard bird. Compared with other wild species it is a heavier and coarser-looking bird and seemingly less inclined to long flights.

It breeds in Eurasia, through the temperate and warmer boreal zones; in western Europe it extends up the Scandinavian coasts and breeds in western Scotland and in Iceland. In winter it moves south to warm-temperate regions and is migratory through most of its range; but some winter around the southern North Sea, and it is resident in parts of the British Isles. The Iceland breeders also winter in the British Isles.

For nesting the Greylag Goose prefers open waters with nearby grassland, and an island or waterside nest-site. It will also nest on small coastal islands. The nest is simply a lined hollow in the ground. The wild British population now breeds only in extreme north-west Scotland and on some of the Hebrides.

It occurs early in British history, being present in the warmer periods of the Pleistocene from the Cromerian Interglacial onwards, and probably breeding at such periods. It was almost certainly breeding in the extensive marshlands of the Iron Age, since it seems to have been domesticated at that time. The readiness of newly-hatched young ones to follow any moving creature and to adopt it as a parent would make them an easy bird to domesticate, especially in the lake settlements of the period. Julius Caesar noted that the British kept geese, and that they appeared to use them as watch-dogs rather than for food.

In spite of continuing domestication, the wild birds continued to hold their own. In later centuries English birds became confined to the eastern counties, being lost to Cambridgeshire and Yorkshire about 1773, and by the early nineteenth century disappearing from Norfolk and Lincolnshire, last breeding as a wild bird in England in 1831. During the nineteenth century the southern limit shrank back through Scotland and by the twentieth century they were restricted to the north-west and the Hebrides. By 1956 it was estimated that only about 175 pairs were left, most of them on the islands. Under protection they have begun to increase again with about 500–700 breeding pairs and as many non-breeders in the mid 1980s. They are still thinly dispersed, mainly in the Hebrides.

In the 1930s some birds were kept ferally in south-west Scotland, where they increased to form a breeding population which began to be an embarrassment to local agriculture. In the 1960s eggs and young were used by wildfowling organisations to create widely dispersed populations in eastern and central Scotland and through midland and southern England. There are also colonies in Anglesey and around Strangford Lough. In England they are concentrated in Lakeland, Bedfordshire and North Kent. These feral flocks tend to be partly tame, and sedentary. It is estimated that they now constitute the major part of the breeding population. They are by preference birds of waterside grassland, but fairly adaptable to circumstances. They will roost on small inland waters. Like the feral Canada Goose they show a tendency to assume the status previously held by park ducks rather than as a shootable element of our wild waterfowl.

Superimposed on these populations in winter there are the Icelandic migrants. The native birds of north-west Scotland move to the east coast at this time. The Icelandic birds occur through Scotland south to England north of Lakeland and to Northumberland; a few are scattered around Ireland. They tend to be concentrated mainly around estuaries, and feed on lowland grasses, stubbles and root crops. The main concentrations are in southern and eastern Scotland and numbers have increased in recent years from about 25,000 in the early 1950s to over 100,000 in the mid 1980s.

White-fronted Goose *Anser albifrons*

Most readily recognisable of the grey geese, this has a boldly barred underside, white around the base of the bill, and a cheerful disyllabic babble: a flock is often likened to a pack of small dogs. Greenland birds have an orange-yellow bill, Siberian birds a pink one. The young lack the distinctive belly and head-markings.

It has a circumpolar breeding distribution in the tundra regions. One population occurs through the Siberian tundra; others are scattered in the Arctic north-west of North America, and one on the east coast of Greenland. The Greenland population winters in the British Isles, and some of the western Siberian birds wintering around the southern North Sea occur in southern England and Wales. As a winter visitor it prefers grassland and cultivated farmland, but also utilises a variety of other habitats of a generally open kind, including bogs and saltings. It roosts mainly in estuaries. Winter flocks may be large, but tend to break up into smaller groups when feeding, a habit particularly noticed in Greenland birds. It shows a broad habitat tolerance in breeding, and although mainly on coastal or inland shrubby tundra, Greenland birds use more montane sites with heath and bog.

It was present in Britain in the past, from the Middle Pleistocene Wolstonian Glaciation onwards, presumably a migrant in warmer periods, but a possible breeder in colder periods. Subsequently, as a bird of saltings and coastal grasslands, it may have had a relatively stable existence.

Certain feeding grounds appear traditionally favoured. About two-fifths of the Greenland birds winter on the Wexford Slobs in south-east Ireland, with another fifth scattered elsewhere in Ireland. The remainder, with the exception of a small number in North Wales, come to western Scotland and Caithness, with about two-thirds of these on the island of Islay in the Inner Hebrides. There is relatively little information on the populations in the recent past. The Greenland birds decreased slightly in the 1960s and 1970s but have increased again and stand at about 16,000 – 17,000 in the mid 1980s.

The Siberian population wintering in Britain varies as an extension of the larger number that move to the east side of the North Sea, mainly in the Netherlands. Their main British sites are to the south and east of those used by Greenland birds. They concentrate in the Towy Valley of south Wales, the Severn Estuary, the Hampshire Avon, Romney Marsh and north Kent, with small numbers in parts of East Anglia. These populations fluctuate with the winter weather, and a scattering of small numbers may be widespread. The North Sea population appeared to quadruple between the early 1960s and early 1970s, but numbers fell in Britain at this period, possibly because of changes in feeding grounds. There are usually some 5,000–7,000.

Lesser White-fronted Goose *Anser erythropus*
NOT ILLUSTRATED

An infrequent migrant, this is like a small individual of the previous species, less heavily barred with black below, with the white of the forehead extending back onto the fore-crown, and with a narrow, fleshy, yellow ring round the eye. Its voice is higher-pitched. In flight and on the ground it appears quicker and more active.

It breeds in a narrow sub-tundra zone of Eurasia, in broken or hilly ground on the edges of scrub and wooded tundra. In the west its breeding range extends part of the way along the mountain range of northern Scandinavia. It winters in warm-temperate regions from Greece eastwards. Western Europe is not a part of its normal migration route or wintering area. However, its route southwards crosses those of westerly migrating White-fronted and Bean Geese in autumn, and individuals appear to be caught up in flocks of these. As a result, stray Lesser White-fronted Geese appear with some regularity in Britain and countries spread around the southern North Sea, usually as single individuals in flocks of the other species.

It does not seem to have had a more westerly distribution in the past, and records of it from Ice Age caves appear to be due to misidentifications.

Ducks

These are the most numerous waterfowl, in numbers and species. The generalised duck is a smallish, solidly built bird with short legs, large webbed feet, and a broad, flattened bill. However, the wide range of species is possible because there has been adaptation to different habitats, and different feeding methods. In addition to the typical surface-swimming and surface-feeding species there are others that dive and swim under water in search of food, while some have become adapted to some degree of terrestrial life and feeding.

Our British ducks may be grouped and subdivided into the shelducks, the surface-feeding or dabbling ducks, a wood duck, freshwater diving ducks, sea diving ducks and the fish-eating sawbills.

Shelducks

Alopochen and *Tadorna* species

These are ducks more adapted for life on land, and sometimes seen as a link between ducks and geese. They are longer-legged and more upright in posture, walking and running more easily than typical ducks. Flight appears a little heavier, and they have a striking wing-pattern with white coverts above and below, black primaries, and glossy green on the secondaries. The sexes are similar, and there is no dull eclipse plumage. They nest in holes or deeply concealed sites.

There are two British species. The Egyptian Goose is a bird of the margins of inland waters and marshes and was introduced from Africa. It has a small feral population. The Common Shelduck is native, and usually occurs on the intertidal mud of coasts and estuaries around the British Isles.

Egyptian Goose *Alopochen aegyptiacus*
NOT ILLUSTRATED

A heavy-looking duck, about the size of a small goose but longer-legged. The head is small in proportion, and the sharply narrowed bill and tapering rufous-brown patch across a pale-irised eye tend to give it a slightly spiteful look. It is warm brown or greyish on the back, pale buff on the underside with grey-washed flanks and a rufous-brown belly-patch. The face is whitish around the dark patch, the nape shaggy and rufous-tinted, and there is a thin reddish-brown ring around the base of the neck. The long, strong legs and stout, tapering bill are pink. In flight the wing-pattern shows in striking contrast to the body. The female has a harsh quack, loud and guttural, but the male can only utter husky panting notes.

It perches freely on trees, and nests for preference in a tree cavity or hole in a cliff or bank, but will exceptionally use thick cover at ground level. This need for a large nest cavity may have restricted its ability to colonise. When not breeding it may flock but it shows a lot of aggressive display, posturing with feathers ruffled and head drawn in against the breast, or with head and neck extended; while in breeding territory it advertises its presence with erect postures and spread wings, and loud calling from the female. It feeds mainly by cropping herbage in open spaces near water, taking refuge on water when threatened.

It is an African species that in the past extended into the Middle East and south-eastern Europe. It was first known as a captive species in Britain in 1678, was breeding on the waters of various parks and estates by 1785, and has continued as a breeder in small numbers for the subsequent 200 years. In the last century it was breeding on the lakes of private estates in Norfolk, at Woburn in Bedfordshire, at Bicton and Crediton in Devon, and with one Scottish locality at Gosford in East Lothian. Bicton birds wandered in the south-west, and birds occurring in the past on the Northumberland coast may have come from East Lothian; but although at present there appears to be evidence of some local dispersal in winter it is a rather sedentary species.

The present-day population is around 500 birds, over four-fifths of them in Norfolk with the main concentration at Holkham. The East Anglian population extends into northern Suffolk; there is a small concentration on the borders of Devon and Somerset, and scattered occurrences elsewhere in midland and southern England. The relative lack of success has been attributed to competition with grey geese, and to predators; it probably shares with another potential coloniser, the Ruddy Shelduck *Tadorna ferruginea*, the problem of a lack of cavities and similar sites for the larger nesting ducks.

Common Shelduck *Tadorna tadorna*

This species, which R.M. Lockley once aptly compared to a painted toy, is the most conspicuous of our ducks, flaunting its simple black, white and chestnut pattern on bare open mudflats, or against green foliage on its inland forays for nest sites. Although a few have moved to nesting on inland waters, its primary distribution is controlled by the presence of shallow muddy and sandy coasts and estuaries. Pairs establish feeding territories, defended by aggressive displays with vertical head-pumping movements or short runs with extended head and neck, accompanied by deep nasal quacking from females and softer fluty whistles of males. It feeds mainly on small invertebrates filtered out of the mud, and to a much smaller extent on plant material.

For nesting it needs a cavity and this may be some distance inland. A rabbit-burrow is preferred, but any sort of hole in the ground, or in or under tree or building may be used. The boldly patterned black-and-white ducklings are led to the nearest water by both parents. Later, broods join in flocks with only one or two adults, most adults moving in a moult migration to the German coastal flats of the Waddensee. A smaller number remain to moult at Bridgwater Bay in Somerset and on some larger estuaries on the east coast.

In autumn birds return, spreading north and westwards, and followed by some of the western European birds, while fledged young disperse around the coasts. However, few use the extreme north-west of Scotland in winter.

Gadwall
MALE

Shelduck
MALE

MALE
Garganey

FEMALE
Mallard

MALE

Teal
MALE

D.M. HENRY

Its very early history in Britain shows some peculiarities. There are single occurrences in the last glaciation in the midlands and south-east England; but there is evidence of its presence around the Torbay region of Devon from the latter part of the next-to-last glaciation, the Wolstonian, onwards to the present. It appears to have occurred there in both warmer and cooler periods, although in the coldest stages of the glaciations the channel was mostly dry land. There would appear to have been some favourable conditions, possibly in terms of local climate and estuarine or lagoon waters, which led to its long-term survival there.

Subsequently there is little information. Conditions for its survival are likely to have changed little over the centuries, although rabbit-burrows would not have been available in very early times. The numbers fell in the nineteenth century, no doubt due to shooting; but although there has been some local variation in success, the numbers overall have steadily increased in the present century, and it has colonised or re-colonised the Shetlands. In winter there are now about 65,000 in Britain and up to 8,000 in Ireland, about half the western European population; but there are only about 12,000 breeding pairs in summer.

Dabbling Ducks

Anas species

These are the typical surface-feeding boat-shaped ducks. The body is rather long, the legs short, and the resultant gait is a waddle; but they swim strongly. The bill is broad and flattened, with fine ridges on the insides of the edges. They feed at the surface of the water with a rapid dabbling motion: the bill is moved from side to side in the water with rapid small opening and closing movements, the fine ridges helping to strain out small particles of food. They also feed a little deeper by up-ending and reaching down, particularly in shallows. They are mainly birds of fresh water.

The females have rather dull dark-streaked brown plumage which helps to make them inconspicuous; but both sexes show the diagnostic bright wing-patch, the speculum, on the secondaries. Breeding males have brightly patterned and distinctive plumage. They display in groups to females that subsequently nest and rear young alone. During the summer, males moult into a duller 'eclipse' plumage resembling that of the female. The nest is a down-lined hollow, usually on the ground, concealed in vegetation and not far from water. They are strong and swift fliers, and most species are migratory over much of their ranges.

The British Isles and parts of western Europe offer tolerable winter conditions for species that are migratory in other parts of their ranges; and with the exception of the summer-visiting Garganey, all are resident in some part of Britain. The Wigeon and Pintail are the most northerly in breeding distribution, nesting in tundra or boreal zones, with midland Britain as part of their southern limits. Teal and Mallard are more tolerant of a wider range of conditions, breeding from tundra to temperate zones. The Shoveler is a more migratory breeding species of boreal to temperate regions, while both Gadwall and Garganey are limited to more temperate regions for breeding and mainly migrate from these in winter.

Gadwall *Anas strepera*

Like a smaller, slimmer and more soberly coloured Mallard, this has a breeding male in shades of grey and black with just a touch of colour on the wings, and a female brown-mottled in Mallard fashion, but both identified by the bold white patch of the speculum. It is a quiet duck of quiet waters, usually on still or slow-moving and shallow lowland lakes, ponds and marshes.

The female has a soft quack, and the male a deep harsh note and a display whistle. The sociable displays include exaggerated head movements, water-flicking with the bill, and rearing the tail end to display the surprisingly black plumage of the posterior body and wings.

The Gadwall occurs through the temperate regions of Eurasia and North America, migrating to warm-temperate of subtropical zones in winter; but it is resident in parts of Europe and the western edge of North America. However, it appears more sensitive to cold and wet conditions than many other species, which may account for its limited occurence in Britain. It was present in the Ipswichian Interglacial of south-eastern England and in the Iron Age in Somerset. Its apparent absence from Britain during historic times may have been due to the colder conditions of the Little Ice Age, but it was probably a winter visitor in small numbers from continental Europe.

Birds introduced to the Norfolk brecklands in about 1850 began to breed and, although they increased considerably, in fifty years the distribution had only spread to northern Suffolk. In 1962 it also colonised Iceland. Birds were not recorded breeding in Scotland until 1909 at Loch Leven. During the warmer period of the first half of this century it spread in southern Sweden and increased in Iceland, birds from both areas wintering in Britain. There was some increase and spread in East Anglia, and also across southern Scotland, while feral populations were established around London and on the Scillies. From 1933 onwards it began to nest in very small numbers in Ireland, mainly in County Wexford.

These feral birds were rather sedentary, increasing but not spreading greatly, and dispersal has been due mainly to human introductions which in more recent times have established scattered sites across England and south Wales with limited spread around them. Even now the breeding population is only in the order of 250 pairs. In winter about a quarter of these birds emigrate, but there is also an influx from Europe. These are much more widespread, mainly in midland and south-eastern England, and several thousand may be present.

Garganey *Anas querquedula*

A little duck, unobtrusive in both colour and behaviour. Females and eclipse males have the typical dark-streaked brown plumage, and it is the wing-coverts, a blue-grey patch in the male, pale grey in the female, that become suddenly apparent in flight and identify the species. Its green speculum, bordered front and back with white, is like that of the Teal. It is not a very vocal bird: the female has a low quack, and the male has an odd mechanical-sounding crackle or rattle, particularly when displaying. Displays include head-waving and vertical head-pumping movements, preening behind the wing and an exaggerated throwing-back of the head to touch the back.

For breeding it prefers shallow fresh waters, particularly the marginal parts where thinly-growing emergent and floating vegetation provide a sparse surface vegetation that helps to hide it. At other times, while preferring a similar habitat, it will use more exposed sites. It feeds on plants and small creatures taken on or just below the surface, often feeding with head submerged. It flies fast and readily. The nest is in thick ground vegetation near water.

It is a migrant, with a broad distribution through boreal and temperate Eurasia, wintering in Africa and south-east Asia. Its earliest recorded occurrence in Britain in the past is on the east coast in a pre-Hoxnian interglacial, and it also occurred in Iron Age Somerset. Subsequently its numbers seem to have been determined by weather, with annual influxes depending on conditions at the time. Breeding takes place opportunistically on sites which happen to be suitable at the time, and flood-lands and fens tend to be most used.

It was probably very scarce in the last few centuries, but in the first half of the present century it increased as a British breeding bird, and in north-west Europe generally, as the climate became milder. In England and Wales it built up from a few pairs at the turn of the century to about 50 in the early 1950s, peaked at about 70 in the late 1960s, but has fallen since. It is scarce in Scotland, with single proven breedings in 1928 and 1979, and scarcer still in Ireland. The British Isles is on the edge of its fluctuating and unpredictable summer range, and its future status will depend on our varying climatic conditions.

Mallard *Anas platyrhynchos*

This is the typical duck, the ancestor of our domestic ducks, and the standard against which all other ducks tend to be measured. It also sets the standard for duck voices, and the coarse loud quack of the female is better known than the higher-pitched and softer notes of the male. Those familiar with the domestic bird may not know its displays. These are often sociable, take place on water, and involve synchronised and ritualised posturing by groups of males. Displays include rearing up with tucked-in head, flicking water with the bill, and raising and displaying the black posterior and distinctive tail-feathers; and these are mostly accompanied by an unexpected fluty whistle.

Although it prefers shallow, still water with plenty of vegetation, it is highly adaptable and can use almost any patch of water, and also look for food on land. It walks well, flies strongly, and can rise steeply in confined places. It also uses a great variety of nest-sites. Coupled with a tolerance of human disturbance and a wide natural range, all this has helped to make it the commonest duck. It occurs naturally from subarctic to warm-temperate zones of the northern hemisphere, and over most of its range migrates to warmer subtropical areas in winter. It is resident in the British Isles and most of Europe, with an influx of wintering migrants as well. As a domestic bird it has been introduced into all parts of the world as a resident. It is the most frequently occurring duck in the British Ice Ages, with its earliest

record in Norfolk in the Pastonian Glaciation, and it is subsequently present in both warmer and cooler periods. Like the Greylag Goose it appears to have been domesticated in Iron Age times, probably by the taking of newly-hatched young which quickly learn to follow a parent-substitute. It was probably domesticated independently in a number of parts of its range.

Its later history is difficult to interpret, tame and feral birds being mixed with wild ones. As a wild bird its population has been more affected by the availability of water than by climate. We may suspect that numbers fell with the drainage of large areas of marshland, but may have increased with field enclosure and the use of small cattle-ponds. In recent decades the picture becomes still more confused with the deliberate introduction of feral birds for shooting. At present it is uniformly distributed throughout the British Isles as a breeding bird, and present in most areas in winter when in some places such as Scotland, nearly half the birds may be winter migrants from abroad. The number of breeding pairs in the British Isles has been estimated at between 70,000 and 150,000, and the winter population at about 550,000.

Teal *Anas crecca*

Smallest and shyest of the ducks, this prefers the muddy and vegetated margins of waters; it is probably best known for the musical fluty whistle of the male, its steep upward rocketing spring when disturbed, and the agile fast flight on whistling wings. It is not easy to get near enough to see the fine head-pattern of the male; and the cream-coloured patches under the tail, white stripe along the side, and white-edged and green-streaked speculum are the more conspicuous marks. The duck is the usual streaky brown, with white belly, and has typical quacking calls.

Displays are similar to those of other dabbling ducks, but the head-feathers are raised to display the pattern as on a laterally-flattened disc, while the rump-raising display is a rocking-horse motion in which the cream and black undertail-coverts are strikingly apparent. Displays usually involve a group of males around a

Studies of Teals

female, accompanied by a confused chorus of short whistling notes. The nests are hidden in thick ground cover near water, sometimes several close together. The birds tend to remain hidden for most of the day, becoming active at dusk. They feed frequently on wet mud, or in shallow pools and puddles, often with the head submerged.

It is present as a breeding bird across Eurasia and North America from subarctic to temperate zones, mostly migrant in winter to warm-temperate and subtropical zones. It is resident in the British Isles and much of Europe. As a breeding bird it prefers the smaller ponds and bogs of acid moorland and peat areas, and is thinly distributed. In the past it occurred early, in the Cromerian Interglacial of the Middle Pleistocene of Norfolk, and in some midland and north-western caves in the last glaciation. It does not seem to occur as a prey species of early human settlements; but this may have been because of its more specialised breeding requirements, and its furtiveness and agility at other times.

Because of its breeding preferences its main concentrations are on uplands of northern England and Scotland, Ireland except the southern quarter, and suitable areas of Wales, East Anglia and south-eastern England. In winter it moves to lowland waters, and tends to be scarce or absent in areas where it nested. The fact that it is not easily seen when breeding, and that there is a large influx of winter migrants from northern Europe and Siberia, make population changes difficult to assess. There is some evidence of a slight decrease during the second half of the present century, possibly linked with colder climate. Estimates of population vary. Breeding birds have been estimated at about 7,000–12,000, but having increased by winter to about twice that number; the winter influx has been estimated as up to 200,000, although this may vary with the season's weather. In general there seems to have been a sizeable increase in wintering birds during the period when residents are decreasing.

PLATE NINE

Pintail *Anas acuta*

Physical elegance is not a usual anatid attribute, and the slender neck, fine head and tapering tail of this species come as a surprise. It is enhanced on the male by the white line along the neck and the spiky tapering tertial feathers lying along the back. The female, more sober in colour, shares the elegance of shape. The white-edged speculum is dull green, buff on the female; and the conspicuous characters are the slim shape, and the white breast of the male. It is a restless, fast-flying bird with narrow wings, long thin neck and thin, tapering tail.

It has the typical dabbling duck displays, but uses in particular those in which the distinctly patterned head and neck are displayed. It is vocally rather quiet; the female quacking, the male using a soft, thin piping, and during displays a louder whistle. It is one of the dabbling ducks in which the male tends to remain with the female during incubation and the hatching period, although playing no active part. The nest is on the ground near water, and at times in a rather open and exposed site.

It has a wide general breeding range from arctic to cool-temperate zones around the northern hemisphere, wintering in warm-temperate to tropical regions. For breeding it prefers shallow waters of open and extensive grassy areas. Because such waters are often temporary in the natural state, it tends to change breeding sites easily, occur sporadically, and often move long distances. In Britain the breeding sites are few and widely scattered, mostly on coastal sites and moorland; while wintering birds tend to occur in large flocks on a relatively small number of estuaries.

In the past it occurred as a Pleistocene species as early as the Cromerian in Norfolk, but is comparatively rare in early remains, possibly because fast flight, wariness and a preference for very open spaces made it a difficult prey. As a species breeding north to the tundra it might have been expected to do well in the colder periods of the fourteenth to nineteenth centuries, but within that period it is first recorded breeding in Britain in 1869 in Inverness, Scotland. Later it was mainly centred on Loch Leven with regular breeding from 1898–1939, but only once or twice since. There are scattered and sporadic records elsewhere, but regular breeding only in Caithness and the south Orkney islands. It bred in the Shetlands until the 1950s but has not done so recently.

In England, it bred in Kent in 1910 and intermittently on Romney Marsh for the next 35 years. It has used the marshes of the Thames estuary since 1947, and has bred in the Fens. There are also scattered breeding records in north-west England, of which some at least originate from feral birds. It reached Ireland in 1917, breeding in County Roscommon where it has bred intermittently since.

Estimates of this small breeding population fluctuate at around 50 pairs. In winter there is a big influx of birds from western Siberia, Scandinavia and Iceland. These birds gather mainly in estuaries, but some penetrate inland up rivers with floodwaters or gravel-pits. The Mersey and Dee estuaries, Ouse Washes and Essex coast have large numbers. Wintering populations have increased in the last few decades and may total about 30,000 for the British Isles.

Wigeon *Anas penelope*

A squat, stubby-billed bird with a high forehead. In flight the warm chestnut colour of the female contrasts with a white belly, but it is usually the striking white patch of the flying male's wing-coverts that identifies the species, together with his exuberant whistled *wree-ou* call, used in excitement and alarm, in displays and between the pair. Males are noisy and agressive in

Pintail

FEMALE

MALE

Wigeon

FEMALE

MALE

Shoveler

MALE

FEMALE

D.M.HENRY

displays, with constant use of the loud whistles, while the female's low purr or growl is like a background undertone. Displaying birds fluff up the chestnut and yellow head feathers, and the pale forehead is ritually displayed to the female. Threatening males tip the closed wings upwards to display the white covert-patch.

The short, stout bill is adapted for grazing, and in addition to feeding in shallow water it frequently crops the herbage on saltmarshes and grassy water-sides. Flocks of hunched birds nibbling steadily over the marsh grass are typical of winter estuaries. Although a widespread lowland bird in winter, it is more limited in its breeding habitat. It prefers the smaller waters of upland moors, preferably on an island site. The few scattered breedings in southern England are probably of feral birds. The nest is usually well-concealed in thick and tall ground cover such as tall grasses, and heather or bracken in more open sites, but in parts of its range it uses open woodland, and hides the nest in shrubby growth and thicker cover. Nesting may not be apparent until the young are seen. As with the Pintail, males are more attentive to the females than in some other species, and tend to remain nearby at least until the earlier part of incubation.

Its overall range is across the tundra and boreal zones of Eurasia and in Iceland, migrating to war-temperate and subtropical areas in winter. Only in Britain does it occur all the year. It was present in Britain in the Pleistocene, with its earliest record in the Cromerian Interglacial. Like the Pintail, it is a subarctic bird that does not seem to have been breeding in the colder periods of the Little Ice Age in Britain, and is first recorded as nesting in the last century. It invaded Scotland from the north in 1934 and spread southwards, mainly inland, to become widespread by the 1950s but most breeding in the highlands. It has reached Yorkshire by 1897, but only established a regular breeding range as far as the northern Pennines. In Scotland, in recent decades, it has tended to breed more to the east and less to the west. Scattered breeding pairs further south, mainly in East Anglia and the Thames valley, may originate from feral birds probably escaped from waterfowl collections. The total breeding pairs may number around 300–500.

Winter sees a big influx from Iceland, Scandinavia and Siberia. Numbers vary from season to season and place to place. It is estimated that 200,000 to 250,000 Wigeon winter in Britain – and perhaps another 100,000 in Ireland – totalling about half the north-west European wintering population. In the past these have congregated mainly on coasts and estuaries, but they show an increasing tendency to move inland, feeding on stubble, winter wheat and similar new food sources, and taking advantage of gravel-pits, reservoirs and protected reserves.

Shoveler *Anas clypeata*

This is the super-dabbler among ducks: its big bill broadly flattened and longer than its head and finely adapted for filter-feeding. The bill is big enough to seem something of an encumbrance. This is a chunkily-built duck, tending to carry the head low and tucked back on the shoulders as though to support the bill. In flight it is bottle-shaped, the body long and bluntly-rounded at the tail end, tapering a little at the shoulders to a strong neck and head and squared-off bill. The wings appear set well back on the body; both sexes show a white-edged green speculum and pale blue wing-coverts, that form a patch conspicuous in flight.

It is a quiet and stolid species. When at rest, the female might be mistaken for a Mallard, but in lateral view, a male in breeding plumage shows a white body with a great chestnut flank-patch that is more conspicuous than the dark head and bill. The calls are subdued: low-pitched notes, chugging, wheezy or hoarse in the male, low and quacking in the female. Displays, involving groups of males, are like those of other dabbling ducks but not unexpectedly they often involve showing off the head and bill. In addition, males have short jump-flights designed to show off the plumage pattern in flight and producing special wing rattling sounds.

Shovelers are of necessity feeders in shallow, muddy-bottomed fresh or brackish waters that produce plenty of tiny organisms. This limits them mainly to lowlands, where they use small pools and ditches as well as larger waters. The nest may be well concealed in ground vegetation, or in a more open site. The male usually remains in attendance on the female until incubation.

It nests in the northern hemisphere boreal and temperate zones, wintering in warm-temperate to tropical zones; but with some present at all seasons in western Europe and the British Isles, although not the same birds throughout the year. In the past it would probably have been a bird of warmer periods, and the only early records are from the Hoxnian Interglacial in the south-east and from Somerset in the Iron Age. Because of its habitat requirements it is vulnerable to lowland drainage, and the widespread drainage of swamps and fens from the sixteenth century onwards, and in the last century, must have reduced its numbers. It became rare, but during the warmer climate of the end of the last century and first half of the present century it showed a considerable increase and spread in the British Isles, paralleling increases elsewhere in northern Europe. Its spread was limited by its need for marshy lowland habitat.

Although the first Scottish nesting has been recorded from the 1840s onwards, the main increase was not until this later period, since when it has extended to the Outer Hebrides and Orkney. Since the 1950s there has been little further increase, and some loss where habitat has deteriorated through drainage. The breeding concentrations are mainly in eastern Britain, particularly in the south-east, and it is infrequent in highland Scotland, Wales, south-west England and most of Ireland.

This breeding population of about 1,000 pairs moves south in winter to France and Spain, and is replaced by birds from Iceland, Scandinavia and Siberia, many of which are also passing through. A fall in late winter numbers may indicate a change of movements in returning migrants. Wintering populations are of about 17,000 birds, now falling to about 9,000–11,000 in late winter.

Wood Ducks

Aix species

Sometimes known as 'Perching Ducks', these are a group of diverse species, possibly diverse in origin, but adapted in varying degrees to perching on trees and nesting in tree cavities. They are therefore able to take advantage of small areas of water in forested habitats, mostly in warmer climates. The only British species, the Mandarin, is an introduced bird that has become established in parts of Britain. It originates from eastern Eurasia and has an ecological and closely-related counterpart, the Carolina or American Wood Duck *Aix sponsa*, in North America. Both have crests, but the Carolina Duck lacks the elaborate cheek plumes and enlarged orange tertial 'sail' of the Mandarin.

Mandarin *Aix galericulata*
NOT ILLUSTRATED

The breeding male of this species is probably the most absurdly ornate of our waterfowl. It is a small compact bird. The female is greyish-brown, slightly crested, with a white eye-ring, white on throat and belly, and white-spotted breast and flanks. The male has a pink bill and yellow feet, and in both sexes the bill has a stout, curved 'nail' at the tip.

The male's elongated crown feathers give him a high forehead and a crest arching back to taper onto his back. The white sides of the crest arch like absurdly emphasised eyebrows from the base of the bill to the nape, and are buff-tinted at the front; while its upper surface is a dark stripe, glossed blue-green on forehead and nape, and maroon in between. The cheeks are bristling fans of fine spiky chestnut plumes, overhanging the sides of a purple breast bordered with black-and-white lines. The vermiculated buff flanks are also bordered black-and-white. The wings appear mainly dark but the innermost tertials are streaked purplish-green and white, with one feather on each wing expanded to form a great orange crescent that stands up above the back like a small sail, counterbalancing the elaborate head plumage.

Although theoretically conspicuous it is less obvious in its chosen haunts. It perches freely and tends to rest by day, hidden on branches overhanging the water in shrubs or low trees. It is agile in flight, often keeping low among the trees. It flights at dusk, the plumage sleeked and much less conspicuous than might be expected, and feeds by streams, pools and marshy areas in woodland. It will also use larger waters where these have heavily-vegetated margins. It feeds on small creatures – fish, snails and insects – and on seeds and nuts. Acorns are an important food, and chestnuts and beechmast are also eaten.

It is a quiet bird, but with a varied vocabulary, the male having various short, sharp whistling notes, the female a coot-like *kek* and some low sharp notes and clucks. In display the male raises the crest, stretching the white brow upwards. Some displays are like those of dabbling ducks. There are also head-flicking, raising and shaking movements that emphasise the head-plumes, the head being tilted so that the crest projects behind, and the spiky cheek-plumes are ruffled in a manner reminiscent of display plumage of a grebe. In the ritualised preening-behind-the-wing display, the orange tertial fan plays a conspicuous part.

Birds may remain paired for a number of seasons, but separate for a time while the female is caring for the young; they meet again in flocking groups later in the year. The nest is usually in a hole in a tree, sometimes up to ten metres or more above ground, and the recently-hatched young clamber to the entrance and drop to the ground. Increasing population pressure and shortage of sites in recent times seems to have led to several females laying in one nest.

Its natural habitat is temperate broad-leaf forest in Manchuria, China and Japan, more particularly where oak trees are plentiful; and it is most successful as a feral species where such conditions occur. Several bones found in the Cromerian forest beds of Norfolk seem to be referable to this species and to indicate its presence in the Middle Pleistocene. (This has been commented on in the section on the Pleistocene in the Introduction, p.14). There is evidence of the presence of temperate oak forest at that time which would have been suitable for it.

Subsequently, there appears to be a gap, until it occurs as an introduced exotic waterfowl from the eighteenth century onwards. It has always been popular as a captive bird and kept in waterfowl collections. A drawing was made from a live one in England in 1746. It is not known when it started breeding freely, but birds were breeding successfully in park at Edenbridge, Kent in 1912. Six pairs released in Surrey in 1928, and another 99 in London in 1930, are thought to have been the basis of our present population.

Although it is migratory in the countries of origin, British birds do not appear to move far. The main feral population is centred on west Surrey, extending into Sussex, Berkshire and southern Buckinghamshire. Elsewhere small numbers have established themselves where birds bred in captivity have been allowed to fly freely. Such centres were to be found in the recent past in east Norfolk, Bedfordshire, Hertfordshire, Kent, Hampshire, Gloucestershire and Cheshire. Numbers are still increasing and birds elsewhere may represent a spread of fresh releases. Recent surveys show scattered sites that extend to the south-west and south Wales, but the distribution is mainly in the lowland parts of the southern half of Britain; an isolate population has maintained itself at Perth, in Scotland, since the 1960s.

Its future distribution is likely to be limited by its need for broadleaf woodland and cavity nest-sites. It has continued to increase in southern England, estimates having more than doubled between the late 1960s and mid 1980s, and the British population is estimated at about 850–1,000 pairs.

Freshwater Diving Ducks

Aythya species

These are squat squarish ducks with short broad bodies, short tails usually held low, and big rounded heads. Legs and feet are large and longish, set well back and well apart, making them awkward in walking but giving a strong propulsion underwater. They dive abruptly and re-appear equally suddenly. In clear water one can see them descend, head down, and body at a slant, the legs raised to the sides of the body, simultaneously kicking up and back. This enables the birds to reach the bottom in deeper water, but appears to be a fight against their natural buoyancy, and once the forward and downward propulsion is relaxed, they bob to the surface like released corks. They have flattened, dabbling-duck-like bills.

Their wings appear smaller than those of dabbling ducks, with a broad white bar across the flight feathers. They are less agile in taking flight, using their feet to help them, pattering briefly across the surface before becoming air-borne. They fly fast and straight with very rapid wing-beats, showing the typical outline of compact body, short neck and large head. The plumage has simple colouring, mainly large patches of black, grey or chestnut. In the eclipse (the summer plumage of males) the plumage pattern resembles that of breeding birds but is duller, especially on the head and breast.

They are rather silent, except in display; even then most vocalisations are subdued. They flock on open waters in winter, and courtship display, like that of dabbling ducks, usually involves a number of males and is directed at one female. Both the pair bond and the parental bond of adult and young appear weak and broken within a short time.

There are three regular British species. The Scaup is a tundra-breeder, visiting Britain in winter, with one or two scarce breedings. The Tufted Duck is resident, with additional immigrants in winter, as is the Pochard.

Scaup *Aythya marila*

This is the least striking species; the male dark at both ends and pale grey around the middle, the female distinguished by white around the bill base that may exceptionally occur also on some female Tufted Ducks. Quiet and unobtrusive, it usually remains out on the water, as a British bird usually seen in flocks on estuaries or coasts. Although it will rest at the water's edge, it is awkward and ill at ease on land, feeding and roosting afloat. Although mainly silent, the male has a soft repeated whistle and the female uses muffled growling notes. The calls used in display are similar and only a little louder. Display is a little less elaborate than in dabbling ducks. Head-raising and puffing-up of the neck occur, and head-lifting, turning, flicking and shaking. The head is also thrown back abruptly with an accentuated cooing call. In the preening-behind-the-wing display the male rattles his bill against the feather quills.

It breeds on large open stretches of water, nesting near the water's edge. An exception among these species, it breeds on fresh water but winters mainly on estuaries and coasts. Although it dives less deeply than the Tufted Duck, it is adapted to diving in the rougher

waters of tidal areas, taking various small creatures – particularly shellfish – and some plant material. Very large numbers have occurred at Scottish sewage outfalls where waste brewery grain was plentiful, and at mussel beds. Its general breeding distribution is circumpolar in arctic and subarctic zones, on tundra and into forest edge. It extends down the mountains of Scandinavia, the northern Baltic shores, and Iceland.

There is no apparent evidence of it in Pleistocene or prehistoric Britain, apart from a record from County Meath, Ireland, about 800 AD, although present-day evidence suggests it might have bred at cooler periods. Like some other tundra-nesting ducks, the Scaup does not seem to have colonised Britain in cooler centuries; but towards the end of the last century, when it was decreasing at its southern limit in Europe with climatic amelioration, it bred in Scotland. The first record was in 1897 in the Outer Hebrides, then on the mainland in Sutherland in 1899, while in the first locality it bred annually until 1902 and occasionally to 1913. Absent during the subsequent warmer years, it began again in 1939 in Caithness. England's only record was in 1944 in Lincolnshire. Then it nested on the Scottish west coast in 1946; bred regularly in Orkney from 1954 to 1959, then in 1965, 1969 and 1973. In 1969 it also bred again in the Outer Hebrides, and in 1970 at Perth.

This pattern of sporadic breeding of one to three pairs indicates that we are at the margin of its breeding range, but it is a regular winterer. Birds come from Iceland, Scandinavia and Russia. They concentrate in estuaries and on shallow coasts; scarce in north-west Scotland, Wales and south-west England. Numbers fluctuate with food supplies. At sewage outfalls in Edinburgh in the mid 1960s and 1970s, the winter peaks normally exceeded the present estimated total for the British Isles, on some occasions being treble that number. They disappeared with changes in treatment of sewage. Average numbers are now estimated at about 5,000–10,000 wintering birds.

Tufted Duck *Aythya fuligula*

The need for water with space and depth for diving tends to reduce the Tufted Duck, in most people's minds, to small groups of squat brown figures well out on the water and disappearing at intervals, identified by the occasional black male with its bold white flank-patch. On city park lakes it may become tamer, and visiting migrants mingle with residents without betraying their origin. Here one can see the purple gloss of the male's black plumage, the slender drooping nape tuft making the head appear bigger and rounder, and the iris like a gold ring on a black head. The female has a vestigial drooping tuft of a crest.

Like the Scaup it is a quiet bird, the male occasionally using a soft whistle, the female a low harsh growling quack. The displays are like those of the Scaup with upward stretching and thickening of the neck, and various movements making the head conspicuous and accentuating the still-drooping crest. Contracting pupils make the yellow iris of the eye suddenly conspicuous. The male has whistles and soft gobbling calls.

It prefers to nest on islands, sometimes many close

Scaup

FEMALE

MALE

Tufted Duck

FEMALE

MALE

Pochard

MALE

Goldeneye

MALE

FEMALE

D.M.HENRY

together, and it will also nest with colonies of smaller gulls or terns. It is sociable, tending to flock at all times. It is a bird of fresh waters, preferring reasonably productive still waters with depths of 3–5 metres although it can dive to depths of 14 metres to feed. It mainly uses waters without floating vegetation or dense marginal growth, and takes mostly small animal life, particularly molluscs and midge larvae. Diving with a small jump it takes food from the bottom, usually swallowed immediately. It will also feed in shallower water, and tame birds learn to take bread and similar food. Where conditions are suitable it uses a wide range of lakes and ponds, including most types of man-made waters. It will also use quiet slow-moving rivers. In winter it may resort to estuaries and inlets but, unlike the Scaup, avoids areas of strong waves and currents.

It breeds from subarctic to cool-temperate zones across Eurasia, and from most of its range migrates to warm-temperate and subtropical zones; but in Britain and northern Europe is present all year round. It was present in the Pleistocene as a species of warmer periods from the Cromerian Interglacial onwards. It seems to have been absent as a breeding bird during the Little Ice Age. Its colonisation of Britain and north-west Europe took place during the warmer period of the late nineteenth century and first half of this century. It has slowed since but there may still be some increase. The expansion seems to have been westerly as well as northerly and may have been aided by increased aridity in south-west Asian lakes.

First nesting was recorded in Yorkshire in 1849, in Scotland in 1872 and in Ireland in 1877. Expansion was rapid, until most suitable waters were occupied. The Tufted Duck tends to avoid the more acid waters of upland areas and its stronghold is in the lowlands. It has taken advantage of new reservoirs and gravel-pits. Its winter range is slightly more contracted than its summer range, with flocks on the larger fresh waters, but the general pattern is the same.

There is some winter shift of population, with Scottish birds moving south-west to Ireland, while the winter visitors come from Iceland, Scandinavia and Russia. The breeding population has been estimated at about 7,000 pairs in Britain with about 2,000 more in Ireland. The wintering population in Britain stood at around 20,000 in the early 1960s, but had trebled to over 60,000 by the mid 1980s. It is difficult to calculate because of annual variations in visitors. Ireland is more difficult still with about another 25,000 generally, to which could be added 30,000 more at Lough Neagh in the mid 1960s which fell to only a quarter of that by 1980. From a nineteenth-century breeding rarity it has become our commonest diving duck.

Pochard *Aythya ferina*

Like the Tufted Duck, the Pochard is another compact duck that seems to live floating in the middle of open water, but which is bold-patterned enough to be recognisable at a distance. The male is black at the back and front, pale grey on the body, and the chestnut-orange head and neck are equally visible on swimming or resting birds. The female is duller: brown on head, breast and rump, and light greyish-brown on the body. In flight both show grey wings and the paler grey wing-bar is not distinct. At close quarters, the high-crowned head with slanting forehead is distinct, and the male has eyes with orange irises that seem to flash when the pupils contract during displays.

In displays the head is raised on a straight and often swollen neck, and turned and shaken in various ways. Calls are secondary to posture. The head is vigorously thrown back with a subdued whistle, and a wheezy whispering accompanies swimming with head and neck extended horizontally. Except in display they are generally silent, and any calls subdued. The male may make a soft whistle, and the female a low harsh growl.

Like the Tufted Duck the Pochard is a bird of open waters, preferring larger ones with a rich bottom fauna and flora but without floating plants. It takes mainly plant material and usually feeds at depths of up to 1.25 metres. However, it prefers waters with marginal emergent and fringing vegetation that is tall and thick. Here it nests by or just in the water, pulling in vegetation for a nest-mound. Where possible, it uses an inland site with suitable vegetation. The male tends to remain with the female through the incubation period. In winter it tends to flock on reservoirs, lakes and gravel-pits, and in hard weather may move to slow-moving rivers, estuaries and sheltered coasts.

It breeds across temperate Eurasia, migrating to warm-temperate and subtropical zones, but is present all the year in western Europe and the British Isles. In the past, it was present in eastern England in the Cromerian Interglacial and also in Iron Age Somerset, but seems to have been less common than the Tufted Duck. Its more recent history in Britain is uncertain, and it seems to have been rare but probably breeding for a long period, possibly restricted to East Anglia. Its spread began in the mid 1800s when it was spreading into, and increasing in, many parts of western Europe.

It bred in Yorkshire in 1844, Hertfordshire in 1850 and continued to spread into suitable sites. It reached Scotland as a breeding bird by 1871 and Ireland in 1907. It continued its spread in the present century, completing the Scottish invasion by reaching Caithness by 1921, but only occurring sporadically through central Ireland. In England and Wales the spread has been slow and patchy, probably because of the habitat requirements. It spread through north Kent in the 1940s, and after the introduction of feral birds bred more extensively in the London region from the early 1950s, and was introduced into Hampshire in 1961. It is now widespread but thinly and irregularly distributed in Britain, more numerous on the eastern side; also in central Ireland. In Scotland, however, there appears to have been a decrease in the second part of this century, possibly linked with colder conditions. The nesting population is estimated at about 200–400 pairs.

The influx of winter birds appears to be a mainly westerly movement from central Europe and western USSR. The birds are more widespread but with a similar general distribution pattern to that of breeding birds. Part of this influx occurs as a moult migration of incoming adults, mainly males, with several thousands on south-eastern reservoirs and up to about 20,000 on a few Irish loughs. Until the late 1970s when sewage treatment changed, the Edinburgh outfalls attracted some 7,000 Pochards as well as many Scaup. Numbers of wintering birds fluctuate considerably, but since the mid 1960s have almost trebled, and by the mid 1980s stand at about 50,000 with another 30,000 more in Ireland.

Sea Diving Ducks

Bucephala, Somateria, Melanitta and *Clangula* species

This varied group have in common the habit of diving for food. They breed mainly in arctic to subarctic regions where they may use fresh waters, but they winter on sea coasts. The bills are stout and their principal foods are shellfish and crustacea. There are five British species. The Goldeneye breeds in the boreal zone, in forest areas, with a small number recently nesting in northern Britain. The Commer Eider is an Arctic nester extending south as a coastal breeder in northern Britain. The Common and Velvet Scoters are typical sea ducks but breed in tundra and northern boreal regions, with a few of the former nesting in western Scotland and Ireland; while the Long-tailed Duck is a tundra-nesting winter visitor.

Goldeneye *Bucephala clangula*

The least marine of the sea ducks, this may also appear in small numbers on inland waters, often in company with other diving ducks but looking longer and lower bodied, with short neck and a large, dark high-peaked head. It rises easily, often steeply, and flies quickly with a musical whistling wing-beat. The inner half of the wing appears mainly white. Usually silent, it becomes noisy in display, the female with low harsh notes, the male with loud disyllabic calls, whistles and harsher rasping notes. The displays are striking, including extended neck and head (sometimes at an oblique angle with head feathers fluffed), a rearing up and throwing back of the head to touch the back, and a similar exaggerated throw-back of the head is combined with a raising of the rear end and backward kick of bright orange feet that throws up jets of water.

It is a strong swimmer, confident in turbulent water where it thrusts forwards with head and neck half-extended, and able to dive and feed in strongly-flowing currents. In its breeding habitat, it probes the stony bottoms of rivers and lakes, taking mainly molluscs and other small creatures. With this tolerance of salt water it is able to use waters of all kinds, from fresh to salt, and still to flowing, but it seems to prefer estuaries and sheltered coasts in winter. It breeds by forest lakes and rivers, and uses tree holes, particularly those of the Black Woodpecker, to which the female must fly directly. It very occasionally uses a low cavity or burrow. It will take to nest-boxes, and in parts of northern Europe these have been used for centuries, some of the eggs being taken for food.

It has a broad breeding distribution through the boreal forest zone of the northern hemisphere, migrating to temperate regions in winter. Although it could have bred here in cooler times, there is not much very early evidence of it in Britain. It was present in the Cromerian Interglacial in Norfolk and in Somerset in the Iron Age. There is no evidence of it breeding, even during the Little Ice Age of earlier centuries, although some birds might have been overlooked in view of the occurrence of non-breeding birds in summer. A pair that nested in rabbit burrows on the Dee estuary in 1931–32 might have been injured birds suffering from impaired flight.

The first real evidence was in the present cooler phase, in 1970, when a pair bred in Scotland, in East Inverness at a site where nest-boxes had been provided as an experiment. It was in typical nesting habitat, and by the mid 1970s, there were three pairs and evidence of spread, with possible breeding in north-west England as well. Large numbers of nest-boxes were provided and some were used, although other pairs used natural sites. By the mid 1980s the breeding population was about 50 pairs, mostly in Scotland with a few in Cumbria, and possibly some birds summering as far apart as Wales and Essex.

Wintering birds come from Scandinavia and western Russia. Present around the coasts of the British Isles, they are widespread on inland waters in most regions. The larger concentrations are on south-eastern reservoirs, some Irish loughs and Scottish firths. Numbers change as birds move around in hard weather. The wintering population of the British Isles is estimated at 10,000–15,000.

Eider *Somateria mollissima*

Heavyweight of the diving ducks, the Eider is a comfortable-looking, stolid inhabitant of rockier coasts. With short but strong legs set well back, it walks rather upright and unwillingly on land, and although it will rest on waterside rocks and sandbanks, it appears much more at ease on the water. The swimming male looks mainly white, the black belly only conspicuous when it rears up, or in flight. Young males, and adults in eclipse, are confusingly piebald. In any plumage, the almost triangular head and heavy wedge-shaped bill identify it. The flight is strong and direct, usually low over the water, and birds travelling for any distance tend to fly in single file.

It is sociable at most times, feedings in parties and flocks along the shore. Displays are by groups of males around a female, and the most typical involves puffing up the breast and throwing back the head to emit a loud expressive crooning double-coo, with a slight tone of surprise. At other times it is a mainly silent bird, the female having a deep throaty *krog* note. Displaying males also swim in front of the female, turning the head to display the nape pattern.

The male accompanies the female until she settles on a nest-site, then deserts her. The nest is just a hollow lined with eiderdown, often in an open site, but hidden by the motionless and cryptically-coloured female. Once the young have been led to the sea, broods may mix and amalgamate in flocks. The main foods are crabs (brought to the surface and shaken to pieces before being swallowed), mussels, and other shellfish such as periwinkles. They are obtained by diving, usually in depths of up to 3 metres, up-ending, or just reaching under the surface.

The Eider requires highly productive shores with some shelter from heavy seas and bad weather. It occurs around the shores of the Arctic, migrating from frozen sea areas in winter. There is little evidence of its presence in Britain in the distant past, apart from an occurrence at a site in Sutherlandshire early in the last glaciation, and records from early human settlement in Scotland. Its association with St Cuthbert would indicate its presence on the Northumberland coast in Saxon times.

It has probably been saved from widespread killing to some extent, because of the value of the down of the nest-lining. However, distribution in the British Isles in recent centuries seems to have been limited to Shetland, Orkney and the Scottish Islands, together with some parts of the north-east coast. From the mid nineteenth century onwards, there was a spread both in the British Isles and elsewhere in north-west Europe. This was southwards, and seems to have been linked with greater protection. Breeding birds spread around mainland Scotland about 1850 and began to colonise the northern coast of Ireland in 1912. Walney Island on Morecombe Bay, the most southerly breeding colony, was not colonised until one pair settled in 1949, but had 300 by 1970.

With the exception of a site in the Solway Firth and that at Walney, a line from Donegal Bay to about Coquet Island off Northumberland would be the southern limit of coastal breeding in the British Isles, which occurs on most coasts and islands north of this.

The distribution suggests something in the nature of a climatic limit. There have been some recent decreases in Shetland and the Firth of Forth. Eiders are highly vulnerable to sea pollution by oil or chemicals. The breeding population around the British coasts is estimated at about 20,000 pairs, and probably half of these are on the east coast of Britain.

In general, British Eiders do not move far. There is a tendency for north-eastern and Orkney and Shetland birds to form large moulting flocks in late summer, with some southward shift later in the year. In winter, there is an influx of birds, and small numbers appear scattered around the English and Welsh coasts. These may originate from the Baltic and from breeding colonies established in the Netherlands since the 1920s. The wintering population of the British Isles is estimated at about 70,000 birds.

Common Scoter *Melanitta nigra*

For the land-based watcher this is the real sea duck. Glimpsed offshore at binocular or telescope range, a flock of jet black males and pale-faced females are briefly seen sliding over a wave and disappearing in the troughs, or diving simultaneously with a sudden show of wing-tips and tails. They fly in long irregular dark lines, fast and low over the sea. It is only when the occasional birds turn up on inland lagoons or reservoirs that one can get a view of the stout bill, ornamented with the swollen knob and yellow upper surface.

It prefers shallow seas, inshore and offshore, often where the sea bed is sandy; and prefers to feed at depths of 3–5 metres, but can go to depths of 10–20 metres and if necessary lower still. Under water it propels itself with the feet, but the wings are partly opened when diving and may be held a little away from the body when under water. Important foods are mussels, cockles, shrimps crabs and sandeels, but a wide variety of other small creatures and some plant material are also taken. It feeds in flocks that tend to drift with the effects of tide and wind, then fly back to begin again. It avoids broken, rough waters and enclosed inlets. In the winter months it lives at sea, roosting on the water and rarely, if ever, coming to land.

Display occurs in the flocks in typical fashion with a group of males reacting to a single female. The males have low plaintive whistling or piping notes, frequently repeated and accelerating when they are excited. A chorus of such notes at varying pitch can be heard from flocks. The female's call is similar but lower and harsher in tone. In display, the birds call with head held high and the spiky tail cocked up vertically. Individuals rush across the water with head and neck extended; or with head drawn in low, back arched and feet splashing. There are sudden short flights in which the wings produce a high pitched whirring or trilling sound.

When nesting, the birds change habitat completely, moving inland. In tundra and boreal regions they occur near fresh water, preferring to nest among tall herbage or in shrubby growth. In the British Isles, nesting is mainly by moorland or acid lochs. Nesting is not easy to determine and the statistical discrepancy between suspected and proven nesting is considerable. After nesting, adult birds move out to form moulting flocks offshore in late summer.

Eider

FEMALE

MALE

WINTER MALE

AUTUMN FEMALE

FEMALE

MALE

Long-tailed Duck

Common Scoter

Velvet Scoter

MALE

D.M. HENRY

Its general distribution is through the subarctic and northern boreal zone from northern Scandinavia to the Alaskan coast, wintering south to temperate sea coasts. It extends down the Scandinavian mountain ridge, and has scattered breeding sites in northern Iceland, and north-west Scotland and Ireland.

In comparison with other species of ducks, records of the Common Scoter are fairly frequent in eastern England in the Pleistocene, from the latter part of the Cromerian Interglacial onwards. Cave remains inland at Creswell in Derbyshire dating from the last glaciation suggest that it might have bred near this site. It also occurred in Iron Age Somerset.

There is no evidence of the Common Scoter as a breeding species before 1855 when a nest was found in Sutherlandshire; others were found breeding annually in Caithness in the 1860s. These may have been evidence of a long established population previously unnoticed. There was a southward spread in Scotland to Invernesshire and Argyllshire in the 1880s, Rosshire in 1913 and Perthshire in 1921. Meanwhile it had spread to County Fermanagh in Northern Ireland in 1905, and to Shetland in 1911. Many of these breedings were sporadic or temporary, and subsequent spread has been slight. A population has been established in County Mayo in north-west Ireland since 1948, and there have been breedings in scattered sites in south-west Scotland since the early 1970s.

At Lower Lough Erne in County Fermanagh, numbers increased from 7 pairs in 1917 to about 150 in the late 1960s, but dropped to about 50 in the mid 1980s. Elsewhere, it is difficult to assess the significance of fluctuations, although there has been a decrease in parts of northern Europe in the last few decades. Scottish breeding was estimated at about 30–50 pairs in the mid 1970s and at about the lower figure in the mid 1980s, with Irish figures dropping from about 130 to 80 in the same period.

Wintering birds come from Scandinavia and Russia and are scattered in suitable coastal areas around most of the British Isles; they are mainly absent from Shetland, Orkney and the rocky shore of north and west Scotland, much of northern Ireland, the southern Irish coast and the Bristol Channel. There are large migratory movements in the English Channel. Once birds have arrived, there seems to be remarkable little movement between chosen areas. The winter population is estimated at 25,000–30,000 birds.

Velvet Scoter *Melanitta fusca*

The rarer of our two scoters, this species tends to be lost among the wintering Common Scoters. It is a winter visitor, joining its sibling species, but almost always in smaller numbers and hidden in the large flocks. The female is easier to detect, a dark brown bird with a small whitish mark between bill and eye, and another slightly larger patch on the hind cheek. On the male the yellow bordering the upper bill, and the small white streak behind the eye are barely apparent at a distance. The white patch on the secondaries is the most conspicuous mark, but this may be hidden on a swimming bird. It becomes apparent in flight, which the Velvet Scoter does with a heavy and more laboured take-off than the Common Scoter. The white patch is more often seen when the birds half open the wings in diving, or when one rears up to flap its wings.

Velvet Scoter

The choice of winter marine habitat is similar to that of the Common Scoter, but the Velvet Scoter will more often feed in turbulent waters among rocks and between islands, or enter estuaries for mussel beds. It is a quieter bird, lacking the piping choruses of the previous species and using a variety of briefer notes, from a high whistle to deep croaks and growls. The display call is a high-pitched double note, and the displays – although generally similar to those of the Common Scoter – lack the short display flights, and include instead ritual diving and underwater pursuits.

It tolerates a wider range of breeding habitats than does the Common Scoter; Over much of its range it breeds further south in the boreal forest zone, and around the northern and central Baltic coasts, so it is surprising that it has not done so in the British Isles, apart from the suspected occurrences mentioned below. It breeds through the boreal zone in Eurasia and western North America, wintering on sea coasts, but not extending quite so far south as does the Common Scoter.

It does not seem to have been recorded in Britain during the Pleistocene, and its earliest records are from Somerset in the Iron Age and Scotland in the Dark Ages. There are no authenticated records of it breeding in the British Isles, although it has been suspected of doing so in the present century, the last suspected occasion being in Shetland in 1945. In northern Europe, the Baltic population increased in the warmer 1920s to 1950s, but in general it has suffered from shooting and disturbance and there has been an overall decrease in the last few decades.

As a coastal bird it occurs early with moulting flocks being present off the eastern Scottish coast in August and September. The winter build-up seems to be slower than that of the Common Scoter, reaching a peak in late winter. The larger flocks occur mainly around Shetland and Orkney and down the east coast of Scotland and England. It is more likely to visit inland waters than the Common Scoter. Both species are highly vulnerable to oil spillages at sea in winter. The numbers fluctuate considerably. The Moray Firth region holds the largest winter flocks and in early 1983, at over 8,000, had more than the estimated normal number for the British Isles. This is estimated at 2,500–5,000, rising at times to 10,000 birds.

Long-tailed Duck *Clangula hyemalis*

After the stout solidarity of Eiders and scoters, this small and fragile-looking duck seems out of place swimming and diving in surging winter seas off some rocky shore. The long slender tail of the male is less conspicuous than might be expected, tending to lie along the surface, but it usually shows a spread tail and part-opened wings as it dives. The small size, neat head with high forehead and stubby bill help identify it.

For us it is a black-and-white or mainly white bird, but in summer plumage, the male has the foreparts dark brown, with a large white face-patch, reversing the pattern. The back, including the slender scapular feathers, is dark brown with lighter brown feather margins, while belly and flanks stay white. The female becomes dark brown on throat, and front and back of the neck, with a large dark brown cheek-patch and browner suffusion on breast and flanks. These changes are produced by more complex moults than in other species, with confusing intermediate plumages.

It flies fast and low, tilting from side to side, with downward wing-beats. The dark wings lack any conspicuous markings. It tends to fly in long wavering lines or shapeless flocks, plopping easily into the water as it lands. It is one of the more strikingly vocal ducks. Both sexes have a loud, yodelling *ah-ooo-gah* call, far-carrying and resonant. This is used at all seasons as well as in display. In displays the male shakes, tilts and turns the head to show off the pattern, and cocks the tail high. The head may be thrown back to touch the back with the crown; occasionally it is swung forwards, while the rear end is raised with tail erect and the feet give a backward-splashing kick. The latter display is accompanied by a special double-yodel.

It prefers shallow seas, feeding at depths of up to about 10 metres, although it is capable of much deeper dives. It takes a wide range of animal and plant foods, with molluscs such as mussels, cockles and winkles forming an important part. It feeds mainly by day, scattering in small parties, but tends to gather in large roosting flocks at night. These are out at sea and most of the activity takes place offshore, sometimes at distances of 3–8 kilometres out, unsuspected and unseen on land.

In breeding it moves to tundra, both on coasts and inland, and upland with similar conditions.

It has a circumpolar breeding distribution on arctic tundra; and also occurs in Iceland, on the mountain chain of Sweden and Norway, and parts of the Baltic coast of Finland. In winter it moves south to ice-free shores; but in Europe goes no further than the coast of Norway, the southern Baltic, the northern Netherlands and the British Isles.

The Long-tailed Duck has the distinction of being the earliest recent species identified in the British Pleistocene, occurring in the Lower Pleistocene Norwich Crag formation. It is not much in evidence otherwise, but does occur in the last glaciation in Derbyshire, and on the south Wales coast early in the Holocene.

Although breeding has never been proven in the British Isles, it is claimed that it bred in Shetland and Orkney in the last century and early in this century; more specifically in 1848 and 1887 at the former site and 1911 at the latter. Individuals and pairs sometimes summer in Scotland and breeding was suspected in the Outer Hebrides in the late 1960s.

In winter its main strongholds around the British Isles are in Shetland, Orkney, parts of the east coast of Scotland, the Outer Hebrides and north-west Ireland. As a species it has suffered from heavy shooting, is vulnerable to being caught in commercial fishing nets, and with its mobility and offshore flocking tendencies is dangerously liable to deaths from oil spillages; it has suffered badly from these in the Baltic. In general, there has been an overall decrease in the northern European population in recent decades.

Winter birds are thought to come from both Scandinavia and Russia, and some may originate in Iceland. Off the Scottish mainland, the Moray Firth is the most important feeding and roosting region and in the early 1980s three roosts there held about 18,000 birds at times. At other places the numbers appear to be much smaller around the coasts, although no-one can be sure what is happening out at sea. Occasionally individuals are seen on inland waters. The population wintering around Britain is estimated at about 20,000 birds.

Sawbills

Mergus species

These are fishing ducks, designed to catch fish underwater and built on somewhat similar lines to the cormorants. The body is long and streamlined, with strong legs and feet set well back on it for propulsion. In front it tapers to a long, thin neck, narrow head and long, slender and very narrow bill. The ridges on the horny sheath of the bill along the inside edges of the jaws are a series of small sharp projections that help the bird to grip a slippery fish more strongly, and give the group its common name.

They have spiky crests that can be raised in display but sleeked away when not required. Males have a summer eclipse plumage in which they are almost indistinguishable from females. In all three, the coverts and secondaries on the inner half of wings of males are mainly white, showing conspicuously in flight. In females, the white is confined to secondary feathers except in the Smew, which has whitish coverts. They are hole-nesting species and the females, particularly those of the larger species, are distinctly smaller than the males. Although their legs are placed well back on the body, they walk well on land and can perch.

There are three British species, all three mainly breeding in the boreal to subarctic zones, but with three size categories. The Smew, the smallest species, occurs only as a winter visitor to fresh waters and estuaries. The middle-sized Red-breasted Merganser may nest on coasts as well as inland, and is mainly coastal in winter; while the largest, the Goosander, is mainly a bird of fresh waters.

Smew *Mergus albellus*

This is the smallest and most scarce of the fish-eaters. On the water the male looks white, the fine black pattern only visible on closer view; while the female and immature birds look grebe-like, a resemblance heightened by the white throat which makes the dark hind-neck look narrow and the head larger. The dark eye-patch gives the face a pinched look and the bill, although narrow and tapering, with hooked tip, is shorter and stouter than that of other sawbills. It is an adept diver, usually in depths of up to 4 metres, feeding mainly on small fish but taking insects and other small creatures in summer. It will often feed in parties and flocks, the birds diving almost simultaneously. It is an agile and fast flier, with groups tending to fly in slanting lines of chevrons.

It is usually silent, but the male has a low harsh note and when displaying uses a soft rapid rattling call; the female has a louder harsher version. The male displays with the forehead crest raised, at times thrusting the body forward as it swims, with the head pressed back until the neck rests on the mantle. It may rear up and then suddenly lower the head forwards, displaying the dark nape pattern. It performs the usual types of head-raising and turning displays, and will also lie along the water facing the female with head and neck extended and tail raised.

Like the Goldeneye, it breeds in tree holes in northern boreal forest in sites close to still or slow-moving fresh water. It prefers the holes made by Black Woodpeckers, but like the former species, it will use nest-boxes where these are available. It likes flooded woodland with dead trees. It has a broad boreal range across Eurasia, but with a peculiarly limited distribution west of Russia, with limited extension into north-eastern Scandinavia. In winter it moves to temperate regions, and in Europe is mainly a bird of inland waters such as lakes, reservoirs and gravel-pits and sometimes much smaller pools, more rarely resorting to shallow salt estuaries and inlets.

It occurred in the British Pleistocene from the Cromerian Interglacial onwards, and through the Holocene at least to the Iron Ages. Its remains occur at more sites than those of the larger sawbills. Its range spread during the last century, when the population in northern Sweden was established; and in the late 1920s there was some spread on the Finnish-Norwegian border. There were also a few breeding on the Lower Danube in Roumania at the turn of the century. In recent times in Russia, the range has contracted northwards due to loss of habitat.

Birds wintering in countries around the southern North Sea appear to come from Scandinavia and western USSR. The bulk of the wintering population is in the Netherlands, which gives them 85% of the world population. The British wintering population is a marginal part of this, occurring mostly in East Anglia and south-east England, with a sparse scatter of small occurrences elsewhere. In the 1950s, up to half those present occurred on the reservoirs around London, although this only involved about one hundred birds. In the next two decades this fell to about a tenth, and the British winter population from several hundreds to a hundred or less, these having shifted to other south-eastern sites. However, numbers fluctuate erratically, and a sudden cold spell in January 1985 raised the London total at one point to between 140 and 200, indicating the marginal nature of our wintering population in relation to the North Sea area as a whole.

Red-breasted Merganser *Mergus serrator*

This shaggy-headed sawbill with its long snaky neck is most typically a bird of sheltered coastal waters. The body lies long and low in the water, and when the crest is sleeked back, the narrow head and slender bill look like little more than a tapering extension of the long neck. It is a sociable species, usually occurring in parties and small flocks.

When hunting, it swims with the foreparts of the head and the eyes underwater to spot its prey, as do other fish-eating birds such as grebes, divers and cormorants. A group will often dive simultaneously. Underwater, it swims with head and neck extended, and unlike other sawbills may use the wings to help the feet which provide the main propulsion. Small fish may be swallowed immediately but larger ones are brought to the surface first. It will also take crustaceans and other small creatures. It prefers shallow and reasonably clear water with depths of up to 4 metres.

It is a quiet bird except when displaying. Then the male uses a very variable wheezy purring or rattling call while the female has harsh croaking and grating notes. The male displays often involve somewhat gawky and

MALE

FEMALE

Smew

Red-breasted Merganser

FEMALE

MALE

Goosander

FEMALE

MALE

D.M.HENRY

angular postures. The head may be raised high, then turned or shaken, or pressed back on the shoulders with uptilted bill. Head and neck may be extended obliquely with the crest depressed, then lowered until the neck rests on the water while the rear end is tilted sharply upwards with the tail depressed. The male calls with open bill, the scarlet lining vivid against the dark head.

The female nests alone in a tunnel or cavity, in the ground, among tree roots, in a bank or under thick vegetation, preferring areas by water and overgrown with trees or scrub. Although mainly coastal it may go far inland up rivers and streams and to small lochs. The flight is agile, fast and usually low. At other times, the Merganser prefers broken shorelines with shallow sandy inlets, straits and estuaries, especially with deeper channels and with islands. When not active it may rest on sandspits or grassy banks. Adults move to brackish and salt waters in late summer for moulting as well as using them for overwintering.

Its general distribution is circumpolar, through the subarctic and boreal zones, and this is continued into the north-western parts of the British Isles. It occurred in Britain in the Pleistocene at intervals from the Cromerian Interglacial to the Devensian, and as human prey from the Mesolithic to the Bronze and Iron Ages, and presumably later. It was noted in the nineteenth century in central and western Scottish highlands and islands south to the Solway Firth, and in north-west Ireland, but was probably present in this breeding range in most of the earlier centuries. In spite of human persecution for this bird's success in fishing, it was not only present in reasonable numbers, but was able to spread to some extent during the period of maximum destruction.

At the end of the nineteenth and beginning of the present century, it began to spread eastwards to highland Scotland, and east and south in Ireland. Although it had spread across to Aberdeenshire and Kincardineshire by 1913, it had not reached the southern borders, in Dumfriesshire, until 1928, and did not cross into England until 1950. In the 1950s it colonised the Lake District and north-west Wales; and by the 1970s outlying breedings occurred in Derbyshire and Glamorgan. In Ireland, it occurs through suitable places north and west of a line from Cape Clear to Dundalk, with an isolated population in the extreme south-east, in Wexford. Breeding pairs in the British Isles are estimated at about 2,000 to 3,000.

Winter distribution is concentrated around the coasts. British breeding birds are thought to move to nearby coasts, joined on the south and east coasts by migrants from Scandinavia, and in the north and west by birds from Iceland. The main concentrations are around the larger bays, inlets and estuaries, with few in the extreme south-west of England and the Bristol Channel. Numbers fluctuate with winter severity, with occasional influxes in bad weather from across the North Sea. Average numbers in winter are estimated at about 11,000.

Goosander *Mergus merganser*

This, the largest of our ducks, has the long low body of the typical underwater hunter. The neck and bill are long and slender, but the solid-looking crest of the male makes the head look bulkier and the long bill even thinner. The female has a shaggy double crest that makes it difficult to distinguish from the female Red-breasted Merganser if its larger size cannot be established.

The Goosander is a bird of cold, clear northern rivers and lakes, strong and active, apparently at home in rushing waters of rivers and streams where it may not only dive, but also dash erratically through the shallows with head submerged, in pursuit of fish. It rises into flight with less ease, but once airborne, it moves in strong level flight with a low whistling wing-beat, often flying low and following the courses of rivers and streams.

Like other sawbills, it is a quiet species except during display, but even then the principle calls of the male are subdued twanging or bell-like notes. The female's call is a harsh *karr*, like the male's alarm call. Postures include a lateral display of the fluffed head feathers, and an upwards stretch of neck and head with bill raised. In addition both display and hostility may include rapid rushes across the surface of the water.

The female nests in a cavity, preferably a tree hole, but holes in banks and among rocks, or artificial cavities such as nest-boxes are also used. The site is usually close to a freshwater lake or river. It feeds in such waters, at depths of up to 4 metres, taking mainly fish, in a similar manner to that of the Red-breasted Merganser. It prefers clear water where fish are visible. Larger fish are brought to the surface and since these may be trout or salmon parr, they induce envy and antagonism in unsuccessful fishermen. In winter it tends to flock on larger lakes and reservoirs, and sometimes sheltered sea inlets. Birds roosting on larger inland waters may disperse along local rivers to feed.

Its general distribution is circumpolar through the boreal zone and into the cool-temperate regions where it may breed in montane area. It winters in the temperate regions, at times not far from the breeding area. It occurred in Britain in the last two major glaciations and in Iron Age Somerset. In theory, like the Red-breasted Merganser, it might have continued as a breeder in parts of Scotland. Possibly its relative conspicuousness and fishing ability were against it. At any rate, it seems to be assumed that it had been exterminated by the mid nineteenth century, and a breeding in Perthshire in 1871 is the first recorded in the British Isles.

After a winter influx in 1875–76, more widespread breeding was recorded, and by the 1920s it had become a breeding bird through most of the highland region in the face of active opposition from fishery interests. It spread to the Tweed Valley of the Border in 1930 although shot out again for a time, and to Dumfriesshire in 1936, colonising south-west Scotland and the border country. It crossed to Northumberland in 1941, Cumberland in 1950, to County Durham in 1965 and into northern Yorkshire and Lancashire by the early 1970s, at which time it also bred for the first time in mid Wales and northern Ireland. It may now almost have reached the limits of suitable habitat. The breeding population has been estimated at 1,000 – 2,000 pairs.

In winter it spreads in inland fresh waters to other parts of Britain, and is joined by birds from continental Europe. Local shifts and fluctuations occur as birds move when waters freeze. The winter population of the British Isles is estimated at about 8,000 birds, two-thirds of them within the breeding range.

Stiff-tailed Ducks

Oxyura species

The Stiff-tailed Ducks are diving ducks, rather small and stoutly-built with short thick necks, largish heads and dabbling-duck-type bills that are as long as the head. Stout legs are placed well back on the body, and a longish tail, narrow and stiff, lies along the water but can be erected vertically at moments of excitement. They have grebe-like habits, living on the more vegetated still waters, diving and dabbling for food, and tending to build nests in emergent vegetation in shallow water. There is an endemic European species, the White-headed Duck *Oxyura leucocephala*, which has a relict breeding distribution in a few isolated areas of south-east Europe and around the Mediterranean but does not reach Britain. Instead, Britain has been colonised by an introduced American species, the Ruddy Duck *O. jamaicensis*.

Ruddy Duck *Oxyura jamaicensis*
NOT ILLUSTRATED

Small and stout, like a Shetland pony of the duck world. The male in breeding plumage is bright chestnut, with white undertail-covert beneath a dark spiky tail. The head has a black cap down as far as the eyes, with two small short tufts over the eyes that can be raised in excitement; the sides of the face form large white patches; and the bill is light blue. In eclipse plumage the white markings are retained, the cap is duller, and the rest of the plumage is drab brown with faint barring. The female is like the male in eclipse but with a warm brown on cap and back, while the face is greyish-white with a narrow dark line arching across it. The downy duckling has a similar pattern and a pair of pale spots on the back.

It often swims with the tail cocked, and may appear to sink underwater rather than dive. It seems reluctant to walk on land although it can do so, and unless leaving a site is also reluctant to fly, moving with rapidly whirring wing-beats when it does so. It feeds chiefly by diving in depths of up to 1 metre to take food from the bottom, which mostly consists of insects and plant material. It tends to move and to flock on larger inland waters or some sheltered coastal site in winter.

It is generally silent, but in display both sexes may use notes that can be squeaky and high-pitched, or low croaking and grating sounds. There is an odd breast-beating display. The male cocks up the tail with white undertail-coverts fluffed, raises the head and inflates the breast. It then lowers the head and drums on the breast with its bill, forcing air bubbles out of the breast feathers. This produces a rattle that becomes a hollow drumming or belching sound. The female may perform similar movements but only makes a rattling noise. In another display, the male forces the head back towards the raised tail, then lowers the tail while shooting the head and neck forward and rushes forwards for several metres, beating the wings in the water to produce a loud ringing sound. The nest is built by the female as a platform in the water among thick fringing vegetation. Resting platforms may also be constructed.

Young of captive birds flew from the Wildfowl Trust at Slimbridge on the Lower Severn in the late 1950s, and breeding occurred in Somerset and later in Staffordshire in 1960 and 1961. It spread to reservoirs, ponds and gravel-pits in Somerset, the Severn Valley, and west Midlands as far as Cheshire. There were 10 pairs in 1968, 25 in 1972, 50 by 1975 and there has been a continued increase. Since 1980 it has nested on waters in the London region, and well into the Midlands. It bred at Lough Neagh in Ireland in 1974. In Scotland, it bred in Angus in 1979 and annually since, has occurred in various localities in the south and east and bred in 1984 at the Loch of Strathbeg in north-east Aberdeenshire.

Wintering birds disperse through the whole of southern and central England, into Anglesey, and along the Essex-Suffolk coast. Some cross the Channel to the continent. Its population after breeding is approaching 2,000 and looks set to continue rising.

Diurnal Birds of Prey

FALCONIFORMES

The birds of this order are mostly active raptors, pursuing and killing live prey, although a few have become scavengers on dead carcasses. They have in common large eyes and very acute eyesight, sharp hooked bills capable of tearing, and large strong feet equipped with claws for gripping prey. The three families in Britain are – Ospreys, Pandionidae; Hawks and Eagles, Accipitridae; and Falcons, Falconidae.

Osprey
Pandionidae

This family contains only a single species, specialised for fish-hunting. The feet have an outer toe that can be turned back to help grasp a fish more effectively, and the swollen spiny pads on the undersides of the bases of claws also help to hold a slippery prey. The bill has a slender and strongly downcurved tip.

Osprey *Pandion haliaetus*

This bird, lost as a breeder for over forty years and regained with a great deal of publicity, has become a symbol of conservation in Britain. At close quarters it does not look like an ideal choice, being scrawny-looking, with staring eyes and a hangdog expression. It appears more impressive at a distance when, after circling over a lake, it plunges down with feet extended, half-disappears below the surface, and then flaps up shaking the water from its feathers and clutching a large fish in its feet. It has long narrow wings and a relatively short tail, sometimes resembling a large gull when seen from a distance.

North-west European Ospreys migrate to West Africa and re-occupy territory on return. It is a bird that needs long stretches of water (fresh or salt), and clear enough for a fish to be seen by a bird soaring overhead. It uses lakes, rivers, estuaries and sheltered coasts. The nest, built by both birds, is used and added to year after year and may become a great drum-shaped mass in a tree top or on a rock outcrop or promontory, but always with a wide view around. The calls are shrill whistles and yelps, and the male has a swooping display flight, rising steeply between swoops and hovering with a fish held in its feet.

It has a wide general range, breeding in boreal and temperate zones of the northern hemisphere and on subtropical coasts, migrating to subtropical and tropical zones. It also occurs in Indonesia and Australasia. Killed off by man, it is now absent from most of Europe and the British Isles.

There is little early fossil evidence of it in Britain, apart from a tentative identification from what may have been the end of the last glaciation in Derbyshire. Postglacially it was certainly widespread in Britain, although possibly not in Ireland. It was destroyed as vermin. There are some last-known breeding dates, 1570 on the Solent, 1678 in Lakeland, 1757 in south Devon, 1838 on Lundy and 1847 in Somerset. Information seems to be lacking from both Wales and Ireland.

It has been common in Scotland until the nineteenth century, but with good guns and preservation of fish stocks it was shot out, many estates offering bounties for it. Egg-collectors and skin-collectors helped the final demise. It disappeared from southern and mid Scotland in the early nineteenth century, and most other areas in the middle of the century, last nesting in northern Perthshire in 1886, Cromerty 1901, south Inverness 1908, and may have bred at Loch-an-Eilean in the Spey Valley until 1916. A similar decline occurred for similar reasons throughout Europe in the nineteenth and early twentieth centuries, the species holding out best in the south-east until the 1960s.

Birds continued to migrate through Britain, but were usually shot if they remained in one area for long. The Scandinavian population – which has also declined – increased with protection, particularly in the 1940s, and more individuals began to appear in Britain. Single pairs are said to have bred in Scotland in the Cairngorm region in 1953 and 1954. From 1955, a more publicised pair nested at Loch Garten in Spey Valley, unsuccessfully until 1959. Other pairs began nesting: 2 were known in 1960, 25 by the late 1970s, and 40 by the mid 1980s, all of them in Scotland. The species is now re-established in spite of continued egg-stealing and shooting of migrating birds abroad.

Eagles and Hawks
Accipitridae

This encompasses a variety of raptors, the species included here having hooked bills and strong, grasping feet. They build nests, and males feed females and young. Variable in size, shape and habitat preference, they can be subdivided into several groups. Broad-winged soaring birds include the stronger hunters such as eagles and the weaker, more scavenging, species such as buzzards and kites. The harriers are gliders: long-winged and long-tailed birds that tend to hunt by gliding low over the ground and surprising fairly weak prey. The short-winged hawks, Sparrowhawk and Goshawk, are birds with short broad wings and long tails, that manoeuvre rapidly among trees to surprise and hunt down prey.

Common Buzzard

Golden Eagle

Common Buzzard

Rough-legged Buzzard

Osprey

D.M.H.

White-tailed Eagle *Haliaeetus albicilla*
NOT IN THE COLOUR PLATE

This great greyish-brown bird, rectangular in outline when gliding, head and tail dwarfed by the wings, a tapering tail that is white in the adult, and a massive yellowish bill, is our lowland waterside eagle. It prefers to be near water, salt or fresh, coastal or inland. Fish, snatched alive from the water's surface, or found dead, constitute about two-thirds of the normal prey but it takes a large range of creatures, from goose-size downwards; it will feed mainly on carrion available.

It has a powerful slow flapping flight and soars well. On the ground it appears heavy and short-bodied, with a large head. It has yelping and cackling calls and some more feeble high-pitched notes. Paired birds show circling, mock-attack and swooping displays, and occasionally they may lock feet and fall in a cartwheeling plunge, separating just before reaching the ground. The nest is a conspicuous, sometimes huge, mass of twigs, in a tree top or more often on a rock ledge, the site often low, and sometimes vulnerable to interference.

Its general distribution is across Eurasia in subarctic to temperate zones, and resident in southern Russia and Europe. It has disappeared from most of its European range in historic times. Its first British record is in Devon towards the end of the penultimate, Wolstonian, glaciation; and it occurs at various sites in the Devensian Glaciation and Holocene. Its bones sometimes occur in caves with a range of possible prey species, suggesting that it might have used some caves or their entrances as nesting or roost sites in the past, although there is little recent evidence.

It was present in Bronze Age and Iron Age settlement remains, and in Bronze Age Orkney may have had some ritual function in burials. It is this species, together with the opportunist Raven, that became part of Norse and Saxon legend through its recognition of the carrion-producing possibilities of human conflict and its attendence at local battles. In these earlier periods, it must have been common in the British Isles around coasts and on islands, along the larger rivers and on lakes and swamps with open water.

As farming developed, it became regarded as a harmful bird with a price on its head. It gradually disappeared from most of Britain, holding out longest in more remote parts. By the eighteenth century, England had only a few relict sites. It appears to have bred near Plymouth and on Lundy in the eighteenth century, and on a cliff of the Isle of Wight in 1780. The Lake District was a last stronghold although eggs, young and adults were destroyed annually during much of the eighteenth century. The last nesting was recorded in 1794, although birds were seen in 1835. There is no evidence of English breedings after the eighteenth century. Wales must have held many pairs, but these probably disappeared by the early nineteenth century, and seem to have left no record other than place-names. Ireland must have held at least 50 breeding sites, which was reduced to about 29 by the nineteenth century, and gradually shot out; a last breeding was on the north Mayo coast in 1898.

Among outlying islands, the last record for the Isle of Man is 1818 and for St Kilda and Fair Isle about 1830; Shetland had at least 12 sites at one time: three used right until the early part of the present century with the last nesting in 1910, while on Orkney it was in 1911.

White-tailed Eagle

There are at least 100 known Scottish sites, of which about two-thirds were still in use by the early nineteenth century. With game-preserving, sheep-keeping and a general movement of crofters to the coasts, the slaughter accelerated in the latter half of the nineteenth century. The White-tailed Eagle ceased breeding in southern Scotland in 1866, and was gradually reduced and exterminated northwards and westwards. The last mainland breeding was probably that in Sutherlandshire in 1901; and the last island attempt was on Skye in 1916, the solitary female remaining at that site, a white-plumaged bird, being shot in 1918.

Subsequently, occasional young Scandinavian birds wandered to the east coast of England in winter, and more rarely elsewhere. An attempted introduction with four young birds on Fair Isle in 1968 failed. From 1975 onwards, a few young birds from Norway were kept and released each year on the island of Rhum in western Scotland; 82 were imported over 10 years. They spread on the west coast and and islands. They take six years to mature. A pair reared the first young one in 1985, two more in 1986, and in that year three other pairs laid eggs, and two or three more pairs held territory. At present the chances of permanent re-introduction look hopeful.

Golden Eagle *Aquila chrysaetos*
This is the resident eagle of mountains and open uplands. In flight it shows big, square-ended wings and a large broad tail, the head appearing relatively small and wedge-shaped. Immature birds have the basal half of the tail and bases of flight feathers white. For a large bird it can be surprisingly inconspicuous, inhabiting a large territory and with long periods of inactivity. Its main prey consists of hares, rabbits and grouse down to quite small creatures. It takes carrion where this is available, dependent on it as its main source of food at times.

It has some yapping calls, but the voice is often weak and shrill for a bird of this size. It has high-soaring and swooping display flights. A territory contains several alternative nest-sites, usually on sheltered ledges, sometimes in trees. Its general distribution is wide, through suitable regions of the northern hemisphere, where for the most part it is a resident.

It probably always had a limited range in the British Isles, restricted to mountain areas. Although sometimes confused with the White-tailed Eagle, the only early remains in the south are from a Cheddar cave at the end of the Ice Ages or early in the Holocene, with no suggestion that it was breeding there. There is evidence from Derbyshire at about the same period and from the Pennines in the early Holocene. The original population is difficult to envisage, but Leslie Brown estimated the carrying capacity never to have exceeded about 500 pairs in Scotland, 50 in England and Wales and 150 in Ireland.

Like the White-tailed Eagle it was killed from early times, but because of its habitat and more elusive habits probably did not suffer badly until upland sheep-keeping became extensive. There appears to be remarkably little information on its decrease. It seems to have disappeared from Wales very early on, with no firm dates. In England it would have been present in the Peak and Pennine areas, Lakeland and Cumbria, and across to the border hills. It last bred in Derbyshire in about the mid eighteenth century in Lakeland in the late eighteenth century, and Cheviot until the mid nineteenth century. In Ireland, it seems to have been widespread and mainly killed in the nineteenth century, with the last breeding in Donegal in 1910, and possibly in County Mayo in 1912.

Its main stronghold was in Scotland. Here it suffered from shepherds, and grouse-preservers, but was tolerated on deer forests. It was exterminated in the southern uplands, and further north it suffered in the eastern highlands in particular and was reduced in numbers or wiped out in many places. However, it began to recover in numbers with the reduction in gamekeeping after the 1914–18 war and increased in irregular fashion through the highlands, also breeding on some occasions in the south-west. Conditions improved again after the 1939–45 war. It increased in the Hebrides in the 1940s, possibly benefitting from the absence of the White-tailed Eagle, and from 1948 re-colonised the uplands of the south-west. Between 1956 and 1960, a pair bred on the north Antrim coast of Ireland. A pair established themselves in Lakeland in 1969 and have bred successfully in most years since.

A lack of data makes it too difficult to establish what is happening to the Scottish population generally. On past estimates there would seem to have been a large increase, but they should have had setbacks with the loss of rabbits after myxomatosis in 1954, and extensive breeding failure due to toxic chemicals in sheep carrion in the early 1960s. The first overall census in 1982 revealed 511 territories with pairs or single birds, and a winter estimate of 1,000 to 1,200 birds.

Common Buzzard *Buteo buteo*

This squat, slow-soaring raptor with its plaintive, far-carrying call is the only large resident bird of prey over most of Britain. In flight, broad rounded wings and tail, and bluntly rounded head contribute to a solid shape. The detail of the predominantly barred plumage pattern varies enormously. It evolved as a forest species, and although venturing into the borders of moorland, mountain and open grassland habitats, it is never wholly away from trees, and is most numerous in landscapes where trees and open space are mixed together.

Although best known for its habit of soaring for long periods, it usually hunts with a low glide, surprising its prey, which may range from rabbits down to earth-worms. It may hunt the latter by trotting over the turf in a rather ponderous fashion. It also takes carrion, and in recent times has taken to waiting on the telegraph poles of busy rural roads for traffic casualties. The loud long *ca-aow* call is used by resident territorial birds and breeding displays involve high slow soaring, slow wing-flaps and a series of deep swoops with steep rises

between them. The large twig nest is usually in a tree, exceptionally on a rock ledge.

It is virtually impossible to separate bones of this species from those of the Rough-legged Buzzard, except that small individuals are more likely to be of this species. Buzzards occur as far back as the Pastonian Interglacial of the Early Pleistocene, and not infrequently from then onwards. It was certainly fairly common and widespread in post-glacial times, and probably benefitted from the early and incomplete forest clearances. However, by the mid fifteenth century it was listed as vermin, taking domestic poultry and the then-protected rabbit. From then onwards it had a price on its head, was certainly killed extensively in parts of southern England in the seventeenth century, and by the eighteenth century was uncommon in the south and east.

The nineteenth century brought the gamekeeper with guns, traps and poison. By the mid nineteenth century, it had disappeared in south-eastern and central England, and was a western bird with residual populations in Sussex to Somerset, inland Suffolk and Lincolnshire, north-east England and east and central Scotland. It became restricted to the extreme north of Ireland, and disappeared in the 1880s apart from a single pair in Antrim from 1905 to 1915. By the 1914–18 war, with gamekeeping at its height, it was further driven back to the New Forest, Devon and Cornwall, Wales, Lakeland; and in Scotland to part of the south-west uplands, west central Highlands and some of the islands.

The breakdown in gamekeeping after that war, the farming recession and the spread of the rabbit all helped towards its recovery. By 1954, it had spread back over much of its ground in the previous century; roughly west of a line from east Sussex up the centre of Britain to the eastern highland, but absent from the west Scottish lowland and Lancashire and Cheshire. It re-colonised the extreme north of Ireland in the early 1950s. The population of about 12,000 pairs was thought to be the highest for several centuries.

When everything looked fine, myxomatosis struck the rabbit population and killed 99% of it between 1953 and 1956. The residual population is still slowly trying to recover. The Buzzard population fell; breeding success was poor in those remaining, and distribution began to retreat on the eastern fringes. In the 1960s and 1970s, the upland populations of north and west which had escaped the worst problems of rabbit loss were hit by toxic chemicals in live prey and dead sheep. By the time pesticides had been brought under control, overall numbers of Buzzards had dropped to about 8,000–10,000 pairs.

Distribution is now mainly west of a line from mid-Sussex to the Wirral Peninsula, in Lakeland and Cumbria, in south-west Scotland with a scatter to the south-east, and through the Western islands and most of the highlands except the extreme east. It nests on Orkney. In winter there is a slight eastward wandering of young birds, but persistant gamekeeping prevents new settlement.

Rough-legged Buzzard *Buteo lagopus*

This is a subarctic to arctic replacement of the Common Buzzard, very similar, although slightly larger. Less variable than the latter, it has more obvious contrast in

79

colour, the head usually pale, the upper tail surface white with a broad dark subterminal band. Underneath the sides of the breast and a patch at the angle of the wing are blackish. Accustomed to hunting over open, treeless tundra, it tends to fly lower and hover more frequently than does the Common Buzzard. It has a circumpolar distribution, breeding in arctic tundra and montane zones, including northern Sweden and much of upland Norway, and migrating to temperate zones in winter. It nests on rocky outcrops or low hummocks, and feeds mainly on lemmings and voles. These have cycles of abundance and scarcity. In years when they are plentiful, the Buzzards also increase; in the subsequent years of scarcity they may appear in larger numbers and for longer periods, and range further, when they move southwards.

Winter visitors to Britain cross the North Sea, usually occurring as scattered individuals on the east side from Shetland to Kent, only exceptionally inland or in the west, and most frequent from East Anglia southwards. It may have been more numerous and may have bred in the colder past, but since the bones cannot be separated with certainly from those of the Common Buzzard, we have no definite Pleistocene records of it. It is unlikely to have occurred more frequently in the post-glacial period. In its present occurrences, the number involved is very small, about 20 annually.

PLATE FOURTEEN

Honey Buzzard *Pernis apivorus*
NOT ILLUSTRATED

This is a weak buzzard, as large as the others, but with wings and tail longer, more slender and more obviously barred, and longer neck and smaller head. The claws are blunter, for easier walking and digging. It is a summer visitor and its main food when breeding is the grubs of wasps and bees, which the birds digs out from their nests. It also takes other large insects, frogs, lizards and sometimes birds. It has a plaintive whistling call, rarely used.

It is a bird of mature deciduous woodland with large glades, or mixed woodland and grassland, where it can find a supply of wasps' nests. It is a rather furtive bird, flying between or just over trees, in inconspicuous fashion. The nest is in a tall tree, for the bird is a secretive nester, intolerant of disturbance. It hunts over a wide area.

It breeds through the boreal and temperate zones of western Europe, but is absent from most areas immediately bordering the Atlantic, and the oceanic climate may be unsuitable for the abundant summer insect life that it needs. It winters in central and southern Africa. These rather specialised habitat requirements, probably including fine hot summer weather, may help account for its rarity in Britain where it is on the edge of its range, and numbers might be determined by weather during spring migration. The few passage visitors may have been deflected from their more usual route.

There are no early records, but it might have been present in continental-type summers that seem to have occurred just before and after glaciations. James Fisher quoted the first British record as 1675. Its population until very recent times is a matter of guesswork, little helped by its secretive nature. At the best of times, it was probably only the south that provided suitable conditions. A handful of pairs seem to have been present in the Hampshire Basin and New Forest areas for most of the time, with random casual breeding of single pairs elsewhere.

These could be in temporarily suitable sites west to Wales and north to parts of Scotland. It bred at Selbourne in 1780. It was recorded breeding in Hereford in 1895, and County Durham in 1897 and possibly to 1899; and it is said to have bred as far north as Aberdeen and east Rosshire in that century. It nested near the Welsh border from 1928–32, and elsewhere in southern England in 1923 and 1932. The only other Scottish record is for north-east Fife in 1949. Over the last fifteen years the estimated maximum population has been under ten pairs, with only up to two proven breeding in any year.

Red Kite *Milvus milvus*

A superb agile glider and manoeuvrer, the kite is an aerial raptor, whereas others spend much of their time simply sitting. With a skilled ability to use small air currents as well as thermals, it hunts by circling and scanning open ground, or low-level gliding over similar areas. Although capable of taking a large range of live prey, it is notorious for its use of carrion; dead sheep forming about half the food of British kites. The call is a shrill double whistle. There is a permanent pair-bond and little specialised breeding display. It is a solitary hunter, but wintering birds form roosting-flocks. The nest is usually built in a tree, old nests of other species being sometimes used.

It prefers extensive open areas, with low or sparse vegetation and some trees present. It is a European species, extending north to southern Sweden, but more numerous in warmer areas. In southern and western Europe, including Britain, it is resident; but it is migratory in the north and east.

There is little early evidence of the bird's history. The only British Pleistocene record is from the coast of south Wales in the last, Ipswichian, interglacial. It is likely to have been widespread in the early Holocene, and in historic times seems to have been present through most of Britain – but apparently not in Ireland – as a scavenger of rural and urban carrion and rubbish. The lack of rubbish disposal around medieval towns may have increased its numbers. By the fifteenth century, visitors from abroad were commenting on the tameness and size of the flocks of Red Kites in London, where they snatched food from childrens' hands, and behaved like the Black Kites of the Middle and Far East. It continued to nest in London, in much smaller numbers, well into the eighteenth century.

Until the eighteenth century, it had been protected as a useful scavenger although disliked as a killer of young

Red Kite

Montagu's Harrier

MALE   FEMALE

MALE

Marsh Harrier

FEMALE   Hen Harrier

MALE

D.M.H.

poultry, but at the end of that century and in the nineteenth century, when game preservation began, it was in trouble. Its numbers would have suffered in any case from a significant decrease in carrion, and the burial of dead farm animals. In addition it was shot, and was easy to poison in large numbers. It had also learned to nest near man and was more vulnerable in this respect. At the beginning of this period it was widely present north to lowland Scotland, and its almost total loss must have seemed as improbable as would that of the Crow at the present day. However, by 1870 it had been exterminated in England.

It was greatly reduced in Scotland by 1850 and had ceased to breed by 1890; there may, though, have been a slight resurgence during the 1914–18 war, when it was said to have bred in Glen Garry in 1917 and was also seen in Perthshire, and was seen in Argyllshire in the summer of 1919. It was wiped out in south Wales in the mid nineteenth century, and persecuted elsewhere, and by the end of the century the total British population appeared to be about 5 pairs in central Wales.

These were given privately-organised protection and increased to 10–12 pairs between 1910 and 1920, with a nesting record in Devon in 1913 and Cornwall in 1920. From 1920 to the 1940s there were less than 10 pairs, but by 1951 there were 13. Breeding was poor due to loss of rabbits through myxomatosis in 1954–55, and toxic chemicals in 1963–64, but by 1967 there were 23 pairs, which gradually increased to 46 by the mid 1980s. Increase has slowed in the last decade and productivity is poor, with the total population fluctuating at about 100–150 birds. There is some vagrancy of young birds but no habitual migration abroad, while some recent winter occurrences in eastern England and Scotland are thought to be wandering continental birds.

Montagu's Harrier *Circus pygargus*

Smallest and most lightly-built of the harriers, this bird seems to glide with the airiness of a paper toy glider, soaring or hanging motionless in light winds. It flies low and slowly, hovering and dropping on small prey, ranging from voles, mice and small birds to large insects. It is a bird of open lowland heaths, swamps and reed beds, also using the early stages of forestry plantations, and sometimes meadows and cultivated fields. It is a summer breeding visitor to such areas. The calls include sharp chattering and thin, high-whistling notes. The pairing displays involve wild acrobatic swooping and tumbling by both birds. Plunging dives with spread wings and tail may produce loud drumming sounds. The nest is on the ground, hidden by tall vegetation.

It breeds in the western half of Eurasia in temperate to warmer boreal zones, but in Europe tends to be absent from Atlantic coasts, and Britain is on the periphery of its distribution. It winters in Africa and India. There appear to be no early British records based upon bones. Historically it was confused with the Hen Harrier. The characters for recognition were finally clarified by Colonel Montagu in 1803, and from then onwards we have some idea of its status. As a summer migrant on the edge of its range, occurrence may have depended in part on weather, and use of sites tend to be sporadic and unpredictable.

It may never have been much more numerous in Britain. Like other raptors it decreased in the nineteenth century through deliberate persecution, and this con-

tinued to some extent until very recent decades. It may also have suffered from heathland and marshes being taken into cultivation in the last two centuries. However, its increase coincides with the warmer period of the earlier part of this century. From the 1890s to 1920 there were usually 3–4 nests, mainly on the Norfolk Broads. Numbers increased, with other breeding in southern England and Wales, to about 15–25 in the 1930s. This increase continued, possibly aided by lack of attention during the 1939–45 war, to about 40–50 pairs in the mid 1950s and possibly half as many more. These were mainly in south-west England with about half in Devon and Cornwall, but with scattered breeding west to Anglesey, and on the east side up to the border. Scottish breeding was reported in Perthshire in 1952, 1953 and 1955, and in Kirkcudbrightshire in 1953; and since 1955 there have been one or two sporadic breedings in Ireland. Numbers dropped back to 15–25 in the late 1960s, to none in 1974 and 1975, but rising to 6 or more in the mid 1980s.

In recent years, there has been an increasing tendency to nest in crops on cultivated land. Numerically it is very rare in Britain but it is questionable whether there was ever a native population, as opposed to an unpredictable periodic extension and retraction of the edge of its overall breeding range.

Hen Harrier *Circus cyaneus*

This is the moorland harrier, a larger version of the Montagu's Harrier. It has made a surprising recovery, progressing as a breeding bird from being absent on mainland Britain early this century, to becoming our commonest nesting harrier. It hunts in typical harrier fashion, gliding low and searching open areas of moorland with an apparent thoroughness that has earned it the dislike of grouse moor gamekeepers. It pounces on its prey (mainly small birds, but also many small rodents), snatching them dexterously with long thin legs. Usually quiet, it has quick chattering calls of varying pitch. In contrast to the normal low flight, its displays may involve extravagant aerobatics with deep plungings, steep upward climbs and rolling. Its nest is on the ground, usually in low thick vegetation. Outside the breeding season a number of birds may roost communally on the ground, usually on open sites without human disturbance.

Its overall breeding distribution in Eurasia is from subarctic to temperate zones, migrating from most of that area in winter, but resident in most of Europe and Britain. It migrates to warm-temperate and subtropical zones, and westwards to Europe. It also occurs in the Americas. More tolerant of cooler temperatures than other harriers, it tends to breed on higher ground in Europe, above 200 metres. In Britain most of the territories are on uplands, but it has bred on the fens and marshy lowlands of East Anglia. In winter there is a general shift towards lowland and coastal areas.

Like the Montagu's Harrier it has not been found in prehistoric deposits, and its early status is uncertain. William Turner in 1544 identified it as taking domestic fowl, presumably young birds, as well as other species, but it does not seem to have suffered active persecution, even though it was regarded as vermin. It was probably widespread as a breeding bird over most of the British Isles until the late eighteenth century. It may have been helped by the earlier forest clearances that had left widespread and sometimes large areas of rough grazing and heathland, and by the fact that many fields were unfenced; there were also large numbers of bogs and marshy areas. The colder climate from the fourteenth century onwards may also have suited it.

In the late eighteenth and early nineteenth centuries, an increase in the conversion of heathland and moors to cultivation, creation of enclosed fields and drainage of bogs began to reduce numbers. This change of land use produced a great decline in the first half of the nineteenth century in southern England, while in the north and west sheep grazing, heather-burning and keepering of grouse moors had a similar effect.

As Donald Watson has shown it was present in most areas in about 1825, except for a belt from Essex to south Wales and parts of central Ireland, although its status in Shetland and Lewis was always in doubt. Forty years later, it had gone from much of lowland England and the Scottish lowlands. It was present but rare in southern England, East Anglia, west and north Wales, and moorlands of central and northern England. It was apparently still plentiful in highland Scotland and the islands, Orkney, and in parts of southern Ireland with a small area in Antrim.

In the second half of the nineteenth century, systematic persecution wiped it out over most the British Isles. Mainland Britain's last regular breedings seem to have been in 1893 in Devon, 1899 in Northumberland and 1902 in Wales. In Kintyre and Arran, a small residue may have held out until at least the 1914–18 war. Ireland still retained breeding birds in parts of the south-western half and in Antrim, and these – together with birds in Orkney and the Outer Hebrides – were the only regular breeding population for the next half-century. At all periods, the picture is complicated by sporadic breedings of single pairs at widely scattered localities at intervals of a few years.

During the decrease of gamekeepering in the 1939–45 war, it re-colonised parts of the Scottish highlands, but in Ireland had retreated to the south-west. Its spread continued: by the 1960s in Scotland it occupied large areas of the highlands and south-west uplands and border, it spread into north Wales and recolonised southern Ireland. By the mid 1970s it was more numerous in Scotland, had spread south to the Pennines, Peak District and North Yorkshire moors with sporadic attempts further south, and was scattered through most of Ireland. Young plantations had become an important nesting habitat. In winter, the birds tend to shift and occur in lowlands and coastal areas of most regions. It does not appear to migrate and there may be a small influx of continental birds.

Nesting pairs have been variously estimated at about 250–550, and winter population for the British Isles at about 900 individuals. Whatever the apparent causes, it should be noted that recent population changes in both this species and Montagu's Harrier coincide broadly with major variations in climate.

Marsh Harrier *Circus aeruginosus*

This species, the largest of the three, is a reed-bed harrier. Although its hunting – and more rarely its nesting – may extend to adjacent areas, its preferred habitat is that of extensive reed-beds, where it also hunts over open water and any bordering marsh or open cultivation. Despite being the biggest harrier, this more vegetated habitat may make it the least visible of the three. It hunts low, gliding with the wings upheld in the shallow V-shape typical of the harriers, and catching its prey with a sudden turn, swoop and snatch with the long slender legs. It takes a large range of birds and other animals.

The bird illustrated is the male; but females and immatures with uniform dark brown plumage, setting off a bright yellow or straw-coloured head, are more often seen. It has chattering calls and thin whistling notes. It shows the same tendency as other harriers in display, switching from its usual low gliding flight to spectacular swooping and tumbling aerobatics. It is sometimes polygamous. Nests are hidden in undisturbed areas of reed-beds, more rarely in growing crops.

The breeding range is broad, from warm boreal to warm-temperate zones, and it is resident in Australasia and Malagasy. It is also wholly or partly resident in southern and western Europe, including Britain. Elsewhere it migrates to subtropical and tropical areas. However, within this range it is usually limited to areas near water, usually with well-vegetated margins, but as a non-breeder may extend to bare marshes and open grassy areas.

It has the only early British harrier records, occurring around the Iron Age lake settlements of Somerset. It must have been widespread and plentiful in post-glacial times in the extensive fens and marshes of low-lying areas. Its population is closely linked with fen and marshland, and shares a history of drastic decline as these areas were drained and cleared. The extensive seventeenth century fenland drainage probably initiated the main decline, and that of the nineteenth century nearly finished it. In the early nineteenth century it was still widespread in England, Wales and Ireland. It decreased rapidly concurrent with extensive drainage, shooting by gamekeepers and collecting of eggs and skins. Its final disappearance in Britain seems uncertain, but it was extinct here by 1900. In Ireland it persisted for a while in some middle and western areas, but the last recorded breeding was in 1917.

Some habitat remained and like other harrier species stray pairs attempted nesting. In the Norfolk reed-beds it was breeding in 1908, 1915, 1919 and 1921. From 1927 onwards several pairs nested annually, and in about 1939 they spread to Suffolk. There had been up to 5 pairs, but by the mid 1940s they were increasing and in 1945 a pair bred in Anglesey, and in 1946 in Kent. By the 1950s there were up to 12 pairs in East Anglia, some intermittent nestings in Hampshire and regular breeding in Dorset for 1951 onwards.

In the early 1960s the numbers dropped suddenly, probably due to toxic chemical residues in their prey. Breeding ceased in Dorset in 1961, and between 1950 and 1961, Norfolk pairs dropped from 5 to nil. Until 1970 only a few pairs remained, mostly in Suffolk. Stray breeding still occurred: Lancashire in 1962, Yorkshire 1963, Scotland possibly in 1966 and 1969, with a later attempt in 1980. Then British numbers rose again from 1 pair in 1971 to 15 in the late 1970s, reaching 28 in 1983. The latter total was mainly in East Anglia, with some in south-east England, and birds were also present in northern England and Wales. Only a very small number appear to remain in Britain in winter. The species seems temporarily safe here, but vulnerable.

Sparrowhawk *Accipiter nisus*

This small fierce-eyed hawk is the least obtrusive of our birds of prey. Its short broad wings with splayed primaries, and the longish tail, enable it to manoeuvre rapidly around obstacles, and it is a woodland bird moving easily among trees. It hunts low, taking advantage of cover to surprise its prey, snatching with strong, long-toed feet. It is usually glimpsed in the act before disappearing into cover again. The food is mainly birds of songbird size; together with some other small creatures. The female is noticeably larger than the male, dark brown with a brown-barred breast where the male is grey with rufous-barred underside. The main call is a sharp chattering *kek-kek-kek* in varying keys. It will soar at times, usually with a few rapid wing-flaps at intervals, and display involves soaring and series of swoops. The nest is in a tree in woodland.

It has a broad breeding range through Eurasia, from subartic to warm-temperate woodland, resident through temperate Europe but otherwise migrating to warm-temperate and subtropical zones. It might be expected whenever trees were present, but is only identified from the end of the last glaciation or early Holocene in Devon, and from the latter period in south Wales. It must have spread with woodland and been most numerous before systematic clearance began, but prefers broken rather than continuous forest, tending to leave mature forest to one of its few predators, the Goshawk. Partial forest clearance might aid it since it prefers the younger stages of regrowth.

Leslie Brown suggested that the medieval population might have been between a quarter and half a million adults. Its numbers must have fallen steadily with loss of tree cover, with gamekeepers helping the reduction from the eighteenth century onwards. Towards the end of the nineteenth century, with tree cover reduced to 5% of Britain and gamekeeping at its height, numbers must have been very low. However, with game preservation reduced, it increased during both world wars, possibly quadrupling during the second when population may have been at its highest since 1800. Modern conifer forestry also suited it.

There was evidence of decrease again in the mid 1950s and of catastrophic decline by the early 1960s, when it disappeared from some south-eastern grain-growing regions, although the fall was slight in highland Scotland. It appeared to be due to residues of toxic chemicals in the birds eaten, which they in turn had received with their seed and insect diets. With increasing controls in the use of such chemicals there was a gradual recovery: with estimates of 15,000 pairs in the mid 1970s and 25,000 by the mid 1980s. This is still short of the 32,000 pairs that Ian Newton estimated as the potential British population. There might be about another 8,000–9,000 in Ireland. Winter figures in the mid 1980s were estimated at about 170,000 birds, including non-breeders but excluding the small number of continental migrants that occur.

Goshawk *Accipiter gentilis*
NOT IN COLOUR PLATE

This is the large hawk of forest, like a huge Sparrowhawk and with similar habits, but taking larger prey. It prefers more open, mature woodland. As in the

Goshawk

Sparrowhawk, the female is much larger than the male, but in this species both sexes have the duller brown plumage, barred on the underside but streaked in juveniles. As prey it will take animals up to the size of pheasants, crows and hares. It is a very sedentary species, even more so than the Sparrowhawk.

It is resident in subarctic to temperate zones of the northern hemisphere. It occurred as remains in caves of Devon and Derbyshire dating from towards the end of the last glaciation and probably in interstadial conditions. It is likely to have occurred at any time when well-grown woodland was present, and appears to need relatively large tracts of undisturbed woodland for successful breeding. Like the Sparrowhawk, its numbers must have diminished as forests were cleared, or cut and replaced with younger growth. It was prized for falconry, being the bird used for practical hunting of potential food such as partridges, hares and rabbits. This must have afforded some protection when nesting, since a supply of young birds was needed by falconers. When woodland reached a low point in the nineteenth century, and gamekeepers could destroy a large sedentary bird liable to take adult pheasants or birds of similar size, the Goshawk was threatened with extermination.

It ceased to breed in Ireland and most of England in the mid nineteenth century, with late breedings in Lincolnshire in 1864 and Yorkshire in 1893. In Scotland it bred in Invernesshire until the late 1850s and Perthshire until the 1880s. In 1939, the *Handbook of British Birds* described it as a rare vagrant, although three pairs bred at a Sussex site from the 1920s or 1930s until 1951. On Speyside in Scotland, it was present and probably breeding in the late 1950s and early 1960s. In the late 1960s to early 1970s there was a systematic unofficial reintroduction of birds by falconers, and rumour suggests that over 50 pairs from northern Europe were introduced to suitable sites in Britain where they began to breed. This was not wholly altruistic since it was hoped that the young would be available for falconry. By the early 1980s, the population was suggested to be about 100 pairs, with a winter population of about 300 birds.

Merlin *Falco columbarius*

The male is the smallest of our falcons, unmistakably blue-grey above and russet-tinted below; but the larger female is brown-streaked and more like a Kestrel in size and outline, but with a faster and more raptorial flight. It is more like a miniature Peregrine, hunting over open country and feeding almost entirely on small birds chased or pounced upon from fast flight. It will hunt low, using rising ground or walls as cover to approach closely; but also indulging in fast and close aerial chases. It has a typical falcon call, a sharp *quic-ic-ic*. Display appears to be limited to swooping performances and chases. The nest is usually on the ground, hidden in heather or bracken, but a rock ledge or old crow's nest in a low tree may be used. The birds leave the higher moorland in winter and scatter to open lowland, in particular to coasts and estuaries.

Its breeding range is in the colder regions, from montane arctic to the boreal zone around the northern hemisphere, with the British Isles on the southern limit of its range. Except in Britain and south-west Iceland, it is a migrant to temperate regions. Its earliest recorded British occurrences are in Devonshire and Derbyshire caves at the latter stages of the last glaciation. It must have decreased subsequently with forest spread but then, like the Hen Harrier, must have increased well into historic times, as clearances gave rise to more moorland and heathland. It may have been reduced to some degree by sheep-keeping on the uplands. Once gamekeepers were used on moorland it suffered from sharing its primary habitat with grouse and was severely and unjustifiably persecuted; its numbers decreased as a result during the nineteenth century. It should have increased like other raptors in the present century, but a slow decrease continued. This was blamed on increased human disturbance – which may certainly have driven it from dune areas of the south-west and Lancashire in the 1930s – and on afforestation; it could also have been argued that it was not suited to the milder climate of the earlier half of the century.

However, the decrease continued and has accelerated since the 1950s. It was then suggested that toxic residues in wintertime prey were responsible, but control of chemicals did not halt the decline. In some areas, birds have fallen to about a quarter of their former numbers, and locally have been lost altogether. In spite of losses it is still present as a breeding species in most moorland regions, with a widespread but thin distribution west and north of a line from Flamborough Head to the eastern border of Devon, but absent from lowland within that range. The range includes the Hebrides, Orkney and Shetland. In winter they scatter to coastal and lowland sites, including agricultural areas, where small birds are more plentiful. They are joined by Icelandic birds and possibly some from Scandinavia. In the early 1970s breeding pairs in the British Isles were estimated at about 600–800, and 2,000–3,000 individuals may be present in winter.

Peregrine Falcon *Falco peregrinus*

This is probably the most powerful of all the falcons; a large compact bird with long tapering wings and fairly short tail. It flies with rapid shallow wing-beats and glides. It hunts by sighting flying prey, rocketing down on it from above, usually striking and seizing it in mid-air. It will take a large range of prey, usually birds, and most often pigeons, ducks, game-birds or other birds of similar size. It has harsh chattering and *kek*-ing calls, usually heard about the nest. The powerful flight is used in displays of aerobatic extravagance at times. The nest is on a rock ledge, sometimes based on large old nests of other species. Basically it is a bird of open country, nesting on crags and cliffs and present in suitable areas in many parts of the world. In Europe, it is mainly a bird of mountainous areas, more widespread in winter. In the British Isles it breeds where crags, cliffs or rock outcrops are adjacent to open areas.

Its earliest recorded occurrences in Britain are from possibly the middle of the last glaciation in Derbyshire and from a Cheddar cave during the Windermere Interstadial towards the end of the last glaciation, the latter interesting in that the body seems to have been buried and lacks skull and claws. It was present on the south Wales coast in the early Holocene, and killed by man at the period in Scotland, and later in the Dark Ages. Falconry, in which this was the prized species in northern Europe, came to Britain in about the sixth to eighth centuries and was an important social activity until the seventeenth century. During this period, the Peregrine received legal protection and a nest-site was regarded as a valuable asset. In later centuries, it lost this special status and as game management increased, it was killed as an unwanted predator.

It has been suggested that range and population decrease since medieval times was considerable, but evidence from deserted sites and population loss suggest that it might have been as low as in the order of 9–16%. From 1900 onwards, population seems to have been fairly constant around minor fluctuations, with about 700 pairs in the British Isles. As a potential threat to carrier pigeons, about 600 birds were shot during the 1939–1945 war, mainly in southern England, with extermination in Cornwall and elsewhere. However, by 1955 the southern population was back to about 70% of its former level.

From 1956 onwards, ornithologists noticed a distinct decrease again, but pigeon-racers claimed an increase that threatened their sport. A survey resulted in 1961–62 that revealed an alarming loss. The cause was toxic chemicals in the bodies of their prey, affecting both the birds and their breeding, and providing some of the most important evidence of such poisoning. With control of chemicals, numbers began to rise and by 1981 the population had risen to about 900 pairs, with an additional 100 single-bird territories. The winter population was estimated at about 4,000 birds. The breeding distribution is around coasts with rocky cliffs, and in mountains and hilly areas west of a line from the Humber to eastern Devon. In winter there is some shift to lowlands, especially coasts and estuaries, but still mainly in the north and west.

Cuckoo *Cuculus canorus* (CUCULIDAE)

Shown here for comparison with birds of prey in flight, the Cuckoo is dealt with in full on page 156.

Game-Birds

GALLIFORMES

Mainly terrestrial and sedentary, these are stockily-built birds with heavy bodies, smallish heads, and strong stout bills. The legs are strong, designed for constant walking and running; the wings short, broad and rounded, allowing fast low flight from an abrupt start, but – with the exception of the Quail – not used for flights of long duration. They are ground nesters with large broods, the downy young running and feeding soon after hatching and flying very early on. Two families are represented in Britain – the grouse, Tetraonidae; and pheasant, partridge and quails, Phasianidae.

Grouse

Tetraonidae

These are cold-country game-birds, mostly occupying more northerly latitudes or higher altitudes. They are stoutly-built and thick-feathered. The feathering extends to the nostrils and may make the bill look short and stubby, and is also present on the legs; in Red Grouse and Ptarmigan the feathering extends to the toes as well. The plumage is cryptically coloured for concealment in rough vegetation, but males of the woodland species are more boldly-coloured and larger than the females. There are four British species. The Ptarmigan lives on tundra-type mountain-tops, the Red Grouse on heather moorland, the Black Grouse on woodland edge, and the Capercaillie in mature woodland.

Red Grouse *Lagopus lagopus scoticus*

The Red Grouse is our isolated representative (subspecies or species according to preference) of the Willow Grouse, a species of open areas in circumpolar arctic to boreal zones of the northern hemisphere, where it is mainly associated with dwarf or scrub willow or birch. At some unidentified time in the past, our bird lost its white wing feathering and all-white winter plumage, suggesting some evolution in less snowy winter conditions. Lacking these distinctive plumages, it appears much the same at all times of year. It has also become a specialist feeder on heather, and in doing so has tied itself to a more limited habitat. Within this habitat, it tends to crouch and hide when disturbed and, for many people, the only view of it is when it rises suddenly and skims away in the low level flight with intermittent glides that has made it a popular target for shooters. In addition to heather, it also feeds on bilberry and crowberry shrubs.

The characteristic abrupt and harsh croaking *go-bak* call is the best known of its notes, but a range of similar croaking and cackling calls are used, particularly in territorial advertisement and display. There is an advertisement flight in which the male flutters up and then parachutes down with fast-beating wings and spread tail, calling as it descends. In ground display the male struts about, the wattle over the eye expanded to a serrated-edged scarlet eyebrow, tail raised and fanned, and wing-tips drooped. The nest is a simple hollow, usually hidden in the taller heather. In winter, birds tend to stay in territory and can burrow in the snow to feed and roost. Younger birds form flocks that may move to lower ground in bad weather, where pairs may sometimes join them. The Red Grouse has a 6–7 year abundance cycle, and may rear no young in bad years and up to 8 per pair in good ones.

There is early evidence of it in the Pleistocene, from the Mendips, in a probably unrecognised interglacial of about 500,000 years ago. It is likely to have been present in subsequent suitable conditions, although the only other ice-age records are from Devensian deposits in caves of the south-west, the Midlands and the north. At some point it became a heather moorland bird. The only present evidence of change in the past is an apparently temporary occurrence of birds with exceptionally large and stout bills, at least indicating that the character is particularly variable, a different bill size being presumably correlated with a difference in diet.

In cooler, but not arctic, Pleistocene conditions, the Red Grouse could have been plentiful in the moorland zone between tree-line and tundra. Its present British distribution on hills extends to an altitude of 600 metres, and to 900 metres in parts of Scotland. As trees invaded, it would have been increasingly limited to a zone of this type on hills and mountains. It would have spread again in early historic times as increasing clearance of trees allowed the spread of heather moorland. It appears to have been valued in northern Britain as a source of food and for hunting, and by the fifteenth century, laws were passed to protect it when breeding. It may have lost ground in the eighteenth century with the spread of cultivation and grazing, but hunting was becoming increasingly important as a social pastime. Systematic burning to maintain moorland became a regular technique in the early nineteenth century. In the second half of that century, more elaborate game control and the slaughter of predators became customary, enabling it to reach optimum numbers. By the beginning of the twentieth century, the population may have been around five million, with about three million shot annually. With such numbers the recurrent population cycles became more apparent.

Attempts had been made to introduce it into Exmoor in the early 1820s, but they failed. However, it was successfully introduced to both Exmoor and Dartmoor in 1915–16. In Ireland, where it was widespread in both mountain and lowland bog areas, it began to decrease in about 1920, and in Britain from about 1940 onwards. This appears to be linked with less rigid control of moorland, reduced keepering, and competition with agriculture, forestry, deer and sheep. The present distribution is in Devon, hill areas of Wales, Peak and Pennines, Lakeland, Yorkshire moors, and across the

SUMMER MALE
Red Grouse

MALE

Capercaillie

FEMALE

SUMMER MALE

MALE

Black Grouse

FEMALE

Ptarmigan

WINTER MALE

D.M.H.

Red Grouse

border country into Scotland, where it occurs as far as the Outer Hebrides and into Orkney and Shetland. By the early 1980s numbers were nearer 800,000–900,000, with a possible 200,000–500,000 breeding pairs.

Ptarmigan *Lagopus mutus*

Resembling a slightly smaller and paler Red Grouse, this arctic bird is a mountain grouse with us, creeping or strutting among the broken rocks and climate-cropped low plant growth of the high mountain-tops. It feeds on plants – leaves, buds, flowers, berries and catkins. It is highly sedentary and achieves the camouflage it needs with three plumage changes a year. Its winter plumage is white, with black tail feathers, conspicuous in flight but hidden by long white coverts when the bird settles. The male is black between bill and eye, with a bold red eyebrow wattle; the female being white-faced with a much smaller wattle. The wings and belly are white all year, but in spring the males becomes a finely mottled dark greyish-buff and the female a more sandy colour with darker markings. In autumn the male is a paler grey, more finely marked, and the female a lighter grey and buff, and as they moult into and out of winter plumage they are mottled with white.

The usual calls are low hoarse croaks and odd crackling notes. It tends to move slowly and deliberately, but can walk and run easily over broken terrain. It may be reluctant to fly, preferring to crouch when alarmed; but when it does, it moves like a Red Grouse with rapidly whirring wings and occasional glides, heading downhill to escape, or across to another high ridge or crag. When it displays, with loud harsh calls and cackles, the male struts with tail raised and fanned, wing-tips drooping, and serrated eyebrow wattle swollen erect. It has short display flights, rising abruptly, gliding, then landing with a flutter, calling as it does so.

The nest is in a slight and sheltered hollow. In both grouse species young are tended by both adults, but pick up their own food. Small flocks form in winter, feeding on bare ridges and sheltered areas; but it can burrow and roost in snow, and grows a thicker layer of feathers that covers legs and feet until they look like rabbits' feet. Periods of heavy snow may force it down into heather moorland, but it normally keeps to the alpine vegetation zone. As with the Red Grouse, their population cycles rise and fall about every 10 years.

Its general distribution is circumpolar in tundra regions, extending into more southerly mountains, and also in the Alps and Pyrenees; it is resident in all areas. It is one of the cold-adapted species that must have been widespread in the cooler periods of the Pleistocene. The earliest record, like that of the Red Grouse, is from an interglacial in the Mendips about 500,000 years ago. It occurs frequently in Devon and the Mendips, and in Derbyshire in the last glaciation. Other bones in the same deposits suggest that the situation might at some periods have been like that of present-day Scotland, with Ptarmigan on the highest ground and milder conditions on lower ground.

During the ameliorating conditions of the early Holocene, the Ptarmigan must have retreated as its habitat receded further northwards and to higher ground. It was recognised as a game-bird, and received protection in the nesting season from the late sixteenth century; but by reason of its habitat it was little known or studied. In England it was present on high ground in Lakeland, and in Scotland in the south-west, the highlands and the islands, and also in Orkney. It decreased in the early part of the nineteenth century, disappearing from some areas. It has been suggested that the increasing spread of sheep may have had some marginal effect, and the more widespread use of guns also helped. The populations were fragmented, it was highly sedentary, and re-colonisation of lost areas would be difficult. It disappeared from Lakeland early in the nineteenth century, from south-west Scotland in 1830 and Orkney in about 1831, from Arran in the 1870s and Rhum in about 1888.

Accessible populations were reduced. By 1938 it had disappeared from the Outer Hebrides. It is present on Skye, Mull and Jura, and Arran was re-colonised in 1977. Attempts were made without success to re-introduce it into south-west Scotland in the late 1960s and early 1970s, but birds from these attempts bred in the Tweedsmuir Hills from the late 1970s to mid 1980s. In parts of the Cairngorm region, disturbance from skiers and increase of predation by scavenging gulls and crows has reduced numbers. The winter population in good years has been estimated at 10,000–15,000 birds and might drop to about 2,500–4,000 in bad years.

Capercaillie *Tetrao urogallus*

This is the turkey of the Old World woodlands, not only on account of its size but in its display strutting, with the big tail raised and spread as a large fan, the wings drooping, and head and neck stretched upwards with throat feathers ruffled, while it emits a weird sequence of clicking, popping and grating notes, and occasional deep bubbling. In spite of its apparent conspicuousness, it can move through trees and undergrowth with surprising stealth, making its alarm flight all the more startling as it erupts with a roar of wings, scattering dead twigs as it bursts up through the canopy to glide and whirr away in more silent flight. It perches easily, and roosts in trees at night, often feeds in trees, and will also perform its display song from a perch.

The great bill with curved tip has a predatory look, but is designed for snipping off the growing tips of plants, in particular the young buds, shoots and cones of Scots Pine which constitute its principal food in winter. At other times it takes a variety of other plants, including all parts of small berry-bearing shrubs. It is a bird of open, mature conifer forest with plentiful undergrowth, and its range is closely linked with that of the Scots Pine. However, there is a population in north-west Spain which relies on holly for its winter food, and another in Siberia occurs in mature oak forest, which both indicate potentially wider adaptations not usually utilised. The males, which are much larger than the females, have areas or 'leks', in which they gather in small groups to display. Mating occurs there, and the more furtive and cryptically-coloured female nests and tends the young alone. The survival of the downy chicks is affected by rainfall and low temperatures, which may limit colonisation of the Atlantic coast areas of high rainfall.

Its main distribution is through the boreal forest zone of Eurasia east to the Baikal region, with outlying populations in the mountains of Europe. Within this range, distribution is limited by the need for woodland with extensive stands of mature trees. Its early distribution in Britain would have been limited by this. The earliest occurrence is in the London Basin in the next-to-last, Wolstonian, glaciation, presumably in an interstadial; while cave remains in Somerset and northern England are in deposits that might be late Devensian or early Holocene. It may well have become widespread once woodland was well-established, and would have retreated again as mature woodland was cleared. W.B. Yapp believed it to be present in England, possibly in East Anglia in medieval times, where in the absence of conifers it might have utilised holly, as does the northwest Spanish population.

By the seventeenth century, it had gone from England and Wales but was still widespread in Scotland and Ireland. It was not held in great esteem as a game-bird, and the flesh was said to be tainted from the pine-shoot diet. Its main enemy was forest clearance and it had largely disappeared by the mid nineteenth century. In Scotland it disappeared from Argyll in about 1765 and from Invernesshire in the 1770s; the last records were from Deeside, Aberdeenshire, in 1785. The Irish population hung on in Tipperary until 1760, and it was still present in Ireland in 1790, but not recorded later. It was then extinct in the British Isles.

Attempts were made to introduce it to Scotland from 1827, and Swedish birds were successfully introduced in 1837 and 1838 at Aberfeldy, Perthshire, where they became established, spreading along river valley forest. Subsidiary introductions were made in some other highland areas in the 1860s and 1890s. It had spread widely by about 1914 when it was constrained to some extent by wartime felling. In the period up to 1950 it had spread south as far as Lanarkshire and occurred sporadically in other counties of southern Scotland, but in the same period had decreased in many places with the felling of mature timber. After its maximum spread, it retreated a little to north of a line from the Firth of Forth to the Clyde, and to the east of a line north from the Clyde, along the eastern side of the north-west highlands, and north-east to Dornock. It had begun to show an increase in the late 1950s but in recent decades has been increasingly shot as a game-bird. It appears to be showing some retreat along the western edge of its range, but whether from climate or shooting is uncertain. Its numbers are estimated at a few thousand.

Black Grouse *Lyrurus tetrix*
This is the most ornate of our grouse. The males gather in early mornings to display at open 'leks', where they posture and leap with the tail raised and spread, showing the curved shape and fluffed white under-tail coverts, while inflating the neck and showing off swollen red wattles. Display are accompanied by a frantic, resonant bubbling cooing, and explosive hisses accompany the upward fluttering jumps. Females visit the leks to mate and then nest alone. The success of the species depends upon maintaining these social displays. When not breeding, males may have a more mottled partial eclipse plumage.

It flies strongly, often through open woodland; perching readily and like the Capercaillie feeding extensively on shoots, buds, fruit and catkins. It inhabits the marginal zone where woodland borders on scrubby or open grassland, moorland or bog. The nest is usually a hollow on the ground, partly hidden in vegetation. In autumn birds tend to form small flocks, the displaying males often keeping together.

This is a woodland edge species of the boreal zone, occurring across Eurasia, and in mountain areas of the Alps and south-eastern Europe. Since it uses a variable habitat bordering woodland, one might expect it to have been plentiful in the past, but in Britain Pleistocene records appear limited to the more wooded periods, in the latter part of the Devensian Glaciation in the south-west, midlands and north. It would have benefitted from the early stages of spread of trees after the Ice Ages, but might have become less widespread as tree cover became more continuous. However, the rather haphazard clearing of forest that followed would have favoured it, but it would then have decreased again later with enclosures and spread of cultivation, more particularly in England. Since its chosen habitat tends to be transient in places, numbers would tend to fluctuate. It seems to have been generally widespread in England, Scotland and eastern Wales until well into the last century, but wholly absent from Ireland.

Towards the end of the nineteenth century, reductions in numbers and local extinctions occurred, probably due in part to a failure to realise the vulnerability of a species that could be shot at display leks. The apparent widespread failure of re-introduction attempts may have been due to the problem of re-establishing leks. It disappeared from many counties of south and midland England in the nineteenth century; but seems to have been successfully introduced into western Wales at this time, although becoming extinct again in Pembrokeshire. In Scotland it was widespread but scarce in the north-west, and absent from the Outer Habrides. It was also absent from Orkney and Shetland.

By the beginning of this century it was still present in Cornwall, Dorset, Hampshire and Wiltshire until about 1920, and disappeared from Norfolk and Nottinghamshire a little earlier; while in Herefordshire and Lincolnshire it remained until the 1930s. In Scotland, numbers had peaked about 1910–15 but decreased again, particularly in the west, over the next 25 years. In Wales it also decreased, disappearing from Glamorgan and the Welsh border in the 1930s. It may have benefitted from the spread of plantations, in spite of being shot as a pest by foresters, and it increased and spread in Wales in the 1940s and in Scotland since the 1950s, although still decreasing in the Pennine and Peak regions of England. The vestigial population in Devon, maintained by recent releases of hand-reared birds, disappeared by the early 1980s, when southern Welsh populations also shrank. The population of the mid 1980s may be in the region of 5,000–25,000 birds.

Pheasants, Partridges and Quail

Phasianidae

These are game-birds of warmer climates. The legs are long and bare, often with spurs. The bills are short and strong. Display patterning occurs on face, flanks and belly. The main plumage colour is usually a cryptic plain brown or a streaky pattern for concealment against grass or leaves. The nest is a scrape on the ground, and broods of downy chicks may be large. There are six British species. The Common Pheasant, similar in size to a domestic fowl, is a bird of woodland edge, scrub and reed-bed; the two ruffed pheasants are birds of dense woodland without undergrowth. The Common Partridge is a smaller short-tailed species of temperate grassland. The Red-legged Partridge is similar, but prefers drier places. These are all resident, but the tiny Common Quail is a migrant summer visitor to well-drained herbage. Only the Common Partridge and Common Quail are original natives, the others were introduced.

Common Pheasant *Phasianus colchicus*
This introduced and cosseted bird, the domestic fowl of the shooting world, has probably had a greater effect on the landscape of England than any other creature, with the possible exception of the horse, and brought about the premature death of more predators and scavengers. It is a bird that rests in thick sheltered cover – undergrowth, bushes or reed-beds – and ventures into more open areas to feed on plants and insects. In the bronzy brilliance of the male's plumage it shares with the kingfisher the claim to be our most colourful bird, but it can be surprisingly inconspicuous among rough herbage; while the buff-and-brown patterned female matches the dead grasses, reeds and leaves among which it may nest. Under natural conditions it is territorial when breeding and often polygamous. It can be surprisingly furtive, the male advertising his presence from cover with a sudden loud *kor-kok* crow and a vigorous wing-whirr. In display, he circles the female with face-wattle expanded and plumage slanted to show off its spread pattern in lateral view. The nest is hidden in ground vegetation.

Constant captive breeding and release make its natural status difficult to determine. It normally occurs in temperate Eurasia from the Black Sea to China, brown-rumped in the western half, blue-grey-rumped in the east. The Green Pheasant *P. versicolor*, the representative in Japan, is better adapted to wetter conditions and has in recent times been introduced to some western parts of Britain, and may interbreed. Western Eurasian birds were domesticated by the Romans and a few may have been kept in Britain, or eaten there. The main introduction was by the Normans in eleventh century, and in the next few centuries they were dispersed and introduced through most of England. They were of this darker-necked, dark-rumped western form. In the sixteenth century they were also introduced to parts of Wales, Scotland and Ireland.

By the late eighteenth and early nineteenth centuries, they had become the most important game-bird, being manageable in the farmed areas around the houses of large estates. Small woodlands and coppices were retained or planted to shelter them, an army of keepers were employed to protect them, and any creature that might conceivably threaten a pheasant's existence from the egg onwards was killed. They were often reared in captivity and released to provide artificially large numbers and, particularly in the last half-century, a wide range of forms from localities in both the east and west of the range were imported, showing considerable plumage variation.

Rearing and shooting was at a peak towards the end of the nineteenth century and birds had been introduced to the whole of the British Isles, from the Channel Islands to the Outer Hebrides and Orkney. In some of these areas it showed its ability to colonise treeless areas with some boggy or marshy vegetation. During the 1914–18 and 1939–45 wars, the numbers decreased with less gamekeeping, allowing it to show an ability to maintain viable, if smaller, wild populations. In general the numbers have slowly but steadily increased in this century, although the rise in predators and crop spraying may have held this back a little. It is now present over most of the British Isles, except in a few areas of bare high upland, and in most of the northern and western Scottish highlands, and the smaller Outer Hebrides. It is estimated that there are about 8 million wild birds, contributing up to three-quarters of the total annual shoot, with around 15 million released annually of which about 3 million might survive the shooting season.

Golden Pheasant *Chrysolophus pictus*
NOT IN THE COLOUR PLATE

This ruffed pheasant is the smallest of the group. It is slim, long-legged and small-billed. The male has a vivid red body, yellow back and scaly green mantle. The

Male Golden Pheasant

Common Pheasant

FEMALE

MALE

Common Quail

MALE

Red-legged Partridge

MALE

Common Partridge

MALE

D.M.HENRY

wings are dark blue, the tail yellowish with a reticulate pattern and scarlet coverts. The head has a narrow golden crest, and a cape of square-ended black-tipped feathers falls from nape to shoulders. In display this is pulled forward to one side, and spread across the face like a great fan with only the pale-irised eye showing above it, the whole accompanied with a loud hiss. The female is pale brown with dark barring.

It is an agile, fast-running bird, flying with great reluctance. Coming from a limited area of inland China, it has been successfully introduced where young conifer woodland has a low dense canopy with no undergrowth, or where yew trees grow in similar fashion. It lives and feeds mainly in such areas. It is incredibly gaudy, but rarely seen, and only the male's rasping *ker-cheek* crow is advertisement of its presence. It may be glimpsed streaking like a startled lizard from one area of cover to another. It has been living ferally in East Anglian breckland pinewoods since the 1890s, and in one locality of south-west Scotland since 1895, with odd attempted introductions elsewhere. It is a highly sedentary species with a British population possibly of 1,000–2,000 birds.

Lady Amherst's Pheasant *Chrysolophus amherstiae*
NOT ILLUSTRATED

A species pair with the Golden Pheasant, this is larger with a much longer, black-and-white barred tail. It is white on the underside, scaly green on neck and mantle, yellow on the back and with blue wings. The crest is green, tipped with red, and the cape is white with black edgings. Its behaviour is like that of the Golden Pheasant, and it comes from another limited area of China. In Britain it occupies a similar habitat of immature conifer plantations with closed dense canopy and no ground cover.

Birds were released at Woburn in Bedfordshire at the turn of the century and at Whipsnade on the Chilterns in the 1930s. It now occupies an area embracing these sites, between Woburn, Biggleswade and Ashridge. It is also present at Exbury and the New Forest edge in Hampshire, and has been released at one or two other sites. There are about 200–500 feral in Britain.

Since the two species hybridise, it is important that their ranges should be kept discrete, and fortunately they are fairly sedentary. The British populations are important, since their status and survival in China is uncertain.

Common Quail *Coturnix coturnix*

Arch-skulker among the game-birds, this tiny stumpy bird is rarely seen, and most records of its occurrence are based on the monotonous ventriloqual *quic-quic-ic* call of the male, which can rarely be traced among the low-growing herbage of crops even when the voice is located. It is well camouflaged in streaky plumage, the breeding male's bold throat pattern only showing if he rears up to look over the plants that hide him. The female arrives later than the male. He displays in a lateral spread of plumage with the nearside wing lowered. The nest is a tiny, deeply concealed hollow, and the young mature rapidly. Although it can fly well, fast and high, it tends to fly only a short way when disturbed, quickly dropping into cover and running. It has a rail-like ability to move through thickly-growing vegetation.

Its general distribution is through the temperate zones, cool to warm, of Western Eurasia; wintering in the tropics, north-west Africa, parts of the Iberian coast, and sometimes elsewhere in the south-west. There is little early evidence apart from one or two occurrences in the latter part of the last glaciation or earliest Holocene. As a species requiring well-drained areas with low herbage, it is likely to have increased as grassland and cultivation supplanted woodland, but as a migrant visitor its numbers would also have been affected by occurrences and climate elsewhere, and possibly by weather at the time of the spring passage.

It is an unpredictable visitor to southern England and south-east Ireland, but sporadically and in good years it might occur, and sometimes breed, almost anywhere. Breeding is very difficult, and often impossible, to prove. Usually it is only the call of the male that establishes its presence. Exceptionally, it occurs in winter in Britain and Ireland and is suspected of overwintering.

In the twelfth to fifteenth centuries, Quail appear to have been reasonably plentiful in the British Isles and regularly caught for food. In the seventeenth and eighteenth centuries it may have been scarcer, but was still hunted for the table as a luxury. In the early half of the nineteenth century, there was a well-marked and continuous decline in numbers, with a drastic and sudden diminution, and disappearance in some areas, in the 1860s. However, in Ireland it increased enormously in the early part of the nineteenth century. There are references to several nests in single fields in the 1840s; and they also remained in large numbers through the winter. In the winter of 1846–47, a Belfast game dealer claimed to have purchased an average of up to 60 a day. This was followed by a sudden decline towards the end of the 1860s, with the Quail almost disappearing from Ireland.

Subsequently there was sporadic non-annual breeding in most counties in Britain, at times north to southern Scotland and in south-east Ireland. 1870 and 1893 were good years, when many were present, but otherwise it was rare until the early 1940s, being scarcest in the mid 1930s. Numbers have increased since 1942 and regular breeding may be occurring in the southern half of England, in eastern Wales and south-east Ireland. 1947, 1953 and 1964 were good years with numbers doubling each time to about 600 calling birds on the last occasion, which may have been equalled in 1970. Attempts have been made to correlate such recent changes with land use or trapping, but other factors such as local shifts might be involved. Breeding birds in the Netherlands have dropped from thousands to hundreds in the period since 1940 when the British population increased.

Red-legged Partridge *Alectoris rufa*

Like the Common Pheasant, this is an introduced game-bird, brought in to increase the targets for guns. It is basically a bird of drier and more open southern habitats and as a substitute for the Common Partridge it tends to provide a more visible prey, but has been heavily criticised for its unsporting tendency to run for long distances rather than take wing in the desired fashion. This tendency to run in the open is one of the limiting factors in its British distribution, since it does not do well in arable areas with wet and sticky clay, or in the wetter part of western Britain.

The bold barring of the flanks and the pale throat with its dark necklace may be less conspicuous in the wild than the bold white eyebrow stripe and the uniform colour of its back. It has a loud *chuk-chuka* and a rhythmic abrasive chugging advertisement call. In aggressive and sexual situations, the male displays laterally, upright and tilting to show off the patterns of face and flanks, and drooping the further wing. Pairs seem to have a long bond, and a female may lay two clutches of eggs in separate nests, one being incubated by the male and the young brought together into one large brood. They may assemble in larger groups in autumn and winter. In general it prefers barer and more open habitats than other game-birds, and is more likely to be seen on arable land.

Its general distribution is through most of France south from the Paris Basin, and in the Iberian peninsula, where it is a bird of drier sunny climate, preferring well-drained soils with scrubby and open vegetation and bare, sometimes rocky areas. The first (unsuccessful) introduction into England was by Charles the Second in 1673 at Windsor, and there were attempts in other south-eastern counties, but the first real success appears to have been with several thousand eggs imported from France and reared under domestic fowl in Suffolk in 1770. It spread in the drier parts of East Anglia where conditions suited it, and during the nineteenth century there were widespread attempts at introductions in various parts of the British Isles, including Ireland and Scotland, where they were unsuccessful.

It had reached its effective limits by the early 1930s, occurring in the eastern half of Britain north to north Yorkshire, in the western half up to Shropshire, and just bordering Wales and east Devon. A scatter of isolated occurrences west and north of this relate mostly to birds released for shooting, and unlikely to establish viable breeding populations. It suffered heavier losses from shooting than did the Common Partridge, but when less shooting occurred, with the decline of the latter, numbers increased. There was a rapid rise in the late 1950s until its population was level with that of the Common Partridge. However, it began to be shot more systematically, and from the mid 1970s birds were bred and released for shooting. Numbers fell again, and the early 1970s population was estimated at about 100,000 to 200,000 birds.

In recent times, releases of Red-legged Partridge for shooting began to be replaced by releases of the Chukar *A. chukar*. This is very closely related. It is a slightly heavier bird, paler, with just a narrow black ring from breast to forehead, less white on the brow and more on the flanks. In the wild it occurs from the Aegean to China. In captivity it hybridises freely with the Red-legged Partridge. The 800,000 or so released annually have been mainly hybrids or pure Chukar for nearly two decades. Releases have occurred throughout the European range of the Red-legged Partridge, with further hybridisation occurring. As a result, it is becoming difficult to discover pure populations of the latter which do not show some evidence of interbreeding in the plumage, although superficially they may resemble the typical species. It may be necessary to identify and conserve pure relict populations.

Common Partridge *Perdix perdix*

This is a small, dumpy and undistinguished bird, the rufous face and black horse-shoe shaped belly-patch of the male only conspicuous at close quarters, and the plumage as a whole finely streaked and barred for camouflage. It is a skulking bird of temperate grassland, that has adapted to the pastures and growing crops of farmland. It walks and runs most of the time and tends to crouch and hide when alarmed. It may easily be overlooked until a group, or covey, finally explode into a short low, level flight. The harsh grating call is the chief indication of its presence, and in the early breeding season this sound may be accompanied by considerable chasing and fighting. It breeds as separate pairs, and the young tend to remain with the adults as a small covey until the next season. The nest is hidden in grass or herbage. The downy chicks, guarded by both parents, feed mainly on insects at first. It does not range far, and may suffer badly in winters with heavy and prolonged snow cover.

In its general distribution it is a grassland bird of western Eurasia, mainly in lowland, and not thriving well in very wet or cold conditions. In Britain its earlier records are from interstadial conditions towards the end of the last glaciation. It may have been scarcer when woodland spread during the early Holocene. However, it undoubtedly benefitted from the clearing of trees and increasing grazing and cultivation of land. It may have suffered from the bad winters of the Little Ice Age of historic times, but in the eighteenth and nineteenth centuries, population increased; this was probably due both to an increase in hedgerows for nesting and arable crops for food, and also to a reduction in mammalian predators such as red fox and stoat to which this species is particularly vulnerable.

Its population peak appears to have been between 1880 and 1914. It was by then widespread through the British Isles; although absent from some upland areas, including much of Wales, a lot of Ireland, and the northern and western highlands and islands, although attempted introductions had occurred in many of these areas. It was also absent from both Orkney and Shetland, but has been successfully introduced there in more recent times.

It began to decrease rapidly in the 1920s, particularly in Ireland, probably mainly through changes in farming practice and gamekeeping. In Ireland this led to protection and a temporary resurgence in the 1930s. However, the general decline continued, accelerating from the 1950s onwards. In addition to loss of hedgerows for nesting and weedy edges of field for feeding, the chemical sprays killed off the insects needed by the growing young and the seeds of weeds eaten by the adults. Even though it is still widespread, the population density has dropped to about a fifth of what it once was. The total population is now about half the excess that was once shot annually, in spite of commercial rearing and re-stocking. Attempts are being made to modify harmful farming practices, but at present it has declined in many areas, particularly along the western edge of its British distribution. It has declined drastically in Ireland to a relict population that is mainly in the south-east. The overall maximum early autumn population is probably less than one million.

Cranes, Rails and Bustards

GRUIFORMES

This order encompasses a disparate group of fairly long-legged birds, ranging from the very large to the tiny, mainly walking in bare open country or wading among swampy vegetation. They are omnivorous in diet, although they take mainly small creatures. They nest on the ground and have downy young that are at first tended and fed by the parents.

Cranes

Gruidae

Tall slim birds, waders and walkers of grassland and open marshy areas. Resembling storks and herons, they have smaller feet however, neater heads with smaller shorter bills, and long feathers overhanging the tail that give the body a longer and heavier appearance. Flight is strong and steady with head and neck fully extended, and they fly in goose-like chevrons and slanting lines.

Common Crane *Grus grus*
NOT IN THE COLOUR PLATE
A tall gaunt grey bird, sufficiently like the Grey Heron for both to have been called 'crane' in the past, confusing old records. It has a bare red nape to a white-cheeked black head, and long curled feathers bunched up like a bustle that droop over the tail. The sonorous rolling and bugling calls and the extravagantly awkward dances of the paired birds are instantly recognisable.

It was certainly a British bird in the past. It nests across a broad temperate and boreal range that would in the past have included Britain and northern France, the birds probably migrating south in winter. It breeds in wet grasslands, swamps and bogs, but winters on drier open ground including arable land and fallows, taking both small creatures and seeds. It has suffered from being large, edible and a good target for early hunters. Its feeding habits may have brought it into contact with farmers and made it more vulnerable than the long-legged water birds. It prefers to nest in scattered pairs, on the ground on small island sites, and is intolerant of human disturbance. With such problems it retreated in the face of human advance.

Since it must also have been a regular migrant, old records and finds of adult bones are difficult to evaluate. Good records of its nesting consist of an incompletely ossified bone from the Iron Age lake settlement at Glastonbury in Somerset, and bones of a half-grown chick from an Iron Age midden on Orkney. It is thought to have nested in Ireland possibly until the fourteenth century, and in the fens and swamps of England until about 1600. Subsequent records depend on the vagaries of weather during migration. Annually about twenty thousand birds move south from Scandinavia in autumn and back again in spring. Occasional birds from this passage stray to Britain, and in some recent autumns several hundred have exceptionally been drifted west by adverse winds and spent a few days in south-east England. Very recently a feral pair have survived in East Anglia and bred, without migrating, so we could probably still regain this species if we wished.

Common Crane

Rails

Rallidae

These are some of the smaller waterside birds, long-legged and low-profiled skulkers in swamps and shallow waters; often furtive and laterally-flattened to slip more easily between the stems of lush vegetation. Bills tend to be short and stout. The wings are rather rounded and short flights appear weak and fluttering, but, although not quickly airborne, once in the air they may make long sustained flights and the Corncrake is a long-distance migrant. Tails are short and partly concealed in coverts, but tend to be frequently jerked erect, and undertail coverts are often patterned to form a conspicuous signal.

The behaviour is often furtive, but in compensation their calls tend to be loud, although abrupt and unmusical.

Five species regularly occur, all wide-ranging in temperate Eurasia. They occupy different, non-competing niches. The Spotted Crake is a small stubby-billed skulker in swampy vegetation, where the Water Rail is larger with a long, probing bill. The Corncrake occupies drier moist grassland. The Moorhen is a shore bird, both in and out of water, while the Coot is mainly aquatic near the shore in fresh waters.

Corncrake

Water Rail

Spotted Crake

JUVENILE   JUVENILE

ADULT   ADULT

Coot   Moorhen

D.M.H.

Water Rail *Rallus aquaticus*

A narrow, streaky bird that seems to be all neck and legs, briefly glimpsed sprinting for cover with head held low, or swimming across a patch of water like a Moorhen, but high in the front and low at the rear. The tail is flicked up in alarm or excitement. The long slender bill is ideal for probing after small creatures in vegetation or mud; but can be swung like a pickaxe, with the whole body and neck as shaft, to deal deadly blows to bigger prey such as frogs, fish or even small birds. It also eats various parts of plants. It is longer winged than other small rails and flies well if necessary.

It is not so much a shy bird as one unhappy in the open, preferring to slide and weave through thick vegetation. It prefers a close growth in or by slow-moving or still water where it can conceal itself, but in hard weather or on migration may temporarily occur by small open waters. Like most marsh rails it is more often heard than seen, being most active in the evening or at night. The sharp *kek* call is less obvious than the harsh squealing in a dying cadence used by a bird in territory. It is strongly and aggressively territorial. The nest is an untidy cup, hidden in thick vegetation, by or in water.

It occurs in marshy areas of warm boreal to warm-temperate zones across Eurasia, mostly migratory, but resident in south and western Europe. Birds winter in western Europe and south in the subtropical zone. The earliest British record is from the Cromerian Interglacial of the Middle Pleistocene and it was no doubt present in suitable periods from then onwards. Its postglacial population depended on marshland habitat and bearable winter conditions. It would certainly have increased as the climate became wetter after the Climatic Optimum of 7,000–5,000 years ago. It may have been rarer in periods of hard winters in the Little Ice Age of later centuries. It would also have begun to lose ground with fenland drainage in the seventeenth century; and this would have become worse in the eighteenth and nineteenth centuries, when drainage spread to affect not only large floodland but also small marshy areas of all kinds.

In the late nineteenth and early twentieth century a warmer climate may have helped it. In more recent times, flooded and overgrown gravel-pits and canals may also have helped to compensate for habitat loss, but there is some evidence of a general decrease since about the 1950s. It still breeds in scattered suitable localities in lowland Britain and Ireland, but is absent from most of Devon and north Wales, and in the Scottish Highlands is limited to a few eastern localities. Although occurring further north in 1968–73 it has not been present in Orkney in summer since 1968, or in Caithness or Sutherland since 1973. Its general winter distribution is similar to that in summer but more scattered, with birds more numerous in the south, scarcer in the north. The breeding population of the British Isles in the mid 1980s was estimated at 2,000–4,000 pairs, more than 1,000 of these in Ireland. Although there is some local movement in hard weather, British birds do not appear to migrate, and there is a winter influx from northern and eastern Europe so that numbers will then be larger.

Corncrake *Crex crex*

This species is best known to British ornithologists for not being present, the rapid contraction of its range in the last century providing a model demonstration of the way in which human activity may inadvertently affect a bird species. It is a summer visitor to moist grassland or mixed herbage, and to young cereal crops. It gets its name from the incessantly repeated, harsh rasping call that may be heard by night and day in the early breeding season. It is more visible when shorter grass or crops may not wholly conceal it, as it creeps along with head held low, while when it calls it stretches up its head with open bill. It can fly strongly but is reluctant to demonstrate it, and if alarmed tends to rush off through the grass more like a rat than bird. The nest is hidden on the ground among grass.

The general breeding distribution is through the warm boreal and temperate zone of Eurasia east to the Baikal region, and it is wholly migratory, wintering in southern Africa. There seem to be no definite British records of it before the very early Holocene in south Wales, although there is evidence of a probably migratory individual in East Africa in the Pliocene period about two million years ago. Originally it must have inhabited the grassy borders of marshland, and must have increased enormously as woodland was cleared and as hay was grown for cattle. In Britain its numbers probably reached a peak in the nineteenth century, when horses were still the major form of transport and extensive hay cultivation was necessary.

In the latter part of the nineteenth century, there was evidence of a decrease in south-east England, and parts of east and central Scotland. By the early 1900s this had also become apparent in eastern Ireland, and losses continued in south-east England until by 1914 it was ceasing to breed regularly in many areas east of a line from Lincolnshire to Somerset, and decreasing west of this.

It had gone from most of southern and eastern England by 1950, hanging on in the Hampshire and Oxfordshire basins and in south Yorkshire until the 1950s, and in Cornwall, south Wales, the Welsh border and County Durham until the 1960s. The Somerset Levels did not lose their regular breeders until the 1970s when they disappeared from the rest of England and Wales leaving only a few along the Scottish border. Such losses may not immediately be apparent, for whereas a resident species might disappear completely, migrants are never wholly discouraged and a few widely dispersed and sporadic occurrences may continue in areas from which regular populations have been lost.

By 1978 there were only 12 birds heard south of the border. The main population, some 700, were on the west Scottish coast and islands, and on Orkney. In 1972 the British population was estimated at about 2,640 pairs with 4,000 more in Ireland. In 1978 the figures were 730 pairs in Britain, 1,500 in Ireland. Numbers are still falling.

The original reason appeared to be the introduction of mechanised grass-cutting instead of the scythe, and cutting at a slightly earlier time in the season, destroying both nests and young. Telephone wires and cables were suggested as a hazard to migration. Further mechanisation, seeded ley grasslands with fewer weeds and insects and earlier cutting, and silage with very early and repeated cutting increased the problem, as did spraying. Even in refuge areas, with loss of habitat variety, birds were forced into unsuitable grassland and crops, with poor breeding results. Finally it seems that even with 'safe' populations, climatic changes and drought in

Africa may also be playing a part. At present, the residual Corncrake population of the British Isles, a significant and substantial part of a disappearing Western European population, continues to shrink.

Spotted Crake *Porzana porzana*

This small, short-billed rail of swampy places is so secretive that its status has always been in doubt. It inhabits sedges and grasses in swampy sites, keeping mainly within the low vegetation, but venturing out to feed on more open margins, rapidly retreating when disturbed with tail cocked and pale buff coverts showing. It walks slowly and deliberately, and runs with head held low. It is rarely seen and the repeated *h'wit* 'whiplash' song of the male is the usual indication of its presence. The nest is concealed in vegetation and rarely found.

It is a migrant breeding in warm boreal and temperate zones of western Eurasia, wintering in tropical zones. Britain is at the margin of its range and like many summer migrants its occurrences are sporadic, scattered and unpredictable. Surprisingly for such an apparently scarce bird it has been recorded from eastern England in the Pleistocene, in the Ipswichian Interglacial, and at the end of the last glaciation or in the early Holocene in north Kent. There is no early information about it, but it is thought to have been more common in past centuries. It declined in the nineteenth century with the extensive drainage that occurred; but seems to have been breeding regularly in some eastern counties of England in the early part of the present century.

However, since then records of apparent breedings have become rare and scattered. It was present more frequently and thought to be breeding between 1923 and 1937 in a number of areas in England and Wales. Numbers decreased again, but it was said not to be rare on the Norfolk Broads in the late 1940s, while numbers bred in some East Anglican coastal marshes in the early 1950s after the sea flooding. The 1968–72 B.T.O. Atlas survey showed scattered occurrences in the south, midlands, mid-Wales, Lancashire, south-west Scotland and the east and north-west Highlands; the Highland occurrences being correlated with an increase in the Swedish population. From 1976 to 1983, records were from east and south-east England with a possible gradual increase, varying from 2–12 singing males at up to six sites; and there was one in Argyll in 1982.

Moorhen *Gallinula chloropus*

A waterside rail and as the name implies a green-legged little hen; long-legged, with the short bill of a general-purpose feeder. The white lateral patches under the cocked tail shown in retreat are a signal; and, when raised and spread, the black-and-white pattern is a territorial threat, two birds often confronting back to back and peering suspiciously behind with lowered heads. Although not obviously modified for it, the Moorhen swims well if jerkily, taking plants and insects at the surface. Preferring water margins or swamps, it seems to manage with a tiny pool, mere puddle, or ditch. It is alert and furtive and given a little cover hides well, can climb into trees, or take refuge under water and just raise its bill at intervals to breathe. However, in suitable circumstances it may become as tame as a park pond duck.

With its relatively simple needs, it has an almost cosmopolitan distribution. It occurred in Britain in warmer interglacials from at least the Cromerian onwards. Its present-day pattern of distribution in the British Isles is like that of the Coot, but denser and more uniform. It avoids the clear, fast-flowing streams of hill areas and is absent from much of north and north-west Scotland, and scattered high hill areas of western Britain and Ireland, but is otherwise present from the Channel Islands to the Outer Hebrides and Shetlands.

A sedentary bird, it suffers from hard winters when water and soil surface freeze, but manages to maintain its numbers. In the colder fourteenth to nineteenth centuries, it was less successful in the north, but increased in Scotland in the warmer decades of the earlier half of this century, and had begun to breed in Shetland in 1890. It may have decreased a little in recent colder times. Its present population is about 300,000 pairs in summer and probably over a million in winter.

Coot *Fulica atra*

A squat, almost tail-less duck-sized rail of open waters. The strong legs, set well back on the body, have lobed toes to aid in swimming on and under water. Diving in water of up to several metres in depth, it brings water plants to the surface, breaking them up with the stout bill. The white-breasted querulous-voiced young are fed in similar fashion. It nests in shallow water near the water's edge, and may come to the land to graze. It is widely successful, using open waters, usually of more than a hectare in extent, provided that they are warm enough to produce vegetation. In breeding it is highly territorial; threatening, chasing and fighting with sharp metallic calls; but at other times birds may gather in flocks, sometimes in hundreds.

It occurs generally from warm boreal to warm-temperate zones of Eurasia and south to Australasia, migrant in much of its northern range, but resident in mainland Europe and the British Isles. It occurred during the British Pleistocene in the Ipswichian Interglacial and subsequently, widespread, but limited by its need for open water to lakes, slow rivers, lagoons and estuaries. Although widespread it would have lost ground in the colder fourteenth to nineteenth centuries, but it extended its range and increased in numbers in Scotland in the late nineteenth and early twentieth centuries, in response to warmer conditions.

More recently it was helped in its coverage by the increase in reservoirs, ornamental waters and gravel-pits, more particularly in southern England. At present it is more sparsely distributed in the west, and absent from most of north-west Scotland. Superficially this absence appears to be linked with areas of mountains and high ground, but the cause is more likely to be an absence of suitable vegetation in the waters. It is forced to move if waters freeze for long, and shift southwards, or to coastal areas, and resident birds are joined in winter by some from other countries around the North Sea. In recent years it has spread into Cornwall, but ceased to breed in Shetland in the mid 1950s, and decreased in Orkney. It may have undergone some general decrease in recent cooler decades. Its population in the mid 1980s might be up to 100,000 birds in summer, but twice that number in winter, when there is the influx of continental birds.

Bustards
Otididae

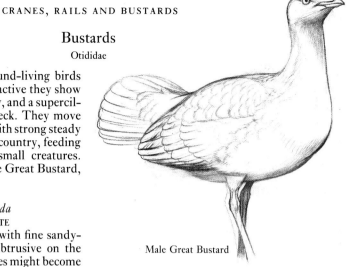

These are large to medium-sized ground-living birds resembling typical game-birds. When active they show longish legs, a body carried horizontally, and a superciliously-tilted head on a long upright neck. They move with a deliberate striding walk and fly with strong steady wing-beats. They inhabit open grassy, country, feeding on seeds, plants, insects and other small creatures. There was only one British species, the Great Bustard, now extinct in Britain.

Great Bustard *Otis tarda*
NOT IN THE COLOUR PLATE

A turkey-sized bird, grey-necked and with fine sandy-mottled body camouflage. Fairly unobtrusive on the ground apart from size, springtime males might become conspicuous by erupting into an extravagant display of white wings and swollen neck. In strong, deliberate flight the wings are conspicuously white. It is a bird of open steppe-type grassland, accomodating to open undulating areas of cultivation and grazing land, and preferring to see and avoid predators from a long way off. Its general range was right across the temperate to warm temperate grassland of Eurasia, with some dispersive movement in hard weather. Through Europe it must have benefitted in the historic past, when woodland was cleared for pasture and cultivation.

Its earliest British records are from south Wales and Cheddar in the early Holocene. Its distribution seems to have been linked with drier heaths and grasslands of

Male Great Bustard

sandy areas and downland. It was present in south-east Scotland until some time before 1526, possibly a relic of the earlier warmer period. In England its main stronghold was in the south-east. Vulnerable because of its size and edibility, needing large open spaces, intolerant of much disturbance when nesting, it nevertheless lasted until the nineteenth century. It was probably finally destroyed because man had become a predator that was able to kill from a distance at which the bird had previously been safe. It last nested, in East Anglia, in 1832. Its requirements are not easily provided in a limited space, and attempts at re-introduction through captive or controlled breeding have so far proved unsuccessful.

PLATE NINETEEN

Waders or Shorebirds, Skuas, Gulls, Terns, Auks
CHARADRIIFORMES

This is a large and varied order of birds, usually associated with the margins of water. Leg length and bill shape vary considerably. They nest on the ground or on rock ledges, with little or no nest material. The young are downy and often independent. Representatives of a number of families occur in Britain: Plovers, Charadriidae; Typical Waders, Scolopacidae; Avocets, Recurvirostridae; Oystercatchers, Haematopididae; Stone Curlews, Burhinidae; Phalaropes, Phalaropidae; Skuas, Stercorariidae; Gulls, Laridae; Terns, Sternidae; and Auks, Alcidae.

Plovers
Charadriidae

A widespread family of waders, living and feeding in large open areas, bare or with very short vegetation that does not impede their fast running gait. The bill is short, with a tapering tip, and the food consists of visible items snatched from the surface with the very typical sudden tilt of head and body. The head is large and rounded, with large eyes enabling it to feed at dusk or at night. The wings are long, usually tapering, and the flight is fast and strong with a typical blunt-headed profile. Legs are long and short-toed. The nest is a bare or sparsely lined scrape on open ground, and the downy chicks are active soon after hatching.

There are seven species. The big Grey Plover is an Arctic bird wintering around the shores, and the Golden Plover a moorland-breeding subarctic species; while the Dotterel uses tundra-type mountain-tops; and the Lapwing the lowland meadows. Of the three sand-plovers, the Ringed Plover is a shorebird, the Little Ringed Plover breeds on inland shingles, and the Kentish Plover is a sandflat species.

Grey Plover *Pluvialis squatarola*
With us, this is a winter visitor. It is a solid, large wader, usually seen spaced out in individually-guarded feeding territories on mudflats or along the shoreline. In winter

WINTER

SUMMER

Grey Plover

WINTER

SUMMER

Little Ringed Plover

Kentish Plover

SUMMER

Golden Plover

WINTER

Ringed Plover

WINTER

SUMMER

SUMMER SOUTHERN RACE

D. M. HENRY

it is an ash-grey and white bird, the black armpit-patches conspicuous on the white plumage in flight. One is fortunate to see it in spring plumage before it leaves for the breeding ground. As with other arctic waders, the black belly plays an important part in its slow and ritualised trilling song flight over its breeding territory. What we hear in winter is the surprisingly human-sounding call note, a plaintive whitled *plee-uu-wee*.

It breeds in the drier ridges of the Arctic tundra, being circumpolar in distribution. It might possibly have bred here in cold Pleistocene periods. Its earliest British records appear to be from Derbyshire in the last glaciation, and possibly from the same period in Sutherlandshire. It is also known from south Wales in the early Holocene, and from the south-east in Roman times. The nearest breeding grounds are in western Siberia, and birds from this region winter around the British Isles. Breeding seasons are short in high latitudes, and by August about 5,000 moulting and migrating birds may already be present in the Wash, which is an important wintering area. Juveniles arrive later. There are movements between areas, and from mainland Europe to Britain and back during the winter period, with birds leaving again in April and May, and a few individuals summering in the north.

The numbers present vary according to the breeding success on the tundra. Numbers had risen steadily in the 1970s and there has been a more recent increase in Scotland. The birds occur around the coasts, wherever there are extensive sands and muds exposed at low tide. They are absent from most of western and northern Scotland, and north-west Ireland. The total wintering population is about 20,000 birds, about one-third of the European wintering population, with the greatest number for any locality on the Wash.

Golden Plover *Pluvialis apricaria*

As a breeding bird this is a moorland plover. In winter it becomes a quiet bird scattered over lowland grass or ploughland, only betraying itself by the plaintive musical *tlui* call-note. In flight small flocks of plain-coloured blunt-headed birds swish over in direct and rapid flight. On its breeding moors it may be equally inconspicuous except for its call note, its gold-spangled plumage providing excellent camouflage. The blackness of face and belly in breeding birds increases as one moves northwards, and is most intense in arctic regions.

Its general breeding distribution is through arctic and subarctic zones of western Eurasia, including Iceland and east Greenland; and on high ground around the Baltic and in the British Isles. It winters in western Europe and from the western Mediterranean to the south Caspian region. Its earliest records in Pleistocene Britain are from south Wales in the last, Ipswichian, interglacial, and from Derbyshire in the last glaciation. It is likely to have bred extensively in earlier cooler periods. Its range would have contracted onto higher ground in southern Britain as the Holocene climate warmed. Its typical breeding habitat is now on moorland at about 240–600 metres in altitude, but in north-west Britain such habitats, and the breeding grounds, approach sea-level. Like other plovers it needs very short vegetation for easy movement and prefers level, exposed areas with very stunted vegetation, or

boggy, burnt-over or well-grazed places. It would have lost ground at lower levels with the early spread of trees. However, it would have increased as tree clearances created moorland, and the colder climate between the fourteenth to nineteenth centuries may have suited it. It is likely to have been at a population peak after maximum tree clearing from high ground, and when extensive grazing of upland areas and regular management and burning of moors for sheep and grouse occurred. This would have been in the mid nineteenth century.

In the late nineteenth century and early half of the present century, numbers began to decrease in Britain and the rest of Europe, and to do so, at the southern edge of its range, in a way that suggested a response to climate. However, the decline seems to have continued into the recent cooler period in some areas, and in others populations have remained unchanged, so other factors may be involved. Obvious possibilities are re-afforestation of breeding areas, changes of use and management of moorland causing changes in vegetation, and perhaps increased predation and disturbance. It disappeared from Dartmoor in the 1850s, and from Exmoor, Bodmin Moor and the Mendips where it had intermittently bred in about the early 1900s. The only position of movement has been a return of small numbers to Dartmoor since 1950. Distribution and numbers have contracted in south Wales where it now tends to breed at higher altitudes. It has been lost from some parts of Lakeland, and from south-west Ireland.

Breeding distribution is now on high ground west of a line from mid Yorkshire to east Devon in Britain; in extreme north-west Ireland, and on Orkney and Shetland. There are about 30,500 pairs. After breeding it shifts to lowland areas, preferring grass and arable land. It will feed on tidal mudflats, but more reluctantly than on other waters, and in some regions may use such areas for roosting. Winter distribution is general throughout lowland areas, native birds being joined by others from Iceland, Scandinavia and Siberia. The winter population is estimated at about 600,000 birds, half of them in Ireland.

Kentish Plover *Charadrius alexandrinus*

Smallest and palest of the sandplovers, it prefers long level stretches of sand, mud or fine stones, and may pass unnoticed in such large spaces until one is suddenly seen scudding across the surface, like a ball of feathers blown by the wind. It is long-legged and plump-looking, with a very white breast that may puff up in threat, and inconspicuous dark face markings. In its fast low flight it shows a white wing-stripe and white outer tail feathers. It has a *wit* call note, and a song trill that is used when it circles low over its territory in slow, tilting 'butterfly' display flight. The nest is just a small hollow in the sand.

It has an almost cosmopolitan distribution, not only on shores, but on the borders of shallow saline inland waters lacking surface vegetation. Its Eurasian distribution is across the warm-temperate region, with an extension up the mild Atlantic coast as far as Denmark. North of Biscay it is a summer visitor. The south coast of Britain is on the north-west margin of its distribution.

There is little evidence of its past status in Britain, and information appears to date from the beginning of the nineteenth century. It bred in Kent, mainly on the shingles of Dungeness, and in East Sussex. In the early part of the twentieth century there were up to 40 pairs breeding on the south coast. Numbers fell in the 1920s. By the 1930s and 1940s there were only sporadic breedings in Kent. In East Sussex, breeding was more rare and had ceased in 1923, but several pairs bred in 1949–56. There was also a single breeding in Suffolk in 1952. Now it is a vagrant visitor to the east and south coasts of Britain. It continued to breed in the Channel Islands until about the mid 1970s. It is decreasing along all parts of the north-west European coast, and although there might be some correlation with trends towards a cooler climate, it is more likely that in all areas it has suffered from the vastly increased use and exploitation of sandy areas and beaches in the present century.

Little Ringed Plover *Charadrius dubius*

This is the gravel-pit plover of inland Britain, having adapted to the shores of such artificial sites from the river shingle and sandspits of the continent. It is confusing like a Ringed Plover but a little smaller, and the extra white bordering on the head and yellow-rimmed eye give it a more shrewish look. Its voice betrays it too. In moments of alarm, instead of the soft anxious *toolee* of the Ringed Plover, there is a sharper and more penetrating *pee-u*, and it has a repeated yipping note of parental anxiety. Its ability to use man-modified sites, not only gravel-pits but industrial sites and tips, sewage works and reservoir margins, is aided by a greater tolerance of human presence than is displayed by most plovers. The bold patterns of head and breast, and patterned tail are displayed in a complex language of signal postures and used in display. It has the typical erratic flight performed over its territory to the accompaniment of a repetitive *cree-ah, cree-ah, . . .* call. The nest is just a shallow scrape that the young leave in typical fashion as soon as the down is dry.

It has a wide distribution through Eurasia, from boreal to subtropical zones, and into the oriental region. Through most of this range it is migratory, wintering mainly in the tropical zone, but with scattered winter sites from the Mediterranean eastwards. Until recent times, its status in Britain was that of a rare vagrant. It was present on the continental mainland and had shown some increase and westward spread in the 1930s.

In 1938 a single pair nested at Tring Reservoir in Hertfordshire. In 1944 it nested in Hertfordshire and Middlesex; and in the next three years spread in the London Basin and nested in central Yorkshire. By the end of the 1940s it had spread through the Thames Valley and Oxfordshire, and into Essex and Suffolk, and Kent and Sussex. By the mid 1950s, southern and northern nestings were joined by a spread to Hampshire, Gloucestershire and the south midlands, Lincolnshire, and from west Yorkshire down to Staffordshire. By 1960 it had included the rest of the midlands and east Yorkshire, with possibly its greatest range. In the early 1960s it was into Norfolk and north Yorkshire, but had begun to breed less regularly in Hampshire, Sussex, the eastern half of East Anglia, and the Severn Valley. There were then about 170–200 pairs. By 1973 there were about 470 pairs in a range relatively unchanged for about ten years, except for a single Scottish breeding in Lanarkshire in 1968. This species is almost wholly associated in Britain with man-made breeding sites, and it has been suggested that this might represent a limiting factor for its further spread.

Ringed Plover *Charadrius hiaticula*

This is the small, worried wader that tends to suddenly appear on an apparently empty beach, making the conscientious holiday-maker almost scared to lower a foot, for fear of crushing a nest that is too well camouflaged. It is small, squat and rounded, the dark eyes almost hidden in the bridled head patterns. In spite of this bold patterning, it is not conspicuous. The dark face-patch provides false countershading that turns the bird's head and body into two rounded pebbles that are lost on a shingle beach. Often it is only apparent when a previously inconspicuous bird, sprinting along the beach, takes flight with the soft *toolee* call and a flash of a long white wing-stripe. It is a widespread inhabitant of our coasts and estuaries, seemingly happy on mud, sand or rock, and beginning to shift inland to reservoirs and gravel-pits where it may come into conflict with the Little Ringed Plover. It has an advantage in being non-migratory and able to move in during winter, when it is a little duller in colour and lacks the bright orange bill of the breeding season.

It is much more sociable than other small plovers, and non-breeding birds will flock in high-tide roosts but may spread out and defend an area when feeding. Aggression is more apparent in the breeding season, with a great deal of chasing and song-flighting. The latter is the typical circling and tilting 'butterfly' flight with slow beats of spread wings, accompanied by a subdued yodelling *toweeoo-toweeoo-toweeoo* note rapidly repeated. Displaying birds show a range of crouching and upright postures that make the most of the black-and-white pattern. The nest is the usual bare scrape, with eggs so inconspicuous on a background of shingle that they are in danger from human feet. The downy young show the typical run-and-crouch in moments of danger, refusing to move again until they have the parental all-clear. Pairs may have a second brood in a season, and young may be moved to better feeding grounds, defended as a kind of mobile territory.

Its north-west European distribution is the converse of that of the Kentish Plover. It breeds in arctic and subarctic zones on the coast and on drier inland sites, extending south in the north-east Atlantic area, along the mountain range of Sweden and Norway, and on coasts south to the Baltic, southern North Sea and British Isles. It is migrant to western Europe, Africa and the Arabian coasts. Britain is on the southernmost edge of its breeding range. From early evidence, it may have been present in south-west England in the Middle Pleistocene, and in Derbyshire in the last glaciation. Its main distribution is almost entirely coastal, on bare shores regarded as being of little value in the past.

Its population is likely to have been fairly stable, responding to climatic conditions, but in view of its present distribution, possibly doing better in cooler conditions. Numbers were probably fairly steady until the late nineteenth century, when travel to the coast became fashionable. At first this might only affect areas near towns, but by the 1920s and 1930s, this had become a significant form of disturbance, with beach huts, caravan sites and similar innovations contributing to it. Decreases began, and continued on many parts of the coast, with some respite during the 1939–45 war.

The species had disappeared from Cornwall and much of Devon by the end of the 1960s. However, it had increased generally in places where it was protected. In parts of the south it also began to breed on safer inland fields near the coast, and enclosed commercial sites, and was also nesting increasingly on reservoirs, gravel-pits and similar sites. In northern England and parts of Scotland, birds have tended to move inland up rivers and use natural shingle banks. However, the sum of these non-coastal sites account for less than 10% of the breeding pairs. There had long been an inland population around waters on the thin dry heathland of the Norfolk Brecklands, with up to 400 pairs in the 1920s, but increasing forestry and agriculture have reduced them to a tiny remnant. In Scotland there is a large and nationally important population breeding on the shell-sand grassy areas, the machairs, of the western islands, but these are threatened by proposals for large-scale agricultural improvement schemes.

There seems to have been evidence of some overall decrease with further potential threats, and serious loss in some areas, but these have tended to be masked by local variations. At present the Ringed Plover breeds around most of the coasts of the British Isles, with the exception of most of the south-west peninsula and Pembrokeshire, and it is scattered on inland sites through the north and east. Numbers have been estimated at about 9,000 breeding pairs. In winter it is mainly coastal and more widely dispersed. At that time there is some westward shift, and also an incursion of birds from the continent, while passage migrants that pass through include birds from Greenland, Iceland and Scandinavia. There appears to be a winter presence of about 35,000 birds, with the largest concentration in the Hebrides.

PLATE TWENTY

Dotterel *Eudromias morinellus*

This is our mountain plover, a bird of the tundra-type conditions of the high tops, famed for its isolation and the tameness that it engenders. It shares with the phalaropes the role change in which the female is the bigger, brighter and more belligerent bird. Having laid a clutch of eggs, she leaves the male to incubate them and tend the young. It is at times polygynous, with the female laying clutches for two males to rear. In display the bold frontal pattern and black belly is emphasised by birds standing upright with belly feathers puffed out. It is a rather quiet species and the calls are mostly soft repeated *pweet* or *pit* notes, but soft twittering calls may be used in display and the female has a display flight with shallow, winnowing wing-beats and a repetitive *peep* call.

It breeds on high areas of mountains, preferring high plateaux and level ridges, where lack of soil and adverse climate reduce vegetation to a low cover of dwarfed heather, grass, moss and lichen, often with areas of bare rock and grit. It feeds on insects, and some plant material. It is necessarily a migrant, coming in late May, leaving in late August. Migrants tend to pause on seemingly traditional lowland areas of short heath or grassland. In late summer it moults into a duller, paler buff winter plumage, with only the whitish breast-band and eye-stripe as faint reminders of the breeding pattern. There is no wing-stripe, but the wings retain their margined pattern.

The general breeding distribution is arctic and arctic-alpine, with a range through the Arctic of Eurasia, and isolate populations in mountains in Britain, parts of southern Europe and Central Asia. It winters in North Africa and Arabia. An unexpected deviation has been the nesting on fields of the newly-drained polder area of the Netherlands in the 1960s. The land is below sea-level, but might reflect local climatic conditions or the physical appearance of the area.

There seem to be no early records of it in Britain, and James Fisher quoted 1450 as the earliest date that it is mentioned. With its specialised breeding habitat, it is unlikely to have been affected much by early human activity. It is more responsive to climate, and numbers may have been fewer in the Climatic Optimum around 5,000 years ago, increasing in the Little Ice Age between the fourteenth and nineteenth centuries. There is little information on breeding birds, but those on spring passage often rest in East Anglia and as far up as Lincolnshire, in south Wales, and on the Solway marshes. In earlier periods up to the first half of the nineteenth century, they were said to occur in hundreds. In the seventeenth century it was netted in numbers by professional wildfowlers in Norfolk, and from the latter part of the eighteenth century onwards, the feathers were in demand for fishing flies. In the subsequent hundred years, it suffered from shooting of passage birds, and skin- and egg-collecting on the breeding grounds. It was suggested that these factors had brought about a major decline, but the overall evidence suggests that the Dotterel has responded to the major climatic fluctuations.

It bred on suitable high ground in the Scottish highlands and may have nested in Sutherlandshire and in south-west Scotland although this is not proven. In England it bred on similar sites in Lakeland and Cumbria, and in the adjacent Pennines, with single records from Yorkshire in 1895 and 1905, and one from County Durham between 1910 and 1926. It also nested on Cheviot in 1911 and 1912. It had begun to decrease by the 1880s and markedly so by 1900. After 1927 it ceased to nest annually in northern England, with just odd single nests in the next thirty years; while in Scotland it has shown a similar decrease and was limited to the main highland region.

The increase began in the 1950s with nests being found more frequently in northern England from 1959 onwards. In Scotland numbers increased and nests were found in Sutherlandshire in 1967, and in the south-west in Kirkcudbrightshire in 1967 and Selkirk/Peebles in 1970. It was suspected of nesting in north Wales in the 1950s and a nest was found in 1969. As with most birds on the margins of normal distribution, numbers will continue to vary. The most active threat appears to be the increased disturbance of high mountains for human

Common Snipe

SUMMER FEMALE
Dotterel

SUMMER MALE
Lapwing

Jack Snipe

Woodcock

D.M. HENRY.

recreation, and an encouragement of scavenging crows and gulls. With a thinly scattered species, numbers are difficult to estimate. In the 1940s to 1960s, the Cairngorm population was estimated at 20–25 pairs. In the early 1970s it was about 50 plus, when the total British population was estimated at 60–80 pairs. In the mid 1980s the Scottish population was estimated at 100–150 pairs.

Lapwing *Vanellus vanellus*

We are fortunate in that the loveliest of our plovers is the commonest: a bird of grassy moors, waterside, pastures and ploughland, appearing as scattered pied figures in spring, or low spreading flocks circling overhead in autumn and winter. Its green glossy back helps it hide when it crouches or broods, with spiky crest slid back. The broad, black-tipped wings and contrasting pattern come into play when it displays in a crazy twisting and tumbling flight over its territory, with thrumming wings and a wild *whullock-weep-weep* call. The *peewit* cry that gives it its other common name is usually heard at moments of mild anxiety, and birds in winter flocks have a nagging, mournful-sounding *peez* note. In spring it uses the pied head and breast pattern in displays, and the male makes the initial nest hollow by literally bowing and scraping and showing off the carroty-red undertail-coverts.

For preference it nests – and prefers to feed – on very short turf or herbage that does not impede rapid running. The food is mostly invertebrates taken from the surface, and the large eyes enable the birds to feed by night as well as day. The nest is a slight hollow, lined with plant stems, often on bare ground. The young need patches of moist grassland or small boggy areas, and are led to these from drier sites, breeding success partly depending on the availability of such places. It is a strong and skilful flier, the large floppy wings giving an unexpected casual agility.

Its general breeding distribution is across boreal and temperate Eurasia where open grassland is present, and it winters in warm-temperate to subtropical zones; but it is resident in the Mediterranean and western Europe, and in the British Isles. Its earliest record in Britain is towards the end of the last glaciation. With its need for open sites and short vegetation, it might have done well in the transitional period, but numbers would have been low in the period of maximum woodland, although they would have benefitted with the clearance of trees, and the spread of moorland, rough grazing and pasture. In the Bronze Age it certainly occurred in coastal and fen areas.

Numbers would have continued to rise over the centuries, although it was hunted for food and its eggs were gathered. The cooler centuries of the Little Ice Age may have kept it below its potential maximum. In the latter half of the nineteenth century and into the present century, numbers in the British Isles decreased, apparently owing to changes in agriculture, increasing cultivation, and systematic egg-cropping. This masked an increase which occurred with the warming climate of the first half of this century. The increase was more obvious in less intensively cultivated regions such as Scotland and the northern isles, with a colonisation of Shetland from about 1930 onwards. A protection Act of 1926 arrested the decline and allowed some increase in England.

From the 1940s onwards, there was a marked overall decrease, probably due to a combination of cooler climate, changing farming practice with increasing arable, more frequent machine cultivation and chemical spraying. It is still a widespread breeder but scanty on the south-west of England, north-west Scotland, and south-west Ireland. Numbers are estimated at over 200,000 pairs for the British Isles, but may be falling rapidly for, like other grassland waders, monitored populations have shown a 30% decrease between 1984 and 1986.

In winter it is absent from mountains and hilly areas, but widespread through lowland, preferring grassland but also on arable land, saltmarsh and mudflats. The largest numbers are in southern and central England, and in Ireland. There is immigration from the continent from June onwards, which is at its height in early winter, and some northern British birds may move to Ireland. Heavy frost and snow may cause considerable local movements and high losses. The winter population of the British Isles is well over a million birds.

Typical Waders

Scolopacidae

These are waterside birds with thin bills and long thin legs. Active, nervous and fast-flying species nest mainly in cooler regions, migrating in winter. It comprises a number of subgroups that have adapted in various ways to their environment.

Snipe and Woodcock

Gallinagininae and Scolopacinae

Bills are often long among the waders, and especially long in the snipe. The bill is plunged into mud or soft damp soil and the prey, mainly worms, are detected by the nerves that extend to the bill-tip. Since these birds do not rely on sight, they can feed at night. The eyes are large and set high at the sides of the head to give a wide all-round view of the approach of potential predators. They are birds of marsh and woodland, relying on cryptic plumage to hide them, crouching and flying up suddenly at the last moment. The downy young are fed at first by the parents.

Of the three species that occur regularly in Britain, the Jack Snipe is a winter visitor to small swampy inland sites. Both Common Snipe and Woodcock are widespread residents, the first in open freshwater sites, the other in woodland and woodland borders with wet areas.

Common Snipe *Gallinago gallinago*
A secretive prober of inland marshy places, from damp
fields to blanket bog, it tends to rest by day in long grass
or similar vegetation where the straw-coloured stripes
on its plumage help to hide it. When alarmed, it
crouches and suddenly rises with a harsh *skarrp* call in a
zig-zagging flight, then rising steeply. It may descend
equally rapidly, with a brief wing-flutter as it brakes and
settles. It feeds at evening and during the night in open,
wet or muddy places, probing deeply with what seems at
times an embarrassingly long bill, taking worms and
other small creatures. It will sometimes wade and probe.
It often occurs in small flocks but breeds in scattered
pairs. It shows a strong preference for open places, such
as wet pasture and moors, marshy edges of waters and
saltmarshes, and tolerates brackish water.

A male in territory uses a monotonous *chip-per chip-
per* call, but its main performance is a switchback song-
flight in which steep rises are alternated with downward
dives or short glides, tail spread so that the rush of air
through the outer pair of tail feathers produces a loud
bleating or whinnying sound. The flying bird tends to
perform in a large circle over the nesting area. The nest
is well-hidden in rushes or grass. The young, usually
four, are brought food by the adults at first, and the
parents later divide the brood between them.

It has a wide range through arctic to cool-temperate
zones in both northern and southern hemispheres.
Northern hemisphere birds are mostly migrant, wintering in subtropical to tropical zones, but resident in
western mainland Europe and the British Isles. It is
recorded from a warm interstadial of the last Pleistocene
glaciation in Derbyshire, and from the end of that
period in the south-west. It was probably widespread
for a long time. It may have benefitted from the clearing
of trees from wet areas, but suffered later from the
increase in drainage of land in recent centuries.

Because of its widespread distribution and secretive
nature, population trends are difficult to determine, and
much of the information is based on the numbers shot.
It appears to have decreased at the beginning of the
nineteenth century, possibly reaching its lowest point
for some centuries at this time. It increased again in the
latter part of the nineteenth century and first forty years
of this century, coinciding with the period of warmer
climate. However, this was also a period of agricultural
recession, with perhaps an increase in scattered, ill-
drained areas. It extended its local range, more effectively colonised the south, and colonised part of the
south Midlands where it had not been present.

Since the 1940s numbers have fallen again, especially
in southern England, possibly due to increasingly
efficient drainage of low-lying fields, destruction of
marginal vegetation, loss of ponds and spraying. It re-
colonised the Isle of Wight in 1967 after 48 years'
absence. It is still very widespread, if patchy in southern
Britain, with about 80,000 – 100,000 pairs estimated for
the British Isles in the mid 1970s. However, by 1982,
numbers in wet grassland were still falling, and snipe
were becoming unusual in these lowland habitats, with
a population in England and Wales about one third of
that previously estimated. Monitored populations have
fallen by nearly 30% between 1984 and 1986. In winter
it moves to lowland areas, shifting around if the weather
freezes hard. A large number of Baltic birds winter in
Britain, and north-west Scotland and Ireland have birds
from Iceland and the Faeroes. For the mid 1980s about
85,000 birds are estimated to be shot in winter from a
population of hundreds of thousands.

Jack Snipe *Lymnocryptes minimus*
This is the small snipe that rises reluctantly, silently and
usually solitarily from the grass and vegetation on the
side of a pond, ditch or small marsh. It flies low for a
short way and then drops down again. If it does call, the
note is shorter and weaker than that of the Common
Snipe. It has the shortest bill of all the snipe and is
therefore more shallow in its probing and takes much of
its food from the surface. On its breeding grounds it has
a switchback display flight with accompanying calls said
to be like the sound of a cantering horse; but in the
British Isles it is a winter visitor.

Its general range is in the boreal zone of Eurasia but
stops short in northern Sweden, with a small isolate
group in southern Sweden. However, it bred in
Germany and Poland in the 1920s and possibly earlier,
and in Poland again in 1977. A displaying bird occurred
in south-east England in 1984. It is migrant throughout
its range with a winter movement westwards to the
British Isles and south North Sea coasts; and southwards to the Mediterranean region and into subtropical
and tropical areas.

Winter birds usually occur singly in all kinds of
marshy, freshwater sites with vegetation tall enough to
provide cover, and occasionally on more exposed sites
when on passage. It feeds at evening and by night,
roosting by day hidden in vegetation and reluctant to
move. With such a furtive, thinly dispersed bird it is
difficult to estimate a winter population. It is claimed
that about 10,000 were being shot annually in the British
Isles in the early 1980s, and the number at present must
be much greater.

Woodcock *Scolopax rusticola*
This big and subtly-patterned woodland snipe is
perhaps the most atypical of the waders. It spends most
of the day resting in a dry woodland site with plenty of
clear open space just above ground level and preferably
some opening nearby. It squats among a carpet of dead
and decaying leaves, beautifully camouflaged, the large
eyes set high on the head giving a wide range of vision.
When disturbed it leaves suddenly with a whirr of
wings, either upwards or weaving among the tree-
trunks. In flight the stout, big-headed body and the
broad rounded wings give it an owl-like outline.

It feeds at intervals from dusk to dawn, either in the
woodland or damp places nearby. It eats invertebrates
and insects taken from the surface, or among leaf litter,
or by probing soft ground. It is secretive in most of its
behaviour, and resentful of disturbance. Breeding males
advertise their presence by a special 'roding' flight,
usually flying just about at tree-top level with a slow
wing-beat and a special double call with a low growl and
higher-pitched sneeze note. In these flights a female is
located, the male remaining with her for a few days until
nesting has started, then apparently roding again for
further mates. The nest is on the ground, hidden in low
vegetation such as bracken or brambles in woodland,
marshes, or more open country; often by a tree-trunk.
The young are led to suitable feeding areas, but may be
fed directly at first.

Its breeding range is through boreal and temperate

zones of Eurasia, resident in southern and western mainland Europe, and in the British Isles. Elsewhere it migrates to the west or to warm-temperate and sub-tropical zones. Its early presence in Britain would be linked with that of woodland. Its earliest record appears to be from fenland peat dating from the middle Holocene to Bronze Age; and it appears oddly frequently in Roman middens, suggesting selective hunting of it for food. It may not have suffered much for early woodland clearing, but in the eighteenth and nineteenth centuries when clearance was at its height the numbers had fallen considerably. Although it was widespread as a migrant and winter visitor, it does not appear to have bred regularly in the British Isles except in England until the early nineteenth century. During the nineteenth and early twentieth centuries it increased and spread through the British Isles as a breeding bird.

From the 1820s onwards it appears to have spread in Scotland, beginning in the north-east and east. It is still thin on the ground in the north-west and absent from the Outer Hebrides, Orkney and Shetland. It also spread to Wales and to Ireland, and consolidated its breeding distribution in England. It was probably helped by gamekeepers preventing disturbance of nesting pheasants, protection in the breeding season, and increase in plantations. Its distribution seems to have been fairly stable since the 1930s, with losses where tree-felling has occurred, and gains in areas of new plantations. Population estimates are mere guesswork, suggested at about 10,000–50,000 pairs.

In winter there is considerable immigration and resident birds appear to be fewer in upland areas. There may be a further westward shift in severe weather, with large numbers in Ireland and western Scotland. The immigrants are from Scandinavia and Siberia. Winter birds feed more actively during the day. Both on migration, and searching for frost-free ground in winter, they may occur in unlikely places. There is no good estimate of winter numbers but in the early 1980s about 200,000 were shot annually.

PLATE TWENTY-ONE

Godwits, Curlews and some Sandpipers

TRINGINAE

This subfamily embraces many of the typical waders, including most of the long-necked, long-billed, long-legged species. It comprises the godwits, *Limosa* species; curlews, *Numenius* species; 'shanks' and sandpipers, *Tringa* species; and Common Sandpiper, *Actitis* species. They breed through a whole range of inland habitats, but winter mostly on shore or estuaries.

Some of the species associated with partly forested regions often perch on trees, and raised nest-sites, such as the old nests of other birds, are sometimes used by the Wood Sandpiper and habitually by the Green Sandpiper. Bills tend to be long and slender but may be modified for specialised feeding.

Godwits and Curlews

Limosa and *Numenius* species

These are the biggest of the typical waders. The bills are long and thin in godwits, strongly decurved in curlews, and this is reflected in their different feeding habits when not on their breeding grounds. From each genus we have a pair of species, one bird more northerly than the other; the Black-tailed Godwit is a temperate-nesting bird, the Bar-tailed Godwit an arctic breeder, and the same is true of Common Curlew and Whimbrel.

Black-tailed Godwit *Limosa limosa*
This is mainly a wet-meadow wader, tall and upright with legs long enough for it to be happy in the taller grasses that would hamper a Lapwing. In some places, however, it uses the wet moorland and blanket bogs as well. In the ashy winter plumage or rufous head and breast of summer, it is a fairly uniform-looking bird, but in flight becomes suddenly pied with the bold black-and-white patterns of wings and tail.

On land it must pick and probe with the long straight bill, but this is seen to best advantage on passage and in winter when flocks feed on estuaries, floodland and shallow, inland waters. They wade out belly-deep into water deeper than that used by most waders, and then probe deeply with head and neck often wholly immersed, and looking rather hunchbacked. It is a sociable but squabbling species, birds sparring with noisy wickering calls, and at other times using a variety of short, nasal notes. Pairs breed in reasonable proximity on moist grassland, bogs or moors, the nest hidden in long grass. A displaying male may strut around a female with fluffed plumage and spread tail, or raise the quivering wings high above the back. It has a complex display flight, rising steeply, and tumbling and banking before plunging steeply downwards to land with wings held high. This is accompanied by a triple note at first, and then a repeated *crweetuu* call. The young are tended by both parents.

Its general breeding distribution is through the warmer boreal and temperate zones of Eurasia, wintering in warm-temperate to tropical zones south to Australasia. Some winter on the west coasts of Europe and in the British Isles. There is an early record of it from Somerset in the Windermere Interstadial towards the end of the last glaciation. It should have done well in the wetter climates of the later Holocene, and as tree-clearing produced more grassland. It would have flourished on the edge of marsh, fen and bog and on

SUMMER   WINTER

Black-tailed Godwit

Bar-tailed Godwit

SUMMER

WINTER

Whimbrel

Common Curlew

D.M.HENRY

lowland permanent pastures, but is large enough to have been shot for food.

By the early nineteenth century, it was suffering from the combined effect of drainage, increased management of meadows, shooting and the taking of eggs. It decreased rapidly and was widely lost by the mid nineteenth century. It does not seem to have been recorded as breeding in Wales, Scotland or Ireland in earlier times, and evidence of breeding was confined to the eastern half of England. By 1830 it had ceased breeding in Yorkshire, Huntingdonshire, and Suffolk, but may have bred in 1847 in Cambridgeshire, 1857 in Norfolk and 1885 in Lincolnshire. After that it was not known to breed for the next fifty years.

There were four scattered breedings between 1939 and 1942, and from the early 1940s the numbers visiting Britain increased considerably. It is suggested that there had been a very considerable increase in the numbers breeding in Iceland during the warmer first half of the present century, and many of the increasing number of wintering birds in the British Isles appeared to originate from this source. In Britain these winterers rose from about 100 in the 1930s to about 4,000 in the 1970s. Recent northern and western breeding in Britain may also originate from this population which is regarded as subspecifically distinct, but south-eastern birds appear to originate from the continent. Breeding began to occur again, usually in wet, tussocky meadow sites. In the overflow washes of the Cambridge Ouse, breeding has occurred since 1952 rising from two or three pairs to fifty at times. In the mid 1980s, it bred as well in Kent, Essex, Suffolk, Norfolk, Somerset, Lancashire and Cumbria. In Scotland it bred in 1946 in Caithness, in Orkney in 1957 and 1975 and in Shetland from 1949 onwards. There were one or two breeding in south-west Scotland in 1972 and later, and in south-east Scotland between 1964 and 1977. It may also be breeding at several sites in Ireland. The present breeding population may be 50–80 pairs but productivity has been poor in the mid 1980s.

Wintering birds occur mainly in a few muddy estuarine areas of the southern half of Britain, and in greater numbers in the southern two-thirds of Ireland. They are scarce in both Scotland and Wales. There is a large winter influx of Icelandic birds. Following the build-up between the 1930s to 1970s, there was a drop in British wintering birds to about one-fifth in the later 1970s, but there has been some recovery since. The combined total is about 12,000–15,000 of which about two-thirds winter in Ireland.

Bar-tailed Godwit *Limosa lapponica*

A little smaller than the Black-tailed Godwit, and with a very slightly upcurved bill, this is a passage and winter visitor to our shores. With birds newly arrived or approaching spring migration, one may have a chance of seeing the rufous-bronze plumage colour, vivid when seen in sunshine on a muddy estuary. More often it is in streaky brown winter plumage, lacking bold marking and with just a white rump and barred tail. It usually occurs in small flocks on the tide's edge, in estuaries or sheltered sandy and muddy bays. It feeds in the water, wading and probing in mud and sand for worms, and sometimes immersing head and neck like the Black-tailed Godwit. At other times, it may feed on the surface of tideline mud. It flies rapidly and skilfully, and flocks are capable of fast manoeuvres like those of smaller waders, including a downward scatter in fast whiffling flight when landing. It is not particularly noisy, but birds calling to each other in flocks use a low abrupt *kirruck* call and various small short yapping notes.

Its breeding range is across the arctic tundras of Eurasia, with winter migration to coasts as far as Australasia and southern Africa; some move westwards to western Europe and the British Isles. There is little evidence of its earlier status in Britain, and as a coastal winter visitor it is unlikely to have suffered from land-use changes, although it was liable to be shot for food. Numbers appear to have been climatically controlled, and to fluctuate with arctic breeding success. Birds assemble to moult in the Wash and Ribble Estuary in late summer and autumn, and are joined by others that have come via the Waddenzee. Winter total may relate to conditions on the eastern side of the southern North Sea. In winter the British Isles may support about 60,000 birds, about 65% of the western European winter total.

Whimbrel *Numenius phaeopus*

This is the smaller curlew of the north, the 'Seven-whistler', often overlooked until it gives the rapidly-repeated whistling note in a tittering trill. For most of the British Isles it comes as a passage migrant, usually occurring singly on coasts and estuaries. It is only separated from the Common Curlew by the characteristic call, and at closer quarters by the striped head and shorter, less curved bill. However, it will also use the *courlee* call and curlew-like bubblings.

In the extreme north of Scotland, and in Orkney and Shetland, it may be a breeding bird. It nests on rough open moorland. On the breeding ground both of the pair are more noisy birds, with whistles and bubbling calls that tend to be more level and higher-pitched than those of the Common Curlew. The male has a circling display flight, climbing steeply with rapid wing-beats, then gliding downwards with arched wings stiffly held. It may continue over the breeding area for long periods. It is accompanied by a series of low whistles, accelerating in frequency and followed by a triple burst of a bubbling tremolo. Similar song may be heard from birds of both sexes on the ground. The nest is a simple hollow lined with bits of nearby vegetation. The young run and feed themselves from the first, but are brooded by the adults. Both tend the young and sometimes divide the brood between them. Insects, and other small creatures including snails, are taken on land, and it also eats small berries such as bilberries and crowberries. On the shore it probes mud and soft soil, but not as deeply as might be expected, taking mainly worms and small crabs.

Its breeding sites in northern Britain are on the margin of its range, which is discontinuously circumpolar in subarctic and cool boreal zones. It is a migrant throughout its range, wintering on coasts from warm-temperate to tropical zones of both hemispheres south to Australia, and the southern extremities of Africa and the Americas. A very small number of individuals, possibly no more than about 30, winter in the extreme south-west of Ireland, with a few in Devon and Cornwall. There is only a single early record of it, from the last glaciation in Derbyshire, although as a cool climate species it could have had a more extensive distribution in parts of the Pleistocene.

It was noted as breeding in Scotland in 1769, but there is little information on its past status. It appears to have responded to climatic changes, breeding in larger numbers and with a greater range in cooler periods. It may have been more widespread in the cooler four-teenth to nineteenth centuries, and certainly underwent a general decrease in the north of Britain from the latter part of the nineteenth century until about the 1950s. It was breeding in Scotland in the nineteenth century, but decreased drastically in numbers and sites in the period 1889–1930. On Orkney breeding mainly ceased after 1880, with one in 1891 and only two between 1918 and 1950. It had bred on St Kilda last in 1905. Inland it may have bred in Invernesshire in 1924, and at a high altitude site in that county from 1931 to 1950.

In the cooler climate of the 1950s and after, it began to increase again. In Shetland there were about 50 pairs in the early 1950s, 150 in 1970 and about 300 by 1980. There were breedings in Orkney in 1968, 1970 and five pairs in 1983. St Kilda had a pair from 1964 onwards, it bred on Fair Isle in 1973 and 1974, and Lewis had a few pairs sporadically from 1957 onwards. It bred in north Sutherlandshire in 1960 and since 1973, and in at least two other mainland sites in recent times. The mid 1980s population would seem to be in the region of 350 plus pairs.

When migratory passage is at its height, numbers sometimes reach 2,000–3,000 in places. The coastal passage is highest on the North Sea coast and in southern England in autumn, while in spring it is highest in western Britain and Ireland; this pattern has been noted north to Scotland.

Common Curlew *Numenius arquata*

This is the largest of our waders; widespread, splendid-ly-voiced and difficult to overlook. It has a striding and dignified gait, and a conspicuously long and decurved bill. Its streaky, brown-patterned plumage, that loses its pale edges and becomes deeper in spring, is not particularly striking, but a white rump is apparent in flight. The flight is steady and level, with the head drawn back and shortening the neck, and groups of birds tend to fly in lines. It is best known for its voice. The loud and far-carrying calls have an unusual throaty, musical quality, and the slightly mournful tone of the calls and exuberance of the bubbling song become associated with the wide spaces – moorland, level marshes, estuaries and coasts – of which they seem a part. It is the frequent *courlee* call that gives the bird its English name; and the shorter, mournful *quorrp*, deep and fluting with a slight upward slide, that gives it the Scottish name of Whaup.

It feeds both on small creatures and berries, seeds and leaves of plants. Inland it uses the long bill like forceps to catch insects and other small animals, and will probe horizontally under an overhang. On estuaries and coasts it mostly feeds on the bare upper stretches of mud rather than in the water, picking and probing but able to reach deep down for burrowing lugworms. It also takes small molluscs and crabs.

Established pairs tend to return to a territory and breed together for a number of years, and territorial displays are not elaborate. In territorial disputes birds threaten in a half-crouching posture, with head and neck raised, and tail raised and spread. The most obvious behaviour is the male's display flight. Like the Whimbrel, he circles widely over his breeding area, rising steeply on fluttering wings, hovering, then gliding down with wings held in a shallow V before rising again. It may be accompanied by an insistent repetition of the *courlee* call at intervals, or by bubbling trills. The nest is the usual shallow hollow, sparsely lined and usually partly hidden in grass, but sometimes quite exposed. Both adults usually share incubation and care of the young. As in other curlews, godwits and most long-billed waders, the downy young have short straight bills, only gradually acquiring the adult shape.

Its breeding distribution is across the open regions of boreal and temperate Eurasia, and it is a migrant except in the Atlantic seaboard and in the British Isles. It winters in warm-temperate to tropical zones. There is little early occurrence of it in the Pleistocene, except in Derbyshire in the last glaciation. It should have occurred on moorland through most of the early Holocene, and it was hunted in Shetland and Sussex in the late Iron Age. As a bird of moorland, and open marsh and bog in forest areas, it would have increased as woodland was cleared, but in the past does not seem to have gained any great advantage from the increase in farmland and pastures. Until recent times it has been regarded as a desirable bird for hunting, big enough to provide a meal, and it would have lost its eggs for the same reason if it nested at a vulnerable site. In Britain – until the end of the nineteenth century – it appears to have been a bird of moorland and hill regions, moving down to coastal marshes in winter.

In the present century it has shown a spread which, since it involves a move down to lower levels and more southerly nesting-sites typical of its general range, does not seem to be immediately correlated with climate. However, resident birds suffer badly in hard winters and there may be a partial correlation. It was originally restricted to the damper parts of upland moors, with a mainly westerly and northerly distribution. In Britain, in the present century, it has spread to lowland heathland, pastures and even to cultivated fields, and has increased throughout its previous range. Breeding densities in some of the new areas are greater than in traditional habitats. It now breeds over most of an area west of a line from the New Forest to Flamborough Head. It first bred in inland Wiltshire in 1916, on heaths in Hampshire and Sussex in the 1930s, and in Norfolk, Suffolk and Cambridgeshire in the 1940s. Distribution is very patchy in the midlands and in south-west England. It has spread to all parts of Ireland, and in Scotland it has moved westwards, first breeding on the Outer Hebrides in 1965, Fair Isle 1968, Foula 1976.

There was some recession in the 1950s, probably linked with increased drainage, and changes in farming practices. Population decreased in some areas and it disappeared from Cambridgeshire again. The breeding population of the British Isles is estimated at about 40,000 to 70,000 pairs. In winter there is a strong movement to coastal areas. In parts of Britain there may be increasing occurrence inland later in winter; while in Ireland birds are normally widespread inland. Some British breeders move west to Ireland or migrate south; while Norwegian birds winter mostly in Scotland, some continental birds occur in southern Britain, and Swed-ish and Finnish birds are generally distributed. The winter population is about 200,000 birds, or about half of the Europe to Africa migrant population.

'Shanks' and Sandpipers

Tringa and *Actitis* species

These are all slender-billed and slender-necked wading and waterside birds – three moderate-sized 'shanks' and three smaller sandpipers – all but one of the last in the genus *Tringa*. The Spotted Redshank is an arctic breeder, the Greenshank breeds in open places in the boreal zone, and the Redshank is mainly a bird of the temperate zone. Of the smaller birds, the Wood Sandpiper breeds in subarctic to boreal zones in open places, while the Green Sandpiper overlaps it, breeding in boreal to cool-temperate zones, but in more wooded habitats. The Common Sandpiper is a bird of the edges of clear fresh waters in subarctic to warm-temperate zones, within the ranges of most of the others but not using the more muddy habitats.

Spotted Redshank *Tringa erythropus*

This is a migrant and scarce winter visitor to Britain, infrequently seen in its striking black breeding plumage. It is usually an ashy-grey bird with white underside, a little larger and leggier than the common Redshank with white brow-stripe, white rump and small wing-spotting visible at close quarters. The loud *chu-wit* call is the most diagnostic character at this time. It usually winters on shores, estuaries and brackish lagoons, wading often belly-deep, picking with the bill or at times swinging it laterally in water. It can swim and up-end like a duck in deeper water, usually doing so in tight groups, and also using group-feeding to drive food in shallow water. A low clucking note is used between birds in flocks.

It has a narrow breeding range through the wooded tundra of Eurasia; wintering around the Mediterranean, in subtropical Africa and the Oriental region. It also winters in small numbers on the Atlantic seaboard of Europe, and around the southern North Sea. There is not early evidence of it in Britain, and James Fisher gave the earliest reference in literature as 1771. It winters at sheltered muddy sites from the Firth of Forth southwards and round the south to Wales and Lancashire, but is mainly absent from the north-west. It is present at a few sites around Ireland. Probably 80–200 birds winter in the British Isles, but this might be half the Atlantic seaboard total.

Redshank *Tringa totanus*

The Redshank is the wader of water meadows, freshmarsh and saltmarsh, a small brown bird with a neurotic and noisy manner, seemingly always on the alert for approaching danger and bobbing its head nervously. Its melancholy musical *tyu-hu-hu* piping call is likely to greet anyone crossing such places, summer or winter, while its wilder single yelping note, often delivered from a post-top, is a sure sign that it has something to hide. In spite of the scarlet bill and legs of breeding birds it is an inconspicuous species until it takes wing, when the white secondary patches on the fast-beating wings, and the white rump, make it easily recognisable.

It feeds mainly at the surface with quick picking movements, on turf or mud, or wading up to belly-deep in water, probing and laterally swishing the bill but not plunging the head under. The upper mud of shores and estuaries is its main winter feeding ground. Birds scatter to feed, but outside the breeding season they may group or assemble into resting parties and flocks at high tide, seemingly always marked by the odd piping notes from uneasy individuals.

Breeding birds often nest near each other, the nest well-concealed in grasses or herbage. Displays performed at the nest-site involve head-bowing and tail-spreading. When landing after display flight, and occasionally at other times, birds break into a yodelling *tullioo-tullioo-tullioo* ... sequence, and as they settle they raise the wings straight up high and may continue calling for a time. This final posture is also used just prior to mating. The quivering white underwings, raised high, are the most conspicuous element, and sometimes one bird's performance seems to stimulate others, and the raised white wings appear like opening flowers across some drab marsh. The male has a typical switchback display flight over the breeding ground, rising on rapidly beating wings and gliding down, the whole accompanied by an insistent single clear *tioo* note. Both of the adults may share incubation and care of the young. They lead the downy chicks to small marshy or flooded sites, and like the Lapwing may be heavily dependent on these for survival of the young.

In its general breeding distribution, the Redshank is a bird of warm-boreal to warm-temperate zones of Eurasia, but extends further north in the region of the warm Atlantic Drift Current in Scandinavia and Iceland. It winters in warm-temperate to subtropical zones, and on the Atlantic seaboard north to Shetland. Surprisingly for a widespread bird there are no obvious very early records, although James Fisher mentioned it as in the Late Pleistocene. It appears to have been fairly well-known in earlier times as a bird of both coastal and inland areas, but it is difficult to even guess at its status because of subsequent striking changes. The evidence suggests that it is sensitive to climatic changes, doing less well in cooler periods, but not benefitting from warmer ones if they are too dry, and suffers badly in cold winters with prolonged hard weather.

In these circumstances, the population may already have been low in the beginning of the nineteenth century. At that time it was said to have undergone a considerable decrease, possibly related to drainage of marshes and farmland, and changes in farming practice. In the early nineteenth century, its distribution in Britain appears to have been confined to the eastern side, from Orkney southwards. The period 1865 to about 1940 saw a continual increase and spread, westwards and southwards, with the main expansion occurring in 1893 to 1915. All counties except Cornwall, Pembroke, and some in southern Ireland had been colonised or re-colonised to some degree by 1925; but Pembroke and Wexford were not added to the regular list until after 1940, by which time the expansion seemed complete. In Scotland the spread appears to have been coastal at first, then inland up rivers to occupy grazings and hay meadows.

From the 1940s onwards there has been a decrease again, particularly marked after hard winters. It may disappear temporarily from areas, and be drastically

SUMMER

Spotted Redshank

Green Sandpiper

Wood Sandpiper

SUMMER

Redshank

Greenshank

WINTER

Common Sandpiper

D.M.H.

reduced in others. In recent times there has been a main and continuing loss on inland, lowland sites where increased drainage of grassland and increased cultivation – possibly combined with other factors – has brought about a significant decrease. The breeding population still appears widespread in northern Britain, very patchy and rapidly decreasing in the south with the main population near the coasts, and scarce in Wales and the south-west. In Ireland the population in mainly inland, and absent from most of the south. The population in the mid 1970s was estimated at about 40,000–50,000 breeding pairs, but is probably much lower now. Monitored population decreased by 30% between 1984 and 1986.

In winter, birds shift out towards the coasts, and are present on most shores. Native birds are joined by others from Iceland, and a more variable influx of continental birds. The wintering population probably exceeds 100,000 birds and may represent one-fifth of the world's population of the species.

Greenshank *Tringa nebularia*

A tall pale wader with the typically nervous manner, and a slightly upcurved bill. It is grey in colour, but in flight the wings appear blackish, contrasting with the white rump. The flight is fast and direct, but it is capable of rapid and erratic movements. Like the Redshank, it has a triple call note when disturbed, but a louder *tew-tew-tew* or *tew-tew-tewk* with stronger emphasis on the final note. It is an active feeder, and in addition to small invertebrate prey may go for larger items, such as small fish or amphibians. It takes most of its food by picking and lightly probing on bare mud and shallow water, or snatching from the air. It may use lateral movements of the bill at the surface of soft mud or in shallow water. When after fish or similar fast-moving prey, it may dash erratically through shallow pools.

When nesting, it occurs mainly where there are slopes with short vegetation and waters and wet areas, which will provide food. There may be some distance between feeding and nest-sites, and territories are large. The most obvious evidence of the birds' presence is the male's display flight, sometimes given high in the air. The bird circles in a switchback display, alternately fluttering up and gliding down, and using a repetitive musical *too-hoo-too-hoo* song. The mating display is like that of the Redshank, with the male quivering the highly-raised wings. Annoyance is indicated by a series of sharp chirping calls. Both adults may incubate, in a nest hollow on the ground, usually by a dead log, rock or similar marker. Both guard the young which are led to a suitable feeding site. Birds begin to leave for the coast in mid-July.

Its breeding distribution is through the boreal region of Eurasia, wintering in subtropical and tropical zones, south to Australia and southern Africa, with scattered sites around the Mediterranean and up the Atlantic coast, with western Scotland as the only region in which it is present at all seasons. Its earliest British record is in the Pleistocene in Derbyshire, in the latter part of the last glaciation. As a bird of cool upland and moorland with boggy areas or pools, it could have been more widespread in parts of the Pleistocene, but subsequently would have been reduced to something like its present range, and possibly even more constrained in the period of maximum spread of woodland. Its range in Scotland

at the present day is in part in transient habitats which may become unsuitable as trees grow, or wet places are drained; but new ones may occur in cleared or burnt-over areas. It was only known from Scotland and should have increased as Scottish woodlands were devastated by the nineteenth century.

In fact, numbers appear to have been lower in the early part of the nineteenth century. Since then there has been an increase which appears to be continuing. The increase has been within the area in which it had long been present. It bred sporadically in southern Scotland in the 1920s, but has not since. Its main breeding range is in the central and north-western highlands and the western islands. Breeding in the Outer Hebrides had decreased and become more sporadic by the 1930s, but it has been re-established again since 1951. It bred on Orkney in 1951 and on Shetland in 1980, but has not established regular breedings.

On the southern edge of its range it has decreased in places, possibly owing to local changes in vegetation and drainage. There is one locality in north-west Ireland where breeding has occurred in recent years. The British Isles breeding population was estimated at 300–500 in 1951, 400–750 in 1970, and 800–900 in 1979.

A number winter in the British Isles, on muddy estuaries and shores. They are mainly in south-west England, Wales and the Scottish Islands, and around much of the Irish coast. About 1,000–1,500 birds may be involved. It is suspected that this represents most of the British breeding population, which tends to return to breeding grounds in early April, well before continental migrants.

Green Sandpiper *Tringa ochropus*

For most people, this is a secretive and often solitary small bird that rises quickly from the edge of a lowland ditch, pool or freshwater stream, looking as black-and-white as a House Martin and rising steeply with a high-pitched *klu-eet-weet* call to seek another site. It is the darkest of these small sandpipers, the wings blackish both above and below, contrasting with a white rump. It is mainly a passage and winter visitor, occurring from about August onwards and only in small numbers in any one place.

On its breeding grounds, it occurs by small muddy-edged fresh waters in swampy areas with trees. In such places it perches freely, and when nesting usually uses old nests of birds such as thrushes, squirrel drays or platforms of tree-lodged material. This makes nesting difficult to establish, but it has occurred in Britain. The species has a typical switchback display flight performed by the male, using a song like a more complex and rapid version of its call. The display is one of the few indicators of possible breeding.

Its overall range is across the boreal and cool-temperate zones of Eurasia, wintering in warm-temperate to tropical zones, and sparsely in north-west Europe. In Britain it has the distinction of a very early record, from the Middle Pleistocene, with what appears to be this species occurring in the Cromerian Interglacial in Norfolk. It is likely to have bred more widely in the past when wooded areas were more extensive; but in recent times it has probably always been a sporadic breeder and a regular but thinly-distributed winter visitor.

It bred in Westmorland in 1917, and has been seen in

summer in Scotland, sometimes in display flight, at intervals in the 1930s, 1940s and early 1950s, mostly on Speyside. Breeding occurred in 1959. As a winter visitor it occurs across England and Wales, rarely in Scotland, and at scattered sites in south Ireland. Although some places are regularly used, there is considerable movement. The winter total for the British Isles is probably about 500–1,000 birds.

Wood Sandpiper *Tringa glareola*

Very like the Green Sandpiper, this is a pale and more speckled bird, with pale underwings, and a softer shrill *chiff-chiff-chiff* call when it rises in alarm in similar fashion to the other species. A small nervous sandpiper with rapid flight, it may occur on small muddy areas and margins of open fresh waters when on passage. In the breeding season it is a bird of swamps and boggy moorlands, or in small marshy areas of woodland clearings. In such areas it perches freely, and occasionally breeds in old bird nests in similar fashion to the Green Sandpiper, although more usually in a hollow on the ground. It has the usual song flight over its breeding area, repeatedly fluttering up and gliding downwards on downcurved wings, while uttering a repeated piping double note. The food is mainly small invertebrates, caught by probing and snatching while it is paddling or wading along the water's edge.

It is a breeding species of subarctic to boreal zones across Eurasia wintering in subtropical and tropical regions. There is practically no information on its early status in Britain, apart from James Fisher's note of its first occurrence in literature in 1784. It may well have been breeding sparsely in the remoter parts of Scotland in earlier centuries. We are on the south-west border of its present breeding range. Like other northern birds, it seems to have retreated from Britain in the latter part of the nineteenth century and earlier half of the present century. There is a breeding record for Northumberland in 1853 and possibly in 1857, and birds were shot in summer in Scotland in the nineteenth century.

Again, like northern species, it has increased more recently. Apart from a singing male in north Inverness in 1947, the next proven breedings were in Sutherlandshire for 1959–65. There were pairs elsewhere in Scotland in the 1960s, with breeding confirmed in 1960 and 1962. From 1968 onwards, pairs were present in each year in various sites in Scotland and except for 1969, 1970 and 1973, breeding occurred each year. In recent years breeding has been confined to Sutherlandshire, Rosshire and Invernesshire. The numbers have at times involved up to 12 possible pairs. It appears to be a summer visitor breeding unpredictably on the edge of its range.

Common Sandpiper *Actitis hypoleucos*

This is the small sandpiper of hill streams. It appears shorter-legged than many other small waders, and has a rapid trotting run and a habit of wagging its tail end vertically up and down when it pauses between activities. It tends to pick rapidly at the water's edge for food, and flies low across the water from one shore to another, often with a shrill *kitti-needi* call. In flight it shows a thin white wing-stripe and white outer edges to the tail. The flight is distinctive, with bursts of small stiff downward beats below the horizontal, alternating with short glides on downcurved wings. Once it has settled, it tends to be quiet and inconspicuous.

Its preferred habitat is on the stony or gravelly margins of clear water, usually fresh water. It occurs along hill streams and the margins of clear hill lakes, but will accept other, similar sites, including the edges of sheltered sea inlets which provide the right conditions. It breeds at such sites, usually nesting near the water's edge on shingle banks or where sparse vegetation grows among stones. In its display flight it usually flies low over the water in a ritualised flight not unlike the normal one, but with more rapid bursts of very shallow wingbeats alternating with glides, and a repetition of a more prolonged and accentuated version of the call. Birds displaying on the ground may raise one or both spread wings high over the back, and show them off to the partner in side view. Both adults appear to share incubation and care of the young, although the closely related American Spotted Sandpiper *A. macularia* is sometimes polyandrous, with the males doing the nesting.

It has a very wide breeding distribution from subarctic to temperate zones across Eurasia, but not in the Faeroes or Iceland. It winters in subtropical and tropical zones, and in scattered sites around the Mediterranean and in western Europe. There appear to be no early records of it in Britain, until Turner wrote of it in 1544. Since it can use streams with open shores through wooded regions of its range, it is possible that its past population may have been fairly stable and, as today, occupied the higher areas of north and west in both Britain and Ireland. Its present breeding distribution is west of a line from the Bristol Channel to north Yorkshire; and in upland areas of Ireland, mainly in the north-western half.

It seems to have disappeared from parts of the south-west, Somerset and Glamorgan early in the present century. There also appears to have been some general decrease since the early 1950s, although this is usually only apparent at local level. Breeding decreased in the Dartmoor area in this period, and ceased in the early 1960s. Scattered breedings have occurred in lowland sites in recent times – in Berkshire in 1955, Hertfordshire in 1955–57, Norfolk 1962–63, and Sussex in 1969.

In general it is still widespread in suitable areas, although it is possible that, like the Dipper, it may come to suffer from the effects of acid rain on upland streams and their insect fauna. Its population in the mid 1970s was estimated at 10,000 to 50,000 pairs. It migrates southwards soon after breeding, and there is a general passage through Britain with individuals turning up briefly at small ponds and unlikely sites. A small number winter in various scattered localities in south-west Scotland, England and Ireland, but is mainly concentrated in the south-west. This habit appears to have increased in the last thirty years, but probably involves only about 100 individuals.

Arctic Sandpipers

Calidridinae

These are shore waders, medium-sized to small, stockier and shorter-necked than the previous group, and with rather stouter bills. They breed in colder regions, migrating in winter and often covering long distances. They tend to have brown or rufous plumages in summer, and to become paler and greyer in winter plumages. Away from their breeding grounds, they feed mainly on the tidally-exposed mud and sand of shores and estuaries, with competition reduced by differences in size and feeding methods. Most of them are grouped in the genus *Calidris*; but the highly-specialised Ruff and phalaropes (plate 25) are usually placed with them in this subfamily.

Of the eight species that regularly reach the British Isles, two are winter visitors, two passage migrants, and one a regular vagrant; the other three – Dunlin, Temminck's Stint and Purple Sandpiper are common, intermittent and rare breeders respectively. The Knot and Sanderling breed in the high Arctic and winter with us. The Little Stint and Curlew Sandpiper are tundra-breeding passage migrants, but although the latter visits us from a limited area of mid-Siberian tundra, the Pectoral Sandpiper which breeds right from the Taymyr Peninsula east across Siberia to Hudson's Bay in North America does not move west, but comes to us from the east as a transatlantic vagrant.

The Purple Sandpiper is another tundra breeder, just reaching us on the southern borders of its range to nest once or twice. Temminck's Stint is a shrub-tundra species breeding into Scandinavia and a new breeder in Scotland, while the Dunlin comes furthest south in the north-east Atlantic region and breeds around the Baltic and in the British Isles.

Purple Sandpiper *Calidris maritima*
A squat and solid-looking rock sandpiper; wholly confined to rocky shores, or rock-like concrete structures of more open places. It is usually seen either huddling a little above sea-level on shore rocks, or down near and into the spray and splash zone, taking small molluscs and other creatures off the rock surfaces or poking among the seaweed. It seems to lack any good distinguishing features until it flies, when it shows a faintly-indicated wing-stripe and white borders to a dark rump. Its voice is subdued. There is a *weet-wit* call and a variety of twitterings, trills and odd purring notes from restless or excited birds.

It nests in stony places among sparse vegetation. In displays it raises one or both wings spread high above the back, and may perform crouching runs. In display flight the male flutters up steeply and then circles, sometimes gliding with wings held in a V, using a series of twittering notes that changes to repeated wheezy trills. The female is the larger and bolder of the pair. She chooses the nest-site and begins to lose interest early in the incubation period, leaving the male to complete the incubation and tend the young.

Its general breeding range is on stony inland areas, or shingly beaches in tundra from eastern arctic Canada across to Severnaya Zemlya, its southern limits through

Iceland and the Norwegian mountains. Apart from a single record in the late Pleistocene to early Holocene of Derbyshire, there are no obvious records of it in Britain prior to 1798, but it could have been present more widely as a breeding bird in Ice Age times and possibly later. In more recent times, its status seems to have been as a passage migrant and winter visitor. Although its overall population does not seem to be fluctuating significantly, it may show some southward shift in cooler periods. It was suspected of breeding in Scotland in the nineteenth century. A few birds are usually present in Orkney, Shetland and in Scotland in summer. In 1978 a pair bred in the Scottish mountains; two pairs in 1979 and 1980, four in 1981, one in 1982, none in 1983 and two in 1984 establish a possibly long-term breeding pattern.

Winter birds restrict themselves to rocky shores, mainly north of Lincolnshire and north Wales, and are scarce in the southern third of Ireland. The main concentration is in the north-east from Shetland and Orkney to Yorkshire. The east coast birds which arrive in July and moult are apparently from Norway; while birds that have already moulted come later to north and west Scotland from Iceland, Greenland and possibly Canada. They mainly leave about April. The number wintering in the British Isles may be about 17,000–25,000 individuals.

Curlew Sandpiper *Calidris ferruginea*
This is a bird from the middle part of the Siberian coastal tundra that might not have been expected to occur with us at all, but is a regular if limited passage migrant. It is often concealed among the Dunlins, for although there are fine differences, this species in autumn plumage looks remarkably like a Dunlin, and since it often mixes in ones and twos in large flocks of the latter it can easily be overlooked. The bill is not as conspicuously slender and curved as one might suppose, both species have narrow white wing-stripes, and the real identification is all-white rump that shows in flight. It is not often seen in spring, when its all-over chestnut breeding plumage would make it conspicuous. It has a subdued *chirrup* call.

It leaves its breeding ground in early July, and winters in subtropical and tropical zones south to Australia and southern Africa. The route to its West African wintering ground lies through the Baltic region and western Europe, and it is birds deflected from the western margin of this route that reach Britain. Its appearance depends on the winds and weather at the time. In some years it is very scarce, while in other flocks may number up to 100 birds. It mostly occurs on the east coast of Britain, with small scattered occurrences inland and elsewhere around the British Isles. Migration appears leisurely and it may be present from about mid July to October. On the return journey in spring, the West African birds usually take a more easterly route through Europe, and numbers in Britain are small.

There appear to be no early records of it in Britain prior to a first mention in literature in 1786, nor of any

Purple Sandpiper

SUMMER

WINTER

Curlew Sandpiper

SUMMER

WINTER

Dunlin

SUMMER

Sanderling

SUMMER

Little Stint

WINTER

WINTER

D.M.H.

change in status, and it may never have formed a more significant part of the British fauna.

Dunlin *Calidris alpina*

This is the commonest of our small waders. A group of small brown birds pottering along and, heads down, energetically jabbing away on mud, in shallow water, or near the tide edge on any estuary, are likely to be Dunlins. And when some small solitary bird takes off from the edge of a puddle or inland swamp or sewage-farm with a short, harsh *screep* call, this is the species most likely to be involved. It may feed by picking at the surface, or by probing in soft mud or soil, while on large areas of soft mud it may feed by rapid and continuous jabbing of the bill into the mud while moving forward very slowly. On most occasions it moves with a rather hunched, head-down look, concentrating on what is immediately in front of it. An upright, alert posture usually indicates alarm and is likely to be followed by flight.

Estuary-feeding birds flock to roost at high tide on dry resting places, and if numbers are large they tend to form tight flocks that perform fast and agile aerobatics, the tightly-packed mass turning, twisting and swooping in astonishing synchronism, flashing white and dark as the birds bank simultaneously, travelling over the water to the resting site. Small parties are equally agile but usually less exuberant. In the flocks the slurred reedy single-note calls merge into a confused twitter.

It shows some degree of sociability on the breeding grounds, where territories may be loosely grouped in an area. On uplands, the preferred breeding sites are like those of the Golden Plover, near which it may nest: level, with fairly short vegetation, and moist, boggy patches, preferably with some pools of water and mud. The sites may range from sparsely vegetated mountain summits and heather moorland, to saltmarsh and the grassy machairs of Scotland's western islands. Displaying males have upright postures with slightly puffed-up breast feathers, to show off the black patch that is present in both sexes. The male's display flight over the territory is a light undulating glide, alternating with rapid quivering beats of the downcurved wings, and accompanied by drawn-out wheezy croaking notes. When descending, and in other territorial flights which may involve both sexes, the birds often glide down with the wings raised in a V, giving a prolonged, high-pitched whinnying twitter. Display in which one or both wings are spread high above the back are also used. Both sexes share the incubation and tend the young.

It has a circumpolar breeding range, mainly on Arctic tundra. However, it breeds in Iceland and extends southwards in the mountains of Norway and Sweden, and parts of their coastlines, occurs discontinuously around the Baltic and into Denmark, and in the north and west of the British Isles. In such areas it tends to breed in open sites with short or sparse vegetation, bare areas and pools and muddy places. It winters widely in temperate to subtropical zones. It was probably a more widespread breeder in cooler Pleistocene periods, but the only early records are from the Ipswichian Inter-glacial sites in Devon and south Wales. Since the present British breeding population belongs to a subspecific form ranging north to Finland and Iceland, it may well have found refuge in glacial periods in, or to the south of, the British Isles.

There is no early historic information on it. It must certainly have wintered here in large numbers. Its breeding population is likely to have increased when upland woodland, particularly that in Scotland, was cleared; and the rough pastures of lowland and shore would have suited it. It would subsequently have suffered a little from changes in farming and increased drainage, but since its breeding sites tend to be in marginal areas, this may only have had a slight effect. It certainly underwent some decrease in the late nineteenth and earlier twentieth century. This has been ascribed to the continuing effect of human activity on vegetation and drainage, and to increased disturbance.

It bred in Lincolnshire until the end of the nineteenth century, and had bred in Somerset prior to 1940. It nested in Norfolk in 1938 and 1939. In Ireland it seems to have been lost from seven counties. In Scotland it was said to nest in every mainland county earlier this century, but began to disappear from the eastern and central lowlands. It had been plentiful in Fifeshire and last nested there in 1937, ceased regular breeding at Loch Leven before 1950 and in East Lothian by 1968. Its breeding range is threatened by afforestation, and agricultural projects such as the 'improvement' of the Scottish machairs.

At present it breeds in Cornwall and Devon, and sparsely from Brecon to north Wales, in the Peak District and Pennines and north Yorkshire, all of these being inland, moorland areas. It breeds at lower altitudes in Lancashire and Lakeland, and is then irregularly distributed through Scotland; it is more heavily populated in the Outer Hebrides, Caithness, Orkney and Shetland. There is a small scatter of sites in central Ireland, but more in the northwest and north. In the mid 1970s, the breeding population of the British Isles was estimated at about 4,000–8,000 pairs.

Non-breeding movements are complex. British and Irish breeding birds appear to leave the country, moving south. Birds from Iceland and Greenland are passage migrants, pausing for a while in autumn and spring; and the main wintering population is from northern Scandinavia and Siberia. Many of these stop to moult on the east side of the southern North Sea before crossing. Birds in winter are almost entirely on or near coasts and estuaries; but they are absent from continuously rocky coastline and scarce in north-west Scotland and Shetland. Fluctuations may be due to weather conditions in winter and to breeding success elsewhere. The winter population in the British Isles has been estimated at about 665,000 individuals.

Little Stint *Calidris minuta*

This is the pygmy of our sandpipers. A compact little bird with a short bill, it can be seen on the mudflats sprinting around among the taller waders and jabbing rapidly at the surface of the mud. It often occurs with Dunlin flocks. It takes off quickly and flies and manoeuvres rapidly, but is tamer and less prone to alarm than the larger species. It is sociable, often occurring in small flocks, calling noisily with shrill *peeps* and twittering. It may occur inland, usually only in ones and twos, and at open sites where there is some exposure of mud.

Its breeding range is on the Eurasian tundra from Finland to the Novosibirskiye Islands. It winters from Africa to India, and in scattered sites around the

Mediterranean. A few hundred winter on the west Iberian coast, mostly in Portugal; and in the last half-century a smaller number have begun to winter in the British Isles. Like most arctic-nesting birds, it spends a relatively short period of the year at its breeding area and a long period on passage, birds being present in Britain from late July until October. It migrates on a broad front rather than channelling itself along more distinct routes, but the smaller number that occur in spring suggest that returning birds travel in a more easterly direction.

There is no historic information on its status in Britain, although it was first mentioned in 1776. However, although there were only 24 records of overwintering individuals in over a century between 1831 and 1937, within the next fifty years there were over 560. There seems to have been a small but steady build-up from an average of one or two in the 1940s, to about 25 in the 1970s. The annual totals vary sharply, but there were about 60 in 1974. Most occur on shallow sheltered inlet areas of southern England, with a few concentrated on the Dee and Mersey estuaries.

Temminck's Stint *Calidris temminckii*
NOT ILLUSTRATED

This might be a very late comer to our breeding birds. It is another small species, like the Little Stint but drabber, appearing slimmer and more like a Common Sandpiper, with a white edge to rump and tail that makes it look longer-tailed. A bird of inland fresh waters, it appears happier in places where a growth of scattered plants around the water's edge and in muddy places provides partial concealment, but is also found in open space bordering water in more sheltered and confined sites. Appearing shorter-legged and more ground-hugging than the Little Stint, it feeds mainly by picking food from the surface. When disturbed it rises steeply, towering up even when not intending to travel any great distance.

The flight appears more erratic and more fluttering than that of other small waders, without the strongly coherent manoeuvering of the others even when in groups. Its call note is a high-pitched dry trill. It breeds in boggy and wet grassland sites in willow and birch scrub. The nest is on the ground, a shallow hollow in the open or hidden in low vegetation. Within the territory, birds habitually perch on shrubs or plants. Display flight begins with a song from a perch. This is a continuous rising and falling trill. The bird begins to flutter the wings, showing the white undersides, raises them in a V above the back and gradually takes off, rising and slowly circling the territory. As it does so, the tail is spread and the raised and rapidly-trembling wings carry the bird around, face to the wind.

There is a complex pairing and nesting system. The female may lay two clutches, leaving the male to incubate the first, while she attends to the second. Sometimes she lays three clutches, the first two involving separate matings with different males who are left with one clutch each, while she incubates the third. The young are tended by the adult that hatches them. The system should enhance the chance of successful breeding, although it might also imply a high level of loss.

It has a breeding range through the tundra zones of Eurasia, and also extends along the mountain range of Norway and Sweden. It winters in subtropical to tropical zones, and in a few areas around the Mediterranean. There is no early evidence of its presence in Britain; James Fisher quoted the earliest reference in our literature as 1832. Nor is there any evidence to suggest breeding prior to the present century.

It nested unsuccessfully in the Scottish Cairngorms in 1934, 1936 and 1956, birds also having been present in 1947. In East Rosshire it bred in 1971, and pairs were present until 1974. It was present in Invernesshire in 1974 and 1975, and bred in subsequent years. It seems likely that breeding or attempted breedings have occurred annually since. By 1980 there were probably six pairs at five different sites, but numbers have fallen a little since. The circumstances suggest that this might be a belated extension of range in this species. It had shown some southward expansion in Norway where it has been increasing during the earlier part of the breeding colonisation of Scotland.

It usually migrates singly or in small groups, the adults leaving before the young are fully fledged, and it is of sparse occurrence around the British Isles as a passage migrant.

Sanderling *Calidris alba*

On many occasions this is the most unmistakable of the small waders. No other would choose a sandy beach and interminably race down the slope in the wake of a receding wave, and then race back up again to dodge the advance of the next one. A winter visitor to Britain, it feeds extensively on the small crustaceans and worms in such places. It appears to use an endless energetic race-stop-and-snatch feeding technique at all times. It usually flies fast and low, showing a conspicuous white wing-stripe and a white rump with narrow black centre band. In winter plumage it looks very white on the ground, and black-and-white in flight. It is fairly silent, but may use a soft *twick-twick* call in flight, and more subdued twittering.

It breeds in north-east Greenland, Spitzbergen, some arctic promontories of Siberia, and the Canadian Arctic. Like most such waders, it spends a short time on the breeding ground and most of the year elsewhere. It winters in suitable areas around most coasts from the northern hemisphere, temperate region southwards. There are no early records of Sanderling bones in Britain, but it was recognised by the sixteenth century, and is likely to have been a winter visitor throughout the Holocene if not longer. However, its present distribution and lack of subspecific forms suggest that its centre of refuge in glacial times was in the northern part of North America, and that its presence in Eurasia may not have occurred until post-glacial times.

British wintering birds are thought to originate from Siberia, with a small number from Greenland. They arrive in July and August, and feed and moult on a few major estuaries before spreading more widely. They occur only on parts of the coast where there are sandy beaches and flats. The main concentrations appear to be in the Outer Hebrides and the Ribble Estuary. There is no evidence of long-term population changes. About 12,000 winter in the British Isles.

Pectoral Sandpiper *Calidris melanotos*
One of the larger but slimmer sandpipers of this genus, it tends to occur singly and unpredictably at the water's edge on marsh pools or sewage farms. It most resembles a small female Ruff in the colouring of back and head, and in its flight pattern with white patches on either side of a dark-centred rump; but it can usually be identified by its well-defined streaky breast pattern. The spread tail feathers show an irregular hind edge. It has an upright walk and feeds with fairly deliberate picking and probing. As a passage bird, it prefers grassy and marshy places where short grass or herbage and pools of preferably fresh water occur together. It has low, grating double or single call notes.

It is a tundra-breeding bird which evolutionarily appears to have been centred on the Bering Strait/North Pacific region. Its breeding range extends westwards through the Siberian tundra to the Taymyr Peninsula, and eastwards in the Canadian Arctic to Hudson's Bay, migrating south to South America and Australasia. It appears to reach Europe from North America, as a migrant accidentally caught up in eastward-moving Atlantic weather systems, usually in autumn, rarely at other times of year. It was first noted in Britain in 1830; and the Handbook of British Birds noted 64 occurrences by 1940. By the 1960s it was becoming frequent, and is now of almost annual occurrence. It is possible that some birds reaching the eastern side of the Atlantic may have remained for several years, migrating to Africa, and may be responsible for some recurring records.

Knot *Calidris canutus*
When a large flock of dumpy, solid-looking waders are seen across mudflats, shoulders hunched and heads down, feeding close together with a steady probing that suggests efficiency rather than urgency, and with the stolid persistence of a herd of grazing cattle, the chances of their being Knots are high. Superficially the Knot is Dunlin-like, but bigger and heavier, and with a shorter, stouter bill. Like some other Arctic waders, it comes in two colours: summer chestnut or winter grey. It prefers the large open areas of slightly higher mudflats or sandy or stony areas of a similar kind. It has a low-pitched, abrupt *knut* call and a whistled *twit-wit*.

Although appearing rather phlegmatic in its feeding habits, it is more spectacular in the wing. At high-tide, the widespread feeding flocks congregate in serried ranks on chosen high-water roost sites until the tide turns. In their movements to and from the roosts, and also when disturbed while feeding, they rise in a tight flock and perform remarkably agile aerobatic manoeuvres with almost simultaneous response throughout the flock. The performance is even more impressive with birds of this size than with smaller waders, especially when a large assemblage swishes past at low level. In flight it shows a whitish rump and narrow white wing-stripe. For the wintering period, it appears to be a specialised feeder on large estuarine flats with the advantage of the abundant food in the form of small molluscs, worms and crustaceans, but is vulnerable to any loss of this habitat.

It breeds mainly in the Canadian Arctic, also in east Greenland, and on a few promontories and islands of Arctic Siberia. It winters on coasts in subtropical and tropical areas to Australasia and southern Africa; and on the eastern Atlantic coasts continues north to the British Isles and southern North Sea. Its earliest record is from towards the end of the last glaciation in Derbyshire. Since our present north-west European wintering birds originate from breeding grounds in eastern Greenland and eastern Canada, it is unlikely that it was present as a breeding bird in the Pleistocene period in Britain. As a winter visitor to estuaries, it is unlikely to have been affected by human activity other than modification of some estuarine areas in the past by human fishing or shipping activities. A more immediate effect on the flocks is the breeding success in the Arctic, and changes in wintering areas.

Part of the British Isles' wintering population comes directly from Greenland and Canada in late summer and moults on the larger estuaries. It is joined later by birds which have moulted on the Waddenzee in the Netherlands, and which continue to arrive between November and February. In spring there is a large movement to Irish estuaries prior to departure, and another north-west to the north Waddenzee. Numbers in the British Isles built up to about 400,000 in the winter of 1971–72 but were almost halved the next year and have not recovered since. This is thought to have been due to a series of poor breeding successes.

Away from the breeding grounds, the current potential threats to this species, as opposed to other estuary-feeding waders, are pollution of the estuaries by oil and chemicals which may do harm directly – or indirectly through the food – and proposed reclamation schemes. About half the wintering birds are concentrated on only eight major estuaries. They are virtually limited to estuaries, muddy or sandy shores and inlets. Overall, the Knot occurs in about 27 areas around Britain, mostly estuaries or groups of inlets. There are few birds on rocky shores, and in most of north-west Scotland and Shetland, and few in north and west Ireland.

Turnstones

Arenariinae

This subfamily has only two species – the common Turnstone, and the Black Turnstone of coastal Alaska and the Pacific coasts of North America. They are strongly-built birds. The stout bill has a slightly upcurved upper mandible, and the neck muscles are strong to aid the stone-turning feeding behaviour.

Turnstone *Arenaria interpres*
This is a small shore wader built for heavy work. It has a rather squat and stout appearance with short, wide-set legs that give it a slightly waddling walk, head held low on shoulders, and a stout tapering bill for probing and pushing. It is sociable, usually occurring in small parties that work over rocks, seaweed beds, sand or pebbles:

Turnstone

SUMMER

WINTER

Pectoral Sandpiper

Avocet

SUMMER   Knot

WINTER

Oystercatcher

D.M.HENRY

WADERS

trotting and peering in a rather fussy manner, occasionaly probing and picking. It flips over small pebbles with its bill, forces head and bill like a chisel-tip under large ones and turns them, and uses the same technique on lumps of seaweed and other beach débris. Immediately the object has shifted, it moves in quickly to snatch at whatever is exposed. Sometimes several will appear to work together when moving a large object. Sometimes it will merely raise the object enough to allow it to probe beneath them.

This turning technique enables it to have access to food sources denied most other feeding waders, but it is only useful where the ground is covered with turnable objects. It is therefore most likely to occur on stony shore habitats, but may occur on a small stony patch or shell-bed on a muddy estuary. Its feeding behaviour is bustling and jerky, and although sociable, it also squabbles as food items appear. The calls include a low *tuk-i-tuk* rattle which may be heard from feeding birds, a twittering *kittick* flight call, and a whistled *teeu* at moments of anxiety.

The flight is strong and direct, but seems less agile than that of other small waders. The pattern revealed in flight is very distinctive. Rump and tail coverts are white, divided by a transverse black band, with another on the tail. There is a white wing-stripe, and a short one at right-angles bordering the body. The whole transforms a dark bird with a sudden harlequin effect as it takes flight. In breeding territory it shows crouching displays and occasional wing-raising. There does not seem to be a distinct display flight with song, but males may circle with slow wing-beats in silent flight over the territory. The nest is a hollow in a reasonably dry site, exposed or concealed. Both sexes incubate, although this is chiefly done by the female. However, it is the male who spends a longer time tending the young.

It has a narrow coastal breeding range around most of the Arctic, but extends south around most of the Scandinavian and Baltic coasts. It winters on coasts of warm-temperate to tropical zones, south to Australasia, southern Africa and South America; and on the east side of the Atlantic, north to the British Isles and the southern North Sea. Its earliest records are in the British Pleistocene, from the Ipswichian Interglacial on the south Wales coast, and from Derbyshire in the last glaciation. In view of its present distribution it might well have bred here in earlier, cooler periods.

In recent centuries it has been known only as a winter visitor. Birds may be present from about July until May, tending to stay in the same area and return to it annually. It is present in winter around the entire coastline of the British Isles, but scarce in north-west Scotland. Migrants from Scandinavia remain a short while in autumn before moving on to Africa, but return by a different route in spring. Birds coming from Greenland and Canada moult on arrival and then remain for the winter. The British Isles' wintering population is around 50,000 birds.

First-year birds often remain through the summer. There is a suspicion that breeding has sometimes occurred in northern Britain. Display behaviour has been seen in recent years in Orkney and Shetland; a pair are thought to have nested in Sutherlandshire in 1976, and nest-making was seen in Orkney in 1978.

Avocets and Stilts
Recurvirostridae

The small number of species in this family show the wader characters in slightly exaggerated form. The legs are very long and slender, and neck and bill are long and slender too. All have bold, simple black-and-white plumage patterns. Basically it consists of two superspecies with a single form on each major continent, and an additional Australian stilt. The Stilts, *Himantopus* species, have exceptionally long thin legs and a slender straight bill. The Avocets, *Recurvirostra* species, have moderately long legs and a very thin tapering bill which is markedly upcurved towards the tip.

There are two Eurasian species – the Avocet which we lost for a while and then regained, and the rare but opportunistic Black-winged Stilt which has occasionally ventured into Britain.

Avocet *Recurvirostra avosetta*
Strikingly and neatly patterned in black-and-white, with partly-webbed feet and a slender upcurved bill, this species is well-known for its attenuated elegance, and for the fact that we lost it for half a century. Its basic habitat requirements are for shallow areas of saline or brackish water, with a fine muddy sediment rich in minute organisms suitable for food, and bordered by bare or very sparsely vegetated ground. In winter it may find this along estuaries, but for breeding it requires still lagoons, saltpans or similar places. It can pick up individual items with its bill, but its most usual feeding technique is to wade with body slightly tilted and head lowered, sweeping the slightly opened bill from side to side through the water as it advances. It moves with quick strides and in deep water can swim for long periods, and up-end like a duck.

The flight is strong and rapid, with the legs and feet trailing beyond the tail; the boldly patterned wings are very conspicuous, making the flight seem more fluttering. It uses a loud, liquid and musical *kluit kluit* call. It nests in colonies in open sites near water. For defence it relies partly on noisy communal mobbing, and may nest in company with other species such as Black-headed Gulls which may help in this respect. Displays are mainly on the ground and are not elaborately conspicuous, tending to involve subtly ritualised postures using the already striking plumage patterns. Both adults share incubation and care of the young. The downy chicks are long-legged but have fairly short, straight bills at first.

It has a wide range through warm-temperate Eurasia and much of Africa, and extends up the western European seaboard to the south-west Baltic. It winters in subtropical zones, with scattered sites around the Mediterranean and along the Atlantic coasts north to the British Isles. There are no Pleistocene records from Britain. James Fisher quotes records as occurring from about 1600. It is a warm climate species, encouraged in western Europe by the warm North Atlantic Drift Currents of the north-east Atlantic. It may never have extended much beyond the brackish seaward edges of the broad marshes of southern England; and there is only evidence of it for East Anglia and the south-east, where large colonies may have been present up to about the end of the eighteenth century.

Like other birds associated with open waters, it fared badly in the nineteenth century. Shallow saline coastal marshes and lagoons were being rapidly drained; conspicuous birds were being shot for plumage and amusement; and colonially-nesting birds could be systematically robbed of eggs for food. The Avocet had probably never been plentiful and it began to disappear fast early on in the nineteenth century. It seems to have been noticed only in the south-east. The last breeding was in Norfolk in 1825, in Lincolnshire in about 1837, and in Kent in 1842 or possibly 1843. As a species breeding on the eastern side of the North Sea it visited Britain at intervals, and in 1882 a pair bred in Suffolk.

In north-east Europe it began to increase in the early part of the present century, possibly aided by the warmer climate of the period. In 1938 two pairs bred in County Wexford, Ireland, the second exception to what was otherwise a century of absence. It appears to have begun colonising the British east coast again a couple of years later, but wartime restrictions prevented a proper search. There was certainly a nesting in Essex in 1944 and in Norfolk in 1946.

In 1947, 28 pairs colonised their now principal sites in coastal Suffolk, Minsmere and Havergate Island. Minsmere, less suitable then, was not used again until 1963, but numbers at Havergate built up to about 60 pairs in the mid 1950s to 1960s. By the mid 1980s there were 115–125 pairs, with half that number in addition at Minsmere. Birds began to occur intermittently at other sites from the Wash to Kent. By the early 1980s, birds were breeding at up to 11 sites with up to 238 pairs involved, but over most of the decade the average of

young reared was about one per two pairs, or less. Natural predation was a problem. In 1984, 52 pairs at Minsmere reared no young. The long-term situation seems insecure.

From the 1947 breeding period onwards, a few birds began to winter on estuaries in the south-west. By the early 1980s, there were about 385 individuals at various sites round the southern coasts from the Humber to south Wales. They appear to be mainly native birds, with some from the continent; while some native birds migrate to southern Europe or Africa.

Black-winged Stilt *Himantopus himantopus*
NOT IN COLOUR PLATE

This is the thinnest wader of them all. The legs are so long in proportion that they invite comparison with the flamingos. The body is slender, the neck long, the head small with large eyes, and the bill thin and straight. Wings and back are black, the crown of the head blackish, and the rest of the plumage white. The legs are pink. In flight, the wings are long and tapering and the legs project way beyond the tail. It has a sharp repeated *kik* call. It feeds by paddling, often deeply, in fresh or brackish water of marshes, pools and shallow lakes.

It occurs widely in warmer regions where such waters may dry up, and is therefore opportunistic and nomadic in feeding and breeding, finding and exploiting new areas temporarily. It nests colonially by water, or on mounds and tussocks in it. It has never regularly been seen, but has been a rare vagrant at intervals since 1684. It might even have nested occasionally, unnoticed. In 1945 four pairs nested on a Nottingham sewage farm, in 1983 one pair in Cambridgeshire, and in 1987 one pair in Norfolk. In mainland Europe it breeds intermittently north to the Netherlands, and as an opportunistic breeder it might occur again at any time.

Oystercatchers
Haematopidae

This family consists of a single cosmopolitan superspecies of very similar forms, which are either black-and-white or all-black. It has a long strong bill, blunt-ended but laterally compressed to a point at the tip to produce a sharp, chisel-like instrument. We have a single, pied species.

Oystercatcher *Haematopus ostralegus*
Biggest, brashest and noisiest of our shoreline waders, the Oystercatcher appears to make a virtue of conspicuousness. The startling simplicity of its colouring would, in any case, make it difficult to hide on the mudflats and shellfish beds where it mostly feeds; and when it flies the pattern is enhanced by a white rump and a bold white wing-stripe. It has a striding walk and strong, direct flight. It is alert and noisy, with a loud penetrating *kleep* call-note.

Its bill enables it to break open shells of cockles, mussels and similar shellfish, and to chip limpets off rocks, but it also takes crabs and small fish, and will probe grassland for earthworms. It is both a specialist and an opportunistic feeder. It prefers open areas – mud, shingle and short grass. It breeds in such areas. Pairs often nest in a group of territories and birds meet in frequent piping displays, standing or running with

head lowered and bill pointing downwards, and uttering a series of sharp *pik* notes which gradually accelerate into a prolonged piping trill. The nest is a hollow, barely lined, usually in an open site with a view around. Both sexes incubate and care for the young; and small young are fed directly by the adults.

It has a discontinuous distribution across the temperate parts of Eurasia, which may represent its original range. On shores warmed by the North Atlantic Drift Current it extends from Brittany, via Scandinavia and the Baltic, to the White Sea, and around the British Isles and Iceland. It is a bird of mild climates and the first British records appear to be no earlier than the ninth century, in Shetland. Up to the end of the nineteenth century it appears to have been a coastal-breeding bird subject to some loss through shooting and the taking of eggs, but probably not suffering significantly until the nineteenth century, when it decreased in southern and eastern England as coastal areas were increasingly exploited.

In the present century, there was a marked increase in population both in the British Isles and northern Europe generally. This has been ascribed both to climatic amelioration and to increased protection. One result has been the spread of breeding birds to inland sites. Inland breeding, particularly on river margins, occurred in Scotland as early as the eighteenth century, but in the present century it has spread with birds not only on rivers and gravel-pits, but also on farmland. Coastal birds also show a tendency to nest in fields. It is now breeding in most inland areas of Britain north of a line from the Wirral Peninsula to the Humber. A similar shift to inland sites occurred through northern Europe at the same period.

In southern Britain and Ireland they breed on most coasts, but are most sparse on the south coasts. It is estimated that in the 1960s about 30,000–40,000 pairs

were breeding in the British Isles, about 70% of them in Scotland. In winter most birds shift to the coast, with immigrants from the Faeroes and Iceland in the west, and from Norway in the east. They tend to assemble in large numbers on big inlets with abundant shellfish, and there have been great fluctuations in numbers locally when food supplies vary. Between 1956 and 1974, 25,000 birds were shot in England and Wales to placate the mistaken beliefs of cockle fishermen that the birds were wholly responsible for fluctuations in shellfish numbers. About 300,000 birds, nearly half Europe's population, are thought to winter in the British Isles.

PLATE TWENTY-FIVE

Ruff *Philomachus pugnax* (SCOLOPACIDAE)
Although thought to be closely related to the arctic sandpipers and grouped with them in the subfamily Calidridinae, this is perhaps the most unusual of all the waders. The female is smaller than the male and she nests alone, building, incubating, and rearing the young. Males gather at an open display ground, or lek, where each occupies a small patch on which he postures and shows off his plumage. The female visits the lek, mates with one of the males and then goes off to nest in secret.

Non-breeding birds are not particularly striking. Males have a thickish neck, and both have rather small heads, short stout bills, and a rather lumpy, hunched-back look when feeding. The Ruff flies with fairly slow wing-beats and occasional glides, showing a narrow white wing-stripe and white patches on either side of the rump. It has a *tooi* flight call, but is generally rather silent. It feeds by picking and probing in muddy places around freshwater pools in grassy places, and less frequently resorting to the water's edge on estuaries or shores.

The appearance of winter birds contrasts strikingly with that of the breeding male. In the latter the face becomes bare. Two big tufts of elongated feathers sweep back on either side of the crown, while a great ruff of elongated feathers extends down over the breast and on either side curves back to the nape of the neck. In display both the large 'ear-tufts' and this great ruff are erected and frontally presented to create a great ornamental fan encircling the face. The colours and patterns of these are individually variable, and ear-tufts may differ from ruffs on one individual. Feathers may be rufous, brown, black or white, and plain, barred or streaked.

In display these feathers are spread; and sudden movements such as wing-fluttering, jumps, feather ruffling, rapid turns or forward thrusts alternate with periods of rigid and seemingly ecstatic posturing. Apart from rare low-pitched and subdued notes the displaying is silent. Where birds have been present for a long time, the lekking sites are usually traditional. There appear to be fewer females than males, and their nest-sites are hollows well hidden in long grass and herbage.

Its breeding range is through the tundra and boreal zones of Eurasia, in open areas with small shallow freshwater pools and grassy areas. It winters in Africa and India, with scattered sites through the warm-temperate zones, and north in western Europe to the British Isles and the Netherlands. Although it is a cool-climate bird that might have been more widespread in the past, there seems no record of it in Britain other than at a mesolithic Derbyshire site, and James Fisher gave 1465 as the earliest reference to it. It could have been present during the transitional periods between glacials and interglacials. It would not have flourished while the British Isles were heavily wooded, but should have fared better later, until the extensive drainage of the seventeenth to nineteenth centuries helped to destroy its habitat. It was shot for food, and a conspicuous party of males on an open lek for nearly two months could probably have been destroyed fairly easily.

It has certainly had a more extensive range in southern and north-eastern England. Its main strong-hold was in East Anglia. It had disappeared from most areas by the 1860s. It bred regularly in Norfolk until 1871 and intermittantly until 1890, and probably nested in Suffolk in 1898. In the present century it nested in County Durham in 1902, possibly 1901–03, in Lanca-shire in 1910, and in Norfolk in 1907 and 1922.

An established lek seems necessary for successful breeding, making it difficult to re-introduce, and attempts with imported eggs in Norfolk in 1937, and again in 1957, failed. However, summering birds occurred, and from 1930 small numbers increasingly wintered. Possible breeding was suspected, and the bird was proved breeding on the Cambridgeshire Ouse Washes in 1963. Breeding is difficult to prove because of the secretive behaviour of nesting females, but would seem to be occurring annually now.

By the early 1980s up to a dozen sites were being used; but records could show a possible 32 females with only two proved to breed. Behaviour still appears erratic and unpredictable. Birds also became more frequent in Scotland with display seen in widely scattered localities. Breeding was suspected in the Inner Hebrides in 1977, the Outer Hebrides in 1980, and a nest was found in Sutherlandshire in that year. These northern birds are suspected to have originated in northern Scandinavia, with the English birds coming from the Netherlands and Denmark.

Up to about 1,400 birds winter around the British Isles, mostly on or near the coasts. They are mainly in eastern England, but the scatter extends to eastern Scotland and central and south-eastern Ireland.

SUMMER MALES

Ruff

WINTER MALE

SUMMER FEMALE

Stone Curlew

WINTER

SUMMER

Red-necked Phalarope

Grey Phalarope   WINTER

D.M. HENRY.

Stone Curlews
Burhinidae

A small family of large to very large waders of bare open ground. The legs are long and strong, the bill stout, straight and with a fairly blunt tip. The head is proportionally large and rounded, with large eyes. The wings are long. All the species are superficially similar, but with some variation in size and bill shape. They are mainly birds of warmer climates. The western Eurasian Stone Curlew occurs in Britain.

Stone Curlew *Burhinus oedicnemus*
Although one of the largest of our waders, this is the most furtive, and one can rarely get close enough to appreciate the malevolent stare of the great yellow-irised eyes in the big round head that seems a little too large for the body. The eyes are designed to function in poor evening light or at night, and by day when the bird is usually resting the eyes may be partly-closed to mere slits. When resting it may squat with the lower part of the legs resting along the ground; and when alarmed may crouch right down with head and neck extended. Chicks and young birds often hide in this way.

In the bare, open habitats that it prefers, it can see approaching danger from a distance, and prefers to run, with head held low, to try to avoid it. In similar fashion it will nest in a site that gives a wide view, and leave it while anyone approaching is still far away. This may have saved its life in the past, but in an increasingly inhabited environment it may prevent successful nesting.

It becomes active in the evening and at night. It hunts by a run-and-snatch method like that of the plovers. Even when breeding, pairs tend to move out of the territory and groups assemble at shared feeding grounds, where calling and display occurs. In contrast to its furtive behaviour, the calls are loud and far-carrying. They are mostly variant on a loud whistling *kur-lee* in which the second syllable is accentuated. There are also a variety of lower-pitched hoarse and strangled calls. Birds often call in chorus at these assemblies. There may also be wild dancing displays in which the tail is raised and spread, and the wings spread and drooped to show the pattern, accompanied by rapid hysterical repetitions of piping triple calls in a galloping rhythm. They may then disperse from such displays merely to feed. Posturing between paired birds is much more subdued. The nest is a very shallow scrape in a rather bare site. Both adults incubate and care for the young, which require the food to be passed to them for the first few days.

It breeds in the temperate to subtropical zones, through western Eurasia and into North Africa and India. It is resident in the southern part of its range, and northern birds may migrate to these areas. Britain is at the north-west extremity of its range, with summer breeding birds migrating to the Iberian peninsula and North Africa. There appear to be no early British records, but it was noted by Merrit in East Anglia in 1666. In Britain it breeds on areas of chalk downland and heathland with sparse or heavily-grazed herbage, or on large areas of shingle or sand. The terrain should be dry, and it prefers a warm climate.

The habitats required are likely to have been rare early on, but it should have increased in range and numbers in historic times as woodland was increasingly cleared, and pasture and heathland created. In more recent times it has used the larger areas of arable cultivation, although this is perhaps from necessity. It was possibly always a bird of the drier, open hill sites east of a line from the Cotswolds to Yorkshire, and on the coastal heaths and shingle areas of East Anglia and Dungeness in Kent. In the nineteenth century it began to be affected by increased cultivation and afforestation. It seems to have disappeared from the Cotswolds, Lincolnshire, Nottinghamshire, Surrey and Essex in the second half of the nineteenth century. In the 1920s and 1930s an increase in uncultivated marginal land, and possibly warmer conditions, allowed some resurgence, although it last bred in Yorkshire in 1937. With more intensive land use from 1940 onwards, it began to decrease again. It also suffered from afforestation of parts of East Anglia, and to a lesser extent elsewhere; and more particularly from the loss of the rabbit through myxomatosis in 1954 which allowed extensive hill areas to revert to coarser vegetation and scrub.

The breeding population is now largely limited to the Salisbury Plain and Hampshire Basin area, extending to the Berkshire Downs and southern Chilterns; the South Downs; the chalk areas from Norfolk and inland Suffolk through southern Cambridgeshire and into Hertfordshire and Bedfordshire; and the East Anglian coastal heaths and Dungeness. In the late 1960s, the British population was estimated at about 1,000–2,000 pairs. On the breckland heaths of East Anglia, numbers had dropped from 300 plus pairs in 1949 to 50 by 1963; and Sussex lost two-thirds of its birds in a similar period. Decreases also occurred elsewhere. Numbers in the mid 1970s were estimated at 300–500 pairs, and records for the mid 1980s suggest it might be down to one-third of this. Its chosen habitats are unlikely to persist except on reserves, and it does not appear to be adaptable. Its population may fall still further.

Phalaropes
Phalaropodinae or Phalaropodidae

Sometimes placed in a separate family, but now tending to be regarded as specialised arctic sandpipers, these are small, slenderly-built birds with thin bills. The female is larger and more brightly coloured than the male and breeding roles are reversed. They swim well and the feet are partly webbed with lateral lobes on the middle toe. There are three species, one is a North American prairie bird, and the other two occur in Britain. The Red-necked Phalarope is a tundra-breeder, just reaching the north and west extremes of the British Isles; while the Grey Phalarope is a high-arctic breeder occurring only on passage and usually unintentionally.

Red-necked Phalarope *Phalaropus lobatus*
This is a small, slenderly-built and very thin-billed swimming wader. It looks deceptively fragile but is far stronger in both swimming and flight than one might expect. It not only spends its winters out at sea, where it

must swim most of the time, but also swims to feed on shallow pools, lake margins and inlets when nesting. It runs around on land with a rapid trot and with a slight rhythmic bobbing of the head, and will pick up food objects, or probe in likely places. On water it floats buoyantly, riding high at the front end as though unable to sink, with slender neck straight up and head held high, bobbing forwards in time to the kicking feet and pursuing a rather erratic course.

It seems to prefer waters with some sparse emergent plant growth, and tends to follow along near the margin when swimming. Its speciality, which it shares with other phalaropes, is a tendency to spin round in one place on the surface of the water, and as it pivots to pick at the water around it as though its action has stirred up small food items. This rotary feeding method appears unique to these species. When feeding, it makes brief and erratic low flights that appear rather weak and fluttering, but sustained flight is stronger and more direct.

This is a species in which the female is the bigger, brighter and more dominant bird. Females will fight each other for males that they select, and there is a short-term pair-bond. There are pair displays with raised or lowered heads. The female performs short, low advertisement flights which begin by rising with legs dangling, tail spread and wings making a loud whirring sound. The breeding sites may be in marshland or rough pastures near water, or centred on tiny pools well away from a larger stretch of water.

Both sexes make nest-scrapes on the ground in vegetation, and the female selects one of these in which to lay a clutch of eggs. The subsequent incubation and the care of the young is done by the male alone. The female leaves after egg-laying and may mate with another male and lay a second clutch, but this seems to be only when there is an excess of males available.

It has a circumpolar tundra breeding range, extending south in central norway and Sweden and in parts of Finland. It also breeds in Iceland, the Faeroes and in the extreme north and west of the British Isles. It winters at sea off the south of Arabia, north of New Guinea, and off western South America. The birds from north-west Europe and Russia fly across Europe to the Black Sea and Caspian Sea, and then down to the Arabian Gulf and the sea off the southern Arabian coast. If these wintering sites reflect distribution during the late Pleistocene period, then it is possible that this species has shown a westward post-glacial spread in Europe, with Britain at its extremity. Icelandic birds might be the eastern end of the South American unit.

At present, there is no evidence of it in the British Isles prior to Pennant's record of it as a British species in 1769, and it was not found breeding until 1804, in Orkney. It is doubtful whether it ever had much more than a limited distribution in the north-west of Scotland and on the islands, and in the north-west of Ireland. As a cold-climate species, it should have increased between the fourteenth to nineteenth centuries; and a decrease in the first half of the present century may be due, in part at least, to climatic fluctuations.

It is often relatively indifferent to the presence of man. This, when coupled with its tendency to breed in groups at a limited number of sites, made it very vulnerable to the nineteenth-century passion for collecting natural objects, for its skin, and more particularly for its eggs. This caused a serious decrease in its breeding population. In the present century, numbers began to increase under protection, but there may have been some counter-effect from a warmer climate.

In Ireland a large colony and two small ones were discovered at the beginning of the century. The large one held about 50 pairs in 1905, 40 in 1929, 1–3 in 1966, 12–15 in 1970 and seemed to have disappeared in 1973, but with a breeding in 1979. The two smaller colonies were lost by 1944. There had been odd pairs breeding in County Donegal in the 1920s, and it has bred south to Kerry and Wexford. In Scotland it was thought to have bred on mainland sites in 1830 and 1848; a few pairs bred at one site between 1963 and 1967, and one or two have bred in places in most years since 1978. In the Inner Hebrides it bred regularly on Tiree until about 1940, then intermittently. It decreased on the Outer Hebrides, but breeds in very small numbers. It nested on St Kilda in 1872.

In Orkney it had bred regularly until about 1930, then intermittently – and on one island only, and has not done so since 1975. Shetland is its main stronghold but here it decreased in the 1920s to 1940s, increased between the 1950s to 1960s and has since decreased again. All but one or two pairs are confined to Fetlar. The British Isles' breeding population was estimated at about 54–65 pairs in 1968, 45 pairs in 1970, and about 25 pairs in the mid 1980s, with four-fifths of these on Fetlar. Being at the extremity of the breeding range, with migrants moving away eastwards and not passing through the British Isles, the British population is unlikely to increase, unless there is a significant rise in the Northern European area.

Grey Phalarope *Phalaropus fulicarius*

Larger and more heavily-built than the Red-necked Phalarope, it has a shorter and slightly thicker bill. Its name refers to its winter plumage since this is how it is usually seen in Britain. The infrequently-seen breeding plumage is bright chestnut over the body, with a white face, blackish crown and a yellow base to the bill. The dark feathers of wings and back are edged with light buff. It appears stronger and more vigorous than the Red-necked Phalarope, but its behaviour is otherwise similar, though in flight it looks more similar to waders such as the Sanderling, and it is more likely to fly at greater heights.

It has a circumpolar breeding range on Arctic tundra, the nearest sites to Britain being in Novaya Zemlya, Spitzbergen, and few around the coast of Iceland. It is one of those species for which there is no past evidence, but which might conceivably have nested in the British Isles in the colder periods of the Pleistocene Ice Ages.

It winters at sea in areas off West Africa, southern Africa and western South America, in places where ocean currents produce an abundant supply of small organisms. It travels to these wintering grounds by sea. Few, if any, normally pass down the North Sea, and the movements occur to the west of the British Isles. Small numbers of individuals may appear, usually on the western side of the British Isles, mostly in autumn and rarely in spring. Strong gales may exceptionally cause large influxes, sometimes several thousand birds, and some may be swept far inland. Such occurrences are usually in Ireland and the south-west, but small numbers of individuals may be scattered widely across the British Isles and may occur briefly on inland waters.

127

Skuas

Stercorariidae

These are brown-plumaged relatives of the gulls – predatory, piratical and perhaps more primitive. Best recognised by the variation in shape of the longer central tail feathers as adults, and by darker colour with a pale wing-patch at all times, they are fast and strong fliers spending most of their non-breeding time at sea, and travelling widely. Three species regularly occur in Britain. The two smaller species are tundra-breeders, the Arctic Skua extending to northern Scotland and the islands, but the Long-tailed Skua only occurs as a passage migrant. The larger and heavier Great Skua also breeds in northern Britain. It appears to have invaded the North Atlantic in earlier times from the Antarctic. All three are better known outside their limited breeding sites as migratory passage birds, often following the coastline and visible to coastal watchers.

Arctic Skua *Stercorarius parasiticus*
A lightly-built skua, this has two distinct colour phases, the paler one shown, and a dark brown one, with occasional intermediates. It is swift, buoyant and raptorial in flight. The two elongated central tail-feathers aid swift manoeuvering, and one of its main sources of food is gained by harrying gulls and terns, closely following their every movement until they drop or disgorge their food in panic. In addition it will take any small creatures, hunting voles and lemmings on its arctic breeding grounds, and will fish for itself if it must. It also takes birds' eggs in the breeding season. It breeds in colonies of small and fiercely-defended territories, usually on short heather moorland in Britain. It has staccato *tuk* calls and a wailing *ki-iiier*.

Its breeding range is circumpolar on arctic tundra and into the High Arctic, extending also to coasts of Norway, Sweden, Iceland, Faeroes and northern Britain. It tends to use coastal tundra and moorland, and although evidence is lacking, it could have bred more extensively in Britain in cooler periods of the Pleistocene Ice Ages. In historic times it seems to have been limited to Scotland.

It appears to have decreased in the nineteenth century, when eggs would have been taken at colonies, and it was disliked for harrying sheep near its nest. It may not be coincidental that populations were also lower in the warmer period up to about 1940. In more recent times there have been considerable increases. In Orkney it increased from 80 pairs in 1941 to 716 in 1945 and 1,034 in 1982. In some areas it is now competing with the Great Skua for nesting sites, although the latter seems to prefer grassier and moister places. The British population was estimated at about 1,090 pairs in 1970 and must now be in excess of 2,700 in the mid 1980s.

Long-tailed Skua *Stercorarius longicaudus*
NOT IN THE COLOUR PLATE
A little smaller and more slenderly-built than the Arctic Skua, usually pale on the underside, with a well-defined dark cap, and two very long, slender and flexible central tail feathers. Breeding birds take lemmings and voles,

Light phase Long-tailed Skua

and population is affected by their cycles of abundance and scarcity. It is agile, with a more tern-like flight, and can hunt insects on the wing. It also takes other small creatures, but harries gulls and terns for food less often than other skua species.

Its breeding range is circumpolar on higher, drier moss-tundra, barren stony ground and moorland. It is an oceanic wanderer in winter. Now breeding no nearer than north Scandinavia and east Greenland, it occurred in Somerset in the last Pleistocene glaciation, and it might have nested widely in Britain in colder Ice Age periods. It is now a scarce passage migrant, more often on the east coast in autumn and west coasts in spring. Individuals have occurred at British Arctic Skua breeding colonies, and two inland in Scotland in June, and a breeding was suspected on the Scottish mainland in 1980.

Great Skua *Stercorarius skua*
This species ranks with the big gulls, being larger than a Herring Gull but smaller than a Great Black-backed Gull. It is rather squat in build, thick-necked and thuggish-looking, with a stout bill. Its vigorous defence of its nesting area, which may include attacking humans, has given it a reputation for fierceness, which is confirmed by its predation of other nesting seabirds, and their eggs and young. However, it often harries gulls (large and small), and terns, forcing them to drop or disgorge their prey; and it will eat carrion and fishing-boat offal. Recently a few have begun to feed with gulls at refuse tips. At sea in winter it must presumably find its own food.

It breeds on islands and shores, preferring higher ground on grass moorland or grazings, often in wetter sites. The nest is a shallow scrape, poorly-lined. Small territories are aggressively defended and adults display with arched necks, open bills and spread wings raised high like banners to show the white patch, while giving a prolonged series of *piah piah* calls. An abrupt harsh note is used in aggression. Both adults share in the nesting.

Its main breeding range is through the Antarctic seas, and its restricted North Atlantic range appears to represent a later extension and colonisation, possibly post-glacial but certainly before the Dark Ages. Wintering birds disperse around the Atlantic Ocean. Its original colonies may have been confined to Iceland and the Faeroes, but by 1774 there were six pairs nesting on Foula in the Shetlands and three pairs in Unst. By 1821 Shetland had 30 pairs, approved of by farmers because they drove off White-tailed Eagles. Later it was disliked and eggs and young were taken and eaten. By 1861 there

Arctic Skua

Great Skua

Great Black-backed Gull

Lesser Black-backed Gull

ADULT

JUVENILE   Herring Gull

D.M.HENRY
1961

were only 9 pairs. It increased later in the nineteenth century and had protection from 1890 onwards.

It spread to Orkney where breeding was proved in 1915, and where it rose to 20 pairs in 1941, and to 1,652 in 1982. It had also spread to Fair Isle about 1921. Like the Arctic Skua, its main increase was from about 1940

onwards. It spread to the Outer Hebrides in 1945, and also bred in Caithness where it did not occur again until the 1970s. In the 1960s it started breeding in Sutherlandshire and on St Kilda. The population was about 3,200 in 1970, and probably over 8,500 by the mid 1980s.

Gulls
Laridae

A large family of scavengers, minor predators and opportunistic feeders of seas, coasts and some inland waters and marshes. They are long-winged, webbed-footed and with strong, slightly hooked-tipped bills. They are here, for convenience, divided into the larger and smaller species.

Larger Gulls
Larus species

Needing a more substantial food supply than smaller species, these larger gulls are more predatory, sometimes killing smaller or injured creatures as the opportunity arises, but also scavenging on carcases, and eating offal and refuse. They are adapted to shore life and to exploiting colonies of nesting sea-birds, but have increasingly found food from man's activities, and increased in numbers.

There are three regular British species and two winter visitors. The Great Black-backed Gull is a purely North Atlantic species with a rather limited range. It is replaced in the Arctic Ocean by the mainly white, similar-sized Glaucous Gull which visits Britain in winter. The slightly smaller gulls of the Herring Gull complex which covers most of the northern hemisphere also have a white arctic representative, the Iceland Gull, which is also a winter visitor. Two species of this complex breed with us. The dark-backed yellow-legged Lesser Black-backed Gull is a north-west Eurasian branch of the group, while our pale-backed pink-legged Herring Gull probably originated from North American stock.

Great Black-backed Gull *Larus marinus*
This is the giant of the gulls, strikingly black-and-white, with slow powerful flight, a hefty bill and deep impressive baying calls. It is mainly a bird of offshore islands and coasts, taking most of its food from the sea. When nesting it also raids nearby sea-bird colonies, and with its powerful bill is able to kill and eat other birds, from smaller gulls to shearwaters, and mammals such as rabbits. It also scavenges and in winter some move to inland refuse tips and similar sites.

It appears wary of human contact, less tame than other gulls, and when nesting tends to use cliffs or headlands where it may nest as solitary pairs; larger concentrations of pairs tend to be limited to relatively undisturbed island sites in the north. The nesting is typical of that of most gulls, both adults incubating, and bringing food to young until they are well-grown.

It has a restricted breeding range across the North Atlantic; on the east coast of North America, south Greenland, Iceland, the Faeroes, Scandinavia, west Spitzbergen, and around the British Isles and Brittany. Its winter dispersal is within the North Atlantic and mainly in coastal waters. We have no Pleistocene records, but it nested on the coast of south Wales in the early Holocene, about 9,000–6,000 years ago. It seems to have been a coastal bird in the past. It may have tried to move inland but would be killed for food and eggs. By the beginning of the nineteenth century, it was also persecuted as an alleged lamb-killer and possible threat to game-birds. There was a massive decrease in England and Wales between 1850 and 1893 which reduced the population to 20 pairs in six counties; and numbers also decreased in Scotland and Ireland, where it may have been less vulnerable.

By the turn of the century it was increasing again, to about 1,200 pairs in England and Wales in 1930, and by 1956 the numbers of some island populations had trebled again. In the 1920s it increased in Scotland, and it spread on both east and west coasts in the 1960s to 1970s. It now breeds around the coasts of the British Isles, except in the south and east between Hampshire and Berwickshire. There are occasional single breedings in East Anglia. It uses some inland sites in northern England, western Scotland and in Ireland. Over 25,000 pairs may be involved.

In winter some birds move south, but most remain, dispersing more to feeding sites, and a big influx of Norwegian birds occurs along the east side of Britain, forming a significant part of the winter population. There is also an increase of birds at inland sites such as refuse tips.

Lesser Black-backed Gull *Larus fuscus*
This is like a dark version of the Herring Gull, with sooty-grey back and yellow legs. It is clearly related to birds of northern Russia and north-west Siberia which also show these characters. These latter birds were regarded as forms of the Herring Gull, but are now treated as part of this species. Its differences from the Herring Gull are subtle. It is of slightly lighter build, the voice is a little deeper, it is less of a scavenger and fishes more often at sea. It has slightly different nest-site preferences and is mainly migratory. When it occurs inland in late summer passage, it is usually on grassy open spaces, and frequently on suburban playing fields. When breeding it is often on the shore or on arable land. In winter it feeds more on arable land than at refuse tips.

It breeds in large and sometimes dense colonies, preferring level sites. It may nest among dunes or on rocky islands, and more frequently inland on moors or islands in lakes than does the Herring Gull. Where it nests with Herring Gulls, the choice of nest-sites may separate it, as on islands where it may use a flat top while the Herring Gull uses the cliffs and rocky sides.

Its breeding range, spanning several populations separable by the depth of the dorsal grey colour, is from Iceland and the Faeroes to the British Isles; and from north-west Spain and Brittany to the Scandinavian coasts, and through tundra and subarctic zones from Finland to the Taymyr Peninsula. It winters in the North Atlantic south to the Mediterranean, Arabia and the African coasts. Often it is not possible to distinguish the bones of this species from those of the Herring Gulls, and there are no useful early records. It does not appear to have been distinguished separately from the Great Black-backed Gull, until by Montagu in 1802.

It may have derived benefit from the increase in arable farming over the centuries, to judge by its present use of it. Its numbers were probably controlled to some extent by egg-cropping. In the late nineteenth and early twentieth centuries, it decreased considerably in Scotland, inland and in the west. Subsequently, in the present century, it has increased generally in the British Isles. Changes are difficult to evaluate, owing to enormous size increase in some colonies and disappearance of others. In northern and western Scotland, and in Orkney and Shetland, it seems to have suffered recently from competition with increasing Great Black-backed Gulls and Great Skuas. Some southern British colonies appear not to have recovered after heavy egg-cropping in the 1939–45 war. On the eastern and southern coasts of both England and Ireland breeding colonies are very scanty. They are most numerous on the coasts of western Ireland, north and west Scotland, Orkney and Shetland. There were about 47,000 pairs in 1970.

It is mainly migratory, and until recently wholly so, with British birds moving down the European coasts to the western Mediterranean, and north-west and west Africa. Birds from Iceland, the Faeroes and Scandinavia also pass through, and may remain for a while. Overwintering seems to have started about the late 1940s with 165 birds in England and Wales in 1953, rising to 54,144 in 1983. Unlike Herring Gulls, these mainly occur inland in winter, with only small numbers in Ireland, southern Scotland, Wales and the south-west; but with a heavy concentration from Lancashire through midland England to the Bristol Channel and London Basin.

They roost on reservoirs and inland waters, and feed mainly on arable land, but also on refuse tips and sewage farms. Autumn ploughing may have encouraged this. Both native birds and immigrants are involved. A continuous southward movement from the British Isles also appears to occur until late winter, with numbers falling until March. They return to breeding sites later than the Herring Gull. The British Isles' wintering total was estimated at about 70,000 birds by the mid 1980s.

Herring Gull *Larus argentatus*

The most numerous of our gulls, and mainly coastal in distribution, this is the bird whose self-assertive yodelling and constant wails conjure up the 'sea-gull' image in the minds of most people. A dedicated scavenger and minor predator, it of all gulls has benefitted most from man's activities.

Our western Herring Gull, with its ash-grey back and pink legs is one of a chain of northern hemisphere forms. The North American bird is of similar colour, as is the north-east Eurasia tundra form. From western China to the Mediterranean, they are pale-backed and yellow-legged birds. In the north-west Eurasian tundra region and Scandinavia, a dark-breasted yellow-legged bird has separated to become our Lesser Black-backed Gull. An offshoot of the pale-backed and pink-legged American form seems to have given rise to our Herring Gull, probably crossing with the warm North Atlantic Drift Current to colonise a vacant area after a glaciation.

It is a general opportunist feeder on a variety of creatures, together with offal, carrion and some vegetable matter. It prefers raised and sheltered nest-sites but will utilise a wide range. Originally nesting on cliff-ledges and broken ground on coasts, it has spread to inland lakes and moorland ground sites. It has also taken to nesting on the roofs and chimney stacks of buildings since the 1940s, and has become increasingly disliked for the noise and mess involved. The downy young learn to hide between the chimney pots and emerge to beg food from the parents. Nests may be bulky or minimal, and both sexes share incubation and feeding of the young.

Its breeding range is discontinuous in tundra to warm-temperate zones of the northern hemisphere. It is migratory through much of its range, moving to unfrozen boreal to subtropical coasts, but present all year in much of the Mediterranean and European regions. There is no British fossil evidence of it. There is also little information on its early history. In the past it must have been kept in check by human activities, including egg-cropping at colonies, and it was mainly a coastal bird, found inland on lakes mainly in some northern regions.

It seems to have held its own until the present century, when persecution ceased and a considerable increase in discarded refuse at dispersed tips provided an assured winter supply, helping to create a massive increase in numbers. Some colonies grew rapidly. Walney Island, off Lakeland, had 35 pairs by 1935, 120 by 1947 and 17,000 by 1970. The Isle of May in the Firth of Forth had 1 pair 1907, 455 in 1936, 3,000 in 1954, 15,000 in 1970. Its general population has probably doubled in the last 20 years, and the recent increment has been in the order of 15% a year, barely affected by local decreases in a few areas.

Rooftop nesting began in the 1940s, and has spread. There are only a few scattered inland colonies, and except for two small attempts in East Anglia, colonies are absent on the east coast from Flamborough Head to north Kent; but the bird is found round all other coasts. About 340,000 pairs were thought to nest in the early 1970s. Its numbers will probably stabilise or fall with the introduction of deliberate control, and changes in refuse disposal techniques.

In winter it is fairly sedentary, but shows some general dispersal and a move inland. It is still mainly coastal, but has a general coverage in all but hill and mountain areas. Northern European immigrants occur along the eastern side, and small numbers of yellow-legged Mediterranean birds also occur in south-east England. There are unexplained variations. Inland birds doubled to about 103,000 from 1963 to 1973, but declined again in 1983. The total of wintering birds for the British Isles is probably about 500,000 birds.

Iceland Gull *Larus glaucoides*
NOT ILLUSTRATED

This is a smaller bird of similar appearance, a little slighter in build, and about Herring Gull size. It has a very narrow red eye-rim in adults. Its breeding ground is actually in southern Greenland and a limited part of the adjacent Canadian Arctic. It is a regular but scarce winter visitor to the British Isles, carried on westerly winds. It tends to be more numerous in Shetland and the north-west Scottish coast, but may turn up anywhere. There may be only 70–80 in normal winters, but up to several hundred on exceptional occasions.

Glaucous Gull *Larus hyperboreus*
This is a great white gull of the Arctic, some individuals as big as a Great Black-backed Gull, with silver-grey on back and wings, and a thin yellow rim around the eye. Immature birds have pale buffish mottling. It has a circumpolar breeding range in the tundra and High Arctic, some breeding as far south as southern Iceland. The British Isles are on the outer edge of its limited winter range. It tends to occur in late winter, mostly as single individuals, mixing with local gulls on coasts, and more rarely inland. Shetland has annual small parties. The visitors to Britain appear to come from the north, from the Barents Sea to east Greenland. Northerly gales and bad winter weather may bring larger numbers. The average winter population in the British Isles is probably between 200 and 500 birds.

Smaller Gulls
Larus and *Rissa* species

The smaller gull species are similar in appearance to the larger ones, but more lightly built, with thinner bills, and taking more small fish, insects and small invertebrates. Several of them are marshland gulls, tending to breed by inland waters, and also tending to occur in more temperate climates. Five species regularly occur in the British Isles. Of two mainly marshland breeders, the Little Gull is attempting to establish a toe-hold, while the Black-headed Gull is our most widespread species. The Mediterrean Gull is a species of steppe and warm-temperate regions that has invaded western Europe to breed in small numbers. The Common Gull is a northern moorland breeder in Britain. The Kittiwake represents a southern extension of an Arctic coastline species, and is a true sea-gull when not breeding.

Little Gull *Larus minutus*
In all plumages it is distinct in its blunt-tipped wings that have a blackish underside with narrow white margin. In winter the hood is replaced by grey cap and dark ear-spot. Young birds are heavily patterned like young Kittiwakes, but with dark cap and no separate neckband. It often feeds like marsh terns, circling and swooping in light agile flight, and moving upwind low over the water and dipping to seize small objects. It probably feeds this way at sea in winter. It is rather quiet, with a sharp *kuk-kuk-kuk* alarm call. It breeds in open freshwater marshy areas with floating and growing vegetation, nesting on plants or tussocks. It nests in small colonies, showing display behaviour very like that of Black-headed Gulls, both adults sharing the incubation and rearing of young.

It breeds discontinuously in inland regions of the warm boreal and temperate zone of Eurasia. There are a few sites scattered around the eastern Baltic and single ones in Denmark and the Netherlands. Most of these, and Russian and Finnish birds, appear to move down the western European coasts and winter offshore around mainland Europe and the Mediterranean. There are no early British records and it was first recognised in Britain by Montagu in 1813.

Breeding populations fluctuate, but numbers occurring around British shores in winter – in England, Ireland and south-east Scotland – have increased since the mid 1950s as part of a general westerly extension and increase. About 350–800 may occur, with many more in spring. A few birds have summered in suitable south-eastern places since 1968, and breeding was anticipated. In 1976 eggs were laid on a nest on the Cambridgeshire Ouse Washes, and there have been two further attempts, and more summering birds, but no real success as yet.

Adult Little Gull in summer plumage

Black-headed Gull *Larus ridibundus*
If the Herring Gull has become the spirit of the seaside, then the Black-headed Gull has in many places become the town gull. In London it first responded to public feeding when hard weather drove it up the Thames in the 1880s. Now, in many towns, feeding the park gulls is a much a ritual as feeding the ducks, and gulls react even faster to the sweeping arm movements that indicate thrown food. The throaty guttural *kak*-ing calls of circling and fluttering birds is a familiar sound, and in suburbs winter birds will take possession of roof-ridges

SUMMER

Little Gull

ADULT

Kittiwake

JUVENILE

SUMMER

Black-headed Gull

JUVENILE

Common Gull

SUMMER

SUMMER

Glaucous Gull

D.M.H.

and chimneys and threaten passing gulls with screams or throaty choking calls.

Inland, in town and country, they search grassy areas systematically for worms, follow ploughing tractors, and haunt sewage farms and refuse tips. In addition they are agile on the wing and can hover to snatch food from the ground or from water, or catch insects in the air. They appear to find enough food to spend most of the day loafing. For many people the gradual appearance of the dark hood in late winter is a sign of spring, and of the birds' summer absence.

In the south most breeding colonies are on estuaries and coastal saltmarsh or sand-dunes, but from the midlands northwards they use vegetated gravel-pits or clay-pits and sewage farms more frequently, with more natural sites on sedge and reed marshes, boggy margins of lakes and ponds, or low islands in fresh waters. Colonies are at times large, and often dense and noisy, but they may rapidly build up in size or disappear as vegetation or surroundings change from year to year. Displaying birds often show mutual posturing, shoulders hunched and head low, or with head raised high and turned sharply away from the partner to display the nape. Nests are usually on the ground, or raised on tussocks, sparse or bulky. Potential predators are vigorously mobbed, and this may encourage other bird species to nest nearby. Both adults share nesting duties.

It is basically a temperate zone nesting species, but its range is a broad one, from warm boreal to warm-temperate zones across Eurasia to Iceland. It is resident in southern and western Europe, including the British Isles; but elsewhere it is a migrant to coasts, south to tropical regions. With no evidence of subspeciation, it is difficult to guess in what parts it may have found refuge in the colder Pleistocene periods. Although it is now widespread, there is no early evidence of it in Britain, and although as a temperate marsh-breeder one might have expected it to be heavily predated, it is not proven to have occurred as a meal until about the tenth century in Shetland.

Its fortunes may not have varied much in past centuries, although it must have lost breeding sites as marshy areas were drained, and until very recent times has been regarded as an important source of eggs for eating. In the nineteenth century, when it also suffered from shooting for sport and from the demands of the plumage trade, it decreased very considerably, so much so that there was a suggestion from south-east England in the 1880s that it might be lost as a breeding species. However, it was surviving better in the north, and from the late nineteenth century onwards, it began to increase. This may have been due to a number of interacting factors, of which the warmer climate from then to the mid twentieth century may have been a critical one, although it has continued to increase in more recent decades. Similar increases have also occurred elsewhere in northern Europe.

As a breeding bird it has only a few inland sites south of a line from Swansea to Suffolk, and on the coast of that region breeds well in Essex and the Thames estuary, but then only at Dungeness, from Pagham to Portland Bill, and one south Cornish site. Further north it is sparse in the Midlands and patchy in the Fens and eastern counties. However, there are more breeding colonies through the higher ground of Wales, northern England and Scotland, (except in the highland mountains), in Orkney and Shetland, and over most of Ireland, except the south and west where it is sparse. Breeding pairs increased from about 35,000–40,000 in 1938 to 100,000 in 1976.

In winter most of the upland breeding areas are almost totally deserted, and in both Britain and Ireland birds are concentrated on coasts and on lowland areas inland, particularly in the south and east. Inland birds roost on or by open waters such as reservoirs or larger gravel-pits, and the increase of these in recent times may have aided the inland spread. There is a big winter influx of continental birds forming about two-thirds of the total, which may be in the order of 3,000,000 birds.

Mediterranean Gull *Larus melanocephalus*
NOT ILLUSTRATED

This is a white-winged Black-headed Gull. Very slightly stouter and heavier-billed than the latter, it lacks black on the wings, and breeding birds have a black hood that comes right down over the nape, as in the Little Gull. Winter birds have a bigger black ear-spot on a white head. Its call notes are deeper and less harsh than the Black-headed Gulls, and more like those of larger gulls. It may feed inshore or scavenge, but also takes insects and small invertebrates on inland grassy area, and a small amount of plant seeds.

It is a bird of open, steppe-type regions and warmer coasts, occurring on low coasts and estuaries, lagoons and shallow inland waters. It does not habitually go to drier inland sites or well out to sea. Like many birds of shallow waters of warm areas, it readily and rapidly moves long distances to new sites. Its original range is in the Black Sea area and the Aegean, wintering in the Mediterranean.

It only occurred in Britain as a vagrant in the past, and the Handbook of British Birds listed only 10 between 1866 and 1940; but it appeared to have undergone a considerable population increase and occurred more frequently in the 1950s. By the early 1960s, it had spread across much of mainland Europe, breeding mainly in coastal countries as for north-west as Belgium and the Baltic coast. These birds seem to have moved to Atlantic coasts in winter.

In 1968 several birds, including one bred in East Germany in 1966, joined a large Black-headed Gull colony on an estuarine coastal island in Hampshire. They bred, two individuals hybridising with Black-headed Gulls for lack of mates. From 1976 onwards small numbers of pairs have occurred and bred; and they were present on up to six sites in southern England by 1983. About 100–150 birds occur around the British Isles in winter, mostly in the south. They mainly occur on coasts with other gulls, rarely inland.

Common Gull *Larus canus*

Although the largest of these smaller gulls, the Common Gull, with its dark eyes, rather slender bill and legs, neat round white head, and rather prominent rounded breast often has a remarkably mild and dove-like look. However, this is belied by the vigorous piracy with which it will rob smaller species such as the Black-headed Gull. Like the latter, it may be seen quartering the short grass of fields or parks or the bare earth of arable land for earthworms. It is the boreal gull of Eurasia and very often an inland bird, haunting the moors and valleys of hill regions, and on coasts preferring low sandy shores with a plentiful supply of worms and small shellfish.

It does not develop a distinct breeding plumage like those of the dark-headed gulls, but the head which is white in breeding birds shows dusky streaking in winter. Its display behaviour is like that of the larger gulls, a hunched posture with head held low between paired birds, or display with arched neck and wailing calls, or head thrown back in a long yodel that is higher in pitch than those of larger species – a shrill whistled *kee-ya*. The nest is a shallow cup of plant material, variable in bulk, usually on the ground among débris and herbage, but sometimes raised on shrubs or-exceptionally-in pine trees. Both sexes incubate and care for the young.

Its breeding range is in a broad belt across the boreal zone of Eurasia and western North America. At its western end it reaches to the British Isles, Faeroes and coasts of Iceland. It is mainly migratory to temperate coasts and inland waters, but resident on north-west Europe from the southern Baltic to France, and in the British Isles and Faeroes. There is a Pleistocene record of it, from Derbyshire in the last glaciation. It is a bird of cooler, boreal conditions that would have been present further south and is likely to have retreated in the post-glacial period.

Its main stronghold has been in Scotland and north-west Ireland where it nests extensively inland, on islands and shingle banks of rivers, islands in lake marshes, and also on moorland, the colonies usually small and rather scattered. It nests, too, on coasts, grassy slopes or dunes; and on inshore islands; it will nest quite high in hill and mountain areas, usually near water.

It is likely to have found more sites for nesting and feeding, and to have increased in numbers in past centuries, as woodland was cleared and more open moor and marsh, and areas of grass and cultivation were available. It should also have flourished better in the cooler centuries of the Little Ice Age. However, it would have suffered from loss of eggs at its more accessible colonies. Like so many other species, its numbers seem to have increased from the late nineteenth century onwards, when colonies grew and spread in both Scotland and Ireland. It is possible that cooler climate has contributed to the more rapid increase since the 1950s, when it occupied Fair Isles and St Kilda and spread into most parts of southern Scotland.

Some scattered breedings have occurred in north-eastern England, and as far south as Anglesey, Nottingham and Norfolk. In the last two counties, the birds may have moved in from mainland Europe, as almost certainly did those that colonised Dungeness in Kent. Here birds began breeding in 1919, rising to about 20–30 pairs in 1939, but have decreased since. In Ireland it has spread around the north-east coastal regions. In general the main distribution of breeding colonies is wide through Scotland, Orkney and Shetland, and in the north-west half of Ireland. In the mid 1970s, the breeding population in the British Isles was estimated at about 50,000 pairs.

In winter it shifts to lowlands and sandy coastlines. It is almost wholly absent from the greater part of its breeding range, as well as from high ground of Lakeland, the Pennines, Wales, and the west of inland Ireland. It is sparse in the English Midlands and south-west. However, it will use well-drained grasslands of the better-drained hilly areas, such as limestone regions. It feeds extensively at this time of year on arable land and short grasses. Earthworms are an important source of food; and in hard weather it may resort to sandy shores for molluscs and worms, or move out altogether. Inland-feeding birds roost mainly on estuaries, but also on the larger reservoirs. There is a considerable influx of wintering continental birds from late summer onwards, and some westward shift and southward migration of native birds. The winter population has been estimated at about 700,000 birds.

Kittiwake *Rissa tridactyla*

This is the species most deserving the name 'sea-gull', and in winter these small gulls with their narrow black-tipped wings can be seen far out in oceanic waters in all weathers. They are skilful and strong fliers, plunge-diving for small fish and other creatures, occasionally swimming erratically and picking up small objects. Their legs are short and designed for perching rather than walking; while the bill is longer and a little more hooked at the tip than in other small gulls, and with a downturned innermost margin that imparts a slightly peevish expression.

It comes to coasts and island shores to breed, using high, sheer cliffs overlooking salt water, and fixing a drum-shaped nest to a narrow ledge or small prominence. With increased demand for sites and less harassment, it has also started to use lower cliffs, and sometimes ledges of waterside buildings or other man-made structures. It nests in colonies, noisy with birds calling with the incessant wailing *kitt-ee-mayke* call and displaying a bright red gape to the greenish bill. The two young huddle facing the cliff, with little space to move, until they fly.

Its breeding range is on rocky arctic shores, south to Britain, northern France, and more recently to the Iberian peninsula. In winter it disperses, and occurs through the North Atlantic and north Pacific. There is an early occurrence in the Pleistocene, in the colder period of the last glaciation in Somerset. As a purely coastal bird with inaccessible nests, it was probably little affected by human activity in earlier centuries. It must have undergone a massive decrease during the nineteenth century. Then birds in breeding colonies were regularly shot for sport and for food, both from land and from the water; and Kittiwake's wings, particularly those of the young, became a standard item in the plumage trade, resulting in systematic and persistant over-exploitation. Legal protection began to be given at the end of the nineteenth century. A very considerable increase took place in the first half of the present century, both in the British Isles and in northern Europe generally. The British increase mainly enlarged the size of existing colonies at first, but it has been estimated that the population increased at a rate of 50% each decade; and new colonies were being formed from the 1920s onwards. The breeding population by 1970 was estimated at about 470,000 pairs, about half of them in Scotland and a quarter in Orkney. The majority were on the North Sea coasts from Shetland southwards.

Most Kittiwakes spend the winter out at sea, and British birds have reached North America. They may begin to return to the breeding colonies by late winter, but only about 1% of the breeding population occur around the coasts of the British Isles in winter.

Terns

Sternidae

These are gull-like birds, but streamlined for swooping and diving, producing something reminiscent of both kingfisher and swallow. Bills are fairly long, sharp and tapering; head and body are narrower, and more elongated and compact; wings are long, narrow and tapering; while the tail is strongly forked for greater agility and the sudden checks and hovering needed before diving. Movement on land is less important and legs tend to be shorter. They are of two types, marsh terns and sea terns. Marsh terns are lighter, more agile and less specialised, swooping to seize food from the surface, and mainly over fresh water. Sea terns are more vigorous plunge-divers for food, mainly in shallow seas.

They are active, strong-flying birds and vagrants of a number of species may visit the British Isles; but we have one regular marsh tern, the Black Tern, a bird of temperate western Eurasia. There are five sea terns. The Common Tern is a warm boreal to warm-temperate breeder of the northern hemisphere; it is replaced in arctic regions by the very similar and closely related Arctic Tern. Their breeding ranges overlap in the British Isles. The remaining three have scattered distributions on warmer coasts of the world. The Roseate Tern of Britain and Brittany shares its west African wintering area with an Azores population. The British Isles are on the northern edge of the breeding range of the Little Tern. The largest species, the Sandwich Tern, has a breeding range in warm-temperate southern Europe, and another in France, Britain and the Baltic.

Black Tern *Chlidonias niger*
This is unmistakably black or strongly pied. It has an easy, light drifting flight, and can soon be recognised in feeding as it moves slowly upwind low over the water, looking down and constantly dipping to the surface to seize some small object. It may feed (more rarely) in similar fashion over land. When resting, it will often perch on a post or similar raised site. It is a rather quiet bird, using abrupt *kik* calls and sharper notes. Louder *krii-er-ick* calls are used by breeding birds. It is sociable, usually occurring in parties or flocks.

It breeds on shallower fresh or brackish waters with plenty of vegetation, with some lying or floating on the surface. The nests are usually built on rafts of floating plants and stems, and only rarely on dry land. Breeding birds may indulge in group high-flying in which a number mount up calling in spiralling flight with exaggerated wing-beats, and after some aerial chasing descend in a gliding spiral. At the nest, pairs may display in upright posture with uptilted head, and a crouching or deep bowing associated with food-offering. Both adults incubate, and feed the young. Before and after breeding birds may move to larger and less vegetated waters such as reservoirs; and on migratory passage they often occur on estuaries and sea coasts.

It breeds in the temperate zone of western Eurasia and across North America, migrants wintering on tropical and subtropical coasts. The range should include the British Isles and appears to have done so in the past. The earliest mention appears to be that by Turner in 1544. It should have found suitable breeding sites in marshes and fens, and habitat would have been increasingly reduced by the extensive drainage in recent centuries. It also suffered from having eggs taken. Although it does not seem to have extended to Scotland and possibly not to Wales, it was present and probably fairly widespread until the nineteenth century, but had mostly disappeared by the 1850s. By then it was lost to East Anglia except for breedings after floods in 1853 and 1858. Its last stronghold was on the marshy levels of Romney Marsh in Kent, where it appears to have bred until about 1885. There are suggestions that it may have bred on Solway in 1855 and Oulton Broad in Suffolk in 1875.

It ceased to breed in the British Isles for about 80 years. In general it has decreased in Europe in recent times through habitat loss, and this may have caused some birds to re-explore Britain. Three pairs bred on the Ouse Washes in 1966, six pairs in 1969, and some at another East Anglian site in 1970. It bred again on the Ouse Washes in 1975, 1978 and 1983. In the same period birds spread to Ireland, where a single pair bred on a rocky islet in a lough in 1967, and breeding occurred again in 1975.

Common Tern *Sterna hirundo*
This is perhaps the typical tern, flying with deep flickering wing-beats, and with harsh *keeyah* call, and suddenly plunging headlong to hit the water with a splash and rise again with a quick flutter of wings; or flying high overhead in a ritualised fish-carrying display; parading around its mate, head and neck raised high, wings drooped and tail cocked up in a sharp spike, and carrying a small fish as an offering. As a breeding bird, it is widespread on coasts and estuaries and into inland waters with stony or sandy islands and margins, and on artificial sites such as rafts in gravel-pits. It also breeds on the herbage of level offshore islands, and on inland moors in Scotland.

It has a broad breeding range in warm boreal to warm-temperate zones through the northern hemisphere, extending north along the Norwegian coasts but not across to Iceland. It migrates to subtropical and tropical coasts. It does not have early records in Britain, and it was not clearly differentiated from the Arctic Tern until this was done by Naumann in 1819, making any earlier comments of limited use. As a coastal species it was probably only affected to a limited degree by early vegetation changes and by man's activities. However, it must have been affected by collecting of eggs at colonies, and by the nineteenth century would also have suffered from shooting for sport and for plumage.

Certainly numbers decreased, but local increase and decrease in colonies is so erratic and unpredictable, as in most terns, that taken together with early problems of species identification, it is difficult to get a clear overall picture. Numbers increased again in the early part of the present century. It may have responded favourably to the warmer climate of that period, since it seems to have

Black Tern

SUMMER

AUTUMN

Arctic Tern

SUMMER

Roseate Tern

SUMMER

Common Tern

SUMMER

Little Tern

SUMMER

SUMMER

D.M.HENRY.

Sandwich Tern

The length of the tail-streamer and of the legs suggest that this uncaptioned sketch was of a Common rather than Arctic Tern.

reached a peak in the 1930s and to have fallen a little in recent decades. In Scotland, in areas of overlap where mixed colonies of the two species occur, the proportion of Common Terns has tended to decrease, and that of Arctic Terns to rise, in the last few years.

Numbers have also fallen, or colonies disappeared, in places where large gulls and skuas have greatly increased. However, numbers have increased in this period in south-west Ireland. There has been an increasing tendency for inland nesting in the east of England in the last forty years, when more man-made sites have also become available. As a breeding bird it is present on most coasts, but absent from the south-west, almost all of Wales apart from Anglesey, and most of the Durham and Yorkshire coasts. It occurs inland in mid and eastern Scotland, south-east England and the north-west half of Ireland. The breeding population in the 1970s was estimated at about 15,000–20,000 pairs. These birds migrate southwards to winter on the coasts of west Africa.

Arctic Tern *Sterna paradisaea*
This is the Arctic counterpart of the Common Tern. It is difficult to distinguish but has shorter legs, slightly shorter bill, more translucent wings, and difference of emphasis and pitch in the *keeyah* call. It is famous for its migration. It breeds around the Arctic Ocean and although some British birds may winter no further south than the southern African coast, many birds travel to the Antarctic seas. It is thought to be the species with the longest regular migration route. Some young birds appear to remain at that end of the globe for the first year, and are suspected of circumnavigating the south polar seas before returning to breed the following year.

Like the Common Tern, it is adaptable to some degree in feeding. It will plunge-dive from up to 6 metres, but also pick small objects from the surface, catch insects in the air, or hunt over land to take insects from vegetation or worms from the ground. It will also rob other birds and scavenge around fishing boats.

Like the Common Tern with which it may share colonies, it is highly sociable, but also highly aggressive at the nest and in group defence of the colony against potential predators. This sometimes attracts other species, such as terns, small gulls, ducks, waders or grebes, to nest nearby and share the protection. It nests both on coasts and on inland fresh waters, and on various typical sites, including small turf-covered or rocky islands. Its overall breeding distribution is on arctic coasts and tundra, extending south on the east side of the Atlantic to the Baltic, southern North Sea and the British Isles. As mentioned for the Common Tern, the two were not separately identified until 1819 by Naumann, and early records are lacking. It may always have been our most numerous tern, and could have been more abundant further south in the cooler fourteenth to nineteenth centuries. Like most colony-nesting sea-birds, it suffered in the nineteenth century from egg-cropping, shooting, and the demands of the plumage trade. Like them it began to recover in the present century, but may have been less successful in the warmer period. It has been an infrequent breeder in the Scilly Isles, where in the nineteenth century it outnumbered the Common Tern, although there has been some recovery recently.

Although mixed colonies occur around the British Isles, the Arctic Tern is the more numerous in Scotland, where 90% of its population is in the northern islands, the Westray group in Orkney having 28,000 pairs in 1969. Its present distribution is mainly around coasts and a short way inland, northwards from Northumberland on the east side, and Anglesey on the west. In Ireland it is scattered around the coasts, and also on inland sites in the north and west. In England there are odd colonies on coasts of north Norfolk and Suffolk, north Kent and Dorset. The British Isles' population, estimated at 50,000 pairs in 1969, had fallen to about 40,000 in 1975 because of disturbance and natural predation on Westray.

Roseate Tern *Sterna dougallii*
This is a more subtly beautiful tern, light and buoyant in flight, appearing much whiter than others and with a fine pale pink wash on the underside. The tail streamers are much longer. These, and the sharp *chiv-ik* and more gutteral *kraak* calls help to identify it, especially since it tends to occur in small numbers in colonies of other tern species. Although it uses colonies in open sites, its nests tend to be partly protected by beach débris, rocks or vegetation. It is essentially a bird of coastal waters, preferring shallow, sandy shores. It plunge-dives from heights of up to 2 metres. At times it will also steal food from other terns.

It has a discontinuous breeding distribution as

separate populations around the warmer tropical and subtropical seas of the world. Overall, the British Isles is its most northerly breeding place, and birds from here and Brittany join those from the Azores in wintering on the coasts of west Africa. It has a very brief history at present, since it was first recognised and described as a new species by Montagu as recently as 1813, from a specimen collected in Scotland. Its status is difficult to assess because it is one of those species that show erratic changes in the use of nesting-sites.

There are few large colonies, and sometimes small numbers appear as subcolonies within those of other tern species. It is also possible that climate may have some effect in view of an increase in the first half of this century, coupled with some evidence of a more recent decrease. It suffered a drastic reduction in the early nineteenth century, and by the end of it was almost extinct as a British breeding bird. Numbers subsequently increased, possibly up to about 3,500 in the early 1960s. It ceased to breed in the Scilly Isles in 1870, returning in 1920; it was absent from Ulster between 1880 and 1908 and from a previously large colony in County Dublin between the 1850s and late 1940s.

In Britain it now breeds in Orkney, around Moray Firth, Firth of Forth and Northumberland on the eastern side; in Hampshire, Anglesey, Morecambe Bay, and one or two sites in south-west Scotland. There are a few scattered sites in Ireland. Population was estimated at about 2,500 in the late 1960s, 1,400 in the mid 1970s, and about 600 by the mid 1980s. Wintering birds in West Africa may be adversely affected by snaring and catching for food or amusement that occurs on the coast, particularly in Ghana.

Little Tern *Sterna albifrons*

A tiny tern of sandy and shingly beaches, circling in rather excited fashion with fast, wing-flickering flight and rapid *kirridic* calls, usually fishing close inshore or performing miniature versions of dramatic plunge-dives in the brackish ditches of coastal marshes, often pausing and hovering longer than the larger species. It tends to nest on low sand or shingle bars, or on the seaward slopes of beaches, nearer the sea than other terns and likely to lose nests on very high tides.

It has an extensive but very scattered breeding range being in north and central America, and Eurasia south to West Africa and to Australia. It winters on tropical and subtropical coasts. There seem to be no early British records and James Fisher gave the earliest written reference as 1671. It should have been little affected in early times except for loss of eggs to people from fishing villages, but even then colonies would have been small and scattered. As one might expect, numbers declined in the nineteenth century and built up again in the first half of this century. Climate may have some effect since the British Isles are on the northern limit of the species, and none breed in Orkney and Shetland. It may have reached a population peak in the 1930s.

However, in addition to suffering from high tides, predation, and possibly from a cooler climate, it also began to suffer seriously from the vastly increased use of coastal beaches by holidaymakers. Even when these last were well-intentioned, the unlined nest-scrapes and well camouflaged eggs made the nests hopelessly vulnerable. It also, as a species with a small population,

began to suffer significantly from egg-collectors. Numbers were estimated at about 1,600 in 1967 and this was regarded as a low figure. It rose to 1,800 by 1970, but subsequently declined steadily. With special protection it has now stabilised but is still under threat.

Nesting occurs on the sandier and shallower shores of the British Isles, with the main population concentrated in southern and eastern England. It is absent from the south-west and south Wales, most of Yorkshire and Durham coasts, and western Scotland except for a few islands, and from south-west and north-east Ireland.

Sandwich Tern *Sterna sandvicensis*

Biggest and noisiest of the sea terns, with a shaggy-naped black crest, and a grating *kireet* call like an unoiled cart wheel. About the size of a Black-headed Gull, it has a slower and more powerful flight than that of other terns, and often flies at a greater height. It will fly further to feed, and plunge-dives vigorously from heights of up to 10 metres, although it will also take food by shallow diving, and dipping at the surface. One of its main foods is sandeels, and like other tern species it may suffer badly in the future from the excessive sandeel fishing now occurring in the North Sea.

It breeds on very open sites, usually coastal – on beaches, sand bars and spits, on shingle beds and in Ireland exceptionally on islands in freshwater lakes. Birds breed in tight-packed, noisy colonies with nests a mutual bill-stab apart, and the breeding cycle very closely synchronised. It deserts easily if disturbed early in the breeding cycle, and may move a long distance to form a new colony. Numbers also vary erratically at regularly-used sites. Display includes high-flying performance, often initiated by males carrying fish; and paired birds posture with closed wings held away from the body, heads raised and crests ruffled, or sleeked crests and upward-pointed bills. Both adults share the nesting, and part-fledged young may leave the nest and gather in closely grouped 'crèches' while waiting for food. Immature birds may still be fed when they are leaving on migration.

One population breeds in the eastern Americas; another through warm-temperate regions of southern Europe to the Caspian Sea, and on the Atlantic coast from France to the British Isles and Baltic Sea. European birds winter on subtropical and tropical coasts south to southern Africa. It is the only tern with an early (Pleistocene) record; occurring on the East Anglian coast area in an early interglacial possibly about 500,000 years ago. The subsequent history is uncertain. Like other terns, it certainly suffered some decrease in the nineteenth century. It recovered in the present century to about 11,800 pairs by 1970 and approaching 15,000 by 1980. Netherlands colonies suffered serious decreases in the 1960s through chemical poisons in food, which with oil pollution of the seas is still a potential threat.

It does not breed on Shetland, but is sparsely present from Orkney to Northumberland, and on the west side from the Clyde to Anglesey. It is present at places round the Irish coast, but in the south-east half is only present in Wexford. It first bred, or returned to, East Anglia in 1920 (and now breeds to Essex), and to Hampshire and Dorset in 1954. The main population is on the east coast.

Auks

Alcidae

There appears to have been a place in the colder but productive waters of both northern and southern hemispheres for birds that could swim under water and exploit this abundant food. The wings tend to become developed for swimming, and are smaller relative to the body size of the bird. The body is elongated and compact, but for these cold seas, legs and necks are fairly short, the feet set well back for propulsion at the surface, and for steering underwater, and possibly also in flight to supplement the small short tail. In the Antarctic seas this niche has been exploited by penguins, which have achieved an extraordinary degree of adaptation to this way of life. In the Arctic regions an offshoot of the Charadriiformes has moved into this niche, but does not show quite such extreme adaptation. However, similar demands of the environment have resulted in the evolution of striking superficial similarities. This group of birds is the auks.

The smallest, the Little Auk, is an arctic breeder, wintering at sea, and a wind-drifted passage-migrant to the British Isles. Of three medium-sized species, the Black Guillemot is a coastal bird of subarctic regions extending to the northern half of the British Isles and wintering inshore. The Guillemot and Razorbill occupy similar ranges in boreal to cool-temperate regions, the Razorbill tolerant of lower temperatures when breeding, and ranging further in winter. The Puffin is a smaller, stout-billed and more oceanic bird of similar regions. The extinct Great Auk appears to have been a flightless North Atlantic relative of the Razorbill.

Razorbill *Alca torda*

A stoutly-built auk with a deep, blunt and laterally-flattened bill with a curved tip. Well-adapted for swimming on and under water, the posteriorly placed short legs give it the typical upright and penguin-style stance; and the slightly reduced wings give some hint of the specialisation that finally produced the Great Auk. It feeds on fish, swimming with its face and eyes submerged to spot them, then after a surface dive with partly-opened wings, swims rapidly underwater using wings held well out from the body and steering with the feet. It dives to depths of about 6 metres, less deep than the Guillemot and catching smaller fish.

It sleeps on the water, well-insulated by dense plumage, and its flight is fast and usually low, with the feet supplementing the tail; but like all auks it has limited manoeuvrability, and is awkward on land, usually waddling and shuffling with feet and lower legs flat on the ground. It is rather silent, except for low growling calls when breeding.

It nests in colonies on cliffs and rocky shores overlooking the sea. It often shares sites with Guillemots but prefers to nest in a sheltered niche, cleft or cave, resulting in more scattered pairs. The large single egg is laid on bare rock or stones. Both adults tend the downy chick which leaves when part-fledged and goes to sea with the parents.

It is a North Atlantic species, breeding from east Greenland to New England, and from Iceland to Scandinavia, the British Isles and Brittany. It disperses to inshore seas and waters of the continental shelf in winter, as far south as the western Mediterranean, but many adults remain near enough to visit nest-sites in winter. It occurred early in the British Pleistocene, in the Pastonian Interglacial in Norfolk; and later bred in coastal caves of south Wales in the Ipswichian Interglacial. It is also present in early Holocene remains and in the peat of East Anglia.

It had been killed for food from the earliest times, but no doubt saved from serious harm by the inaccessibility of many of its breeding sites. It suffered more severely in the nineteenth century, when increasing ease of transport coincided with the sport of shooting sea-birds off their nests at breeding colonies, and the taking of eggs for food and souvenirs. It seems to have disappeared from the chalk cliffs of Sussex about 1878. In the present century numbers seemed to have been fairly stable, or possibly rising.

It was lost from the eastern Isles of Wight about 1920, and there has been a decrease in numbers in the south of England and Wales since about the 1940s, but some increase in northern Britain. This may reflect changes in fish populations and ranges. It breeds on a succession of sites around the British Isles where cliffs or rocky coasts occur. It is absent from Northumberland to the Isle of Wight, except at Flamborough Head in Yorkshire, and from the Bristol Channel, Lancashire and most of Lakeland. The breeding population is estimated at about 150,000 pairs.

Great Auk *Alca impennis*
NOT ILLUSTRATED

The Great Auk is now extinct. It looked like an oversized and flightless Razorbill. It was similar in colour but had a white oval patch on either side of the forehead, and was said to be 'red about the eyes'. Twice as tall as a Razorbill and larger in proportion, it had wings reduced in size and used only for swimming. It caught fish underwater. To rest on land, and to nest, it needed low shelving rocks and islands where it could leave the water easily. It evolved as a marine bird nesting on islands free from mammalian predators, and it died from the attentions of an insatiable predator – the human being.

Its breeding range was from islands near Newfoundland to Iceland and Scotland; possibly to the Faeroes and east Greenland. It dispersed to sea within this region. Remains from Florida and the Mediterranean may be evidence of the necessary southward shift that must have occurred during Pleistocene glaciations.

Within the British Isles, there is only evidence of its breeding from the extreme north-west, on St Kilda, and on Papa Westray in north Orkney. Martin Martin's account of its breeding on St Kilda in 1698 describes a typical auk, and gives its breeding period from the beginning of May to mid June, and indicates that it was not resident. By the eighteenth century it was said that it did not visit annually, suggesting a decrease, unless it infers that it bred only once in two years. By the early

Razorbill

WINTER

Puffin

SUMMER

SUMMER

SUMMER

Little Auk

SUMMER

Guillemot

Black Guillemot

WINTER SUMMER

WINTER

D.M. HENRY

nineteenth century it was very rare, and by 1840 so little known that the last British Great Auk was caught and killed there in the belief that it was a witch. Demands for skins and eggs from collectors hastened its end. On Papa Westray the last female was killed about 1812, and a male in 1813. The last pair of the species were killed in Iceland in 1844.

Guillemot *Uria aalge*

This is the most spectacular of our auks. It breeds on open sites – the broad ledges of steep cliffs and the flat bare platforms and tops of rock stacks. It packs into such spaces in a seething close-huddled mass of pied bodies and thin heads peering on snaky necks, the whole shuffling, sparring and squabbling with a massive chorus of deep throaty growls and harsh trumpetings. The crowd turns its back on the sea; and under and among it, laid on bare rock, are huge single eggs that the birds seem to have some difficulty in incubating. The eggs show exceptional individual variation in colour and pattern, and possibly aid recognition by the owner in the absence of a nest. It is difficult for birds to move, land or leave; but the crowd stimulus seems to aid and synchronise successful nesting.

The large downy chick is tended by both adults. Nesting ledges face the sea and the young flutter down and leave with the parents when still only half-fledged. Adults moult at about this time so that all are swimming but flightless. Although they leave the nest-site after breeding, adults visit the colony during the winter, although least in mid-winter, and it is immature birds that roam furthest.

Like other auks it feeds by peering under water, then diving to chase fish. It may swim down to depths of up to 60 metres. In some areas large numbers are trapped in fishing nets. Fish are usually swallowed underwater when caught, but it brings to the nestling larger fish than those taken by Razorbill and Puffin, carrying them lengthwise and head-first in the bill.

Its breeding range is in the North Atlantic and North Pacific in subarctic to temperate waters. It appears more localised than other auk species, and a number of subspecies are recognised. The north-east Atlantic population extends from Novaya Zemlya, west Spitzbergen and Iceland to north Finland, the Norwegian coast, the British Isles, Brittany and the west coast of the Iberian peninsula. In winter it is dispersive in nearby seas.

Its early records in Britain begin in the early Pleistocene in the Pastonian Interglacial in Norfolk; and then in the last glaciation in the south-west. Subsequently it, and probably its eggs, were taken for food. Inaccessibility of some sites may have helped it survive. Like many sea-birds it suffered, often very severely, from the systematic shooting and egg-cropping of the nineteenth century, although this may have been localised in its effect. It lost some breeding sites through the erosion of the soft chalk cliffs of the south-east, and ceased breeding in Sussex about 1878 and in Kent about 1910. In more recent times its fluctuations have paralleled those of the Razorbill, sharing a similar breeding distribution, but much more numerous. It has decreased in the south and west of the British Isles, but shown a steady increase in the north and north-east. It has been suggested that oil pollution, to which it is particularly susceptible, may have been a factor.

Its largest colonies are in north-west Scotland and the islands and in Orkney and Shetland. In England it occurs in Northumberland, Flamborough Head in Yorkshire, from the Isle of Wight round to north Devon, and at St Bees Head in Lakeland. It occurs on western promontories of Wales, the Isle of Man, and intermittently around Ireland but with only two east coast areas. It seems to have increased at about 5% per annum in recent decades overall, but this may have levelled out. The total breeding population is estimated at about 550,000 pairs, 80% of them in Scotland and the northern Islands.

Some Norwegian and Faeroese birds occur on British coasts in winter, when birds are widely distributed on all coasts.

Puffin *Fratercula arctica*

Accidents of adaptation and ornamentation have made this the most endearing of our sea-birds. Short vermilion legs support a plump and portly bird with a short tail and a large head that in the breeding bird is ornamented in the manner of a traditional circus clown. The great parrot-bill is enlarged by bands of bright decoration, while a false triangular eyebrow over a red-rimmed eye on a whitened face gives it an air of earnest bewilderment. This is accompanied in social groupings by deep conversational *aah*'s in what sounds like a rural human accent. Its displays include birds facing each other and solemnly rapping bills, and a slow and exaggerated walk with body bolt upright, breast puffed up and bill tucked into it, and tail cocked.

It flies rapidly with fast whirring wing-beats, showing dark underwings. It fishes like other large auks, ducking its eyes under to see first, then shallow-diving and swimming underwater using its wings and going down to depths of up to 15 metres. When feeding young, it accommodates a number of fish crosswise in the bill. Like other auks it moults at sea.

It breeds in colonies, sometimes huge, but requires a substrate into which it can burrow. It honeycombs the turf cover of islands and coastal cliffs with horizontal burrows, or (rarely) uses a natural cleft or cavity. It can dig its own burrows, but will take over those of rabbits or shearwaters.

Its breeding range is in the North Atlantic from Greenland to north-east U.S.A., and from Spitzbergan to north Finland, Norway, Iceland, the British Isles and Brittany. In winter it disperses widely over the North Atlantic ocean, and in inshore waters to the Canary Islands. Its earliest British record is from Derbyshire in the latter part of the last glaciation, and it was killed at breeding colonies from the Stone Age onwards.

Its breeding colonies are mainly on inshore islands, at times they may be enormous but numbers fluctuate wildly, although apparently not through human interference. There are also large local increases and decreases. Factors involved appear to be predation by rats, soil erosion from too much burrowing, oil and chemical pollution, failure of fish stocks from human or natural causes, and possibly underlying climatic factors. Population variation may be as complex in its causes as in other auk species. It was lost from cliffs in Kent in the early nineteenth century. Early numbers were rough estimates, but Annet Island in the Scillies dropped from 100,000 in 1908 to under 100 in 1970. Similar decreases occurred in places such as Lundy Island, St Tudwal's

Islands and Ailsa Craig. An overall picture suggests heavy losses, particularly between the 1920s and 1950s, in the south and west, but some increases, at times considerable in the north and north-east.

It breeds most numerously in Shetland, Orkney and north and west Scotland. It breeds around Ireland, and on the Isle of Man. English sites are limited to Northumberland, Flamborough Head, Dorset, Cornwall and the Scillies, on Lundy and the western extremities of south and north Wales, Anglesey and St Bees Head. The British Isles' population is estimated at about 700,000 pairs, with about 90% of them in Scotland and the islands, and about 300,000 of them on St Kilda.

Black Guillemot *Cepphus grylle*

This is a less penguin-like auk, often looking rounder-bodied and with a small sleek head; and a more squatting stance. Its display strut is in its strong contrast, when it trots along bolt upright, exposing a vivid red gape as it utters a disyllabic peeping call. The more usual call is a thin long-drawn whistle.

It is a bird of rocky shores, nesting in small loose colonies of scattered pairs in cavities among rocks or under boulders. It will also nest under debris and driftwood, and nest-sites may be at low enough levels to be in danger of flooding on very high tides. Unlike larger auks it lays two eggs, and both adults share nesting duties. Off duty birds join others in a 'loafing flock' on the colony's edge, where resting and display occurs. It has rather rounded wings, and the white wing-patch and white underwing are conspicuous in flight in all plumages. It feeds in clear shallow water off rocky shores, where seaweed is present on the bottom. It dives from the surface to depths of up to 40 metres and feeds mainly near or at the bottom. It remains at such inshore feeding grounds during the winter months and does not move far from the breeding colony.

It breeds around arctic shores, and in the north-east Atlantic around Scandinavia south to the Kattegat, and round Iceland, the Faeroes and British Isles. There appear to be no British records prior to one from Devon about the end of the last glaciation, and another from Derbyshire. The next might be Ray's record of it at the Bass Rock in August 1661. Its habitat can have changed little and with its dispersive habits it would not seem a

Black Guillemot in summer plumage

very vulnerable species, even to the nineteenth century sportsmen who shot up colonies.

However, it disappeared from south-east Scotland in the nineteenth century, and from North Wales in the middle of that century. It last bred in Yorkshire in 1938. In England a few pairs breed at St Bees Head in Lakeland, and in Wales a few pairs have returned to Anglesey since about 1962. There are a few sites in the Moray Firth, and it bred on the Scottish north-east coast twice in this century. Otherwise its range is from Caithness round north and west Scotland and Orkney and Shetland, on the Isle of Man, and around most of Ireland.

It is subject to local fluctuations and has increased in recent times in south-west Scotland and eastern Ireland. Since oil operations began in the northern islands, it has been increasingly vulnerable to inshore oil pollution. Its breeding population was originally estimated at about 8,340 pairs but is now thought to be nearer to 17,000–25,000 pairs, possibly rising to 58,000–80,000 individuals in early winter.

Little Auk *Alle alle*

A very small compact bird, not much bigger than a starling. With narrow wings, often no apparent neck, blunt stubby bill, and a tiny white brow-spot over the dark eye, it can look more like a child's toy than a seabird. However, it is surprisingly tough and spends the winter in northern and arctic seas, whirring near the surface in rapid flight, diving and rising easily, bobbing and bouncing over and through waves, and swimming underwater after small planktonic crustaceans.

It is a breeding bird of the High Arctic, its breeding colonies no nearer than Spitzbergen and off northern Iceland. It nests in huge colonies in cavities in screes and fallen rocks, and is thought to be the world's most numerous sea-bird, in spite of a limited range. It is absent from breeding grounds between late August and May. As arctic seas freeze, birds are forced further south, and it winters in the Norwegian Sea and into the northern North Sea. Although not particularly sociable when feeding, suitable conditions may bring them together in thousands. Stormy weather makes food less readily available and as birds weaken they are carried downwind. In periods of exceptionally bad weather they have been forced inshore, dying birds occurring on coasts and individuals appearing inland on widely scattered inland waters.

There is a Pleistocene record of it from the latter part of the last glaciation in the Mendips, and it also occurred on the south Wales coast and in Devon in the very early Holocene. There is nothing to suggest breeding, although this could have occurred in glacial periods. Subsequently its history is one of sparse but annual occurrences offshore on northern coasts, regular appearances in Shetland waters, and sporadically elsewhere – but more often on eastern than on western coasts. Prolonged and severe winter weather may wreck several thousands on our shores, and it is also vulnerable to oil pollution. When 'wrecks' do occur, stray birds may turn up anywhere.

Pigeons

COLUMBIFORMES

Columbidae

These are basically seed-and fruit-eating birds, mostly ground-feeding, but perching, roosting and often nesting in trees. They have simple sketchy platform nests, lay two eggs, share incubation and feed the young when small on a milky crop secretion. They are therefore able to nest quickly, and to rear young easily even when only dry seed is available. Two of our species are specialised nesters in cavities, and one of them prefers perching on rocks.

In general pigeons have compact bodies, plump-looking and with dense plumage. The head is rather small and rounded with a short blunt bill and a soft cere of bare skin over the nostrils. The flight is swift and strong, with a quick take-off. The feet are small and designed for perching and walking. In walking the head bobs rhythmically in time with the steps. Displays involve bowing and tail-spreading, there are advertising display-flights, and the calls are cooing notes.

We have five species. The larger three are resident: the Woodpigeon is a bird of areas with trees in boreal to warm-temperate regions, the Stock Dove a cavity-nester in trees and rocks of similar regions and the wild Rock Dove occurs in warm-temperate zones of western Eurasia, with an extension up the mild east Atlantic coasts as far as Shetland and the Faeroes. This last is also the ancestor of the domestic pigeon. Of the two smaller species, the Turtle Dove is a summer visitor to temperate to subtropical western Eurasia. The Collared Dove is a species of warm Middle Eastern regions that in the present century has colonised temperate and boreal Europe.

Stock Dove *Columba oenas*

Often overlooked as a smaller, stubbier and bluer version of the domestic pigeon, the Stock Dove is perhaps better known either for the series of deep gruff double-coos with which it advertises its presence covertly from the shelter of some tree, or when it emerges from a nest-hole where a pigeon had not been expected. Although pairs may breed in small colonial groups, they do not share sites, and since cavities are always in short supply there are often fierce fights for possession.

Its original niche seems to have been as a bird of forest edge, nesting in holes in mature trees and feeding in open areas, but it can adapt to much more open country, using holes in rocks, buildings, or rabbit burrows, and on coasts in cliffs and outcrops. It feeds mainly on weed seeds and grain which it takes from the ground. The male has a display flight like that of the Rock Dove: horizontal, with slow deep wing-beats and some wing-clapping, followed by a glide with slightly raised wings and spread tail. It also has a deep bowing display with the tail raised and spread. Like other larger pigeons it may have several broods in a year.

It breeds in the temperate zone of western Eurasia, is resident in western Europe and the southern edge of its range, migrating to those areas in winter. It is absent from Norway, and from much of the Atlantic seaboard within its general range. In Britain its earliest records are from the south-west and from Derbyshire in the latter part of the last glaciation, in interstadial conditions when trees would have been present.

It might have been expected to become widespread as trees were cleared and areas were cultivated. With the more extensive clearing of woodland and removal of mature timber numbers might have been expected to fall as potential nest-sites were lost. However, its early nineteenth century distribution in the British Isles, limited to south and east England, coupled with its present absence in the extreme western edge of Europe, suggests that some other factor such as climate may have been involved.

Throughout the second half of the nineteenth century and early twentieth century, it steadily extended its range. This appears to have consisted of rapid advances and pauses for consolidation. It reached Scotland in 1866 and Ireland in 1877, also spreading into Wales, and north and south-west England from the 1870s onwards. It rapidly spread through eastern Scotland in the late 1870s and 1880s; but westward movements were slow. In Ireland it did not reach the western side until 1950; but the spread generally has been attributed to an increase in arable farming.

In the late 1950s and early 1960s, there was a sudden drop in numbers and in some areas a total disappearance. This was particularly noticeable in south and east England, but extended also into Scotland. The cause was the use of organochlorine chemicals as seed dressing in agriculture. With control of chemicals, numbers began to build up again but do not seem to have reached their former level. Crop spraying that prevents weed growth, and the loss of mature trees – particularly through Dutch Elm disease – may have a depressing effect on the species.

Present distribution is widespread, although populations are lower in mountain areas. It extends north in Britain to a line from Clyde to Buchanness, with a population in the Moray Basin. In Ireland it is absent from most of the north-west. Winter distribution is similar in the British Isles, but with birds fewer in the west, and on high ground. Populations in the early 1970s were estimated at 100,000 pairs, but in the early 1980s the winter estimate (with some continental influx) of this sedentary species appeared to correspond to only 30,000–65,000 birds.

Rock Dove *Columba livia*

This is the pigeon we know best, whose wild population has been almost obliterated by the spread of fugitives from its domestic form. It is also the one which has promoted a misleading idea of pigeons in general. For birds, our buildings are rock outcrops and cliffs containing caves; and the Rock Dove is a cliff-dwelling, cave or ledge-nesting, species that is forced by the limitations of such sites to be a sociable bird, pairs

Stock Dove

Rock Dove

Woodpigeon

Turtle Dove

Collared Dove

D. M. HENRY

having to nest in close proximity. In this it differs from almost all other pigeons.

The wild birds still occur in the cliffs of western Irish and Scottish coasts; but elsewhere, and even in these cliff colonies, a mongrel horde with larger heads and lumpier ceres, and plumages chequered with black, splashed with white, or coloured chestnut, have moved in. Behaviour is similar in both. The call is a repetitive deep throaty cooing note, and the ground display is a rather upright pirouetting with swollen neck and lowered, spread tail. It has a horizontal display flight, like that of the Stock Dove. The wild birds continue to live on coastal cliffs, flying inland to feed in fields and pastures; while feral birds exploit similar sites inland and all the other options for nesting, but may have problems finding food in urban and suburban areas, relying on spillage, waste, and food offered by people.

The world-wide presence of feral birds confuses the picture, but the original wild distribution is in warm-temperate to subtropical zones, from western Eurasia into India, Arabia and Africa. It is present through southern Europe and has extended up the Atlantic coasts to the western coasts of Ireland and Scotland. It is sedentary. In Britain it has been recorded from the Pleistocene in the latter part of the last glaciation in caves of the south-west.

Domesticated birds could have been around by Roman times, probably as imports, and could have been kept subsequently. By medieval times, they were kept in large numbers for food, breeding in dovecotes and allowed to forage freely. From then onwards, it appears to have been widespread in town and country, with the possibility of feral birds occurring anywhere. They were a part of the agricultural scene until about the mid nineteenth century. In more recent times they have been kept mainly for pigeon racing or for pleasure. Every year large numbers of young racing pigeons perform their natural dispersal, remaining where they settle.

It is difficult to be certain of the situation. The wild Rock Dove appears to be present in a narrow coastal zone around western Ireland from Waterford to northern Antrim, and from Arran and Bute northwards on the Scottish coasts and islands to northern Caithness, and through Orkney and Shetland. The feral birds have a patchy distribution through the rest of Britain. They are absent or very scarce in mountain regions, and in open pasture areas, and most numerous in regions of heavy human occupation. In winter there may be a shift away from some of the more exposed areas. The total population is difficult to estimate, and is probably highest in urban areas. It might exceed 100,000 pairs, and could still be increasing.

Woodpigeon *Columba palumbus*

The largest of our pigeons, it tends to look heavier still because of the small head and short legs. On the ground it moves with ponderous solemnity; but in trees, for which it is adapted, it can be surprisingly agile, and strong feet allow it to clamber or even hang with flapping wings in order to reach acorns or ivy berries. It is the agricultural offering of a winter food supply of green crops, just at the time when natural sources are getting scarce, that has enabled it to increase its numbers, and to appear as small grey armies steadily cropping their way across fields, and giving an exagger-

ated impression of their capacity for damage.

Were it rarer, the soft colours of the plumage and the deep soothing voice would have made it seem a highly desirable bird. Much of its behaviour is inconspicuous, but in display flight a flying bird suddenly rises with a series of deliberate deep wing-beats that produce a clapping sound, glides down, and may perform an undulating series of such movements. In ground or perched display the male may bow deeply, raising and momentarily fanning the tail. The nest is a twig platform in a tree.

It has a widespread breeding range in western Europe, migrating for much of it into western European and warm-temperate parts of its range. Its British Pleistocene records, from caves of Derbyshire and the south-west in the last glaciation, were presumably from interstadial periods when trees were present. As a reasonably wary and widespread woodland bird it is likely to have maintained reasonable numbers once woodland was established. It is also likely to have increased with scattered clearing for farming, although this would also have reduced available nesting-sites. With the great increase in leafy winter crops, such as clover and turnips, numbers increased considerably from the eighteenth century onwards. In Ireland and Scotland it was scarce until the nineteenth century, when it began to increase and spread. In Scotland it spread in the north-west and bred in the Inner Hebrides and Orkney. It also spread over most of Ireland, but the final colonisation of south-west Ireland was not until the 1950s and 1960s. In Shetland it bred intermittently after 1939. Its present breeding distribution covers most of the British Isles except the higher mountain areas of northern Scotland, the Outer Hebrides and the Shetlands. In winter it tends to shift from north-west Scotland and from much of the west. The population of the British Isles is estimated at about 4,800,000 individuals in summer.

Turtle Dove *Streptopelia turtur*

The soft, soothing, crooning coo of this bird is the spirit of warm summer in the south. The bird itself is not conspicuous until in display it rises steeply, with spread tail, and glides down again, as does the Collared Dove. Its flight is fast, low and direct, with quick flipping wing-beats. It is a bird of scattered low trees, scrub or tall hedgerows bordering on open weedy areas. It feeds for preference in open ground with short herbage, or on arable fields. It takes plant seeds and grain, and appears to be heavily dependent on weed-seeds. It has been suggested that Fumitory, which has a similar distribution to the bird, might be of importance to it.

It seems intolerant of close human presence and disturbance, more so than other doves. The nest is usually in a low tree or high shrub, fairly well hidden, but of the usual platform type. It comes as a summer visitor, present for about four summer months in which it often manages two broods.

Its breeding range is from the western Eurasian temperate zone south to the mid-Sahara; and it is almost wholly migratory, wintering in the Sahel zone of the southern Sahara. It lacks early records in Britain, and James Fisher quoted the earliest records as from the ninth century. It is a bird of warmer, drier climates, that may have done well prior to the fourteenth century, and less well in the colder Little Ice Age of the fourteenth to nineteenth centuries. By the early nineteenth century, it appears to have been limited to England, and absent from most of the north and west of it.

As a summer visitor it would be influenced by the weather during migration, and with less well-defined areas of distribution. It spread west to Cheshire and Wales, and north to Yorkshire in the earlier half of the nineteenth century. It moved into south Lancashire in 1904, consolidating its hold there in the next 30 years. There have been later small incursions into Ireland and south-east Scotland. It bred in County Dublin in 1939 until the early 1940s, and mid 1950s, County Wicklow in 1962, and having been said to breed in County Kerry in the south-west and County Down in the north-east, it bred in scattered sites between those areas in 1968–72. In Scotland it bred in Berwickshire in 1946, and from 1968–72, and possibly in 1982; in Roxburghshire in 1951 and probably in 1968–72; and in East Lothian in 1958, and 1960–66.

At present it is widespread in the British Isles, absent from urban areas and from high ground. It is also absent from much of Cornwall and the western half of Wales, and from the Pennines and Peak District, and infrequent beyond south Lancashire and Yorkshire. There are sporadic nestings in south-east Scotland and on the south and east Irish coasts. It declined in Wales in the 1950s and early 1960s, with local decreases elsewhere, probably due to toxic seed-dressings. Numbers increased again during most of the 1960s and the 1972 population estimate was over 125,000 pairs. However, it appears to be decreasing again. Climatic change, crop-spraying that destroys weeds, shooting in Europe on migration, and drought in the southern Sahara may all be having an adverse effect on it.

Collared Dove *Streptopelia decaocto*

This is a relative newcomer to our avifauna, but not wholly unexpected, since it arrived in the 1950s after a half-century of spread across Europe. Its mournful penetrating and monotonous *kuk-coo-ku* call is frequently heard, and the disyllabic version used at the nest has made many unsuspecting non-ornithologists think they had heard an unseasonable cuckoo. It also uses a distinctive muffled squall as it lands. In some areas it has now ousted the domestic pigeon as a bird of house and garden.

It is limited in some respects by its needs. One is for a reliable food supply, preferably grain; but it hangs about for food put out for chickens, or other farm and domestic animals, and food on bird-tables. This makes it very much a hanger-on in the human environment. In addition it seems to have a need for evergreen trees to roost in, probably in order to escape both winter winds and hunting owls, and also as a place in which to nest. When it finds the right place it nests repeatedly, and quickly builds up a small local flock.

Its displays are like those of the Turtle Dove. It has a rising display flight with deep wing-beats and spread tail, followed by a glide back down onto a perch. In these doves, as in the Woodpigeon, this flight display shows off the more conspicuous pattern on the underside of the tail. The male bows deeply to the female with swollen neck, but with tail unspread, uttering the cooing call. The nest is the usual flimsy platform, which may be used for a succession of broods.

Its progress across Europe was rather spasmodic. Its original breeding range, in which it is resident, is across the warmer side of Eurasia discontinuously from Turkey to China. It seems to have been introduced by the Turks to the part of south-eastern Europe that they occupied, and it was recorded prior to 1900 in the southern Balkans. By 1930 it had spread only a little further and was extending up the Danube valley to Hungary. In the next 10 years it spread through the Hungarian basin. Its big spread was in the 1940s through Austria and Germany, reaching the French border, and into the Netherlands and Denmark. In 1952 the first bird appeared in Britain, in Lincolnshire, and was viewed with deep suspicion as a possible escaped cage bird.

In 1955 a pair bred in Norfolk and it was formally welcomed to the British List. It invaded on a broad front from the east. By 1958 it was breeding in Morayshire in north-east Scotland, having started the previous year, was in four east-coast counties in England, and in Sussex, Hampshire and Ayrshire. In 1959 it bred in north-east Ireland. It continued to spread rapidly and by the mid 1960s had colonised virtually all the British Isles except for a few mountainous areas. It is resident where it has settled.

It increased in the first ten years by about 100% per annum, dropping by the early 1970s to 50 – 25% per annum, and levelling out by the 1980s. Its general distribution still indicated a bird of lowland areas, absent from high hills and moors. Its population is estimated at over 50,000 pairs.

Owls

STRIGIFORMES

Tytonidae and Strigidae

These are nocturnal birds of prey, mainly night hunters with large eyes and acute vision, and a keen sense of hearing that can enable them to locate prey in total darkness. They are raptors, taking a wide range of prey. They do not build a nest. Their clutches are often large and the young hatch at intervals. If food is short, only the older and larger ones survive. They are wholly or partly dependent on the adults for a long time after fledging.

The Barn Owl, a representative of a widespread, cosmopolitan species, is separated in the Family Tytonidae. Of the Strigidae, we now seem to have fewer species than most of northern Europe. The Eagle Owl *Bubo bubo* was present through most of the Pleistocene and possibly early Holocene in Britain. Tengmalm's Owl *Aegolius funereus* and the Hawk Owl *Surnia ulula* occur in the last glaciation in Derbyshire. We have five Strigidae species. The Snowy Owl is an arctic bird recently nesting in north Shetland, the Little Owl a recently introduced resident of mainland Europe. Our three medium-sized species are the Tawny Owl mainly in broadleaf woodland, the Long-eared Owl in woodland not used by the previous species, and the Short-eared Owl in bare open country.

Barn Owl *Tyto alba*

This occasionally hunts in daylight, and although when seen perched, one is more conscious of the elongated monkey face and knock-kneed look, seen in the air it shows a beautiful airy wavering flight and long-legged stoops, with an air of concentrating on some private world of its own rather than worrying about a human bystander. Its voice is weird, long quavering screeches, and snoring and hisses from nesting birds. It roosts and nests in dark cavities, in trees, rocks or caves, using buildings as cave substitutes.

It is basically an open-country hunter with small rodents as its principal prey. In areas with annual fluctuations of rodents such as voles and mice, breeding success also varies. Like most owls it will take almost anything that moves, from small rabbits and thrushes, down to insects, and where possible, food is swallowed whole and large pellets of small bones encased in fur and feathers are regularly cast up. It owes some past success to the provision of nest-sites in the roofs of farm buildings, to keep down rats and mice.

It has a wide although discontinuous world range, but in Eurasia is only present in Europe and south to the Mediterranean and Middle East. It is resident throughout this range. It was present in Pleistocene Britain, in the last glaciation in Derbyshire and in Devon; and also in the early Holocene; assemblages of small bird and mammal bones in other Pleistocene cave deposits may originate from cast food pellets of this species. It is not particularly cold-tolerant, Scottish birds representing its northernmost occurrence. It appears to have always been widespread in most of the British Isles.

However, there have been general and local fluctuations in abundance. On higher northern sheep-grazing reas, and present-day young plantations, numbers have varied with abundance cycles of Short-tailed Voles, and this may have been more marked in the past. It could have increased with some clearance of woods for agriculture, and was certainly sustained by the rodents and birds around earlier farmsteads.

A slow decrease had been noted since the early nineteenth century. In the earlier period, this was probably linked with loss of nest-sites and food with more organised farming, persecution by gamekeepers, and an increase in shooting, trapping and poisoning generally. It continued over much of the British Isles in the earlier part of this century, but on the northern limits, in northern England and Scotland it began to increase between 1910 and 1940, probably responding to the warmer climate.

After the 1940s the decrease accelerated, apparently due to further loss of nest-sites and roosts, reduction of rodents in urban areas, and on farms, and return to a colder weather cycle with some severe winters in which many died. It is also very prone to be killed on roads. By the 1960s it was being heavily hit by toxic chemical poisons from the bodies of its prey. This seriously reduced numbers particularly in south and east England. The general decrease apparent elsewhere had not been seen in Ireland until the 1950s. Numbers for England and Wales alone were estimated at 12,000 pairs in 1934. Some populations are thought to have been halved by the 1960s, and by the 1970s the British Isles population was estimated at 4,500–9,000 pairs, and still seems to be falling.

General distribution seems unchanged, generally present north to the Scottish highlands, then scattered sites north to Dornock in the north-east, and a few on the western side. In Ireland it is generally present, but sparse in the north-west and middle of the south.

Snowy Owl *Nyctea scandiaca*
NOT IN THE COLOUR PLATE

This is a large and solidly-feathered owl of open arctic tundra. The need to keep warm has produced a bird in which the only extremities exposed beyond the squat rounded figure are claws and a dark bill-tip. With the deep-set and often half-closed gold-irised eyes, this sometimes produces an un-bird-like appearance, sometimes described as cat-like. It hunts and nests on bare, open tundra or moor terrain, perching on small eminences. Its numbers are linked to availability of lemmings and voles, and in years when they are in short supply it may disperse southwards beyond its usual limits.

It breeds on tundra around the Arctic Ocean, dispersing erratically and nomadically to subtundra or steppe in winter. In the British Isles it must have bred widely in the cold periods of the Pleistocene Ice Ages but was presumably not vulnerable to cave-dwelling predators, and is only known from two specimens, one populations had decreased, but as the latter increased in the present century so the Long-eared Owl decreased. It has maintained numbers in Ireland, where the Tawny Owl is absent.

Unlike the Tawny Owl, it extends to the limits of the British Isles but is far scarcer overall with only scattered occurrences; it is least numerous in western England, Wales, and north-west Scotland. In winter there is a south-eastward shift of birds and a continental influx, small or very large according to vole numbers in northern Europe. It is suggested that the breeding population might be 10,000–50,000 birds.

Short-eared Owl *Asio flammeus*

Unlike typical owls this has become a long-winged hunter of open country, resting and nesting on the ground. It hunts mainly in low searching flight, sometimes hovering before pouncing; and it has a peculiar light flight, as though the body were too light for the strength of the downward wing-beat, and with a tendency to drift and waver. In flight it shows a big golden-buff area on the primary feathers and a dark patch at the angle of the wing.

It has a display flight over territory with a series of wing-claps. Its advertisement call is a rapid series of low hollow hoots. Its main food is Short-tailed Voles and its numbers vary dramatically with fluctuations in vole populations. In the south of Britain it takes more rats and other rodents, and varies less obviously. It is a bird of open moorland and hillsides, rough pastures, open marshes, and marram dunes; and in winter it moves to open arable land with grass-bank verges rather than hedges.

It nests on the ground in heather, grass or tall herbage. Young plantations with longer grass encouraging voles, and also providing undisturbed nest-sites, have become an important habitat for it.

It breeds in tundra to temperate zones, across Eurasia and North America, with populations in South America and some Pacific islands. It winters in warm-temperate to subtropical zones, but is resident in south Russia, Europe north to Denmark, and the British Isles. In Pleistocene Britain it is known from caves in Derbyshire and Somerset in the last glaciation. It is unlikely to have entered them voluntarily and was probably prey of a larger bird such as the Eagle Owl.

In early times it was probably on such moorland and marshes as existed, and should have increased as woodland clearance provided more rough pasture and moorland. Population should have been high by the early nineteenth century, but it would have suffered from killing by gamekeepers. It last bred in Shetland in the early nineteenth century. Its status as a partial migrant, winter visitor, resident and nomad in search of the high vole populations that encourage temporary fast breeding, make it a difficult species to assess.

It has increased and spread a little in recent times, and benefitted from new plantations on uplands, although these are only temporarily usable. It is absent from Shetland, Lewis, and the extreme north-west of Scotland; and absent from Ireland except for sporadic winter occurrences although it bred in Mayo in 1923 and Galway in 1959. In England it is present on northern and central moorland south to Derbyshire.

It colonised north Norfolk and the Brecklands from the 1930s, has only bred regularly in Yorkshire since the 1940s, and it moved into Suffolk, Essex and Kent coastal marshes in the 1940s–50s. It has bred in the Wash region since the 1960s. In winter it is more widespread, shifting to coastal regions; and there is a variable but sometimes large immigration from the continent. Although seemingly nomadic, traditional wintering areas and roost sites seem to be used. The British Isles breeding population was estimated at 1,000–10,000 pairs, depending on vole numbers; and winter population at about 5,000–50,000 birds.

Tawny Owl *Strix aluco*

This large-headed, dark-eyed owl is the one whose quavering double hoot, inadequately rendered as *toowhit-toowhoo*, haunts our literature from childhood onwards, while the equally conspicuous *ke-wick* call seems to have gone unnoticed. It prefers mature trees with cavities, being originally a bird of woodland but it seems able to manage in sparse parkland, field hedge-rows or city squares, provided that a few suitable trees are present. It hunts from a series of look-out perches in trees from which it can see or hear its prey. It feeds mainly on a wide variety of small mammals, but also takes roosting birds, particularly those that become visible when the trees are bare. It will also take insects, and earthworms are a frequent food.

The nest is in a bare cavity, usually in a tree. The young leave when barely able to fly, and still heavily dependent on the parents. The adults are aggressive in defence of their young at this time, but the long period of learning to fend for themselves is the main period of mortality in this species.

Its range is in the broadleaf forest zone from warm boreal to warm-temperate western Eurasia, and in the latter zone continues across the China and Korea. It is resident. In the British Pleistocene it occurs in caves of Derbyshire and the south-west in the latter part of the last glaciation, presumably in interstadials when trees were present. Its greatest spread is likely to have been at the time when woodland was most widespread, and its numbers would have decreased in historical times as the area was progressively cleared or denuded of more mature trees.

When gamekeeping reached its height in the nine-teenth and early twentieth centuries, it was one of the birds regularly shot, and numbers decreased. With the decline of this persecution from the First World War onwards, its numbers increased, mainly between 1900 and 1930, and in some areas towards the periphery of its British range continued to increase until the 1950s. The climatic amelioration during this period may have played an important part in this increase.

There have been local decreases since. The owls must have suffered like other raptors in the 1950s and 1960s, from an accumulation of small amounts of toxic chemicals in the bodies of their prey; and also from the increasing shortage of mature trees with nest-cavities. Nest-boxes have been designed for their use. The Tawny Owl is not successful at sea crossings. It has not yet been proved to breed on the Isle of Wight, although individuals are present. It is absent from Ireland, the Isle of Man, the Outer Hebrides, Orkney and Shetland. Elsewhere it is widespread except in the Scottish mountains and the English Fens. Its breeding popula-tion is thought to be within the range of 50,000–100,000 pairs.

Nightjars

CAPRIMULGIFORMES

Caprimulgidae

These are large-eyed and large-mouthed birds that catch insects on the wing, feeding mainly in the late evening and at night. Most are birds of warm climates, but a few are summer visitors to cooler regions. Only one species occurs in northern Europe and Britain.

Nightjar *Caprimulgus europaeus*

Like most nocturnal birds this is more often heard than seen, and the song, a peculiar rising and falling whirring sound, almost more like a machine, is difficult to locate. The bird tends to rest by day, sometimes lying along a branch, but more often on a patch of bare ground covered with a litter of twigs and dead leaves. Its plumage is beautifully patterned to aid concealment against such a background, and when it closes its eyes to mere slits, as it customarily does in daylight, it is difficult to detect that a bird is there.

The wings are long and narrow, with blunt tips, and the tail is long. The bill appears tiny and curved, but opens up into a gape fringed with bristles, that seems to split the head in half. The eyes are large and see well in poor light. The flight is light and easy, with steady wing-beats, glides, and rapid twists and hovers to catch insects. In flight the male shows a white patch on the underwing, and a pair at the tail-tips. The food is chiefly moths and beetles, mostly caught on the wing, but occasionally snatched from plants or from the ground.

It appears to occur in a variety of habitats which are dryish, and combine well-spaced trees with partly bare open ground, and with patches of vegetation. In Britain this is most often the edges of heathland, or of conifer plantations on old heathland. There is no nest and the two eggs, also camouflaged, are laid on the ground. The young are downy and crouch motionless if danger is near. Both adults share nesting duties.

It is a migrant; breeding from warm boreal to warm temperate zones of western Eurasia and into Africa.

There are no Pleistocene records, and James Fisher quoted the first reference as that of Ælfric the Grammarian in about 998. We have little information on its past. Natural open woodland in drier places might have provided breeding sites, and these are likely to have increased as woodland was felled and opened up by grazing stock. Casual references suggest that it was common and widespread in the past, but absent from Shetland, Orkney and the Outer Hebrides.

Although sometimes shot by ignorant gamekeepers, it was apparently still plentiful in the nineteenth century, but was said to be decreasing early in the present century, and this had become general by about 1930. The decrease became much more pronounced after 1950. It has been argued that it cannot be from climatic causes, since it spans both warmer and cooler periods. However, there has been a drastic reduction and fragmentation of the heathland and heath-type habitats which were its main area of abundance, and a decrease in the larger flying insects. Interaction between habitat, climate and food may be involved.

By the 1968–72 B.T.O. census, it was limited in Scotland to the Moray Firth borders, some western islands and promontories, and the south-west; it was thinly scattered in northern England, the midlands, central Wales and Ireland; but more plentiful in the rest of England. A total guess of 3,000–6,000 pairs was regarded as optimistic. By 1981 it was further reduced to only the south-west of Scotland and the Strathclyde area, with one in north Sutherlandshire; and there was only a single sighting in Ireland. In England it was even more thinly scattered, with its main areas in the heathland of Surrey to Dorset, the East Anglian brecklands, and smaller areas of Devon, the Nottinghamshire Dukeries, Staffordshire, and Yorkshire. Total population was now estimated at 2,100 singing males, possibly paired. Its loss appears to be continuing.

Swifts

APODIFORMES

Apodidae

Aerial-feeding birds with compact, elongated bodies and narrow tapering wings. Bills short with very wide gapes. Legs very short and feet small with sharp claws for clinging to vertical surfaces. Food is caught in the air, and most species spend the greater part of their lives flying continuously. Because they rely on insects available in the air, they are mainly limited to warmer regions, with a few extending into temperate regions in summer. Only one species breeds in northern Europe.

Common Swift *Apus apus*

This is a bird which, were it not for its need to nest, seems to have severed most of its connections with solid earth. It feeds on the wing on flying insects. Birds that are not on the nest rise to higher altitudes and sleep on the wing at night; and it is suggested that non-breeding birds just keep on flying. It can be threatened by rainstorms which might waterlog its plumage, and with large isolated storms it may fly round them. In a final emergency, it appears able to crawl into crevices or cavities and, if necessary, to become torpid for a while in order to survive unseasonable wet and cold weather.

The seemingly tiny bill opens into a wide gape, the width of the head, and small insects are collected in a ball under the tongue. The nest is in a hole that can be approached easily in flight: in a cliff, rockface, or

Kingfishers
Alcedinidae

These have long bills, tapering or blunt, large narrow heads, wings that are relatively short and rounded, and small legs and feet. They watch for prey from a perch. Blunt-billed species are mostly terrestrial insect-eaters, while those with long tapering bills plunge-dive for fish. The plumage is often bright, glossy and iridescent. They are mostly birds of warm regions, with one species occurring in Europe.

Kingfisher *Alcedo atthis*
Perhaps the most brightly-coloured of our birds, it loses most of its brightness against the reflections and sparkle of water, and the most conspicuous mark is the luminously sky-blue rump, visible as a moving spot of blue light as it races low over the water. In moments of self-assertive display the chestnut breast, enhanced by an upright bobbing posture, forms a bolder splash of colour. It flies fast and straight, usually from one perch to another. It watches for fish from a perch over water, or momentarily hovers in flight, plunging down to seize its prey head first, using its wings to swim under water for a short way if necessary. The prey is carried back to a perch and usually beaten against it before being swallowed. Its call is a shrill whistled *ti*, which may sometimes be repeated in rapid series.

It nests by boring a tunnel into a bank over or near water. There is no nest material, other than an accumulating layer of cast-up fish bones. The eggs are round, white and shiny. The young are fed on whole small fish, presented singly, head first. They have their feathers encased in spiky sheaths until they are ready to fledge.

It feeds mainly on small fish, but if the water freezes, it may be forced to move down to coasts or estuaries, where it will also take small shrimps. As a highly resident species, it is vulnerable to hard winters which kill many; it relies on an ability to produce several broods in a year to replace them.

It breeds from the temperate zone of Eurasia to North Africa, India and the Oriental region. It is a migrant from north-east Europe and across to China, wintering in the west and south of its main range and beyond the southern margins of it. It has one British Pleistocene record, from Derbyshire in the last glaciation. As a waterside bird of small waters, nesting in a raised bank, it is probable that its status has only altered slightly over the centuries; however, the later drainage of marshy areas may have reduced its habitat.

In the nineteenth century it was netted and shot by gamekeepers for alleged harm to young fish stocks, and because the demand for fragments of its feathers for fishing-fly-making, and of its wings for the plumage trade had put a price on its head. Within the present century, numbers may have been restored to some extent, and increases were noted in some regions. However, since the 1940s it has suffered badly from intermittent severe winters, from which it may take years to recover, assuming they are not too frequent. It was estimated that the 1980–81 winter produced a 64% decline in England.

It has also suffered from water pollution. It is now present over much of Britain, with pockets of scarcity; it is absent in extreme north-west Ireland, and in Scotland north of the Clyde-Buchan line, except in the lower Moray basin. In 1972 numbers were estimated at 5,000–9,000 pairs.

Hoopoes
Upupidae

This family contains only two very similar species, separated by minor plumage pattern differences.

Hoopoe *Upupa epops*
This is one of our accidental overflows from the warmer summers of the continent. In aggressive squabbling with another, it looks as gaudy as a butterfly. The pinkish-buff plumage is framed in the spread crest, the broad, black-tipped tail, and the bold-barred wings that in spreading reveal a broad rounded tip with a great white patch on the primaries. When it is feeding on bare ground, this is largely lost. The crest is laid back as a folded narrow strip on the crown, the plumage tends to merge with the bare earth (especially sand or reddish clay), and the bold graduated transverse striping, like the stripes on a zebra, tend to merge into an indistinct greyish tint at a distance. It runs, feeds and dust-bathes on the ground. The bill is ideal for probing into the burrows of crickets and beetle larvae. It feeds on larger insects, and other creatures of warmer, drier areas, such as small lizards.

It nests in holes in trees, banks, walls and buildings. The eggs, with drab-coloured pitted shells, are incubated by the female, fed by the male. The young are downy at first, retaining feather sheaths as a spiky covering on the feathers until they are well-grown. They usually remain as family parties or, where enough are present, form small flocks.

It has a wide breeding range from temperate Eurasia south to Malaya, India and Africa, wintering from warm-temperate regions southwards. Its north-west limit is from the southern Baltic shore to northern France, but in the nineteenth century it bred to Denmark and south Sweden. It has no very early records in Britain, and its first mention appears to have been about 1600, suggesting that it was never widely known. As a migrant, with Britain just beyond the edge of its normal range, it appears to be a potential victim of spring weather: if fine enough at the right time, this may cause it to overshoot its normal range, and – given suitable conditions – to breed for a season further north.

Hoopoes tend to feed conspicuously on open places and are generally noticed. Up to the early part of this century, they were usually shot as a result. Well into the middle of the present century, the excuse that a gamekeeper had mistaken one for a Jay was considered an adequate defence for having shot one. It appears to have occurred regularly in small numbers on migration and attempted to breed at intervals. From the 1830s it had about one breeding record each decade, but in the period 1895 – 1906 there were 8, and in the 1950s there were 4, 2 of these in 1955. In recent times, there have been about 100 recorded on passage each spring in the British Isles. Most counties can boast the odd one, but the majority are in the English south coastal counties, with smaller numbers on the east coast north to Yorkshire, in Pembrokeshire and Anglesey, and in County Cork in south-west Ireland. Some stay on.

Its recent breeding pattern has been single breedings in 1968, 1969, 1971, possibly 1975, 1976, 4 in 1977. There were possible breedings in 1980, 1983 and 1984. This peripheral pattern of one or two breeding attempts may continue indefinitely, unless some conditions – weather, food, or the actions of man – change significantly.

Golden Oriole *Oriolus oriolus*
(ORIOLIDAE IN PASSERIFORMES) See page 200.

PLATE THIRTY-THREE

Cuckoos

CUCULIFORMES

Cuculidae

This group encompasses birds very varied in structure and habits. Some nest normally, others breed as a group sharing one nest, others are brood parasites, laying eggs in other birds' nests. Their only consistent character is a reversed outer toe. They feed on insects and other small creatures. One species occurs in western Europe.

Cuckoo *Cuculus canorus*
Usually unseen but clearly heard, this has been the recognised announcer of the coming of spring in Britain since early times. It is less easily recognised; slender, with narrow tapering wings and long tail, it has a level flight with downward wing-beats and might be taken for a small falcon. However, the relative weakness of flight, and the upward taper from breast to narrow bill at the front end helps to identify it. The male is grey, the female has some brown on the breast, and some individuals are barred chestnut and black overall, while the heavily barred brown young bird has a white nape-patch. Apart from the *cuckoo* call, there is a gruff *gowk* note and the female has a bubbling call.

It feeds on insects, and is adapted to cope with hairy caterpillars that other birds find inedible, but which form the major part of the cuckoo's diet. Females lay single eggs in the nests of small birds, removing and eating one of the host's eggs. The young cuckoo, hatching first, relieves the irritation of eggs and nestling sharing the nest by squirming under them, and heaving them out to have the host pair's undivided attention. Breeding success must depend on a suitable supply of hosts, preferably insect-eaters. They range from woodland Robins and Dunnocks to waterside warblers and wagtails, and moorland Meadow Pipits, enabling it to occur through most major habitats.

It is a migrant, breeding through Eurasia from subarctic to warm-temperate zones and into China. It winters in southern Africa, Indomalaya and the Philippines. It was first recorded in Britain, according to James Fisher, by the Anglo-Saxon Saint Guthlac in 699, in the Fens of eastern England. With its potential range of hosts, it can adapt to long-term environmental changes, provided that nesting birds do not become too scarce. There is no suggestion of significant changes in its numbers until recent times. It may have been affected a little by spread of towns, and random shooting in the nineteenth century. There was some decrease in the south-west in the 1940s, and in the 1950s a more general decrease was noted, although more particularly in the east, perhaps related to the greatly increased use of chemicals to control insects, affecting both the Cuckoo and its hosts. Cuckoos appear to have decreased elsewhere in northern Europe. There is still a general distribution in summer in the British Isles, the population estimated at about 17,500–35,000 pairs.

Woodpeckers and Wrynecks

PICIFORMES

Picidae

These are birds in which the strong, tapering bill and well developed neck muscles allow the bird to tunnel into wood, while the tongue can be extended a long way, and may be barbed or sticky to catch insects. Large, strong feet with a reversed outer toe allow them to cling upright to trees, while a stiffened tail forms a prop. Wings are rounded and the flight is undulating. They nest in holes in trees, without nest material. The eggs are round, white and shiny; the nestlings naked. Nesting duties are shared by both adults. Young fledglings can climb better than they can fly. Wrynecks are less specialised than typical woodpeckers.

There are only two wryneck species: one is in Africa, the other is in Eurasia and occurs in Britain. The British Isles has noticeably fewer of some groups of woodland species than does the European mainland. Owls are one example; the woodpeckers are another with only half the potential species, and none breeding in Ireland. The Green Woodpecker is widespread in more open, woodland-edge areas; the Greater Spotted is a bird of trees, and the Lesser Spotted is a smaller counterpart, preferring broadleaf trees and only in southern Britain.

but more common by the 1970s. Dutch Elm disease in the late 1960s provided a great number of slowly dying trees and sample bird counts in 1960–83 showed a two-and-a-half-fold increase. These trees are ceasing to be useful or are being cut down, and numbers may level or fall. An estimate of the population of the mid 1970s was about 30,000–40,000 pairs.

Winter birds are mainly sedentary and may show some southward shift. There are intermittent irruptions of northern continental birds.

Lesser Spotted Woodpecker *Dendrocopos minor*

Like its larger cousin, this little, boldly-barred woodpecker should be a conspicuous sight, but a habit of feeding in the thinner branches high in trees makes it easily overlooked. Its series of shrill notes might be mistaken for those of a Kestrel or a distant, frightened Blackbird. It shares with the Greater Spotted Woodpecker a sharp *tchick* note and an advertisement drumming, but both are weaker. In this species the male has a scarlet crown, the female's is white, and young resemble the adults.

It feeds mainly on insects, taken from rotten wood, and from branches, twigs and leaves; and less often on seeds. Because it searches smaller branches, it uses smaller trees along hedgerows and in small patches of woodland; it prefers more open broadleaf woodland. It uses parkland, and trees in older, less commercialised, orchards and in gardens, and may feed low in them. It excavates frequently, making holes for roosting as well as nesting, the nest-hole often in the underside of a branch. In addition to suffering from Starlings, Nuthatches and House Sparrows as potential hole thieves, the Greater Spotted Woodpecker can be a serious threat to it and its young.

Although generally avoiding conifers, its breeding range is through to subarctic to warm-temperate zones of Eurasia, where it is resident. It has a British Pleistocene record, in Derbyshire towards the end of the last glaciation. It should have been widespread from the time when birch woodland first moved in at the end of the glaciations, but may have suffered from competition with the Greater Spotted Woodpecker. As a bird of smaller tree growth it might have had an advantage in the subsequent period of cutting and clearing of woodland, with some periods of local regrowth. It is likely to have suffered where trees were mainly or wholly lost, but in general may have maintained something approaching its present distribution.

It is thinly distributed overall, using not only the more open woodland, but areas where trees are scattered in parkland, or in belts along streams or on farmland. Most of its fluctuations have been local. Its attachment to old orchard trees led to decreases in Herefordshire before 1938, and in Somerset during the Second World War when old cider orchards were grubbed up.

It increased in the early 1970s when the elms dying with Dutch Elm disease provided a temporarily rich supply of wood-feeding invertebrates. It may have suffered in some areas from hard winters, and from the increase in Greater Spotted Woodpeckers. It is mainly a bird of southern England, present mostly in lowland areas north to north Yorkshire and Cumbria, and scarce in the Fens and Lincolnshire, and in the western half of Wales. Its population is estimated at about 5,000–10,000 pairs.

Wryneck *Jynx torquilla*

This species looks more like an overweight and exotic warbler than a woodpecker. It has the turned-back outer toe, but lacks the stiffened tail, having a longer, square-ended one. It perches in a more conventional songbird manner, but tends to sag a little on the perch. The bill is tapering but stubby, and the crown feathers of the rather full-throated-looking head can be raised into a small erect crest. The grey and brown plumage has a delicate camouflage pattern that should conceal it against leaf débris or tree bark. The call, a repeated *quee-quee-quee* ... is described as similar to that of a falcon, but resembles more a weak and exhausted Green Woodpecker, softer, slow and with a slight dying fall to it.

It is an insect-eater, but like the Green Woodpecker specialises on ants, and has a long sticky tongue that it can protrude into small holes and insect burrows. It feeds mainly on the ground, moving in jerky hops, taking ants and other insects from the surface or from holes and crevices. Its tendency to spread the tail, and rather odd sinuous head and neck movements help to identify it. It often perches on twigs, but can cling to vertical surfaces. Its bill does not cut wood, and it must use natural holes or old woodpecker holes for nesting. If alarmed it has a hissing threat display, erects the crest and twists head and neck in a weird fashion. It is capable of producing several large broods in a season.

It breeds through boreal and temperate zones of Eurasia, wintering in subtropical zones. The first reference to its presence in Britain seems to have been by Turner in 1544. It is difficult to guess its early history, which must have been closely tied to that of the ants on which it feeds. It is likely to have increased when clearing of woodland began to create more woodland edge habitat. It prefers open areas with scattered trees which may be fairly small; and it can use hedgerows with old trees, and may have done better as enclosed lands matured. Up to the mid nineteenth century, its range was through most of England and Wales, with the possible exception of Cornwall and Northumberland. It did not occur in Scotland or Ireland except as stray birds on passage.

By the 1900s it had disappeared from Wales, Gloucestershire, Cumbria and Durham. In the earlier warmer part of the present century, up to the 1940s, it disappeared from most of the north and Midlands down to Warwickshire and Bedfordshire, persisting in Northamptonshire and Huntingdonshire. In the 1940s it disappeared from most of the west, and by the mid 1950s was limited to East Anglia, and Oxfordshire, Berkshire, Surrey and Kent. By 1960 it was only present in Kent, and there it dropped by 1965 to about a dozen pairs, with only two certain breedings, and has been absent since 1979.

No plausible cause of the decline has been established, but in Britain it has shown one of the most dramatic distributional turn-arounds of any species. During the 1960s singing Wrynecks were increasingly seen in the Scottish Highlands. These were thought to have moved across from Scandinavia and were centred on the old pine forests. In 1969 three pairs were present on Speyside. Since then, there have recently been only single records from various places in southern England, but up to a dozen possible breedings per year in Invernesshire, although no proven breeding since 1980.

Song-Birds

PASSERIFORMES

The birds in this great order are the typical small perching birds that have adapted to a wide array of differing habitats and modes of feeding, without having lost their basic standard similarity. This includes the syrinx that enables them to produce their musical and often elaborate vocalisations. They seem to have had their main adaptive, evolutionary spread later than many other bird orders, possibly in response to the evolution of the great variety of flowering plants, and the insects that went with them.

Martins and Swallows

Hirundinidae

These spend most of their time on the wing, feeding on insects caught in the air. Their need for insects makes them mainly tropical birds, or summer species to cooler regions. Less totally committed to the air than swifts, they nevertheless have long bodies, relatively small legs and feet, and long narrow wings. The tails tend to be less forked. We have the three widely-distributed migrant Eurasian species. The Sand Martin nests in colonies of tunnels bored into sandy banks. House Martins stick mud nests to vertical sites under overhangs, while Swallows nest in buildings and caves.

House Martin *Delichon urbica*

This boldly-patterned martin is the most accomplished builder of our three species, making a large half-cup of mud pellets stuck to a vertical site close under an overhang, to leave only a narrow space between the cup edge and surface above. House eaves have proved themselves an ideal site, the House Martin being fairly tolerant of humans and, as a result, man has provided suitable nest-sites spaced across almost every part of the British Isles. To build the nest, it needs sticky mud, and that is the primary limitation on its distribution. However, it can obtain mud from the margins of small ponds or even puddles.

At good sites it nests in colonies, the nests sometimes touching. Nest-sites apart, it is a bird of open country, tolerating scrub and trees but absent from forest. It is highly sociable at all times. It has a more fluttering flight than the Swallow and tends to feed higher in the air. The flat chirruping twitter and *sweet* alarm note identify it, but the soft twittering song is often obvious only at the nest. It perches on wires and bare branches, and clings easily to walls and roofs.

It is a migrant; breeding across Eurasia in boreal to warm-temperate zones, wintering in Africa, India and south-east Asia. James Fisher referred to it as occurring in Britain in the latter part of the Pleistocene Ice Ages. It is likely to have been present in most of earlier warm periods, but not a likely prey species. It originally nested on cliffs, crag and rock outcrops, and was likely to be confined to coast, hill and mountain areas. The eaves of buildings provided it with ideal sites to which it has progressively transferred, with continuing limited use of more natural sites. It must have increased and spread enormously over the centuries, as human settlement and building increased. These would ultimately have provided an almost even-spaced coverage over most of the British Isles; and the early population can only have been a fraction of that of recent times.

Its only setback in this respect may have been through heavy smoke and industrial pollution, destroying insects. It was absent for this reason from central London between 1889 and 1965. As a breeding bird it is present over all the British Isles, but scarce and an intermittent breeder in Shetland, Orkney, the Outer Hebrides, the extreme north of Scotland and some Scottish mountain areas. Its number show local fluctuations and it is vulnerable to severe bad weather while migrating. In recent years in Britain, it is likely to have suffered from a steady reduction in ponds and muddy places, and a reduction in insects. Its breeding population is estimated at about 300,000–600,000 pairs.

Sand Martin *Riparia riparia*

Small and drably-coloured, with a low flitting flight and usually seen hunting insects over water, this martin may not attract much attention, but becomes much more conspicuous at a large nest-site, where a swarm of birds may circle, flutter and twitter harshly in excited activity around a vertical area of bank riddled with holes. It has rapid wing-beats and, when feeding, a more fluttering flight.

It needs sandy, stony or clay banks soft enough to burrow into, hard enough to remain stable, and usually feeds over water where possible. As a result, it is mainly a lowland bird. Where unmolested, it will nest at fairly low sites and ignore nearby human activity. At suitable sites, a number of pairs will burrow simultaneously at adjacent sites, producing close groups of holes. This communal activity may help to space them. The song is a harsh twittering. It begins to breed early, and may raise several broods; and it moves on to form big seasonal roosts in reed-beds bordering open water, where it can feed before migrating south.

It has a slightly more northerly breeding range, from subarctic to temperate zones across Eurasia and North America, wintering in subtropical to tropical zones. Its earliest record in Britain seems to be from about the eighth century. Its array of natural sites cannot have changed much over the centuries, and would have been in river banks, cliffs and eroded steep banks. Its first extension would have been through the larger-scale quarrying, digging and bank-making activities of humans, where these involved relatively soft substrate.

The greater need for sand, gravel and clay in more recent centuries has probably been its greatest aids in spreading. Unfortunately, some of these sites have a limited period of usefulness, and although showing fidelity to a good site, the Sand Martin is also an

Sand Martin

House Martin

Swallow

Shorelark

SUMMER

Woodlark

Skylark

D.M. Henry.

opportunist because of this potential instability of nest-sites from year to year. There may have been a small long-term overall decrease. It was said to have bred in the last century in Shetland and the Outer Hebrides, where it is now absent; and it last bred in Orkney in 1918.

It winters in the semi-desert Sahal zone along the southern side of the Sahara Desert. In 1968–69, that region suffered a severe drought. The Sand Martin population dropped suddenly and it was thought that 75% had been lost in the British Isles. It began to build up again, but the Sahal suffered another drought. In the 1982–83 winter, Sand Martin numbers dropped again by about $7\frac{1}{2}\%$, but in 1983–84 they fell by 71% of the previous total. Estimates suggest a loss of 90–95% since the mid 1960s. The early population had been estimated at about 1,000,000 pairs, now falling to about 50,000–100,000 pairs. The birds are still widely distributed as a breeding species over the British Isles as a whole, but much more thinly, and at risk in their winter quarters.

Swallow *Hirundo rustica*

This has a special place in European tradition, not so much for the beauty of its plumage or the small exuberance of its song; but for the fact that early on it moved from caves and shelters as nest-sites to occupy the artificial caves of houses and, in the days before window glass was usual, would enter rooms and nest inside the house, as it will in sheds and barns today. Presumably because it is an aerial feeder adapted for rapid manoeuvrability, it seems to feel less threatened by humans and adapts more easily to living with them than do most earthbound birds.

It prefers open country and occurs more frequently near water. It often skims low in pursuit of insects. Flight is fast, agile and powerful, with intermittent glides and frequent twists and turns. The forked tail with its long outer streamers permits quick pauses and turns when in pursuit of insects, or moving within limited space. The legs are short and it is less agile at walking than the martins. Its usual call is a loud *swit*

often repetitive as a twitter, and the song is a rambling, warbling twitter with short intermittent trills, but rather quiet. The nest is usually built on some small support or projection; it is a cup of mud pellets, and lined with feathers. Rafters and supports under roofs inside buildings were ideal for it; but it has lost many such sites as buildings change.

It has a wide range from boreal to warm-temperate zones in Eurasia and North America, wintering in subtropical to tropical zones. It is a bird of open country, usually near water, needing a sheltered site or cave for nesting. Possibly because of this, it has several Pleistocene records. It was present in the Mendips in an early interglacial about 500,000 years ago; and it nested in caves on the south Wales coast in the last, Ipswichian interglacial about 120,000 years ago. In warmer interstadials it occurred in caves of the south-west, Kent and Derbyshire.

It would have had a low population in the early Holocene. Increased spread of woodland might have had a slightly adverse effect, but overhanging banks with tree-roots or even root masses of fallen trees might have been used for nest-sites. Once clearance began and Swallows were associated with human settlement, numbers must have increased steadily, to a point where it becomes difficult to envisage the earlier state of affairs. Over most of its range in the British Isles, it is dependent on human structures for nest-site, and to some extent its history is tied to the history of British human population.

Numbers fluctuate from year to year, affected by climate – in particular by sudden cold weather during migration, and by variation in breeding success. There is a suggestion of an overall decrease in areas where it was more numerous in the past, and where insect food and breeding sites may be scarcer. Overall distribution has seemingly altered little, and covers most of the British Isles, although it is scarcest in north-west Scotland and the islands. Total breeding population in the early 1970s was estimated at 500,000–1,000,000 pairs.

Larks
Alaudidae

These are small and usually cryptically-coloured terrestrial species of open places. They have short, strong bills, and feed on seeds, plants and insects. The nest is on the ground. They have strong, broad wings for sustained flight and their advertisement songs are delivered while on the wing. Britain has three regular species. The Shorelark is usually a winter visitor from tundra regions; the Skylark is a widespread grassland species, and the Woodlark a temperate species of open ground with trees, on the edge of its range in southern Britain.

Shorelark *Eremophila alpestris*

The summer male is a boldly-marked bird, but the female lacks the 'horn' tufts and has a smaller black bib. In winter the dark markings are reduced and obscured, and it is undistinguished in appearance, pale buffish, white below, and dark-tailed in flight. It has thin *seep* and *si-di-wi* calls. Although often bold and self-assertive when breeding, at other times it tends to move in a

crouching posture, head low, although it can run swiftly if it wishes. It has a tendency to crouch and feed in hollows that makes it difficult to see in winter haunts. The male has a display flight, rising steeply and silently, then gliding and singing short phrases of a few notes with a jingling finish. The nest is a cup built into a hollow at the side of a stone or plant tuft. The female builds and incubates, the male helps feed the young.

It has a circumpolar distribution in the tundra zone, but extends to temperate North America, where competing lark species do not occur. In Eurasia, another population extends through mountains of the warm-temperate zone. Western Eurasian tundra birds winter around the southern North Sea. Its earliest British records are from towards the last glaciation, the Devensian, in north Kent and Derbyshire. It could have bred here, but there is no way of guessing at its status. Its apparent occurrence in similar strata to the Snow Bunting and Lapland Bunting, in uncertainly dated cave deposits from Devon that might extend back into the last glaciation, might be an indication of a tundra-breeding community. However, it is only recorded as having extended the western limits of its range into Scandinavia in the last two centuries, and its earliest references in British literature are from 1830 onwards. It occurs in winter in small numbers on the east coast, usually where areas of sand dunes mix with saltmarshes. The numbers fluctuate but are usually very small.

In 1969–73 there was a considerable increase in British numbers, with flocks of over 100 at some east coast sites, and a spread of birds around the coast of England south to the west coast. Although flock numbers have subsequently dropped back to an average of 10–12 birds, and southern coastal occurrences are rare, there is still a wintering population on the North Wales to Lancashire coastal area. Winter numbers are low, and may vary from about 250–1,500 individuals.

In 1972 during this period of winter increase, a singing male also occurred inland in the Scottish highlands: in a bare rocky mountain area, similar to Scandinavian breeding sites. A pair was suspected of breeding in 1973, but was absent in 1974. Single birds appeared again in 1975 and 1976, and a breeding was proved, with at least one more bird present, in 1977. They have not returned since.

Woodlark *Lullula arborea*

A squat-looking bird, broad-winged and short-tailed, the crown feathers at times forming a high crest and showing the creamy eye-stripe. Quiet and unobtrusive, it has a liquid *t'luee* call-note. In song the male circles widely over territory, singing phrases of repeated musical notes, and pausing noticeably between each phrase. It will also sing from a song perch with a wide view, on a tree or bush. It prefers to feed on areas with sparse, dryish vegetation, and the nest is usually tucked against a tuft of grass or heather.

A European bird of temperate to warm-temperate climate, extending north-west to the southern parts of Britain, Sweden and Finland, it migrates from the north-east part of its range into the warmer warm-temperate and western European areas, and into the Middle East. It has an early British Pleistocene record, in Derbyshire in the last glaciation. It was subsequently recognised by Turner in 1544. In Britain it appears to require well-drained, often sandy or gravelly, sites with very short sparse vegetation of grazed or mown turf, some taller herbage to nest in, and scattered trees for song or observation posts. This not only limits its range but makes it unpredictably discontinuous. It likes heathland and has been shown to rely on recurrent fires in such areas to clear ground vegetation.

It seems to have been more widespread at times in the past, since it is said to have bred in Lancashire and Cumbria in earlier times. It was at a low ebb in the nineteenth century, having been noted as decreasing in southern England and Wales; and it increased and spread in the warmer period from the 1880s to 1940s. It bred in Yorkshire in the early 1900s but not again until 1945; and in Ireland it bred in Wicklow in 1894, Wexford about 1905 and Cork in 1945. It also spread in Lincolnshire in 1946.

It is a partial migrant, perhaps more than is usually recognised, but may suffer if hard winters extend to the continent. It suffered from cold summers at the beginning of the current cold cycle in the early 1950s. In the London region of the Thames Valley, a pair were first recorded breeding in 1920; by 1954 the area had 45 pairs; by 1964 none again. Similar rises and falls occurred elsewhere. It may also have suffered loss of habitat from heathland cultivation, and spread of scrub after Myxomatosis in 1954. It may have recovered to some extent since, but is still scarce. There were about 100 known pairs in Britain in 1965, but about 200–450 in 1972, and about the same in 1981–83. The extent of breeding occurrences shown by the B.T.O. 1968–72 survey is surprisingly close to that mapped in the Handbook of British Birds in 1938. Its general distribution is through the south coast counties, but rare in eastern Kent; also in Surrey and Hertfordshire, the East Anglian brecklands and south-east Suffolk; a small area in Nottinghamshire, and south-west Wales.

Skylark *Alauda arvensis*

With a song famed for exuberance and length rather than melodiousness, this is a bird best heard singing as it circles high in an open sky. It is broad-winged, helping it to hang in the air, but the sometimes fluttering flight is considerably stronger than it looks. In flocks, one more often hears a softer *chirrup*, or the harsh *tschirr* of squabbling birds. It probably owes its widespread abundance to man's agricultural modification of Britain. It prefers open ground to feed and nest on, but is more tolerant of growth of grass, herbage or young corn than are most other lark species. It feeds on grain as well as weed seeds, and is commoner in grain-growing areas than on grass. At times it eats a considerable amount of plant material – leaves and shoots – arousing the enmity of farmers. However, it does not like trees, and is suspicious of small hedged fields.

Its breeding range is from boreal to warm-temperate zones across Eurasia. It is resident in the warmer parts of its range and in western Europe, with some migration into its subtropical range. Throughout the range, it is linked with open grassy areas and cultivation. In Pleistocene Britain it occurred in the last, Ipswichian, interglacial in south Wales, and in the latter part of the last glaciation in Derbyshire, Kent and Devonshire. Its British range must have been limited by the spread of woodland, but it would have increased and spread as this was cleared, and may have reached its maximum population in recent times.

It has benefitted from widespread arable agriculture. It suffers in hard winters, although there is some local migration. There is a large continental influx in winter. Many of these may have been involved in the trapping (usually netting) for food in winter, that continued until the beginning of the present century. This seems to have been concentrated in regions where flocks occurred. Richard Kearton mentioned 12,000 trapped in a single morning around Brighton in January 1897, after a westward hard weather movement.

They do not appear to have suffered as much from toxic seed-dressings, and weed and insect sprays on crops as might have been expected. As breeding birds, they are present over the whole British Isles, including all the islands. In winter, there is some shift away from mountains and high ground, and a greater concentration in the east. There seems to be no recent significant change in a breeding population for the British Isles of about 2,000,000–4,000,000 pairs. The winter population could be about 25,000,000 birds.

Crows, Magpies and Jays

Corvidae

The largest of our song-birds, these are strong-billed and strong-footed, fairly intelligent and adaptable and able to utilise a variety of food sources although, with the possible exception of the Jay, primarily taking animal rather than plant food. They are able to use their feet to hold down food items while they deal with them. They both walk and hop, again with the exception of the arboreal and hopping Jay. Flight is slow and powerful.

There are seven British species. The Raven is a large scavenger and generalised-feeder, once widespread and now driven back to wilder parts. The Crow is a smaller version that has been more successful in maintaining a wide distribution. The Rook is specialised as a grassland feeder, nesting colonially in trees, and mainly limited to farmland. The Jackdaw is also a bird of grassland, but a cavity-nester that has spread with farmland and human settlement. The Red-billed Chough is a bird from more southern montane areas, extending north on the Atlantic coastal zone and in Britain now confined to western coasts and mountains. The Magpie is primarily a bird of forest edge and scrub, that has exploited human activities and is widespread; the Jay is closely linked with the distribution of oak woodland.

Carrion Crow *Corvus corone*

This has two forms, the all-black one to which the name Carrion Crow is usually given, and the grey and black Hooded Crow that is almost, but not quite, a separate species. However, in general behaviour they are indivisible. As a species, it generally feeds on a variety of small creatures down to insects and earthworms, seeds, vegetable matter and fruit. It is also a scavenger, but it is as a carrion-eater suspected of killing young lambs, and as a petty predator that it has always been disliked. This has been enhanced by confrontation with the intelligence and suspiciousness that has enabled it to survive alongside human society. It feeds mainly in the open, and breeds in solitary pairs, the cup nest placed high in a tree; but where this is lacking and isolation permits, nests may be built on low sites. The deliberate flight and deep loud caw are recognisable features. Non-breeding birds may form large flocks where they are not persecuted, and may gather to feed on rubbish tips, sewage farms or shores. Pairs may join them in communal winter roosts while retaining territories.

Its distribution is across Eurasia in boreal to warm-temperate zones. In some period of the Pleistocene Ice Ages, it had been separated in different refuges, and differentiated there. The eastern Eurasian form is all-black. The western bird (our Hooded Crow) has a grey body. However, in a south-western refuge area in a cold climate, probably in Spain and Portugal, another all-black form survived and in warmer times spread back in the western half of Europe north to the British Isles. This is our Carrion Crow. It meets the Hooded Crow along a zone through northern Italy, up through eastern Germany and Denmark. The Hooded Crow might have already extended across to Ireland, but the Carrion Crow intruded in Britain, pushing it north. The Hooded Crow is now in Ireland, the Scottish islands and

north and west highlands, Orkney, Shetland and the Faeroes. Where the two meet they hybridise, producing intermediates that appear less fertile and less successful than the parent forms. As a result, a limited hybrid zone is maintained. This zone moved northwards in Europe with the climatic amelioration of the earlier half of this century. In Scotland, the southern end stayed put on Clydeside, but the northern end shifted westwards over 45 years from Aberdeenshire to the western side of the Moray Firth, and with hybrid birds through most of the highlands.

Its bones, apart from the skull, are like those of the Rook. Crow/Rook remains occur in the British Pleistocene from the next-to-last, Wolstonian, glaciation onwards in the south-west, and in the last glaciation in Derbyshire. Able to use both woodland and open country, it would have been widespread from the first, but over recent centuries was killed with increasing success on farmland. With the advent of organised gamekeeping in the late eighteenth and nineteenth centuries, attempts were made to wipe it out by all means available, without success. However, the numbers must have been drastically reduced over the whole of the British Isles. With the cessation of gamekeeping in two world wars and general reduction in game preservation, numbers began to increase, although it is still being killed to the present day.

It spread locally as it increased. By the late nineteenth century, it had already begun to nest in parks of large cities, and numbers continued to grow in urban areas. Increases have continued in recent times, although with some reductions in areas such as East Anglia, where intensive game preservation still continues. It is present throughout the British Isles as a breeding bird, the hooded form occupying Ireland, the Isle of Man, the north-west half of Scotland and the northern islands. A few Carrion Crows also occur in north-east Ireland. The total population may be about 1,000,000 pairs. There is a small winter influx of Scandinavian Hooded Crows, and possibly some continental Carrion Crows.

Rook *Corvus frugilegus*

This is a crow that has become specialised in probing turf and soil for worms, cranefly larvae and other invertebrates. For this, it has a slightly longer bill and lacks facial feathering. The bare white skin of the face and high-crowned look help identify the adult, although young birds have a feathered face and look more like crows. The caw is deeper and more deliberate.

As a grassland feeder in areas of few trees, it nests communally: a rookery of many pairs crowded into a clump of mature trees with nests slightly spaced. In addition to small creatures, it also eats grain in autumn and winter, and like other corvids takes a wide variety of foods, seeming to have an addiction to walnuts. In winter the Rooks within a large area form a big communal roost, often with Crows and Jackdaws, but still make a brief daily visit to the rookery.

It has a breeding range across Eurasia in temperate regions. It is resident in most of Europe, but further east

buildings as nest-sites in others.

While it seems to have suffered less persecution than other corvids, it appears more susceptible to climate, and this may have depressed numbers in the colder fourteenth to nineteenth centuries. In the warmer part of the late nineteenth and earlier twentieth centuries, it showed a marked overall increase. This was particularly strong at its northern limits in Scotland. It began to colonise Orkney by the 1880s, and the Outer Hebrides by 1895; but it did not reach Shetland until 1943 and is only a sporadic nester there.

In the 1960s, there seems to have been a considerable expansion on western coasts and islands from Scotland to south Wales, but there was some decrease in eastern England where grassland gave way to grain-growing. Similar increases and northward expansion appear to have occurred in Europe generally. In addition to a west and southward movement in Britain in winter, there is a continental influx to south and east coasts. During the big Jay irruption in the autumn of 1983, over 20,000 Jackdaws were seen moving through Cornwall in one day, but this is rare.

Its present distribution is throughout the British Isles; it is only scarce in the western and north-west Scottish highlands, and on some smaller islands, with one Outer Hebrides colony, and occasional Shetland nesting. The breeding population is about 500,000 pairs.

Red-billed Chough *Pyrrhocorax pyrrhocorax*
At a distance, this can pass as a Jackdaw until the high-pitched and more explosive *kee-ow* call betrays it. It is a bird of dry open hillsides, probing among stones and thin turf for ants and small insects. In the British Isles, it is precariously at the northern extremity of its range, and vulnerable to hard winters when the ground freezes and birds die. It inhabits cliffs, and inland outcrops and quarries, nesting on a ledge in a deep crevice or cave. It is a sociable species, pairs and non-breeders feeding in small flocks.

It occurs through the uplands of the warm-temperate zone of Eurasia, from Spain to China; and it extends up the mild Atlantic coasts to France and the British Isles. Although a cave bird, its Pleistocene records are only from the warm Ipswichian Interglacial in Yorkshire, and late last glaciation and early Holocene in Somerset and the south Wales coast. As a coastal and rocky-area breeder, it should have been little affected by human activity. Early written records are confused because the name 'chough' is used both for this species and the Jackdaw.

It seems to have been common within the limits of rocky coasts with short turf, and mountain sheepwalks, until the end of the eighteenth century. Quarrying may have offered it a few additional nest-sites. Numbers subsequently declined gradually for nearly two centuries, with no apparent reason other than a vulnerability to hard winters, and poor rate of recovery in small scattered populations.

On the east coast, it had bred at St Abbs Head in Berwickshire since at least 1578, but disappeared soon after 1866. It disappeared from the Yorkshire coast in the first half of the nineteenth century, and in this period was also lost from the Kent and Sussex coasts and many inland and coastal sites in western Scotland south to Kincardineshire. In the later nineteenth century, it

disappeared from the Isle of Wight, Dorset, south Devon and Cumbria; after 1910 from north Devon; and by 1930 from south-west Scotland, Skye and Mull. It last bred in Cornwall in 1952.

It occurs inland in a few places in north Wales and parts of extreme western Ireland. Otherwise it is on Welsh coasts from Pembrokeshire to Anglesey; the Isle of Man; Islay, Jura, Colonsay and tip of Kintyre in Scotland; and on north, west and south Irish coasts. The population in 1982 was about 900–1,000 pairs, with about 1,000 more non-breeding individuals. Its British population seems to be stable and increasing slightly although other western European populations, which also declined, may still be decreasing. Apart from winter weather, its most likely threat is from agricultural 'improvement' of feeding areas.

Magpie *Pica pica*
Admired for its bold, bright colouring and jaunty manner, but disliked for raiding birds' nests, the Magpie has always suffered from the ambiguity of human attitudes. Where tolerated, it is prepared to feed and nest close to human settlement, and has begun to find a place for itself in some of our cities. Where circumstances permit, it is resident. Although mainly an insect-eater in summer, and a seed-, nut- and fruit-eater in winter, it is an opportunist and at times a carrion-eater and petty predator. It is a bird of open places, but needs a bush or tree to hold its bulky nest with the protective dome of twigs. Sites may vary from isolated thorn bushes to dense conifer plantations.

It has a broad range across Eurasia and western North America in boreal to warm-temperate zones, and into arctic Scandinavia. In Pleistocene Britain it occurs in the last glaciation, probably in interstadial conditions, in Derbyshire and the south-west. As a bird of woodland edge, scrub and open spaces it would have become limited during the early spread of woodland, but must have increased as woodland was cleared and farmland spread. It did not start its successful colonisation of Ireland until about 1676, in Wexford. With the advent of widespread game preservation, it was extensively shot and poisoned from the late eighteenth century onwards, and by the late nineteenth century was scarce or extinct over much of Scotland outside the industrial lowlands, almost extinct in East Anglia, and greatly reduced elsewhere.

It began to increase with the reduction in gamekeeping during the 1914–18 war, and continued to do so in spite of persecution. It did not increase in East Anglia until the 1930s. A larger and more widespread increase occurred during and after the 1939–45 war. In the 1950s and 1960s, it spread into urban areas. However, destruction of hedgerows and use of pesticides has caused a decrease in some parts of the south-east, especially in East Anglia. It now breeds throughout England, Wales and Ireland, although sparsely in East Anglia and the Pennines; and in Scotland mainly in the lowlands and Aberdeenshire regions, sparsely in the south and in the Moray Firth. The British Isles population is estimated at 250,000–500,000 pairs.

Jay *Garrulus glandarius*
The brightest of our crows, it is best seen when it flaps over, with broad rounded wings and bulging throat, toiling to and fro in its autumn acorn-

planting activities. In some open stretches of grass it buries enough acorns to last it through the winter, finding them again without difficulty. If it dies we have an embryo oak plantation. If acorns fail it may store sweet chestnuts, hazelnuts and beechmast. In spite of the occasional egg or nestling, its diet is mainly insects, seeds, acorns, nuts and fruit. It is a bird of open woodland, preferably oakwood, but it will also use the edges of conifer woodland and plantations. Although furtive and often silent it may betray its presence by its raucous, screeching alarm call. Its cup nest is hidden in a tree or tall shrub. It is normally resident.

Its general range is across Eurasia in boreal to warm-temperate zones. Its uses broadleaf and mixed woodland, but not pure conifer woodland. It is resident, but being reliant on acorn and nut crops for winter storage, there are irruptive movements from the northern part of the range in autumn, when these fail. In Britain the Jay occurs as far back as the Middle Pleistocene, in temperate oakwoods of the Cromerian Interglacial in Norfolk, and later in presumably interstadial conditions in the last glaciation in Derbyshire and the south-west. In the post-glacial period, it may not have been common until the oaks invaded Britain about 8,000 years ago. It would then have become numerous. It would have

decreased again as woodland was cleared. Like the Magpie, it suffered seriously from game preservation, that involved shooting and poisoning, the former still continuing to some extent. Although more evasive, it underwent an overall decrease, and numbers were lowest at the turn of the century.

Aided by a reduction in gamekeepers during the two world wars, it steadily increased again in the present century. It colonised urban areas earlier than the Magpie, in the 1930s. Since the mid 1930s, it has re-colonised ground lost in Ireland. It is now generally distributed through England and Wales, but absent from areas of the Fens and high bare uplands. In Ireland, it is scarce or absent from much of the north and west. In Scotland its distribution is limited, although afforestation has helped it to spread. It is present in the south-west and border regions, and through the southern edge of the highlands from Argyll across to Aberdeenshire. The British Isles population has been estimated at about 100,000 pairs.

Although not regularly immigrant, continental birds may come to the British Isles during periodic irruptions. In 1983, thousands temporarily moved westwards through Britain when acorn crops failed.

PLATE THIRTY-SIX

Tits

Paridae

A family of small, often brightly-coloured birds. They have strong, stubby bills and strong feet which enable them to cling acrobatically to twigs in order to search for small insects; these can also be used to hold down food items such as seeds and nuts, while these are dealt with. They build a cup nest in a hole, and raise large broods. They are mainly resident.

There are six species in the British Isles. Broadly speaking, based on their wider distribution, three are mainly conifer forest types and three from broadleaf forest. In Britain they must extend into mixed woodlands, or show a greater tolerance for the other type. Of the conifer forest birds, the Crested Tit is a bird of more mature trees, only present in Scotland; the Coal Tit can adapt to both types, and the Willow Tit is a bird of borders of damp lowland conifer woodland and the scrub associated with marshy places.

Broadleaf forest birds are the Great Tit and Blue Tit, both able to extend to woodland edge and sparsely wooded areas, but the Blue Tit is more able to adapt to an extreme reduction of vegetation. The Marsh Tit is a closely-related replacement of the Willow Tit, in more typical broadleaf woodland. Both Marsh Tit and Willow Tit are absent from Ireland.

Great Tit *Parus major*
This is a big, bold, rather thuggish-looking tit. Larger and less agile than the smaller species, it may search more on the ground for food such as fallen beechmast or nuts. It is able to manage well beyond the confines of woodland, and this may have helped it to adapt to parkland, hedgerows and gardens. Even so, it still seems

to need a few trees in its immediate surroundings. In spring and summer, it feeds mainly on insects taken from trees and bushes. It is resident and terrestrial and its short repetitive song, often consisting of alternating high and low notes, is heard for a long period of the year. Nesting depends on the possession of a nest-hole, which may to some extent control density and distribution in this and other tit species.

It has a broad range across Eurasia in temperate to warm-temperate zones, extending into boreal and subarctic zones in northern Europe. It is resident except along the northern limit of its range from Scandinavia eastwards. It had an early appearence in the records in Britain in a Middle Pleistocene glaciation in Essex, probably about 500,000 years ago, and also occurred in the latter part of the last glaciation, probably in interstadial conditions in Derbyshire and the south-west. As a bird of predominantly broadleaf woodland, it could have spread in Britain as woodland spread. It would have needed to manage without winter beechmast, since the beech was a latecomer in the British flora, too late to reach Ireland unaided. It would have lost some ground in historic times with the increasing clearance of woodland, but might then have adapted to more scattered trees and taller scrub where this existed. While it may have remained widespread, its population is likely to have been smaller.

With the enclosures, it could have exploited the nineteenth century pattern of hedgerow trees and coverts, and parkland. In more recent times, it has spread widely into the more vegetated gardens. In the warmer first half of the present century, when it also

Great Tit

Blue Tit

Coal Tit

Crested Tit

Willow Tit

Marsh Tit

D.M.H.

spread northwards in Norway, it colonised mainland Scotland north of Invernesshire where it was previously absent. From the 1950s it nested sporadically on Rhum and Eigg, and nested at Stornaway from 1962. It is not on Orkney or Shetland, but is otherwise present throughout the British Isles, save for a few mountain areas mostly in northern Scotland.

Although its woodland population is fairly stable, the farmland population fluctuates strongly, possibly through greater vulnerability to hard weather. After reaching low levels in the early 1960s, probably due to two hard winters, farmland figures nearly doubled by 1972, and the population has increased overall by about 11% between 1972 and 1984, now estimated at about 3,300,000 pairs. In winter birds may join small local flocks, and there is some general movement away from higher ground or more exposed areas to woodland. There is no regular significant immigration, but continental birds may occur after irruptions in years when beechmast crops are poor. One such year was 1957, when the native population was also at a high level, and involved some British birds in movements as well.

Blue Tit *Parus caeruleus*

Small, fussily-active and tame, the Blue Tit has found a woodland and scrub-edge habitat in gardens, and readily adopted the nest-box as a substitute for the always scarce nest-hole. In a man-modified environment its readiness to investigate unfamiliar food sources has helped, and it has become an accepted part of the human environment, catered for as a kind of uncontrolled pet or garden ornament. Its acrobatic agility and stout, stubby bill enable it to exploit broadleaf vegetation as a source of its mainly insect food.

It is basically a bird of open woodland that can move out and adapt to almost anywhere with some saplings or shrubby growth, beyond the Great Tit's limits. Even within its more typical habitat, the provision of nest-boxes can increase its population density considerably. It also uses holes for roosting in winter. It can use the fringes of conifer woodland and plantations, increasing its range. It has a small song-phrase, with repetition, of two sharp notes and a shivery flourish.

It has an European distribution east to the Urals, and from warm boreal to warm-temperate zones, and is resident except on its north-east fringe. The earliest British record is uncertain, bones in a Middle Pleistocene interglacial in Essex, about 500,000 years ago, being either of this species or the Coal Tit. Extrapolating from other bird species present, the Blue Tit is the more likely of the two. Apart from this, its British record would appear to date back to the eighth century.

It is likely to have been numerous and widespread over most of the last 9,000 years, and possibly more numerous when oak woodland became a climax vegetation. It must have decreased as woodland was cleared, but is even more adaptable to lack of trees than the Great Tit. It showed the same tendency to increase in the earlier part of this century, but was already in the extreme north of the Scottish mainland at the turn of the century. It has bred on Stornaway since 1962, and the Scillies since the 1940s.

Apart from this, it is widespread and numerous throughout the British Isles, but absent from Shetland, Orkney and a few mountain areas of Scotland. Like the Great Tit, pairs on farmland doubled between 1962 and 1974, but unlike that species, numbers fell again. The 1972 population was estimated at about 5,000,000 pairs, but by 1982 was reduced by about 7%. In autumn and winter it may join local roving bands of birds, and there appears to be a movement away from high ground. Like the Great Tit, it takes beechmast where available and feeds more on seeds in winter. Irruptive movements of continental birds sometimes occur, and in a major western-European movement in 1957, British birds were also involved.

Coal Tit *Parus ater*

A little bird, less conspicuous than the commoner tits, this is likely to be noticed as a small sad voice in a pine tree, calling with a plaintive *tsuu* note, or using thin shrill, Goldcrest-like squeaks. It tends to feed within conifer trees and high up, difficult to see except when it hangs upside-down and the white nape-patch shows. Its disyllabic song is like a higher-pitched version of that of the Great Tit. It can also utilise broadleaf woodland, and is numerous in the west of the British Isles, but finds it difficult to compete with Great Tits and Blue Tits, and its thin bill gives it an advantage when feeding in conifers. With its small size, it tends to avoid other species by feeding high, but in winter will come down to collect and hide beechmast or other seeds, to feed on a little later. It may also nest low, and often uses holes in stumps, walls or banks, some at ground level.

Its range is across Eurasia in warm boreal to warm-temperate zones. There is evidence in the Middle Pleistocene, in an Essex interglacial about 500,000 years ago, of either Blue Tit or Coal Tit, their bones being similar. From the other species present, the former is the more likely, in which case the first British reference to the Coal Tit, according to James Fisher, was by Ælfric the Grammarian in about 998. The British Coal Tit is yellower than continental birds (although the difference is not clear-cut), but even if it is not a specialised isolate, it would have needed to adapt to broadleaf woodland, for fairly early in the Holocene the pine was being limited to Scotland, as the climate warmed and broadleaf trees became widespread.

Being at a disadvantage in competing with other species, the Coal Tit is likely to have been widespread in marginal areas, surviving better on uplands, and perhaps in specialised vegetation such as yew woodland. It must have lost ground with woodland clearance, but had an advantage from the early nineteenth century onwards, with the planting of conifer plantations, and of exotic conifers in gardens, parkland and around estates. Its increase and spread was rapid in such areas.

Like other species, it had been absent in northern Scotland, but spread there by the end of the last century. Although breeding at higher altitudes than other tits, its small size makes it vulnerable to cold weather. After losses in the winters of the early 1960s, its population trebled in sample counts in the next five years. It appears more stable now at an estimated 1,000,000 pairs. It is now present throughout the British Isles except on the Scillies, Orkney and Shetland, and a recent sporadic breeder at Stornaway on Lewis. It colonises more of the mountain areas of Scotland than other tit species, but is less in evidence around the Fens and Humberside, and north-west extremities of Ireland. As with other species, there are occasional, usually small, irruptions of continental birds.

Crested Tit *Parus cristatus*

This is a pine-wood specialist, a small bird with patterned face and spiky crest that tends to spend much of its time in the outer twigs and branches of pine trees; but it advertises its presence by the unmistakable purring trill. It also has typical tit-type high-pitched squeaky notes. It nests in a hole, and if necessary will excavate one, often in a dead pine sapling or rotten wood of an old post, as well as using higher sites. In Britain it is closely linked with scots pine, feeding mainly on insects taken in the trees, but in winter it hunts more at ground level, also taking pine seed which it may store with other food, hidden in crevices or wedged into bark.

It is a European bird, in conifer woodland, from Spain and Greece north to the Arctic Circle and White Sea. It may have been present in pinewoods of interglacial or interstadial periods; and it is likely to have been present in southern Britain about 10,000 to 8,000 years ago when pinewood was present further south, and to have retreated with it to Scotland. The first reference to Scottish Crested Tits seems to have been by Willughby and Ray in 1678. All verifiable records seem to refer to the scots pine woodland of the Spey Valley. It is agreed that it must have been more widespread, but as woodland was cleared this became its last refuge.

Cut off from communication with woodland elsewhere, and in small numbers, there it has remained. In recent times, maturing conifer plantations have allowed it to spread a little around the Moray Basin. It may also have been present for a long period in the small population in north-west Inverness. With a little human help, it might have done well in the pines of Surrey, East Anglia or possibly Keilder Forest. It is susceptible to hard winters and numbers fluctuate strongly. The average population is thought to be about 900 pairs.

Willow Tit *Parus montanus*

The two black-capped tits are difficult to separate. The duller crown, whiter cheeks and paler wing-edges of the Willow Tit are not easy to see, and it is usually the loud triple *tchay-tchay-tchay* call with its nasal tone that is needed for identification. In Britain it is usually a bird of swampy woodland and thickets of alder, willow and birch, or in waterside trees. Possibly because damp wood is more rotten, it habitually excavates its own nest-hole, unlike the Marsh Tit. From its riverine tree belts it has extended to damper hedgerows, and is more frequent on farmland than the other species. It has a thinner bill, less able to cope with beechmast and nuts than other tits, but stores food items in winter, including small invertebrates.

It occurs across Eurasia in boreal to temperate zones. Since the British birds were not identified as separate from the Marsh Tit until 1897, it has little history. It is a bird of montane damp conifer woodland, and broadleaf swamp thickets. Its past history is difficult to guess at. It would have lost most of its conifer woodland at an early stage in the Holocene. If it then turned to alder and willow carr woodland of a fen type it is possible that it would have found a fairly extensive habitat on some of the larger marsh areas such as the Cambridgeshire fens and Somerset levels. It would then have lost much of this during sixteenth to nineteenth century drainage. It seems to have adapted to damper hedgerows and farm thickets.

It now has a widely spread population through England and Wales in a variety of such sites, absent from higher ground and from much of the more extensive open marshland and fen areas that might have provided tree cover in the past. It seems thickest in the west, in Wales, and in the north-west. In Scotland it is limited to the south-west and a few scattered sites north into the lowlands; and for no apparent reason it is absent from Ireland, and also from Scillies, Anglesey, and the Isle of Man. It is very sedentary and the winter distribution differs little from summer, but there may be some westward shift of young birds. Its breeding population is estimated at about 50,000–100,000 pairs.

Marsh Tit *Parus palustris*

Difficult to distinguish except by its drabness, the Marsh Tit is the black-capped tit with the loud *pitchou* call, the small explosive note its best mark of identification. Primarily it is a woodland bird, holding territory all the year, and in competition with species such as the Great Tit. It therefore tends to occupy the lower bushy strata of woodlands. It prefers broadleaf woodland, particularly beech and oak, and occupies drier and more open areas than does the Willow Tit. It also has a stouter bill, capable of dealing with beechmast, and in winter hides and hoards these and other seeds, as well as insects, sometimes for a few days or less; but it forms a reserve to aid survival.

It uses a natural cavity for the nest, and like those of the Coal Tit they are often very low down. In addition to territorial pairs, there is a drifting population that forms winter flocks with other birds, and these may be joined momentarily by resident birds as they pass through. As with most species of tits, winter is the time of greatest mortality.

This has a slightly more southerly and lowland distribution than the Willow Tit, discontinuous, in Europe and again in eastern Eurasia, and extending from warm boreal to warm-temperate zones. It is mainly a bird of broadleaf woodland. There are no very early British records. According to James Fisher, birds of this type, either Marsh Tits or Willow Tits, were mentioned in the tenth and eleventh centuries; a definite Marsh Tit was reported by Willughby and Ray in 1678, although the Willow Tit was not recognised here until 1897. Like other tits, Marsh Tit history would be linked with woodland, presumably becoming numerous and widespread as broadleaf woodland spread in the Holocene, and retreating as woodland was cleared in prehistoric and historic times.

It has adapted to some extent to hedgerows, orchards and small coverts where suitable trees are present. It is highly sedentary. In broad outline its British distribution is very similar to that of the Willow Tit, although extending less far north, but in detail they replace each other in differing habitats. It is absent from Ireland, and present in England and Wales, but not in Anglesey, the Isle of Man or the Scillies. It only extends north of the Scottish border in a small part of Berwickshire. It is widely present in the south, very scarce in the Fens and near the coast from the Wash to Yorkshire and County Durham. It is also sparse in south-west Wales and absent from most of its west coasts, and from south Lancashire and north Cumbria. It was more numerous in the 1970s than the Willow Tit, with a 1972 estimate of 70,000–140,000 pairs; but this dropped 20% by 1984.

Long-tailed Tits

Aegithalidae

A small family of seven species of tiny, insect-eating birds. They are strong-footed and agile, taking food mainly from twigs and leaves of trees and bushes. The nest is domed. Four species occur in the Himalayas and China with another across Eurasia, its range overlapping one of the eastern four.

Long-tailed Tit *Aegithalos caudatus*

A small fluffy ball of feathers with an overlong tail; almost constantly and fussily active, searching the surfaces of trees and bushes for items as small as aphids and insects' eggs. It is sociable, and one is usually conscious of the sudden appearance of a party of them, trees at once alive with small rocketing forms swinging acrobatically on twigs, calling with a fusillade of low, sharp notes and high, squeaky calls, then passing on equally suddenly. At night they huddle like a multi-tailed feather ball on a sheltered perch. The nest, in a tree or bush fork, is an elastic domed structure of moss and spiders' webs, lined with feathers. It may have to expand to accommodate a growing brood of up to 12 young. These help to compensate for losses through cold winters. Pairs defend breeding territories, helped at times by supernumerary adults, and in winter locally-roving flocks defend flock territories. They use woodland, open woodland and scrub, and can move to overgrown hedgerows and lower growth.

It occurs across Eurasia in boreal to warm-temperate zones, but is limited to mixed woodland areas of conifer forests. It has differentiated in past isolation. It has a dark back and striped head in the British Isles and mainland Europe, and in Korea and Japan; a grey back and striped head in southern Europe to Iran and China; and a white-headed form, probably from the east, is found right across the Siberian range to Scandinavia.

There is a British Pleistocene record from the last glaciation in Derbyshire; otherwise it is known from the eighth century onwards. It needs some thick shrubby growth for shelter, and would have spread with woodland. It would have decreased with widespread clearing, although adapting to parkland, taller hedgerows and coverts. In general, it is affected only by destruction of woodland cover. There is some evidence of recent decreases where extensive hedgerow destruction has occurred. Its main enemy is cold weather, and in severe winters its population has dropped by up to 80%, taking some years to recover. Distribution is determined by vegetation, and it is absent from barer high ground in northern England, Scotland and Ireland, and from windswept parts of some western Scottish islands. It is absent from Shetland, Orkney, the Outer Hebrides and Scillies. In a good period (in 1972) the population was estimated at about 150,000 pairs.

Nuthatches

Sittidae

Mainly tree birds, these have large and strong feet, enabling them to grip the irregularities of tree bark or rocks, and travel over them in any direction, head up or head down. The tail, not needed for support, is short. The bill is stout, sharp and straight. They can open and feed on nuts and woody fruits of trees, by wedging them into crevices and hammering them open. They are mainly adapted for life on trees, and there are a number of species in the warmer parts of the Old World, but only one has spread through Eurasia.

Common Nuthatch *Sitta europaea*

An active species, moving in fast jerky hops in all directions over tree-trunks and branches, taking insects and hacking open hazelnuts, chestnuts, beechmast, and hard seeds such as hornbeam and yew. It wedges them into crevices, swinging the bill like a pickaxe, with loud rappings. It may store food in winter; and it can take peanuts from a bird-table at an alarming rate to hide them. It is mainly found in well-grown trees, likely to produce food, in broadleaf woodland, parkland, or more scattered sites. It uses a natural tree cavity to nest, reducing the entrance to size by plastering mud around it. It has loud, clear, repetitive calls: a whistled *kwi-kwi-kwi* ... and long trills being typical.

It extends across Eurasia in warm boreal to warm-temperate forest zones. It has an early record in the British Middle Pleistocene, in temperate oak forest

conditions in the Cromerian Interglacial; and also in the latter part of the last glaciation, presumably in interstadial conditions, in Derbyshire and Devon. Its post-glacial history would appear to be linked to that of nut or acorn-producing trees. The hazel, as the earliest coloniser, would presumably be the key species, with others added later. It would have lost ground with woodland clearing, then shifted to using isolated patches and rows of mature trees, and in more recent times, parkland, hedgerows with large trees, and similar places.

Its present distribution is similar to that of broadleaf woodland such as oak and beech. It was limited to England and Wales, and in the nineteenth century appears to have been absent from north-west Wales, sparse eastwards from there towards the Wash, absent from the fen country, with an outlying population in Yorkshire. There seems to have been a small extension of range from the 1940s onwards, into the last part of Wales, and shifting northwards in the Midlands. The range is now south and east of a line from the Mersey to the Tweed, with birds mainly absent in a band from south Lancashire to south Yorkshire, and in Lincolnshire and the fen region. There is a scattering of breeders in Lakeland, and more recently single birds have begun to appear in parts of Scotland. The population is estimated generally at about 20,000 pairs.

Bearded Reedling

MALE

Long-tailed Tit

Wren

Common Nuthatch

Common Dipper

Common
Treecreeper

D. M. HENRY

Treecreepers
Certhiidae

Small birds adapted like woodpeckers for climbing upwards on trees, with well-straddled legs, and strengthened shafts to the spiky tail feathers. The bills are long and decurved, for probing into crevices after insects and invertebrates. Flight is relatively weak. There are five species. Two occur in Europe. The Short-toed Treecreeper *C. brachydactyla* probably differentiated in the Pleistocene in the Iberian peninsula, and now occupies European broadleaf woodland. The Common Treecreeper is distributed across Eurasia mainly in conifer woodland, but in the British Isles, as the only species, uses both conifer and broadleaf.

Common Treecreeper *Certhia familiaris*
This is a small streaky-bodied and silvery-breasted traveller over tree-trunks and branches, furtive and squeaky-voiced. It moves in small rapid hops, spiralling upwards, or upside-down along the underside of a branch. A short undulating flight takes it from high up in one tree, to low down on the next, to resume its upward hunt. It roosts pressed into a hollow on a tree-trunk, and builds its nest behind loose bark, or in a crevice. It is solitary for much of the year, but may accompany flocks of tits in winter woodland. It uses both broadleaf and conifer trees, finding more on rough and flaky bark.

Its range is across Eurasia in boreal to temperate zones. In Britain, its earliest record is from about the eleventh century. It is thought that it may have returned in post-glacial times, when conifer woodland was dominant; and, as this was increasingly replaced by broadleaf woodland (from which the Short-toed Treecreeper was absent, unlike that of the European mainland), it perhaps adapted to this also. It would have been reduced in numbers in historic times, when woodland clearance became more extensive, but since it can adapt to more open places with scattered trees of various sizes, its main problem may have been the need for nest-sites. It is also susceptible to hard winters, which strongly reduce its numbers. After bad winters in the early 1960s, it increased dramatically over the next ten years. A probable slight increase since the nineteenth century would have been obscured by these responses to climate.

The Short-toed Treecreeper, extremely difficult to separate, has been noticed increasingly in southern England in recent times. It has been suggested that a few might be breeding, but the actual situation seems uncertain. The Common Treecreeper occurs through the British Isles, but is absent from Shetland, Orkney, the Outer Hebrides and Scillies. It is scarce in the fen country, on barer mountain areas, and the extreme north-west of Scotland and Ireland. The population is estimated at about 150,000–300,000 pairs.

Wrens
Troglodytidae

A family of medium-sized to small insectivorous birds of the Americas. They are typified by short bodies, largish heads, strong legs and feet, thin bills that are sometimes long, and short tails. They build domed nests. One form invaded Eurasia during the Pleistocene, presumably via the Bering Straits, speciated there, and partly re-colonised North America.

Wren *Troglodytes troglodytes*
This is a very small bird, designed to exploit ground cover. It moves easily and rapidly over and through low woodland vegetation, looking like something between a mouse and an animated walnut. It will peer and probe at ground level, crouching flat, and enter under overhangs and into cavities. It will also search ivy and creepers on trees and rocks. It needs an overgrown, low shrubby layer, preferably within woodland or scrub; and is unhappy in hedgerows and in wooded areas with poor ground cover. The nest is a domed structure. The male defends a territory with bursts of loud song, that seem to shake its whole body, the small erect tail sometimes moving as though pumping it out. He builds a number of outer structures of nests within the territory, and tries to induce more than one female to occupy them. The female lines the nest and incubates the eggs, the male helping to feed the large broods. Territories are often maintained in winter, but it suffers badly in cold weather. Birds may be forced to more sheltered sites, and in very cold weather territorial birds may join others in crowding into small roost-holes, up to 50 birds on occasions, in order to keep warm.

It occurs across the southern part of Eurasia in warm-temperate zones, and both in the far east and Europe extends northwards into warmer boreal regions, and as far as Iceland. Its earliest British record is in the latter part of the last glaciation, in Derbyshire and Devon. However, its history is more complex. Slightly distinct forms which have been named as subspecies are present on Iceland, the Faeroes, Shetland, Fair Isle and the Outer Hebrides and St Kilda. These suggest a period of isolation – when these islands were mild enough to support wrens – and a secondary colonisation of mainland Britain from the continent.

Once here, it was able to occupy woodland, scrub and every area of low cover. Like other species, it must have been reduced in numbers and distribution by clearing and cultivation of land. It still remained widespread, and would have flourished in outlying areas. The proliferation of coverts and planting would have helped it to spread back again. Otherwise, its only serious enemy is cold weather. Like most small birds, it dies in large numbers in cold weather. They are replaced by the production of more than one large brood in a year. After two bad winters, the B.T.O. censuses showed a rise in ten years of eight to ten times the initial population, but it could presumably fall faster and more abruptly. It is distributed throughout the entire British Isles, and the average breeding population is thought to be about 4,000,000–5,000,000 pairs.

Dippers
Cinclidae

A small family of five species, in the main replacing each other geographically. Superficially like large wrens, they are closely related to thrushes. They live on fast-flowing waters, mainly in hill regions, and are adapted to feeding in and under flowing water, and nest nearby. Two species occur in Eurasia, overlapping in the Himalayas; the Common Dipper is the western Eurasian species.

Common Dipper *Cinclus cinclus*
A squat, strongly-built bird, stout-billed and short-tailed, with a large head. It has long, strong legs and tends to stand in a half-crouched stance, frequently flexing the legs and bobbing the body up and down. Its strong feet enable it simply to walk into and under fast-flowing water. It can swim, and in addition can use its wings to swim under water and grip with its feet, enabling it to feed on insects such as caddis-fly larvae, molluscs and small fish. It is limited to fast-flowing streams with clear water, pairs usually well-spaced along them, and it usually flies low over water with rapid beats of the short, strong wings. The nest is a large domed structure of moss, with an internal cup and a slight entrance hood, usually in a crevice or cavity overlooking water. It has sharp shrill calls, and a loud warbling song.

It occurs discontinuously, in hilly areas, across Eurasia to China. In Europe, it occurs in appropriate habitats from subarctic to warm-temperate zones, and up into high arctic/alpine altitudinal zones. There was some differentiation in isolated populations in Pleistocene times, and Scandinavian and Pyrenean birds have black bellies. Its earliest British Pleistocene occurrences are in the latter part of the last glaciation, in Derbyshire and Devon. It could have been an early coloniser after glaciations, and as a bird feeding in hill streams and nesting on their edges, it would have been affected only slightly by later human activity. It must have been reduced, when it was killed in the nineteenth century for eating trout and salmon eggs. However, it appears to have maintained its numbers. Its fast-flowing waters rarely freeze and it appears able to survive most winters; but it may have shown a slight response to climate in recent times.

In the warmer first half of the present century, it bred on Orkney from 1919 to 1940, but has done so only sporadically since. It also spread slightly eastwards in southern England and the Midlands. It had ceased to breed on the Isle of Man by 1950. However, these breedings might have been restorations of nineteenth century losses. It now faces a new threat, which may seriously affect its numbers, in the increasing acidification of waters in the north and west. This can kill off insect life and could seriously restrict Dipper distribution. In Wales, it appears to have initiated a progressive decrease since the 1950s.

It is absent from Shetland, the Isle of Man and the Scillies, but is otherwise present on most suitable waters north and west of a line from Teesmouth to Poole Harbour, together with birds on the north Yorkshire moors and the wolds. Its 1972 population was estimated at about 30,000 pairs. Occasional black-bellied Scandinavian birds occur on the eastern side of Britain in winter.

Babblers
Timaliidae

A large and very varied family of song-birds, mainly in the African and Oriental regions. One subfamily, the Parrotbills, Paradoxornithinae, consists of species specialised for feeding in reed-beds and bamboo thickets, which often have short and very stout bills. Most have very limited ranges crowded into the south-east of Asia; and the Bearded Reedling (or more accurately the Moustached Reedling) is the only one extending well into Eurasia.

Bearded Reedling *Panurus biarmicus*
This reed-bed babbler has a plain-headed female, but a male adorned with staring eyes and a pair of theatrical Victorian moustaches that can be bristled out in display. The depths of reed-beds offer microclimates, warmer and shut off from the wind, and all too often the birds are hidden with only the characteristic twanging *ping* call as evidence of their presence, or a brief view of a whirring flight just over the heads of reeds. With strong feet and long tails, they rapidly ascend and descend vertical reed stems in alternating hops like small clockwork toys. They feed on reed-seeds taken from the fluffy heads in winter, and take insects in the summer. The cup nest is built deep in the reeds. With several broods a year, and rapidly-maturing young, they are able to compensate for winter losses. This rapid build-up of numbers in a circumscribed habitat gives rise to these irruptive dispersals, when a flock may rise and, flying high and fast, set out in search of another reed-bed, only pausing temporarily if it proves inadequate.

Its range extends discontinuously across Eurasia in temperate to warm-temperate zones, in areas of reed-beds. According to James Fisher, its earliest British record is in 1662. Its past occurrences in the British Isles would have been determined by the presence of *Phragmites* reed-beds. However, although these would have been extensive in the past and extended to areas such as the Somerset levels, there is no evidence of it outside south-east England. Within that region, it could have had a much more extensive range, but would have lost large areas of its habitat with increasing large-scale drainage from the seventeenth century. In the nineteenth century, it still occurred from Lincolnshire south over the fen regions of Huntingdonshire and Cambridgeshire, in the Broads and along the East Anglian coast, in the Thames Valley up to Berkshire, and from Kent to Hampshire and possibly Dorset.

Drainage began to reduce its range; it suffered badly from cold weather; and once populations were low the nineteenth- and twentieth-century egg- and skin-collectors helped to depress its numbers further. By the 1930s and 1940s, it was limited to Norfolk and parts of Suffolk. Its lowest point was after the winter of 1946–47, when there were four or fewer pairs in Suffolk and one male in Norfolk. It had been assumed that they were sedentary, but it was discovered that they could cross between England and the Netherlands.

After 1959, extensive reed-beds on new polders in the Netherlands produced surplus birds, some of which irrupted westwards. In Britain, under protection, it also increased and birds began to disperse, exploring new reed-beds. Its main stronghold is now from East Anglia south to Kent; but also inland to Bedfordshire, Hertfordshire and Cambridgeshire, in coastal Hampshire and Dorset, on the Humber and in north Lancashire. Irruptive birds have occurred north, to south and east Scotland. The population may now be over 600 pairs, but is still vulnerable to bad winters and cannot rely on back-up populations abroad.

PLATE THIRTY-EIGHT

Thrushes and Chats

Turdidae

These are birds with narrow bills, a well-developed, usually square-ended, tail, and strong swift flight. The legs are long and strong, most species hopping, but more terrestrial species may also run. For convenience they are subdivided here into thrushes and chats.

Thrushes

Turdus species

These are moderate-sized, solidly-built birds, mostly with loud musical songs, taking fruit in trees and bushes, and insects, worms, and snails on the ground. There are six British species. The Blackbird is a widespread species, originally of forest edge and scrub. The closely-related Ring Ousel occurs at higher altitudes in treeless areas on rocks and screes. The Song Thrush is a woodland bird, and the Mistle Thrush prefers open areas with larger scattered trees. Redwing and Fieldfare are smaller and larger replacements in colder areas, moving south in winter. However, the British Isles seems to be a region where many of these generalised divisions are modified.

Blackbird *Turdus merula*

This is the typical song-bird of gardens with even a small amount of shrubby cover and a worm-rich lawn, and similar minimal habitats. The lazily-whistled, rich, musical song phrases with their careless finish are one of the few signals of urban spring. It is conspicuous, and noisily hysterical in its everyday alarms. It hunts grassland and lawns, and scratches and throws leaves about, as it scuffles under trees and bushes. It is also quick to take advantage of fruit and berries. The bulky nest is tucked into a fork or niche, high or low, in a tree or bush or on a building.

It breeds in warm-temperate to subtropical zones of Eurasia, but in Europe extends north into the boreal zone, from which it is migratory to warmer parts of its range, and into the Middle East in winter. In bones from the British Pleistocene, this and the Ring Ousel cannot usually be separated. Blackbird/Ring Ousels occur in the Middle Pleistocene Cromerian of Norfolk (possibly Blackbird), in the Ipswichian Interglacial in Devon, and frequently in the last glaciation in the south-west and Derbyshire, and in the early Holocene on the south Wales coast.

As a bird of scrubby forest edge tending to feed in the open, it could have spread with the first woodland. Until the mid nineteenth century, it was still tied to a woodland habitat and must have decreased as woodland was cleared, although able to use modified areas such as coppice. In the later nineteenth century it became a garden bird, beginning to spread to urban shrubberies. Towards the end of the century it spread and completed its colonisation of the British Isles, beginning to breed in Orkney and Shetland, and moving into the western extremities of Ireland.

It was not until the present century that it finally colonised the urban areas, and at the same time showed a general increase. In this warmer period it had spread north in Europe generally, and extended to habitat limits in the British Isles. It now nests over the whole of the British Isles, with a few vacant areas in the Scottish mountains. In winter, there is a complex southern and western shift, with many – mostly young birds – leaving the north, some movement into Ireland and a smaller one across the Channel. The majority of adults stay put, surviving winter weather and maintaining territories. There is also a large influx of birds from northern Europe. The British Isles population has been estimated at about 7,000,000 pairs, and the wintering population at 14,000,000–20,000,000 birds.

Ring Ousel *Turdus torquatus*

For this mountain blackbird, the necessary element in a territory is an outcrop of rock or a gully, and the odd stunted tree or bush is an irrelevance. The male sings from an exposed prominence that gives a wide view over territory, the song consisting of repetitions of a few simple notes, loud, clear and sometimes beautifully amplified by the site. Flight tends to be stronger than that of a Blackbird, and it hides among rocks and scree. Although the female is duller, sexes are less dissimilar than in the Blackbird, and both have the white chest-

Blackbird

FEMALE

MALE

Ring Ousel

FEMALE

Mistle Thrush

Fieldfare

Redwing

Song Thrush

D.M.HENRY

crescent. The nest is usually on a ledge of a rocky outcrop or slope, sometimes in old quarries or buildings if these are present, or just tucked into the grass of the steep bank of a stream.

Basically a European bird, its breeding distribution is discontinuous in mountain areas. It is present in mountain ranges from southern and central Europe to Iran, and through uplands of Norway and Sweden, the British Isles, and Brittany. It migrates to warm-temperate and circum-Mediterranean regions. Its bones cannot be distinguished from those of the Blackbird, and Pleistocene records of both are listed under that species. James Fisher quotes the first written record as 1450.

As a montane bird of rocky areas, it may have been affected only slightly by human activities. Clearing of woodland, and spread of upland sheep grazing in the eighteenth to nineteenth centuries may have increased its food supply; quarrying and mining may have provided additional nesting-sites. It is a higher-altitude replacement of the Blackbird, and as a summer visitor possibly more able to cope with the colder environment. It seems to have been more widespread in the nine-teenth century, decreasing in the warmer period towards the end of it and in the first half of this century.

It appears to have been previously widespread in Ireland, and considerably reduced in this warmer period, disappearing from many areas. It also decreased in south Wales, and disappeared from Cornwall and the Isles of Man. In Scotland, it was considerably reduced in numbers and distribution. In recent, colder, decades it might be expected to spread again, but may have been supplanted by the spread of the Blackbird while at a low ebb. In Scotland, a decrease in the south and lowlands and Inner Hebrides appears to be continuing although sporadic nesting still occurs.

However, if one takes about 300 metres as its lowest altitude, it appears to be nesting in all areas above this limit, occurring on high ground north and west of a line from the north Yorkshire moors to Dartmoor. In Ireland, it is very scarce and scattered on a few high sites. In the British Isles the population may be 8,000–16,000 pairs. In addition to the complete migration of breeding birds, there is a small passage of Scandinavian birds in spring and autumn.

Fieldfare *Turdus pilaris*

Although a scarce breeder, this is mostly a winter visitor, moving in as big restless flocks, constantly moving on with gruff *chaking* calls. They spread out over farmland and short grass, spaced out and alert, or gather to strip a bush of berries. The flight is strong, with easy but hesitant wing-beats. It is highly sociable, but a bird discovering a rich food source, such as a crop of windfall apples, will try to appropriate them with single-minded territoriality. It will roost on open ground as well as in trees or shrubs.

Breeding birds occur in woodland edge, open wood-land, birch scrub, small plantations and farmland trees, and often nest colonially. Although sociable, they tend to be noisy and squabbling. The song is an odd mixture of squeaks, whistles and chuckles.

It breeds across Eurasia in the boreal zone, wintering in the warm-temperate zone and west to the British Isles and eastern Iceland; but it is present all year in Europe, north to the Baltic and coastal Norway. In the British

Pleistocene it occurred in an interglacial, possibly about 500,000 years ago in Essex, and in the last glaciation in Derbyshire and the south-west. It typically occurs in Britain as a winter visitor, and in this respect its status is unlikely to have changed much over the centuries, the numbers probably being dependent on Scandinavia and Siberian populations.

It has extended its range in recent times, apparently beginning in the mid to late nineteenth century. As a boreal bird, its range had ended in north Poland and Prussia, at the south-east end of the Baltic. It spread westward across temperate Europe reaching Switzer-land in the 1920s, eastern France in the 1950s and Denmark by 1965. In the latter period there may have been a southward, as well as a westward shift. In 1967 a pair nested in Orkney. Since then scattered pairs have been breeding sporadically, about half a dozen a year, in scattered sites from Shetland south to Yorkshire and Staffordshire.

In winter it is nomadic. Large numbers occur over most of the British Isles. They are more dependent on fruit than are Blackbirds, and more vulnerable to cold weather, moving when conditions are hard and tending to shift southwards through the winter. The average winter population may be about 1,000,000 birds.

Mistle Thrush *Turdus viscivorus*

This, the largest, boldest and noisiest of our thrushes, is mainly a bird of woodland edge and parkland, with mature trees and open grassy ground. It adapts to farmland with hedgerow trees, but also extends to marginal heathland and moorland where trees are small, scarce or absent. It holds a large territory and sings from a high perch, with short fluted phrases – loud and musical, if a little off-key. The cup nest, usually in a tree fork, is fiercely and noisily defended, and the loud rattling alarm is often heard.

Later the family party may join others to form small flocks feeding on open grassy areas. However, when winter comes, adult birds will select a food-source such as a well-berried holly tree, or other fruit-bearing tree or shrub, or one adorned with large mistletoe bunches where these are plentiful. The latter habit probably gave the bird its common name. It drives off all other fruit-eating birds, and defends this as a private source of food to sustain it through the winter. Most young birds migrate instead.

Like the Song Thrush, its breeding range is through Eurasia east to Lake Baikal, and it occurs in boreal to warm-temperate zones; it winters, where migrant, in the southern part of its range, and is resident in mainland Europe and the British Isles. Its earliest British record is from the latter part of the last glaciation in Derbyshire, and it was present in south Wales in the early Holocene. As a bird of more open woodland, and woodland edge with grassy feeding areas, it may have found a less plentiful habitat in very early times, but partial clearing, and grazing within woodland, may have increased its numbers in historical times.

It seems to have decreased, possibly with woodland clearance; and by the eighteenth century it appeared to have retreated mainly to southern England and Wales, being scarce or absent in northern England and Scotland, and absent from Ireland. It began an unex-plained recovery. First seen in Ireland in 1800, it started breeding soon afterwards. At the same time it moved into south Scotland, with scattered breeding further north. By the mid nineteenth century, it was through all Ireland. By the 1870s, it had extended its range north to Caithness and Sutherlandshire. In the subsequent period up to the 1950s, it consolidated its numbers.

It is now present through most of the British Isles, except some mountain or treeless areas of Scotland; but has only bred rarely and sporadically in the Outer Hebrides and Orkney, and never in Shetland. Although well-established, it suffers in hard winters; in 1962–63 it lost three-quarters of its population but recovered within five years. Breeding pairs are estimated at about 300,000–600,000. In winter, most Scottish birds migrate to Ireland and France, and young English birds are migratory. There is only a small influx from the continent, and numbers may be about 400,000–800,000 birds.

Redwing *Turdus iliacus*
Smallest and quietest of the thrushes, this is usually first identified by the pale creamy eye-stripe, and the carroty-coloured flanks that are only conspicuous when if flies. As a winter visitor it appears in unpredictable nomadic flocks, feeding extensively on fruit and berries, but when these are scarce, it may hunt in leaf litter under trees and bushes, or search open ground for worms. At this time of year, many of their movements are nocturnal and the thin, high-pitched *see-ih* call of birds passing over can be heard on clear winter nights.

Like the Fieldfare, it is a woodland-edge bird tending to feed in the open, but more prepared to enter thicker and bushier woodland. As a nesting bird, it is more solitary. As well as using trees and shrubs it may place a nest in the side of a bank, or in roots of a fallen tree. The song is a clear, descending series of up to seven fluty notes with a final low flourish, and it has a sharp *chittuk* of alarm.

It breeds across Eurasia in the boreal zone, in broadleaf woodland and scrub borders. It migrates to warm-temperate zones and through western Europe north to south Norway, the British Isles and Iceland, being resident in parts of these last three. It has British Pleistocene records in the last glaciation in the south-west and Derbyshire. Primarily a winter visitor, its past population is likely to have been dependent on conditions in Scandinavia and further east. Britain is along the northern edge of its wintering range, and it is very vulnerable to hard winters, birds often dying in large numbers.

In the present century it has been discovered breeding in Scotland. It was first found in Sutherlandshire in 1925. Sporadic breedings were recorded in 17 of the next 41 years, involving about 30 pairs. In 1967 seven pairs were found, and in the B.T.O. Survey of 1968–72, up to 20 pairs were found in one year, with as many more holding territory. It was suspected that pairs had often been overlooked, and the 1972 Scottish population was suggested to be about 300 pairs. The subsequent picture is of 50–70 pairs a year (perhaps fewer in bad years), and at best up to 30

confirmed breedings, with a suggestion of some overlooked. They are almost all in the highland area of Scotland and into Orkney and Shetland. In addition pairs have been seen behaving suspiciously in northern England, and there was a single Irish nesting attempt in County Kerry in 1951, and one in Kent in 1983.

In winter, the majority of the darker subspecies that nests in Iceland and the Faeroes moves into Ireland and Scotland, and there is a considerable influx from Scandinavia. Movements are nomadic and unpredictable, but the average British Isles winter population may be over 1,000,000 birds.

Song Thrush *Turdus philomelos*
A skulking and unobtrusive bird of thickets, low cover and woodland, it compensates with its song: a vociferous and prolonged repetition of various short phrases. It sings from a high perch, but is usually a ground feeder. In addition to worms, slugs and insects, it is able to eat snails, beating them against a stone until the shell breaks. This might give it an extra food source in critical periods. Outside woodland, it appears to need some tall but shrubby growth in which it can hide, but there is a population in the Hebrides and Orkney that appears to have adapted to tall heather and dykes. It can use parkland, shelterbelts, tall hedgerows and gardens with plenty of shrubby growth.

It breeds across Eurasia as far as Lake Baikal in boreal to temperate zones; it winters in the warm-temperate zone, and along the southern edge of its breeding range and in western Europe. It occurred in Pleistocene Britain, in Essex in an early interglacial about 500,000 years ago, and in the last glaciation in the south-west and in Derbyshire. It was probably an early colonised bird of encroaching woodland, and must have been widespread and numerous through much of the post-glacial period. It would have lost ground as woodland was cleared, although it could use small residual areas in farmland. It may have gained some respite when pheasant coverts became fashionable in the nineteenth century. Its general distribution suggests that although it may penetrate a little further north as a summer visitor, it is less tolerant of low winter temperatures, or bad weather, than is the Blackbird.

This may explain some evidence of a general decrease – although no significant change of range – since the 1940s. It occurs throughout the British Isles, apart from Shetland, but is absent from a few Scottish mountain areas. It ceased to breed regularly in Shetland after the hard winter of 1946–47; and following the 1962–63 winter, numbers dropped by 41%, although recovered during the late 1960s. The 1972 breeding population was estimated at about 3,500,000 pairs, but could drop to about one-third after severe winters.

In winter it tends to move down from high ground, and northern birds may move west into Ireland. There is an influx of continental birds, and a through-passage of Scandinavian ones, with a few staying. In really hard weather, southern birds may move to France. The total winter population may be similar to the summer one.

Chats

Oenanthe, Saxicola, Phoenicurus and *Luscinia* species

These are small, often brightly-marked insectivorous birds with slender bills, specialised as breeding birds for a variety of habitats. The Wheatear occurs in very open, often rocky country; the Stonechat on heathland and marginal land with shrubby growth; the Whinchat on more open rough grassland; the Black Redstart in rocky places; and the Common Redstart in trees in open habitats. The Robin is a bird of the floor and lower strata of woodland, the Bluethroat is limited to moist shrubby montane and tundra areas; and the Nightingale occurs on or near the ground in low, thick woodland cover.

Wheatear *Oenanthe oenanthe*

This is a bird of short turf and the scanty vegetation of open stony places, where it nests in holes, burrows, rock crevices or stone walls. It moves over open ground with swift, springy hops and short flights in which the black-and-white rump and tail flash into view. It has a short musical warble, and sharp *tac* calls.

It is a summer visitor, breeding across Eurasia from Greenland to Alaska, and from tundra to warm-temperate zones. It winters in Africa. In Pleistocene Britain it was present in the last, Ipswichian, interglacial on the south Wales coast, and in Derbyshire and Kent towards the end of the last glaciation. Its range is likely to have become restricted to coasts and moorland as woodland spread in Holocene times. When woodland was cleared and pasture increased, particularly hill-grazing, it would also have increased, more so when large-scale sheep-grazing on uplands occurred.

On the chalk downland areas of the south, it may have been restricted to some extent by the lack of nest burrows or holes, and tended to rely on rabbits. Population is likely to have been high by the nineteenth century. It was one of the small birds regularly caught for food on an appreciable scale, although this may have mainly affected passage migrants. Numbers may have remained fairly stable over a long period, except in England, south of Yorkshire and Lancashire. Here there has been a steady and striking decrease. The major cause was a change in farming practice, including the plough-ing up of sheep walks and rough grazing; secondary ones may have been increased by human disturbance, and cessation of grazing on heaths, commons and marginal areas. Increased afforestation would have affected it adversely in the north as well. The 1939–45 war accelerated activity, and in the subsequent decades most of the chalk grasslands were ploughed. In addition, the myxomatosis outbreak and loss of rabbits produced a countrywide rapid growth of vegetation that rendered many areas unusable. Outside the Peak and Pennine districts, it is now very sparse in most of England, except the East Anglian breckland, Hampshire Basin and the south-west. It is also mainly absent from most of central and eastern Ireland. Apart from this, it breeds through-out the British Isles. The population has been estimated at about 80,000 pairs. The larger Greenland subspecies, also breeding in Iceland and the Faeroes, passes through in spring and autumn, as do Scandinavian birds.

Stonechat *Saxicola torquata*

This is a small, stout, round-headed sentinel on a tall plant stem, or low bush in areas of heather or coarse grass with some bare ground. It swoops to pick up insects from its perch, and when excited, it tends to twitch wings and tail, showing off its markings. It scolds with a chacking *tac tac* and a *hweet* call. The cup nest is tucked into ground vegetation. It is a resident, greeting intrusion with conspicuous suspicion at all times of year. Its needs limit it to heathland, moorland, marginal land or abandoned cultivation. It also occurs on bare cliff areas and sparsely vegetated coastal shingles.

It breeds across Eurasia from Ireland to Japan. Separation in part of the Ice Ages appears to have produced eastern and western forms. The former extends through eastern Eurasia, north to the boreal zone. The latter has a more restricted distribution in Europe, with the Whinchat occupying more of the northern region. In Europe, it occurs in temperate to warm-temperate zones; and over most of Europe except the western seaboard and British Isles, it is a migrant to warm-temperate and subtropical zones.

Its bones are similar to those of the Whinchat, and Stonechat/Whinchat remains are known from the latter part of the last glaciation in Derbyshire and the south-west, and from the south Wales coast in the early Holocene. It might have had a wide distribution at that period but would have become restricted with the spread of woodland. With woodland clearance in historic times it could have spread, but only on marginal land and moorland, where cleared land was poorly grazed and scrubby growth occurred. Its history is probably linked with marginal lands, and the imperma-nence of them may have caused frequent shifts.

It suffers badly from hard winters, when numbers may be heavily reduced and recover gradually. The increased fragmentation of rough heathland and mar-ginal land from which birds could be wiped out in bad winters, and to which they might not easily return, may account for its virtual absence over much of England. It is found on drier heathland areas through the southern counties, sparsely in East Anglia, and otherwise in a broad coastal zone from Cornwall to Orkney (but not Shetland), with a thinner zone down the Scottish east coast to Northumberland. It is present through the islands, and most of Ireland except inland north-east. There is a very thin inland scatter of pairs in western England, more numerous to the north. In winter, birds move out of Scotland and Lakeland mountains, and more occur in the south, some migrating southwards. Irish birds shift towards the coasts. Many pairs defend winter territories. The British Isles breeding population was estimated at about 30,000–60,000 pairs in 1972, but might be down to a quarter of this after hard winters.

Whinchat *Saxicola rubetra*

Slimmer-looking, but Stonechat-like in habits, this displays more white on tail and shoulders. It is a bird of more open rough grazing areas, with fewer bushes. It will use tall plants and wire fences for perching. It can

Wheatear
MALE

FEMALE

MALE

Stonechat

Robin

MALE

Whinchat

Black Redstart
MALE

Common Redstart

FEMALE

MALE

D.M. HENRY

utilise rough meadows, marshy grassland, grassy road-sides and field borders, railway embankments, hillsides with thin bracken, moorland and the early stages of young plantations. Combined with migration that avoids winter weather, all this enables it to exploit a wider area than the Stonechat. It has a short but varied warbled song, and softer *tic tic* alarm calls. The nest is in ground vegetation.

Its breeding range is in western Eurasia, from the boreal to temperate zones, migrating to the Sahel zone of the southern Sahara, and east Africa. Its bones resemble those of the Stonechat, and possible early occurrences are listed under that species. Like the Stonechat, its early Holocene distribution would have been restricted by the spread of woodland; but it might have been better able to exploit in cleared areas the rough grazing or farmland fallows. It should have survived well and been widespread in past centuries, having an advantage as a more cold-tolerant species moving south in winter.

Although always scarcest in the south-east of Britain, its numbers have declined there in the present century. There was also some decrease elsewhere, but in general it seems to have recovered after reaching low levels in the 1950s and 1960s. Its south-east decline was probably due to a 'tidying-up' of the environment, and it does not thrive well in areas of intensive farming and grass mowing. However, loss is not wholly linked with habitat, and a climatic element may have been involved, or something else that has not been detected. East of a line from the Solent to Flamborough Head, its distribution is very patchy and it is sometimes absent, and similarly in English counties of the Welsh border. In Ireland it has a limited distribution, mainly in central and north-western regions. It is also scarce in north-east Scotland and absent from Shetland, Orkney and the smaller Outer Hebrides. Its main strength is in northern and western uplands. The population has been estimated at about 20,000–40,000 pairs.

Robin *Erithacus rubecula*

The bright-eyed inquisitiveness of the Robin has given it a false reputation for friendliness. Among themselves both sexes hold individual territories, only coming together to breed, and that cheerful silvery winter song is really a warning challenge to all comers. The sexes are similar. It is a woodland bird, snatching insects in the air and feeding on the woodland floor. It can hover and snatch berries as well as insects. In the past, it followed the rooting wild boar to benefit by its digging. Now it sees the human gardener as a rather poor substitute. It has a *tic* alarm note. The nest cup is hidden in a low cavity in a bank, hedge, tree-root or garden shed. Young birds are brown with a dark-spotted throat.

It breeds in western Eurasia in boreal to temperate zones, resident in mainland Europe, North Africa and the British Isles; it is migrant in Scandinavia and Russia to Mediterranean and subtropical areas. There are British Pleistocene records from the last glaciation in Derbyshire and the south-west. It would have been widespread when woodland was at a maximum extent, but as a resident bird it has adapted to small, scattered patches of bushy cover, although it still needs somewhere to hide, and prefers some trees to be present.

It is absent from Shetland, but otherwise present as a breeding species throughout the British Isles, save for a few Scottish mountains. In winter there is a shift down from uplands and southwards, a small proportion migrating, but most holding winter territories. Migrants hold winter territories in other countries. Numbers may fluctuate by up to 40% and were lowest recently in mid 1960s and mid 1980s. There are probably between 3,500,000 and 5,000,000 pairs. Occasionally large numbers of autumn Scandinavian migrants are diverted on passage and temporarily appear in Britain.

Black Redstart *Phoenicurus ochrurus*

This would be an inconspicuous bird, the females and immatures being dull sooty-grey, were it not for the typical rufous tail, frequently quivered vertically by perched birds, and suddenly conspicuous in flight. This is a bird of rocky places, searching for insects, sometimes fluttering up after them. Like the Rock Dove it has recognised buildings, particularly the large, rambling concrete commercial structures, as just another kind of rocky outcrop. The male sings its odd warble-and-rattle song from a high point; and it has a sharp *tic* alarm call. It tucks its cup nest into a raised cleft or cavity. In the southern part of its range, it occurs widely from rocky coasts to mountain-tops, but in Britain seems limited mainly to cliffs and buildings.

Its breeding range as a resident is across the warm-temperate zone of Eurasia, from southern Europe to Mongolia, and in western France north to Brittany. As a migrant it extends across most of mainland Europe, and winters from warm-temperate to subtropical zones. It has early records in Britain, in the latter part of the last glaciation in Derbyshire, and on the south Wales coast in the early Holocene. It is unlikely to have been much affected by human activity in this country, but is susceptible to cold weather; and its range may have contracted widely in the Little Ice Age of the fourteenth to nineteenth centuries. It is closely linked with stone buildings and settlements in Europe, and these may have helped its inland spread.

It showed a northward spread in the latter part of the last century, probably linked with ameliorating climate, and spread north into northern Germany and Denmark; and by the early part of this century it was extending to southern Sweden. It was also occurring more frequently in south and east England. There are said to be nestings in 1845 and possibly 1909. In 1923–25 pairs bred on the Sussex coast, and in 1927–29 in Cornwall. Several pairs bred at Wembley in north-west London from 1926 to 1942. There were scattered sporadic breedings in the south-east, and after war-time bombings had created stretches of shattered masonry, colonies were created in London and Dover from 1940, that scattered during post-war reconstruction.

As a breeding bird it is mainly centred on the London region and Norfolk to Sussex coasts, with scattered inland industrial sites in the Midlands and Humberside and north to Yorkshire. Numbers tend to fluctuate, but showed an increase from about 50–60 pairs, in the mid 1940s to mid 1970s, to about 100 pairs more recently. There is still a slight northward and westward spread. In winter some birds migrate, and others scatter mainly along coasts, from Kent around the south and west coasts to Lancashire, and on the east and south coasts of Ireland. The winter population might be about 500 individuals.

Common Redstart *Phoenicurus phoenicurus*
One of the loveliest of our summer birds, this shares
with the Black Redstart the frequently-quivered tail,
also used in tail-spreading displays. Its song is a short
cheerful warble with an uncertain finish. Its loud *hweet*
and *wee-tuk-tuk* calls are more noticeable. It feeds, sings
and flits on exposed twigs, with flycatcher-like flights,
as though anxious not to be overlooked. Its most typical
habitat is the edges and glades of open mature, broadleaf
woodland such as oakwood, but with the human
fragmentation of woodland, it has adapted to hedgerow
trees, parkland, orchards and gardens. Its fairly bulky
cup nest is built in a tree cavity or woodpecker hole, or if
necessary a lower hole in bank, wall or rocks.

Its breeding range is across Eurasia from Britain to
Lake Baikal, in boreal to warm-temperate zones,
migrating south to the Sahel zone of the southern
Sahara. It has Pleistocene British records from the latter
part of the last glaciation, in the south-west and
Derbyshire. It would obviously have done well in an
early period with more extensive woodland cover, and
would have lost ground as woodland was cleared; but its
ability to make do with a few trees may have enabled it to
survive in cleared but farmed areas. In full woodland it
may suffer competition for nest-holes in trees, which are
always in short supply and contested by various species.

It is a summer visitor and its overall population has
tended to vary considerably. Wild fluctuations from
year to year have been noted from as far north and far
back as Speyside in the 1890s. There was a general
decrease, more marked in southern Britain, in the earlier
half of this century, but no serious loss. However, it is
scarce and very patchy in the region from the London
Basin north to Humberside. After the mid 1940s, it
stabilised and began to increase a little.

As a Sahel-wintering bird it lost over three-quarters
of its numbers in Britain in the early 1970s during
Saharan droughts, and has received some more recent
setbacks; but it does not seem to be as deeply affected by
these droughts as some of our other passerines, and it
has been able to recover and maintain numbers. It is
more numerous in western and northern Britain, scarce
in the south-east and in eastern Scotland. It is a very
sporadic nester on the Outer Hebrides, last breeding in
1914, and does not nest in Orkney or Shetland. Ireland
has only very occasional breedings by one or two pairs.
Its population is in the range of 10,000–100,000 pairs.

Bluethroat *Luscinia svecica*
NOT IN THE COLOUR PLATE
A slim, redstart-like chat, this can be as bold as a Robin
on its northern breeding grounds, but incredible
skulking as it slips through on migration. It is drab
above, with pale belly- and eye-stripe; it is usually
identified by the chestnut panels at the base of the tail,
briefly glimpsed as it darts into cover. The breeding
male has throat and breast a vivid blue, thinly bordered
with black and chestnut below. The blue breast has a
large distinct central spot, chestnut on Scandinavian

Studies of male Bluethroat

birds, white on European mainland birds, and seemingly lacking on Spanish birds. It has sharp scolding notes
like a Robin's; and a high-pitched rich, musical warble,
sometimes described as like a 'silver bell'. It is a bird of
low, swampy growth; birch and willow scrub on damp
heaths and tundra of the north; wet woodlands and
thickets, or the edges of woodland streams, in more
temperate regions. The nest is tucked into vegetation at
ground level.

In its Ice Age past, separation produced three forms.
An eastern form, in tundra and temperate zones across
Eurasia west to the uplands of Finland, Norway and
Sweden is red-spotted; while isolates in the Caucasus
and Spanish mountains are unspotted. Between the last
two, a European form occurs with a white-spotted
breast, and meets and interbreeds with the red-spotted
form in Russia. It has a temperate distribution and is
scarcer in the west. Both red-spotted and white-spotted
birds migrate to warm-temperate and subtropical
zones.

There seem to be no early records, with the earliest
published British references from 1826 onwards. Scandinavian birds pass through in spring and autumn,
mainly on the east coasts, and a few white-spotted birds
may occur in spring, possibly deflected from their usual
route. Breeding was not expected, other than as part of
the general south-west shift of species in the colder
recent period. The first breeding attempt was in 1968,
when a female with eggs was found in Inverness. In
1979 an apparently unspotted male held territory in
Nottinghamshire. A red-spotted male was in song in the
Spey Valley in 1980; and a white-spotted male sang and
displayed on Humberside in 1981. A female was present
in summer in south-east England in 1983.

Nightingale *Luscinia megarhyncha*

This is a chat of low thickets, reluctant to show itself, and maintaining a territory and attracting a mate by a loud and varied song, that often contains beautifully musical phrases. It is notorious in that the song continues to be delivered through the night, when there is little competition from other birds. Its alarm note is a frog-like croak. The deep cup nest is built low, just above the dead leaf and debris layer in brambles or bushes, more rarely in nettlebeds, or in more heathy territories, in bracken or gorse.

Its breeding range is across western Eurasia in temperate to warm-temperate zones, and it winters in Africa. Its earliest British record is from about the end of the last glaciation in Devon. Basically a bird of broadleaf temperate woodland, it requires some fairly thick low cover, and prefers damp sites. Its British range is limited to the south and east, and may not have been more widespread in the past. It would then have had a more continuous habitat that decreased with woodland clearance, but it could use coppiced woodland and denser hedgerows where available, and would have been widespread, although at lower densities, by the late nineteenth century.

In the first part of the present century, its numbers increased although distribution remained relatively unchanged. Population seemed to have reached a peak in the 1950s, then fallen. Numbers in 1972 were guessed as possibly about 10,000 pairs, but a census by the B.T.O. in 1976 revealed 3,200–4,000 singing males, while by 1981 it had risen to 4,770. It obviously varies with spring weather, and with breeding success elsewhere outside Britain. Its present range is roughly from mid Devon and the Severn Valley to the Humber, with an absence in the industrial north midlands and Greater London. The majority of birds are in Kent and Sussex. There may have been recent decreases in the Severn Valley, and in Lincolnshire and Norfolk.

Warblers
Sylviidae

Small insectivorous birds with slender bills, usually feeding and nesting above ground in trees, bushes or reed-beds. They are mostly dull and cryptically coloured, identifying themselves with loud musical songs. Britain has fourteen regular species, all but two are summer visitors. The typical woodland warblers, *Sylvia* species, include the Blackcap in high woodland, the Garden Warbler in lower woodland and scrub, the Lesser Whitethroat in scrub and bushes, the Common Whitethroat in bushes and hedgerows, and the Dartford Warbler in heathland gorse. Reed-bed and marsh haunters, *Acrocephalus* species, include Marsh Warbler, Reed Warbler and Sedge Warbler; the low thicket-skulkers, *Locustella* species, the Grasshopper Warbler, and in marshy areas, Savi's Warbler. The arboreal leaf warblers, *Phylloscopus* species, have the Wood Warbler in high woodland, Chiffchaff in any tall trees, and Willow Warbler in lower open scrub. A newcomer is Cetti's Warbler, *Cettia* species, on marshland edge.

impossible to guess its past distribution, although this might have been wider, and lost ground with increased drainage. However, in view of its present distribution it may also have been scarce in colder periods of past centuries, and most records date from the warmer 1890s onwards.

Between 1900 and the 1920s, it seems to have ranged sporadically as far as an area embraced by Devon, Somerset, Herefordshire, Staffordshire, Warwickshire, Oxfordshire, Buckinghamshire, Middlesex and Kent. From the 1920s onwards, it bred regularly only in its principal area of Worcestershire and Gloucestershire, and in Herefordshire, Somerset, Dorset, Sussex and Kent. Its limits now are through southern counties to Dorset and Somerset, but mainly in the Severn Valley, with odd nesting north to Nottinghamshire in midland counties. It would seem to fluctuate between about 45–70 pairs, with about four-fifths in Worcestershire.

Marsh Warbler *Acrocephalus palustris*

Confusingly like a Reed Warbler, this is one of the species whose song and habitat are clues to its identity. It is a bird of reed-bed borders and marshes, nesting in willow withy-beds where stems are thin, and in tall marsh herbage around bushes and saplings; but it is limited to the damp lowlands of southern river valleys. Its song is a typical rambling and rapid outpouring, but more musical, and with an impressive range of mimicry that separates it from Reed and Sedge Warblers' more monotonous efforts. It does not seem short of nesting-sites, and climate presumably limits it in Britain. It nests low in vegetation and in withy-beds, its nest cup slung between twigs or stems.

It breeds in Europe, in temperate to warm-temperate zones, but is absent from Spain and Portugal and most of south and west France. It appears to avoid the milder, damper Atlantic climate zone, which may affect its British distribution. It winters in Africa. It was not identified as present in England until 1871. It is almost

Reed Warbler *Acrocephalus scirpaceus*

This is a slender brown bird of reed-beds, rather furtive and adapted for clinging, sidling and moving among vertical reed stems. However, it may rise to higher reeds to sing, and its presence is usually announced by a rather monotonous chorus of rapidly repeated churring, jangling and twangy notes, low in pitch, and lacking the variety of Marsh and Sedge Warbler song. Apparently stimulated by the presence of neighbours, it can be heard during the night more frequently than by day for much of the season.

It occupies reed-beds in colonies of small territories, birds sometimes overflowing into nearby herbage or shrubs. The cup nest is bound to vertical stems of young reeds, rising as they grow.

It breeds in western Eurasia in temperate to warm-temperate zones, and in Europe extends north to the southern Baltic. It winters in Africa. It was first noted in Britain by Willughby and Ray in 1676. Its history is linked with reed-beds, presumably where they were dense enough to maintain it, for there appears to be

FEMALE

MALE

Reed Warbler

Blackcap

Garden Warbler

Marsh Warbler

Sedge Warbler

Grasshopper Warbler

Nightingale

D.M.HENRY

some limiting quality which determines those it finds suitable as colony-sites. Since it relies on insect food, the microclimate created by the reed-beds might be important. It seems never to have colonised Ireland. It would have been more numerous in the larger marshes and fens of the past, and has seen a steady reduction of habitat from the seventeenth century, as drainage increased.

Cessation of widespread reed cutting in the present century may have helped it, and the growth of new gravel-pits provided new colony-sites. Since the 1930s it has spread in south Lancashire, and on the north Wales coast to Anglesey, and it has consolidated in south Yorkshire. In the 1950s and 1960s it spread from south Devon, through Cornwall to the Scillies. It has increased and spread in south Sweden and into Norway since the 1940s, and there is a small passage through Scotland, which may account for a stray breeding in Shetland in 1973. It is now present south from south Lancashire and south Yorkshire, with a scattering up the Lancashire coast; but it is absent from high ground and hill ridges, including much of Wales and the south-west. Its only Irish breeding was in County Down in 1935. The 1972 population was estimated at about 40,000–80,000 pairs.

Sedge Warbler *Acrocephalus schoenobaenus*
This is a bird of the scruffy and overgrown edges of reed-beds and marshes, inquisitive, noisy and easily startled into song. The song itself is an interminable rambling medley of high and low notes, some nasal or twanging, and occasional mimicry. It breeds on reed-bed edges, where other vegetation and shrubs invade, in overgrown marsh, and in waterside vegetation generally, sometimes overlapping with the Reed Warbler; but at times it extends to drier habitats. The nest is low-down in a bush or thicket. In late summer, northern birds may shift to southern England to put on fat prior to migration.

Its breeding range is across western Eurasia in warm boreal to warm-temperate zones, but to the Arctic in Finland and northern Norway. It winters in Africa. Its first British record appears to be by Pennant in 1766. As a bird of the edges of marshes and reed-beds, its distribution might have remained little changed in the Holocene, until the drainage of marshes in the seventeenth to nineteenth centuries, and the drainage of small areas in the nineteenth and twentieth centuries, which must have reduced its habitat and numbers.

It appears to have been widespread, and to have increased in the first half of the present century, when it spread in the Scottish islands, and established itself more firmly in Orkney. It may have lost habitat through drainage but has gained some from the vegetated margins of gravel-pits and reservoirs; and it has tended to move into marginal habitats such as bushy hedge-rows, growing crops, and in Scotland into damp rough grassland, scrub and the early stages of conifer plantations. It is now widespread through the British Isles, except on high hill and moorland areas; and it is absent from Shetland.

Its population is affected by the droughts in its wintering area in the Sahel zone of the southern Sahara. It peaked in 1968, declined severely in 1969, rose in the early 1970s and dropped more recently. Its numbers had been estimated at about 300,000 pairs in the British

Isles in 1972, but it had dropped in 1981, and in 1984 by another 30% and it continues to fall.

Grasshopper Warbler *Locustella naevia*
Although widespread, this is a rarely-seen bird. It hides in the low tangles where shrubs and herbage meet, in grasses and brambles, and in swampy areas. It can also use drier areas of similar low growth. It moves stealthily and easily through cover, and usually rises to a higher perch only to sing. The long, reeling, grasshopper-like sound of its song is difficult to locate, varying in volume as the birds turns its head. It is more often heard at early morning or dusk.

Its breeding range is across western Eurasia in warm boreal to temperate zones; and it winters in Africa and northern India. Its first British record appears to be by Willughby and Ray in 1678. Much of the habitat it uses is associated with the overgrown margins of water, or swampy places, and in an earlier period of extensive woodland, it would have been mainly limited to such areas. The clearing of woodland, probably replaced in some areas by low, scrubby growth, would have been advantageous to it, and enabled it to spread. It would have lost much of its marshy habitat with the drainage of major areas from the seventeenth century onwards.

The spread of plantations in the last century and a half has been helpful to it, in that it can use the early stages of them. It has improved and extended its range in the present century in eastern England, northwards in Scotland and westwards in western Ireland, and populations have increased; while in some parts of the south-east it has decreased from habitat loss. It is widespread through the British Isles, albeit rather thinly; and it is absent from high ground, and oddly enough from the Fens also. It is very scanty in northern Scotland and Orkney, and absent from Shetland. Its population tends to fluctuate unpredictably, presumably responding to weather, and changes in habitat availability. It was high in the late 1960s, and early 1970s, and the 1972 estimate of numbers was about 25,000 pairs.

Savi's Warbler *Locustella luscinioides*
NOT ILLUSTRATED
This is a Reed-Warbler-like bird, plain brown with a white throat, pale eye-stripe, a tendency to cock its tail, and more jerky hopping movements. It is a skulker of sedge and reedy growth in swamps and shallow water with small scattered trees, and in lush waterside herbage. Its reeling song is lower-pitched than the Grasshopper Warbler's, a more mechanical buzz, more insect-like and easily overlooked. It may sing from a reed top or tree perch, and sings frequently at night, less by day. The cup nest is hidden deep in reeds or rushes, usually just above ground.

It breeds discontinuously across western Eurasia in temperate to warm temperate zones; and it winters in east Africa. It was not described until 1824, and was recognised in England in 1835. It was then a breeding species of fenland, present in the fens of Norfolk, Cambridgeshire and Huntingdonshire. It may have been present for centuries in this region, but was suffering from the latter stages of extensive drainage that had gone on for several centuries, and from activities such as reed cutting. It was extinct in Britain by 1856. Its general range may have contracted, but in the 1940s and 1950s, it was extending or re-extending its range in north-west Europe.

It was though to be present in north Kent in the 1950s, and a male sang in Cambridgeshire in 1954. By 1960 there was evidence that it bred in Kent, and that up to 12 males were present in the next few years. In the early 1970s it also bred in Suffolk and singing males occurred in south and midland England. It has bred in Norfolk, Suffolk, Kent, Hampshire and Dorset, rising to a peak of about 30 possible pairs in the late 1970s, decreasing a little recently.

Blackcap *Sylvia atricapilla*

This species, with black-capped male and chestnut-capped female, is the most strikingly marked of a rather drab group of birds. It is also pre-eminent for its song, a loud rich warble, reminiscent in tone of a Blackbird's song, but softer, without the harsher terminal flourish, and rambling on for much longer periods. The closely-related Garden Warbler approaches it in vocalisation, but lacks the bold head colour, and prefers slightly different habitats. The Blackcap is a bird of areas with mature broadleaf trees and a good shrub layer, although the former seems more important than the latter. It sings and feeds in the tree-tops, taking insects from leaves and twigs; but it nests low in shrubs, or sometimes in tall herbage. Where some tall trees are present it can adapt to coppice, hedgerow, scrub and plantations.

Its breeding range is across western Eurasia, from warm boreal to warm-temperate zones, and it winters in subtropical to warm-temperate zones and on the milder seaboard of the Atlantic, north to the British Isles. It has British Pleistocene records, in the latter part of the last interglacial, probably in interstadial conditions, in Devon and Derbyshire. As a bird of mature broadleaf woodland, its spread in the British Isles may have been a little delayed until this was widespread.

With the advent of man's activity in woodland clearance, its habitat must have been reduced through historic times; but it would have been able to survive where more mature trees may have persisted, in coppice woodland with taller standard trees, and later in wooded hedgerows. Both this and the Garden Warbler may have done less well where grazing stock in woodland removed the lower shrub layers. Its numbers do not appear to have undergone any distinct changes since the nineteenth century, other than periodic fluctuations, although population has risen since what may have been a low point in the early 1980s, and has spread in Scandinavia since the 1950s.

It is widespread in the British Isles, but sparse in northern areas, very scarce north of the Scottish lowlands, absent from the Hebrides and a very sporadic breeder in Orkney and Shetland. It is thinly dispersed in Ireland, and absent from much of the west. Its 1972 population was estimated at about 200,000 pairs.

It winters further north than related warbler species, and some occur in Mediterranean Europe and western Europe, north to the British Isles. Our breeding birds migrate south, but some from northern and eastern Europe winter here. Originally confined to the south and west, they have spread more extensively, north to Orkney, the numbers varying with the severity of winters. They are frequently seen at bird-tables, although it is not certain how significant such food-sources are. The overwintering was first noticed in the 1820s. In the mid 1940s to mid 1950s there were about 22 records a year, in the 1970s nearer 400, and by the mid 1980s it was thought that about 3,000 might occur in Britain and Ireland.

Garden Warbler *Sylvia borin*

This is a warbler lacking good distinguishing features, apart from the song which is like a Blackcap's but less rich, less varied, with longer phrases and sometimes a little harsher. The difference is not perfect and one needs the song to limit it to two species, and a sight of the bird to decide which one. Both occur in broadleaf woodland with a good shrub layer, but the Garden Warbler prefers lower, more open trees and shrubs, and thick bushy undergrowth with brambles. It will extend to coppice, shrubbery and tall thickets. The cup nest is low down in thick cover, often in brambles, sometimes in tall herbage. Occasionally there are two broods. Mainly an insect-eater, it turns to fruit to fatten for migration; and autumn migrants seem to pause in the Mediterranean area to refatten on fruit before the Sahara crossing.

It breeds across Eurasia in the temperate zone, extending north in Europe into the boreal zone. It winters in Africa. It has an early British Pleistocene record, in the warm penultimate interglacial, the Hoxnian, in Kent. It would have been widespread once the broadleaf woodland spread. It would have been reduced in later times with woodland clearance, possibly relying more on coppice woodland, small shrubby areas, and young plantations. It may have increased in recent times, but this is masked by periodic fluctuations in numbers.

It is widespread north to lowland Scotland, absent from some mountain areas, more particularly in southern Scotland, and also from lowland areas of the fens and west Lancashire. In Scotland it extends to Argyll in the west, and in the east has spread since the 1960s up the eastern side to around the Moray Firth, with scattered sporadic occurrences of individuals further north and west. It is oddly absent from most of Ireland, with a scattered presence around some larger loughs and lakes. The population fluctuates from year to year, more markedly on marginal farmland areas. It was low in the early 1960s and mid 1970s, high in the mid 1960s and early 1980s. The 1972 estimate was about 60,000–100,000 pairs.

Lesser Whitethroat *Sylvia curruca*

In some ways the antithesis of the Common White-throat, this is a skulker in tall thickets, overgrown hedgerows and small trees, usually where bordering on an open space. It tends to emerge from such cover only to sing at the top of it. It is likely to be recognised by the song, a short quick warble followed by a prolonged, tuneless rattle. The cup nest is built inside a shrub, often a metre of two above the ground. Once the young are out of the nest the sharp *tak-tak* alarm note is likely to betray its presence.

It breeds across Eurasia to western China, in warm boreal to warm-temperate zones, but is absent from south-west Europe and western Norway, possibly avoiding the moist Atlantic climate. It was not distinguished as separate from the Common Whitethroat in Britain until about 1780. In natural vegetation it is a bird of scrubby, broken woodland edge, and the borders of clearings, and was probably limited to these when woodland was widespread. It would have occupied the borders of the woodland clearance that later increased, and in the eighteenth and nineteenth centuries would have been able to move into taller hedgerows, and later to young stages of plantations. The British distribution seems determined by climate rather than habitat, and may not have changed greatly in the last century and a half.

In recent times it has been mainly a bird of the south-east, absent from Ireland, very scarce in Scotland. It is difficult to confirm nesting. In the warmer, earlier part of the present century, it showed some westward spread into eastern and northern Wales, and sporadically into Pembrokeshire and Cornwall. Absent from the Peak and the Pennine ridge, it extends sparsely in lowlands to Cumbria and Northumberland. In Scotland a few pairs appear to be breeding in scattered sites to Argyll in the west and Aberdeenshire in the east. It has gained habitat by the spread of scrub in areas such as the chalk downlands, following the disappearance of rabbits after Myxomatosis in 1954.

Unlike the Common Whitethroat, it has not been affected by climate in its winter quarters; and increased for example, by 26%, after the 1983–84 winter. Its 1972 population was estimated at about 25,000–50,000 pairs.

Common Whitethroat *Sylvia communis*

Until recent disasters of landscape and climate this was the common Whitethroat, the bird that could be flushed from low field hedgerows everywhere or from bushes of heaths and commons, puffing up its white throat and shaggy crown, and warbling a short scratchy song, or rising and falling in a hesitant fluttering display flight and song. In some ways it was the least regarded of our warblers, a common bird of nettlebeds and overgrown places, readily emerging into the open to scold with a harsh grating *tscharr* call, or *tuk* alarm-note. The cup nest is hidden low in scrub and tall herbage. Like many insect-eating warblers it would turn to berries for its late summer food.

It breeds across western Eurasia in warm boreal to warm-temperate zones; and it winters in the Sahel zone bordering the southern Sahara. Its first British record was by Turner in 1544. In earlier times it must have been a bird of marginal areas, but in historic times, with the clearance of forest, should have found suitable sites in many places, since it could use any low thicket. It would have increased still further in the eighteenth to nineteenth centuries with the proliferation of hedgerows. It also used the youngest stages of forestry plantations. By the end of the nineteenth century it was regarded as the most numerous and widespread of our warblers.

In the last three decades, it has suffered considerable habitat loss from the massive removal and degradation of hedgerows, particularly in the arable areas of the east and south. This would have lowered the population. Then in 1968 the first serious drought occurred in its wintering area, the Sahel zone of Africa. By the next year, the numbers in Britain had decreased by 77%. They fell still further in the early 1970s and by 1974 were still a sixth of the 1968 figure. In the early 1980s they had risen to almost a third of their 1960s high, and were hit by a further Sahel drought in 1983–84, with a 21% drop in their 1983 total.

The estimated overall drop in the possible pairs in the British Isles over this period is in the order of from 5,000,000 to about 400,000–650,000. In spite of this overall decrease, it is still widely distributed through the British Isles; but it is sparse or absent in the Scottish highlands (other than valleys and peripheral lowlands), only on Stornaway in the Outer Hebrides, has not been on Orkney since 1941, and is very occasional on Shetland.

Dartford Warbler *Sylvia undata*

This small dark warbler, most atypical of its genus, exaggerates the Whitethroat characters. The throat is puffy, the crown shaggy, the long tail, tapered at the tip, is frequently cocked up. It is a bird of dry scrub of Mediterranean hills that has strayed north and only found gorse-covered heathland and long heather as acceptable substitutes. Within this cover it skulks, protected from the weather, occasionally emerging suddenly on the top of a bush to scold with grating or churring notes, or making short jerky flights from one bush to another. The song is a harsh musical warble, based on a short complex flourish of its churring notes. It takes such insects and spiders as it can find in the bushes, and builds its nest in them. They form a shield against the wind and a canopy against rain and snow.

It is resident in the western Mediterranean, from Italy to Spain and Portugal, south to north Africa; and extending up western France to Brittany and southern England. Some small migratory movements may occur in the northern part of its range. It was first described from a specimen from Kent in 1787. Its distribution seems to have been more widespread then, but was based on the more extensive tracts of gorse and heather heathland, with shorter distances between them.

It occurred on heaths and was common around and into London in the nineteenth century. A greater scatter of heathland might explain isolated populations at Cannock Chase in Staffordshire in 1870, at one locality in Shropshire, and on Suffolk heaths. Otherwise its nineteenth century range seems to have been north to Cornwall, Devon, Dorset, Wiltshire, Oxfordshire, Berkshire, Middlesex, London and Kent. It was periodically decimated by hard winters, documented from

Chiffchaff *Phylloscopus collybita*

For many people, this shares with the Wheatear the special status of the mid-March migrant, eagerly looked for after a hard winter. It is a dull olive-brown bird, and to confirm identification one needs the monotonously repeated, but unpredictable, sequence of two notes that give it the common name. However, typical songs of some of the other forms of this species differ from this. The typical alarm call is a plaintive *hweet*. It is widespread, with fairly simple habitat requirements.

The basic needs appear to be a very few tall trees for song posts, and shrubby undergrowth. These conditions may occur from heathland edge and hedgerow to woodland, parkland and the more mature plantations. It appears less affected by cold than related species, but in some of the further north and west limits of its British range, it appears to prefer rhododendron as an undergrowth. The domed nest, like that of other leaf warblers, is placed in tall herbage of low shrubs, but in more instances slightly above ground level.

It breeds across Eurasia in warm boreal to temperate zones, and into the warm-temperate in Europe. It seems to have undergone a Pleistocene separation that produced four forms, with a decrease in yellow pigment and a more greyish brown, as one goes east: a resident Iberian and north African form, the typical European form, a Scandinavian and west Russian form, and an eastern Eurasian form. It winters further north than the other two species, in the Mediterranean region, the Middle East and northern India; with some through western France to Brittany.

Its earliest British record seems to be by Willughby and Ray in 1678, but bones which might be referable either to this species or the Willow Warbler occur in the latter part of the last glaciation, probably in interstadial conditions, in Derbyshire. It may have been less widespread in climax woodland in the Holocene, but would have used the borders of woodland, edges of higher ground, and clearings. It is likely to have increased in historic times with woodland clearing, but probably decreased when this became extensive. It could, however, use coppice woodland, hedgerows with trees and rough ground where these were present, together with plantations with a few mature nurse-trees.

In Ireland, where its range had been limited, it increased in the second half of the nineteenth century and at periods in the present century, and is now through all except for a few corners of the north-west. It is through England and Wales, except in the mountains and Fens. In Scotland it is absent from higher ground and very sparse elsewhere. It spread northwards from the 1950s onwards, but is still scattered and sporadic from the highlands northwards. It increased rapidly from the early 1960s to a four-fold population in the late 1960s to 1970; since then it has fallen back by about half,

with little recent change, and a population of about 300,000 pairs.

A small number of birds persist in winter, in waterside ditches, reed-beds, and sewage-farms, sometimes joined by others from the continent in late winter. They are mainly in England and southern Ireland and are most numerous in southern English counties. On average about 500 birds may be involved.

Cetti's Warbler *Cettia cetti*
NOT ILLUSTRATED

This newcomer is a stout, stubby warbler with short tail; brown deepening to chestnut on the rump, and with a pale eye-strip. Briefly glimpsed, or in rapid flight from one patch of cover to another, it looks like an overgrown wren. It is only easily recognised when a sudden and unexpected short song-phrase, a loud musical flourish of a few repeated double notes, is shouted from a bush a few feet away, before the singer moves on unseen.

It is a bird of shrub and thicket growth in and around marshes and reed-beds, and wet hedge and ditch areas. The male is a little larger than the female, and it appears to be polygamous, having up to three mates. The deep nest cup is built at the edge of low cover in tangles of stems and herbage, near the ground. All the nesting duties from building onwards appear to be done by the female. It feeds low among vegetation; and remains in similar habitats in winter.

It breeds across western Eurasia in warm-temperate zones and is mainly resident. Although restricted to southern Europe up to the end of the nineteenth century, at the western end of its range it moved slowly up through western France to reach Belgium by 1962. It was first seen in north Brittany and the Channel Islands in 1960, and the first British singing male occurred at Tichfield Haven on the Solent in 1961. Birds were seen at various localities in southern England, and one in County Cork in the 1960s.

Some birds colonised reed-bed borders in east Kent and Dorset. By 1972 breeding was suspected in Kent, and by 1973 was verified there and in one other locality. Since then numbers have risen steadily, with occasional temporary setbacks during hard winters. However, it appears to survive cold weather better than some of our other small birds. After a scatter of exploring birds, some north to Yorkshire, in earlier years, its range appears to be from inland Cambridgeshire and the Norfolk Broads, south to Kent, and west to Devon and Somerset, with occasional single breedings in counties such as Hertfordshire, Middlesex and Berkshire. This limit had been reached by the late 1970s, but has changed little since. However, numbers continue to increase, reaching up to over 300 possible pairs in the mid 1980s.

Goldcrests

Regulidae

This group of six tiny species are usually regarded as warblers, but more recent studies suggest that they are a little separated from them. They occur in northern hemisphere woodland, with two species widespread on each continent, and two others on small islands. They are characterised by their small size and brightly-coloured crown feathers. Eurasia has a widespread species, the Goldcrest, and a European species, the Firecrest; both of these occur in the British Isles. The North American Golden-crowned Kinglet *Regulus satrapa* is very similar in appearance to the Firecrest, although the crown colour is more like that of the Goldcrest, and the song differs from both. It is possible that the Firecrest, with its more limited distribution, might have been derived from an earlier, probably Pleistocene invasion of Golden-crowned Kinglet stock into Europe.

Goldcrest *Regulus regulus*

A tiny, thin-voiced bird. A small energetic scrap of activity, hunting almost constantly, and often acrobatically, on leaves and stems of trees for tiny insects and spiders and their eggs, and sometimes hovering momentarily to snatch something. It tends to pass people with the slightly myopic air of something for which a human being is too large an object to be noticed. It seems intent on finding sufficient fuel for the energy to keep itself going, and one wonders where it finds and carries enough to permit the migrations shown by Scandinavian birds. This is something we only become conscious of when an overnight weather-diverted movement brings them in hundreds or thousands to our shores.

Although migrants or weather-driven birds may appear in any vegetation down to ground level, its normal needs seem to be for the presence of conifers or evergreens of some kind, and outside Britain its habitual preferences are even more closely linked with this. It can use conifer twig-tips and foliage more efficiently, and with less competition, than other species in its search for food.

The crown-streak, yellow and orange in the male, yellow in the female, is often barely visible; but a displaying or quarrelling male will lower its head and not only raise, but laterally spread, the head feathers, producing a sudden blazing patch of flame-orange. It has thin, very high-pitched calls that are sometimes hard to hear, and the song is a long phrase with a final flourish. Its nest is a rather bulky structure of moss and lichen, glued together with spiders' webs, bound to the drooping twigs on the underside of a conifer branch, and concealed by the foliage. As with most vulnerable small birds, the broods are large, up to ten or twelve eggs.

It breeds discontinuously across Eurasia in temperate to warm-temperate zones, in Europe extending into the boreal zone in the north, and in montane areas in the south. There are some migratory movements from the north of its range, and from higher altitudes to southern and lower levels in winter. In Britain it was first noted by Turner in 1544. It is likely to have been present in woodland where conifers or yew occurred through much of the Holocene, but may have been increasingly restricted in the south as clearing progressed. It would have increased again in the nineteenth century, with the growth in the planting of conifers both as plantations and as scattered exotics in parklands, woodlands and gardens.

It appears to have increased in the warmer period of the late nineteenth century and earlier part of the present century. Conifer plantations helped it to extend its range into the northern end of Scotland and to the islands, although it is still sporadic on Shetland, Orkney and the Outer Hebrides. Its overall range depends on trees, and although widespread throughout the British Isles, it is absent from the Fens and from some large urban and industrial areas.

As a resident its population fluctuates with severe winters, although varying according to snow and ice conditions rather than direct temperature. According to sample censuses, from the mid 1960s to mid 1970s numbers rose four-fold, while in the late 1970s they dropped by about two-thirds after two severe winters, but rose by 60% between 1979 and 1980. It is estimated that the average breeding population might be over 1,500,000 pairs, with a winter population of about 2,500,000–5,000,000 birds; about one-fifth of this might be overwinterers from the continent.

Firecrest *Regulus ignicapillus*

The black-and-white streaking on the face of this species gives it a more alert look than that of the Goldcrest, but its behaviour is very similar. In theory it is a bird of lowland broadleaf woodland as opposed to the montane conifers preferred by the Goldcrest, but in fact Firecrests appear to show no particular preference, and most of them breeding in Britain have been in conifers or yew trees. As a feeding bird, it tends to take a slightly larger size of prey than the Goldcrest, and hunts more frequently along the larger twigs and branches of trees rather than at their extremities. In display the fiery red of the male's spread crown is striking. The ordinary call note is harsher than that of the Goldcrest, and the song is an accelerated fizzling phrase. Like the Goldcrest it tends to build its nest in a semi-suspended site under a branch, but uses a greater range, including twig forks and ivy on tree-trunks.

It breeds in mainland Europe and north Africa, resident in the south and west of its range, and migrating in the north-east. It was not recorded in Britain until 1832, twelve years after it was first described. Its European range had been extending northwards during the first part of this century, spreading to the Netherlands in 1930, and to Denmark in 1961. In addition, three singing males were present in the summer of 1961 in the New Forest in Hampshire, and in 1962 breeding was proved, with five localities known by 1965. In 1971 a colony was discovered in a conifer plantation on the Chilterns in Buckinghamshire, and singing males occurred from Dorset to Kent.

After initial exploratory dispersal which took singing birds as far as North Yorkshire and south Wales, the larly early fly-ridden farms, may be of some long standing.

In the nineteenth century it appears to have spread a little in northern Scotland and the islands. By the turn of the century it was generally distributed, only affected by local fluctuations. It appears to have suffered more serious decreases since the mid 1960s. From 1962 to 1965 it gained about 10%, but from 1965 to 1974 lost about 50%, and from 1974 to 1985 lost another 40%. Although numbers are decreasing, it is widely distribut-ed throughout the British Isles, but absent from Shetland, and sporadic in Orkney and the Outer Hebrides. Its breeding population might be about 60,000–120,000 pairs and still falling. It appears to be suffering in a similar fashion to some of the species wintering in the African Sahel zone of the southern Sahara, but since it does not winter in that area, it is either suffering some of the problems in its migrations further south, or else the flying insect population of the British Isles is showing an increasing deterioration.

Dunnocks
Prunellidae

This is a small family of insect- and seed-eating birds. Most are skulkers in low cover. The main evolutionary centre of the family appears to be centred on the Himalayas and Tibetan regions. It produces montane and lowland forms. The latter tend to replace each other across Eurasia. The Common Dunnock is the western representative which extends to the British Isles.

Common Dunnock *Prunella modularis*
As a small, unobtrusive and streaky-brown bird this is sometimes compared with the sparrows, but more closely resembles a chat of some kind. However, it differs from both in its ground-hugging tendencies. Although it may be more sprightly in its self-assertive moments, it tends to move in a slight forward crouch, as though all its activities were carried on while moving against a strong headwind. It is a furtive, thicket-haunting species and even when feeding on open ground, it tends to keep close to the shelter into which it can quickly retreat. It takes small invertebrates and seeds, mostly picked up from the ground.

It is rather silent, but males have a short, tuneful but not melodius song-phrase that they tend to repeat for too long. Its other frequently-heard call is a loud *tseep* piping alarm-note. Its social life is rather complex and open to varying interpretations. There appear to be dominant and subordinate males, and the sight of a female escorted by two males, both of whom wave a single spread wing above the back like a banner, is not unusual. Breeding patterns have been variously inter-preted as a dominant pair with subordinate pairs in their territory, the dominant male fathering all the young, or a variable pattern with males having more than one female in good territories, and females having more than one male in poor ones.

It is a sedentary bird of low bushy cover, feeding on the ground under trees and shrubs and in nearby open spaces. It feeds a lot on tiny and barely noticeable insects and seeds, and appears to subsist on small weed seeds in winter. It occurs from low shrubby growth in more open woodland, through scrub, to hedgerows and down to bramble thickets. The rather bulky cup nest is usually concealed in thick cover a metre or two from the ground. It may have several broods a year.

Its breeding range is through Europe, from boreal to temperate zones. It is resident in most of Europe, and migratory from Scandinavia and Russia to warm-temperate zones. Its earliest British records are in the Pleistocene, in the last glaciation, presumably in interstadial conditions, in Devon and Derbyshire. A bird of woodland undergrowth, mostly in more areas, and of all kinds of low scrub and bushy cc likely to have found a large range of margins even if it decreased to some extent as w as cleared and agriculture took over. It c dge-rows, coppice woodland, plantation e nd and orchards.

Already widely distributed, it he Hebrides and Orkney, where it is still v n the latter part of the nineteenth century. y to have shown a general increase in th nineteenth and early twentieth centuries. It nt to be still increasing a little, more particu the south-west, and in suburban areas w bs have become increasingly fashionable. It buted throughout the British Isles with th on of Shetland, where there may have been of recent breeding attempts. It also tends to nt from the higher mountain areas of Scotl ve a limit of about 500 metres. The bre opulation of the British Isles is thought to be 00,000 pairs. It is rather sedentary, but in r, birds tend to move to lower ground away from e north and west, in both Britain and Ireland. Although continental migrants may pass through on passage, there is no evidence of a winter influx.

Pipits and Wagtails

Motacillidae

These are slender, nervously-active birds of open places. Mainly terrestrial and insect-eating, they have slender bills, longish legs and tails, and they walk and run rapidly. There are six breeding species in the British Isles, three pipits and three wagtails. The wagtails are more brightly patterned and tend to prefer the waterside; the pipits are dull and cryptic and occur in ground vegetation. All are birds of more open country, using grassland, steppe and tundra regions of the north.

Within these regions the two groups have shown a similar pattern of divergent adaptation, producing three species in each with broadly similar types of specialisation – one in rocky places, another in more open grassland, and the third with a greater tolerance of more mixed habitats.

Pipits

Anthus species

These are birds inhabiting areas with mainly short ground vegetation and some more open spaces. The drab-coloured streaky-brown plumage reduces their conspicuousness in such habitats. The three species overlap broadly in their general ranges, but occupy specialised habitats within them. The Rock Pipit is a coastal species, the Meadow Pipit a grassland and moorland bird, the Tree Pipit a bird of open areas with scattered trees.

Rock Pipit *Anthus spinoletta*

A large, dark drab pipit with strong legs and feet, this can be seen, often solitarily, searching coastal rocks and tide edge for tiny creatures, or on the turf of cliff-tops or ledges. It has sharp, loud monosyllabic *tsip* calls and alarm notes. Its flight is strong, and it has a typical song flight, fluttering up with sharp squeaky notes that merge into an accelerating trill, as it parachutes down with spread wings. The cup nest is tucked into a rock recess.

Its strong flight and voice are adapted to an exposed coastal habitat; and it probably evolved as a distinct dark form on the north-west European seaboard. It utilises the vertical open spaces provided by high and rugged sea cliffs, but will also make do with low coastal areas with fewer rocks, and may visit flat and marshy coasts in winter. As a winter visitor, the paler Water Pipit seems more at home on the edges of still waters of reservoirs or watercress-beds.

It has a widespread breeding range, separated into several distinct subspecies, suggesting a long period of dispersal and fragmentation. It is present in arctic North America west to Kamchatka and into the Rockies, migrating south. In Eurasia a mountain form, the Water Pipit, occurs through the temperate zone, discontinuously from the Pyrenees and Alps to eastern Siberia. In the north-west the coastal Rock Pipit breeds from the White Sea and Baltic coasts to Britain and Brittany, northernmost birds migrating to west coasts of Biscay, Iberia and Morocco. Its earliest British records are from the end of the last glaciation in Devon, and the south Wales coast in the Early Holocene.

It occurs round the rocky coasts of the British Isles. It is absent from the east coast between Flamborough Head in Yorkshire and the North Foreland in Kent, and the west coasts of most of Lancashire and Lakeland. It is present on other coasts, including all islands. It is unlikely to have been affected much by human activity at any time, with the possible exception of the more recent use of coasts by holidaymakers. It disappeared from the Sussex cliffs in about 1891, with one nesting in 1923, and re-established itself in 1932. It seems to have nested regularly in north-east Kent only since 1967.

The breeding population of the British Isles has been estimated at about 50,000 pairs. In winter it is more widespread around the coasts, with an influx of immigrants from Scandinavia. The winter population is over 100,000–150,000 birds. The southern European Water Pipit disperses from mountains to lowlands in winter, and about 100 birds annually overwinter in Britain. Almost all are at inland sites in south and central England north to Lancashire and Humberside.

Meadow Pipit *Anthus pratensis*

This weak-looking, squeaky-voiced pipit, usually seen in open grassy places where a small party of them will rise and flit a short distance before settling again, is a bird of extensive open habitats with short vegetative cover – grassy moors, heathland, lowland grazing, saltmarshes and dunes, where it is one of the most typical birds. It also breeds on sparse mountain-top vegetation and is the commonest breeding song-bird of uplands. It can utilise borders of rough grass in cultivated areas; but it does not seem to do as well as might be expected on well-kept lowland meadows and pastures. Its food is almost entirely small insects. Its shrill *tsip* call is weaker and thinner, and like that of the Rock Pipit is repeated in a towering song-flight, fluttering up and parachuting back to the ground with an accelerating series of notes. Its cup nest is well hidden in or under grass and herbage.

It breeds in western Eurasia in tundra to temperate zones, extending into Russia, Iceland and east Greenland. Lacking subspecific variation, it is probably of European origin. It is mainly resident in western Europe but otherwise migratory to circum-Mediterranean and warm-temperate areas. Its earliest British records are late in the Pleistocene, from towards the end of the last glaciation in Derbyshire and Devon. Its earliest distribution must have been limited to upland and moorland where trees were absent, and coastal marshes and dunes. It would have increased with the clearing of woodland and extension of pastures.

As a breeding bird it is present throughout the British Isles, but scarce and sometimes absent on heavy clays of the Welsh borders, English midlands and East Anglia.

Rock Pipit

Tree Pipit

Meadow Pipit

Pied Wagtail

SUMMER FEMALE

Grey Wagtail

SUMMER MALE

SUMMER MALE

Yellow Wagtail

D.M.HENRY

It has lost some ground recently with the increasing cultivation of marginal land in the south, and afforestation in the north. It tends to increase in areas of newly planted trees, decreasing again as they close up in growth. There are widespread indications of some local decreases, more apparent in southern Britain. In addition, decreases of over 20% in sample censuses after recent bad winters indicate a vulnerability to bad weather.

The breeding population has been estimated at about 3,000,000 pairs. In winter there is a general movement to lower ground from the uplands, and a considerable southward movement with a large immigration of passage birds and visitors from the north, some of which may move on again if severe weather occurs. The winter population is probably about half that of the summer.

Tree Pipit *Anthus trivialis*
Although deceptively like a Meadow Pipit, its habit of flying into trees when disturbed, perching in them when nesting, and occasionally walking along branches, usually identifies it. It needs areas of relatively short herbage or open ground, with scattered tall song perches such as trees, tall shrubs and, *in extremis*, poles and posts. At the other extreme, it will occur in open woodland and into the edges of thicker tree growth. It also uses coppiced woodland with scattered mature trees, and the early stages of young plantations.

It has a distinct, rasping low-pitched call note and performs its song flight up from, and back to, the top of a tree; the final descent accompanied by a series of loud *seea seea* notes more musical than those of other pipits. Although arboreal, it feeds on the ground in open areas like other pipits, and roosts on the ground. It also nests on the ground, in a cup hidden away in herbage, most often on a bank or slope. At other times it is less sociable than the Meadow Pipit.

Its breeding range is across Eurasia in boreal to warm-temperate zones, and it is wholly migrant, wintering in subtropical to tropical zones in Africa and India. It has Pleistocene records in Britain, both in the last, Ipswichian, interglacial and at the end of the last glaciation, both in Devon. It is likely to have been present during early woodland spread, in open birchwood, particularly on hillsides. Where more extensive woodland occurred, it would have been limited to edges, thin open woodland or the borders of clearings. Gradual haphazard clearing of woodland would have enabled it to increase its population, which would have fallen again where areas were wholly cleared. It is likely to have done well where woodland became open through grazing by stock.

It does not seem to have been recorded from Ireland except as a vagrant. It is present through England and Wales, but although only susceptible to summer temperatures, population seems to have been lower in the north in the nineteenth century, when it was said to be scarce and local in Scotland. In the warmer part of the present century, it became more plentiful and spread in Scotland north of Inverness, although remaining sparse in the Scottish lowlands. It did not colonise Caithness until the end of the 1960s. It is absent from Shetland, Orkney and the Outer Hebrides. In England and Wales its general distribution is patchy, and it is absent from the Fens, and much of East Anglia. Numbers seem to have declined in the southern British range. Its breeding population may be 50,000–100,000 pairs. It migrates south in winter, with Scandinavian birds also passing through in spring and autumn.

Wagtails

Motacilla species

These are more conspicuous than pipits, with brighter colours. The frequent vertical wagging of the white-edged tail when excited is the feature that gave them their name. However, it is possible that they may be less obvious on the edge of moving water in their preferred environment. Like the pipits, the three species overlap broadly in general range, but are separated by habitat preferences. The Grey Wagtail is widely resident alongside running water, mostly on uplands. The Yellow Wagtail is a summer visitor to lowland moist grassland. The Pied Wagtail has greater tolerance of mixed, discontinuous habitats and of less open spaces and is a widespread resident.

Pied Wagtail *Motacilla alba*
Strikingly-patterned, fairly tame, and often living around human settlement, this is the typical wagtail seen trotting around lawns and farmyards with nodding head and wagging tail, the latter suddenly raised and spread, as it brakes and swerves after flies. The loud *chissik* call helps advertise its presence. It has the typical strongly undulating flight. It is partly resident, partly migratory, and although its basic habitat is probably open grassy places, often near water, it is also tolerant of a wide range of varied and less open environments. It occurs on forest edge, in clearings, and more especially around farmland, gardens, buildings and other man-modified areas.

Like the Yellow Wagtail, it is one of the few birds to have a distinctive, easily-recognisable form, that is confined to the British Isles as a breeding bird. It is treated as a subspecies, *M. a. yarrelli*, named after one of our early ornithologists. The male is grey-backed in winter as is the female all year round, while in the continental White Wagtail, *M. a. alba*, both sexes have ashy-grey backs at all times. The cup nest is tucked into some raised cavity or niche in a building, wall, bank or tree. Territorial and aggressive in summer, it may also defend a winter feeding territory, but non-breeding birds often roost together in sheltered sites, sometimes in seemingly incongruous places such as trees along busy streets, or in commercial greenhouses.

The overall distribution of the species is through Eurasia from Iceland and Bear Island eastwards, in tundra to warm-temperate zones. It winters in warm-temperate parts of its range and in western Europe, and southwards to tropical zones. The pale-backed White Wagtail occupies most of the range with another black-backed form in the far east. There are Pleistocene records of Pied/White Wagtails in Britain, in the last interglacial in Essex, and the end of the last glaciation in Devon.

The pied form is a British isolate; like the Yellow

Wagtail, it probably differentiated as a breeding isolate in colder Pleistocene periods, in some western low-lying area when sea-levels were also lower, such as that around the English Channel and the west coast of France south to Biscay, and perhaps the Iberian peninsula. The White Wagtail spread back to occupy the European mainland, and passed north of Britain to the Faeroes and Iceland. Since 1900 it has bred occasionally in Shetland, where equally sporadic breeding of the Pied Wagtail occurs. The Pied Wagtail has established small populations in one or two mainland localities in north France and south-west Norway. In such places, birds appear to pair preferentially with those of their own subspecies.

In early times it would have bred on coasts, along waterways and on marshes. Its increase would probably have come, not so much from woodland clearance, as from the increase of human settlement. For centuries it has been closely associated with farms. It breeds in buildings and walls. Its numbers must have been fairly stable for a long period. It has increased in Ireland in the present century. In recent decades there have been decreases in southern Britain, in particular in the south-east. A change from cattle to arable and a considerable and widespread decrease in farmyard ponds, together with insecticide sprays, have helped to cut its numbers. Sample censuses have shown that it is also very vulnerable to hard winters, and may take a few years to recover. It decreased in farmland by 55% after the 1961–62 and 1962–3 winters, by 12% after the 1978–79 winter, and by 25% after 1981–82. The general breeding population in good periods in the British Isles is estimated as about 500,000 pairs.

In winter the southern population is resident, but that of Scotland and northern upland areas moves south, many emigrating into western Europe and Morocco. Winter population may be about 750,000–2,000,000 individuals.

Grey Wagtail *Motacilla cinerea*
Slightly larger and longer-tailed than the other two, this is typically a bird of running water with stones or rocks. Its most usual habitat is a hill or mountain stream. In southern Britain, it is usually resident but since it takes much of its food from the water's edge, it may be forced to move in winter if this freezes. It has the typical bounding flight and a loud *tzitzi* call. It usually occurs solitarily or in pairs or families. The nest is tucked into a raised hollow or cavity in a stream bank, rock cleft, wall or tree-roots, and often close by water.

It has an oddly discontinuous distribution, mainly in upland areas, across Eurasia in boreal to warm-temperate zones, but absent from most of Scandinavia and Russia. Mainly migrant in the east, it is present in Europe all year in most of its range, but with some migration to circum-Mediterranean regions and into Africa, eastern birds moving to India and south-east Asia. In Britain it is partly-resident, partly-migrant. Its earliest record in Britain is from about the end of the last glaciation in Devon. As a bird feeding and nesting by fast-flowing streams, it has probably been affected only slightly by man's activities over the centuries. One small aspect of importance is likely to have been the innumerable small watermills and mill-races, created in areas of otherwise slow-moving waters in historic times. In recent periods, they have held pairs in otherwise

unsuitable areas, and might have done so in the past. As a mainly resident species associated with water, it is very vulnerable to cold weather. Its numbers may have been lower in colder recent centuries, since it showed a general increase in the earlier part of the present century – both in Britain and in Europe – that seems to have reached a peak in the 1950s. It is mainly absent from an area of England north-east of a line from Yorkshire to Oxfordshire and across to north Essex. In the 1950s it was spreading into this area. However, bad winters in the 1960s and subsequently made periodic drastic reductions in its numbers. For example, there was a decrease of 33% in the winter of 1978–79, and of 42% in 1981–82. Hard winters occurring too frequently could permanently reduce its numbers. Its other potential future problems are pollution and acidification of streams, especially in upland areas.

In its general distribution it is still absent from much of eastern England, patchy in Essex, Kent, the Midlands and south Lancashire. Since the 1950s it has nested sporadically in the Outer Hebrides, and in Orkney where it had sometimes nested earlier. It is absent from the Shetlands and from the Scilly Isles. The British Isles breeding population in a good year has been estimated at about 25,000–50,000 pairs. Most birds in Scotland, and many from northern England, move south in winter to more lowland areas, or migrate into Europe. There is some influx of continental birds. Many appear on still, lowland waters, or farmyards, or sewage farms, or around urban areas. The total winter population may be about 40,000 birds.

Yellow Wagtail *Motacilla flava*
Like the Pied Wagtail this is essentially a British breeding bird, and one of our brightest. Although the male in autumn, like the female and immatures, is a drab olive-brown, the spring bird is as vividly yellow as a dandelion against the green grass. It is conspicuous both in its plumage and the loud *tsweep* call. It is even more conspicuous when in display it throws back its head and puffs up the yellow breast; and it sings its short song from a post, or in flight. It feeds mainly on small insects, caught on marshes, pastures and arable land. The nest is a cup on the ground, sheltered by plants or grass tufts.

It is a migrant species, breeding across Eurasia in subarctic to warm-temperate zones, wintering in Africa, India and south-east Asia. Because of its need for low-lying moist grassland, its breeding range is limited. In the past, presumably in some colder phases of the Pleistocene Ice Ages, it must have become fragmented into smaller local populations, breeding in scattered suitable places. These evolved differing head colours in breeding males, which still persist and can be recognised now that they have spread back to occupy a range that is superficially more continuous overall, but locally limited. The European mainland bird, the Blue-headed Wagtail *M. f. flava* has a blue-grey head and white eye-stripe; northern Scandinavia has the Grey-headed Wagtail *M. f. thunbergi*, possibly an invader via the north from further east, and Britain has its own form, the Yellow Wagtail *M. f. flavissima*.

To maintain this isolation from the rest of Europe, our bird must have had a separate breeding refuge in the past. Since Spain and Portugal have their own blue-headed form, it is unlikely to have been there. With sea-levels low and much more land exposed, the area of the

English Channel and possibly the western coastal regions of France may have provided a separate breeding range during glacial periods. Possibly the Yellow Wagtail and Pied Wagtail are the only relics that we have of the lost land of Lyonesse.

The earliest British record is from the end of the last glaciation in Kent. In post-glacial times, as woodland spread, the Yellow Wagtail must have been limited to the borders of freshwater marshes and swamps of low-lying areas. It takes readily to pasture, catching insects around the feet of cattle, and would have spread subsequently as woodland gave way to pasture and cultivation. For this reason, it would probably have suffered less than other marshland species from the loss of wet areas through increased drainage.

Its general distribution is in England and Wales, and into southern Scotland. Odd scattered pairs of Blue-headed Wagtails occasionally breed, mostly in the south-east; and there are instances of interbreeding. Small numbers of both European forms pass through on migration. In Ireland it bred in two sites, one on the Mayo-Galway border, the other Lough Neagh, but the first disappeared in the 1920s and the second more slowly between the 1920s and 1940s. Sporadic breeding has occurred since on the eastern side. In Scotland it bred north to Aberdeen, but has contracted to the Clyde valley and the south-east, with sporadic occurrences elsewhere. In the first half of this century it tended to become scarcer in southern England, and disappeared from most of Cornwall and Devon. It is generally absent from hilly areas. The British Isles population has been estimated at about 25,000 pairs.

PLATE FORTY-FOUR

Waxwings

Bombycillidae

A family of only three species, occurring in the cooler forest regions of the northern hemisphere. They are plump birds with a black face-mask, and a tapering, erectile crest. The wings are tapering, the tail short, and in flight they resemble Starlings in both outline and movement. One species extends across Eurasia and into western North America, where its range overlaps that of the smaller Cedar Waxwing *B. cedrorum*. The Japanese Waxwing *B. japonica* breeds in extreme eastern Siberia.

Waxwing *Bombycilla garrulus*

A winter visitor, this is a plump, starling-sized bird, the sober plumage set off with touches of red, yellow and white, and the row of odd, waxy-red feather-tips on the wing. Flocks tend to appear suddenly and unexpectedly, when restless moving in level flight using a soft shrill whistling trill, but when hungry becoming relatively silent and tame, concentrating on stuffing themselves with berries. They will take rowan berries, haws, crab apples, cotoneaster and berberis berries and rose-hips. When nesting they take mainly insects and will take winter ones when available; they are surprisingly adept at flycatching from an open perch. They are highly sociable, both in moving and feeding.

Their breeding range is in the conifer forests of the boreal zone across Eurasia and into western North America. In winter they shift south from the northern part of the range. They feed on berry-bearing shrubs and trees within and bordering the boreal forest, but spread south into the temperate zone. These movements are irruptive and difficult to predict in terms of timing, size and direction. However, they seem to be triggered off by some factor prior to the occurrence of potentially inadequate berry crops. It is suggested that the climatic factors producing a good berry crop also produce a large number of young birds in those years, and that when these become adult, they create an irruptive tendency through over-population, coinciding with the poorer berry crop in a short-term cycle.

Britain is on the periphery of the normal outward waves of irruptive movements. It is possible that in the colder, boreal-type climate stages during and towards the end of the Pleistocene, the Waxwing may have been a breeding bird in the British Isles. The earliest records are from the last glaciation in Derbyshire. It has been noted as a winter visitor since 1662. In the past it tended to be noticed only when large-scale invasions occurred, but by the 1940s it was suggested that it might occur annually in small numbers with periodic large irruptions. It had been suggested that these occurred about every ten years, usually around the beginning of a decade, but the pattern does not seem to be predictable.

In years of small numbers, scattered flocks may be of around ten birds, while in major irruptions they might number hundreds or over a thousand. The birds come to us as part of south-westerly movements, mostly arriving from across the North Sea on easterly coasts. These may be throughout the length of Britain. In years of major irruptions they may occur right across the British Isles, and it is only in these years that they occur in any numbers in Ireland. The main areas of occurrence are eastern Scotland to north-east England, and East Anglia.

Starlings

Sturnidae

Common Starling *Sturnus vulgaris*

As one of the commonest of our birds, we undervalue the beauty of its plumage, both with its autumn pattern of fine spotting, and the more worn spring plumage with its green and purple glosses. The weird array of ecstatic noises that pass for a song are almost unnoticed. For most of the time it appears to need two things – a nest-

Shrikes
Laniidae

This is a family of passerine raptors. Although typical song-birds, and although the principal prey is insects, they have evolved short, stout bills with hooked tips, and some may take prey up to the size of small rodents and birds. They inhabit open areas and hunt by watching from an elevated perch, swooping down on prey. They have a habit of killing more than they immediately need, and such surplus prey is often impaled on thorns of bushes, trees or barbed wire. Of the five species that occur in Europe, only two are regularly found in the British Isles, occupying the same heathland habitats: the smaller Red-backed Shrike in summer, and the larger Great Grey Shrike in winter.

Red-backed Shrike *Lanius collurio*
The male is one of our more beautiful birds, and all the more striking when seen balanced on the tip of some small bush on open heathland. Like other shrikes it tends to swing the tail laterally at times, pendulum-fashion, and to partly spread it. Its principal prey is larger insects, beetles, butterflies, moths and grasshoppers; but it may also take small frogs, lizards and fledgling birds. Like its larger relative, it hunts from a number of prominent perches with a wide view, watching for its prey, and flying out in fast swooping flight to seize it. Some prey is impaled on spikes, often on hawthorn, sloe or gorse bushes. Its bulky nest cup is built in a thick shrub, usually two or three metres up.

It breeds widely across western Eurasia, from warm boreal to temperate zones, wintering in Africa, the Arabian Gulf and north-west India. It is part of a superspecies, with a rufous-tailed form in south-eastern Eurasia, and replaced by the Brown Shrike *L. cristatus* in eastern Eurasia. According to James Fisher, its earliest reference in literature in Britain is from the eighth century. As a bird of open, heathland-type areas with a few scattered bushes, scrub or trees, it would have occupied only marginal areas in the early Holocene. When woodland was cleared in historic times, it would have found an increasingly available habitat in heathland, common land, rough grazing and scrub. This may have been at its most extensive in the seventeenth to nineteenth centuries. However, from the mid nineteenth century onwards, it seems to have gone into a long decline, which appears to have accelerated after the 1940s. There is also evidence of a significant decline through north-west Europe as a whole from the 1930s onwards.

It is difficult to suggest a simple explanation. A species that appears to have shown a parallel decrease in the Wryneck. At first sight they seem very dissimilar, but the two may share a rather specialised insect diet, and rely on visual detection of their prey. Both are summer visitors, and the Atlantic seaboard of western Europe often has milder but usually moister and windier summers. They may not only affect insect populations, but more particularly the large day-flying insects that may rely on summer periods of hot and calm weather in order to thrive.

We should, perhaps, add to this the recent extensive use of insecticides. Since the early 1940s there has been an enormous spread, and an enormously increased use, of insecticides of all kinds. These would appear to be reducing the availability of insects in general, and possibly having a greater effect on larger insects with smaller total populations. No serious attempt seems to have been made to quantify the change in this biomass of visually available insects, on which quite a number of our summer bird species depend for the feeding of their young, and for their own survival. We may be seeing a long-term and persistent deterioration in this part of our environment, which may in turn have a serious effect upon others.

The Red-backed Shrike's British breeding range appears to have been restricted to England and Wales. By 1900 it had become absent from Northumberland and Durham, south Yorkshire and south Lincolnshire. By the end of the 1930s, it had further contracted and was lost from north Yorkshire, Cumbria, Lancashire, Anglesey, Pembrokeshire and Cornwall. By the end of the 1940s it had gone from north Devon, south and north Wales, and from Derbyshire to Leicestershire and Lincolnshire. By the end of the 1950s, it was mostly south of a line from the Wash to the Bristol Channel, and absent from Northamptonshire, Oxfordshire and most of Sussex.

Within the south-east it has continued to shrink. From 300 pairs in 1952, it dropped to 250 in 1960 and 80–90 in 1971, more than three-quarters of these being in East Anglia. By the mid 1980s it was down to about 10 pairs in East Anglia, and in 1986 only three pairs bred.

During this catastrophic decline which may result in a loss of the species as anything other than a scarce visitor, a pair bred in 1977 in Orkney, and other birds were seen in north Scotland. In 1978 two pairs nested on the mainland and another five males were present. A further pair bred in 1979, with scattered birds seen elsewhere south to Perth and Angus. Birds were present without breeding in 1980 to 1982, but not after that. It is suspected that this small temporary northern enclave, like the Scottish Wrynecks, may have originated from diverted south Scandinavian birds.

Great Grey Shrike *Lanius excubitor*
In Britain, this is a regular rarity of open heathland country. A long-tailed, thrush-sized bird with heavy head and bill, it spends most of its time perched on the tops of bushes and small trees, from which it can dash out after prey. The flight is fast and low, with a series of undulating swoops, showing large white wing-patches. Larger insects are pursued and caught in the air, as well as being snatched from the ground. It will take small voles, shrews and mice, and also small birds, which it will sometimes pursue and fly down. As a winter feeder in open and rather sparse areas of this kind, it needs a lot of hunting space, and Great Grey Shrikes in Britain usually occur singly, with one bird in each suitable area, and some evidence of individuals returning to particular sites.

It has a very extensive range in boreal to subtropical zones around the northern hemisphere. In Europe it is absent from the countries on the northern side of the eastern Mediterranean: along the Atlantic seaboard, from south Norway, Sweden and Finland, and from the British Isles. However, it is migratory in the northern, boreal, part of its range and winters south into these areas. Its first British record is by Turner in 1544.

It appears to have been absent as a breeding species from Britain, and the western edge of Europe, because of the milder Atlantic climate. Since there is evidence of continental-type climates with hotter summers in Britain at the transitional stages to and from Pleistocene glaciations, it is possible that it could have bred in Britain at these periods, the last probably being about 10,000 to 9,000 years ago.

As a winter visitor to open heathland, it might have found this habitat more extensive during the seventeenth to early nineteenth centuries, although the weather is likely to have been colder. As a visitor from cold boreal regions, its population fluctuations may be linked with cycles in abundance of its prey in these regions. There is little information on its numbers in Britain. In the 1930s it was said to be a winter visitor to eastern Britain, irregular in the west and a very rare casual in west Wales and the Hebrides. Present evidence suggests that there may have been a slight westward extension in its general wintering range, with individuals scattered through Britain except in the extreme north-west, but absent from Ireland. The winter population may be only a little over 150 individuals.

PLATE FORTY-FIVE

Finches

Fringillidae

This is a family of small birds feeding mainly on seeds of various kinds, and with a range of bill adaptations which allow them to feed in slightly differing ways and reduce competition. Their breeding habitats range from woodland to moorland; and they build simple cup nests. There are fifteen British species, in two subfamilies. Two are fringilline finches, almost identical but in different climatic zones, the Chaffinch in woodland, the Brambling near its northern limits. The remainder are cardueline finches. The Hawfinch is a large, massive-billed woodland bird, able to crack cherry stones; the Bullfinch is a woodland edge bud-eating specialist. Feeding in more open places on low plants and on the ground, the Greenfinch is a large-billed woodland edge bird taking larger seeds; the Linnet a feeder in open and bushy places with a small and stubby bill; the Twite replacing it on high moors and north-western coasts. The Serin is similar to the last two, but in drier areas and ranging into trees. The narrower-billed Goldfinch, feeding on seeds from herbage and from birch and alder, links with the birch and alder seed-eating Siskin of conifer woodland and the Redpoll from arctic and alpine birch scrub. The crossbills are specialists on pine-seed, with bills adapted for opening the cones. The Scarlet Grosbeak is a bud and seed eater of moist scrub.

Greenfinch *Carduelis chloris*
From woodland edges, this has moved through farmland into suburbs and gardens, and the exuberant musical twittered song is now a typical spring sound in such places, and the long-drawn harsh *dweezhe* note is even more familiar. It has a wide feeding spectrum on seeds taken from plants and on the ground, and with its heavy bill is able to deal with larger seeds and berries as well, taking seeds up to the size of cultivated sunflower seed. It appears ready to explore and utilise new seed and fruit sources planted in gardens, and this—combined with a willingness to accept winter feeding—has both aided its spread and brought it into closer contact with people. The bright yellow wing and tail markings, present also on the dull brown female, help identify it, accompanied as they usually are by the twittering flight note. The nest, rather bulky for the size of the bird, is usually in a shrub or tall hedgerow, two to three metres up. There may be several broods in a season.

It is a European species, through warm boreal to warm-temperate zones, with some migration from its northern limits in Scandinavia and Russia in winter. Its earliest British record is from the last glaciation, presumably in interstadial conditions, in Derbyshire. In the Holocene it would have found plenty of areas on woodland edge and clearings. As woodland clearance proceeded in later times, it would have derived some advantage from the increasing edge created, and from its ability to use the more limited tree and scrub growth still remaining. It might have gained from the availability of weed seeds and waste grain. However, its numbers overall would probably have fallen. It is also vulnerable to colder weather and this may have depressed its northern population to some extent.

In the present century, it increased and spread northwards to some extent in northern Europe as well as the British Isles. This led to an increase in north-west Scotland, a spread into Cornwall and the Scillies, and into the north-west of Ireland. Its spread into suburbs and towns may date from as late as the 1950s or 1960s. It might, or might not, be connected with the fact that about this time a change in farming methods was bringing about the end of traditional stackyards.

It is now widespread throughout the British Isles, but absent in some mountain areas, scarce in the Outer Hebrides and Orkney, and absent from Shetland. In winter there is an eastward and southward shift to lowlands and coasts. There may be a very small migratory movement. Its 1972 population was estimated at about 1,000,000–2,000,000 pairs; but there has been a drop of 10–15%. Although its numbers appear to be fairly stable, it might be affected by the drop in availability of weed seeds from crops, a drop that has already hit the Linnet.

Goldfinch **Carduelis carduelis**
The Goldfinch is adept at feeding above ground: fluttering, clinging and extracting seeds from tall thistleheads or from alder cones, and the colourful flicker of the black and gold wings and black-and-white tail may be an enhanced signal for others of a food-hunting flock. When feeding it moves with a quick, bouncy, undulating flight from one plant to another, usually feeding sociably in parties or flocks. It is agile

Greenfinch

MALE

Goldfinch

Hawfinch

Bullfinch

MALE

FEMALE

FEMALE

MALE

Chaffinch

D.M.HENRY

both in clinging and in holding down food objects with the foot. The thin, tapering bill-tip enables it to dig deep into thistle-heads, or with cunning vibrations withdraw the seeds from spiky teazels. It has loud liquid *tswit-wit* twittering call notes, and a pleasant and musical song of vigorous and varied warblings and twitters. The neat nest is usually built in a twig fork in a tree.

Its breeding range is across western Eurasia, in warm boreal to warm-temperate zones, but in general it is a little more southerly in its limits than other British cardueline finches. It has been isolated at some time in the past to produce two populations, one which lacks the black-and-white on the head occupying the eastern, Transcaspian, part of the range. It is mainly resident in Europe, but migratory from most of the north-east, including south Sweden. Its earliest records in Britain are from the latter part of the last glaciation, presumably in interstadial conditions, in Devon and Derbyshire.

It may have been reasonably widespread, at least in southern Britain, during much of the Holocene, but probably less numerous. When woodland was progressively cleared and farming spread, weed seeds might have become more widely available together with the more open habitat that it prefers, and numbers are likely to have risen. However, its need for trees–even low trees–for nesting might have limited the options available to it, compared with species like the Greenfinch and Linnet. It has readily adapted to hedgerows with trees, orchards and gardens; and roadside verges provided a source of food, at least until weed-spraying became a local government obsession.

Its brightly-coloured plumage, musical song and simple seed diet had made it a desirable cage bird since early times. There was a very considerable decrease in the British Isles in the nineteenth century. This has been attributed to the constant trapping of very large numbers for sale as cage birds. The demand would presumably have risen with the increase in human population and urbanisation, and since the birds did not survive very long, it was continuous. Commercial trapping of migrant flocks occurred, and other trapping went on all year. This was finally legally banned in Britain in 1888, although not in Ireland for another half-century. There was a marked increase in birds almost immediately, but this merged into the period of climatic amelioration, when the population would also have increased for that reason.

It has undergone a general increase throughout its range in the British Isles and during recent times, like other species, it has shown a slight spread in the south-west, colonising the Scillies, and in western Ireland. Although most numerous in the south, its breeding range extends through Ireland and north to the borders of the highlands in Scotland; but it is local and scarce from Mull and Arran, through Argyll and Aberdeen and to the Moray Firth. It is absent from the higher mountain areas generally. In winter about 80% of the birds emigrate to the continent, wintering from Belgium to Spain. The majority of these are females. Remaining birds shift to more low-lying areas, where food is available. It suffers loss in cold weather, and migrants could be affected if severe winter weather extends far into Europe. In general it has shown a gradual increase from the early 1960s to mid 1970s, and it still retains a high level. The population is estimated at about 300,000 pairs.

Hawfinch *Coccothraustes coccothraustes*

In spite of its massive bill and striking appearance, this is a quiet and retiring bird, seldom seen. In flight the large head, stocky body, big white wing-stripe and stubby tail identify it, but it tends to sit high in trees and its sharp *tzic* call may be unnoticed except by another Hawfinch. The song is just a series of subdued creaks and call notes. When it feeds on the ground, the subtle colouring of its plumage tends to merge with the dead leaf background as its searches for fruit stones and seeds; only highlighted if the sun catches it.

It is a bird of broadleaf woodland, of cherry, beech, hornbeam, sycamore, wych elm, holly and yew, of all of which it can crack the seeds. Its bill is exceptional in its ability to crack cherry stones. It will also take haws and rose-hips in hedgerows, berries of garden shrubs, and in spring and summer takes buds, peas and similar softer items, as well as insects. The nest is in a twig fork well up in a tree; and the young, with their pale, greenish plumage are as unobtrusive as the adults.

It occurs discontinuously in wooded regions across Eurasia, in temperate to warm-temperate zones. In Europe it is mainly resident, but migrates from the north-east to further south in its range and into the Mediterranean region. Its earliest British records are in the Pleistocene, from the latter part of the last glaciation, presumably in interstadial conditions, in Devon and Derbyshire. As a bird of fruit- and seed-bearing trees, it may have had limited opportunity in the Holocene, until the general spread of such trees from about 6,000 years ago. Subsequently it could have been widespread, but limited climatic tolerance may have kept it mainly in southern Britain. It must have undergone some decrease in the later historic period of woodland loss.

It could have been present and breeding in small numbers, but there is little evidence apart from a single sixteenth century East Anglian reference to it as a summer garden raider. It might have been affected by the colder Little Ice Age period of the fourteenth to nineteenth centuries, since it does not seem to have been noticed as a breeding species until the nineteenth century; and until about the 1850s it appears to have been limited to south-east England and the Midlands.

It appears to have undergone a considerable, although sparse, spread in the late nineteenth and early twentieth century, with relatively little recent change, and this might also be linked to long-term climatic changes. Although its main concentration is still in south-east England, it has bred since the 1920s in scattered localities west to Somerset and Devon, into eastern Wales, and north to southern and eastern Scotland. It spread to south Devon in 1953 and further west in Wales in the 1960s. There was a small occurrence in Ireland with a breeding in County Kildare in 1902. Its numbers were broadly estimated in 1972 at about 10,000 pairs. In winter it tends to form small flocks and to move unpredictably, mostly for short distances and depending on tree seed crops.

Bullfinch *Pyrrhula pyrrhula*

Like the Hawfinch, the even more boldly-coloured Bullfinch is also an unobtrusive bird, a frequent skulker in woods and shrubby cover, and the most that may be noticed may be a brief flash of red breast and white rump, or the easily-imitated, hoarse little piping call notes. It is a woodland edge bird, that has moved to hedgerows and shrubbier growth in quite recent times. It tends to take berries and larger, softer seedheads such as sowthistle or groundsel, or those that can be stripped from a stem like dock and nettle. There is a long and strong bond between the pair and it is a secretive nester, building a thin twig nest with a small, finely-lined internal cup in a tree or shrub. It is not strongly territorial.

In winter it feeds on weed seeds and berries, with tree seeds such as birch and ash. It takes buds later, as well as seed, and it is the failure of seed supplies that may force it to rely almost wholly on buds in late winter and early spring. The stout, short bill is designed for taking and crushing buds, to eat only the embryonic flower-bud at the centre. Its ability to strip buds from trees has earned it the hatred of fruit-growers and gardeners. It had a price on its head for this habit as early as the sixteenth century.

It occurs in woodland right across Eurasia, in warm boreal to temperate zones, mostly resident but migratory along the northern edge of its range and into warmtemperate areas. The other four species of the genus have limited ranges in the Himalayas, China and southeast Asia. Its earliest occurrence in Britain is in the last glaciation, presumably in interstadial conditions, in Derbyshire. As a woodland bird it could have been widespread through most of the Holocene period. Its numbers and distribution would have been reduced by woodland clearance, and may have been lowest towards the end of the eighteenth century. Since then it would seem to have increased and spread. Originally this was in woodland edge habitats, but beginning in the 1940s, the Bullfinch showed an increase in numbers, accompanied by a tendency to move out of woodland into cultivated areas–and orchard areas in particular–and to nest in sites such as overgrown hedgerows. Its weak territoriality allowed higher concentrations of nests. It also increasingly began to exploit suburban and urban areas. By the late 1950s and early 1960s, the increase and shift was causing problems in fruit-growing areas because of the amount of buds eaten. The killing of large numbers has been permitted since then.

It has been suggested that this spread to more open spaces has been correlated with the decrease or absence of the Sparrowhawk in many areas. In the 1970s the Bullfinch began to spread noticeably in the conifer plantations in Scotland, but sample censuses show a general decline from the mid 1970s to mid 1980s in populations outside woodland, with only a slight recent reverse of this. The population in 1972 was calculated at about 600,000 pairs, but has fallen since.

It is widely distributed throughout the British Isles at present, but absent from upland areas, and from most of the extreme north of Scotland and the north-west extremities of Ireland. It is absent from Shetland Orkney, the Outer Hebrides, Isle of Man and the Scillies. The overall winter distribution is very similar to that in summer, although there is considerable local movement of birds in response to available food supplies.

Chaffinch *Fringilla coelebs*

This is the commonest bird in Britain, or rather it was, until toxic agricultural chemicals came along. For much of the year it is soberly inconspicuous in spite of the many colours in its plumage, feeding mainly on the ground and mixing small hops with a short-stepped and slightly swaggering walk. It is only when it takes flight, with soft *tsup* calls, that the bold patterning of white wing-bars and white outer tail feathers becomes apparent. It forms small, sociable flocks feeding on seeds and insects, often with other birds.

In spring the male becomes territorially aggressive, showing the chestnut-pink breast from a high perch and repeating a brief and vigorous song-phrase, with limited variation but immediately recognisable. It consists of a series of sharp and rapidly repeated notes, quickening to a rattle and finishing with a flourish. A monotonous *yeap* call is sometimes given instead. It is a bird of open woodland and woodland edge, that has spread to hedgerow and scrub, and for which even a few sparse and scattered small trees will serve as a wood. After breeding, it tends to form small feeding flocks near its home territory. The larger flocks that feed in open fields and use large roosts are continental birds wintering in Britain.

It occurs through western Eurasia, in boreal to warmtemperate zones, resident through much of Europe but migrating from the north-east to the warm-temperate zone and the temperate west of Europe. Its bones are often impossible to separate from those of the Brambling; early records which might be of either bird are known from the latter part of the last glaciation, presumably in interstadial conditions, in Derbyshire, and in the early Holocene in south Wales. The first definite Chaffinch record in Britain would appear to be by Aldhelm of Malmesbury in about 685.

As a woodland and woodland edge species, it must have been numerous and widespread from early on; and with its ability to use even small and isolated trees (assuming this to have been a character of its early behaviour) it could have survived well through most of the woodland clearing period, becoming a bird of manmodified areas where trees occurred. During the warmer period of the first half of this century the Chaffinch's range extended further north in Scandinavia, while the Brambling retreated. The recent nesting of Bramblings in northern Britain presumably indicates that a retreat is in progress.

During the late 1950s and early 1960s there was a widespread and significant decrease in the number of birds. This was most apparent in the south-east. It coincided with the use of toxic chemicals for seeddressing, and in earlier occurrences the Chaffinch was a species notably affected. In addition, there was a widespread use of toxic insecticides. These badly affected a bird which eats a lot of insects and rears its young entirely on them. From 1962 to 1965 there was a slight increase in numbers, then a stabilisation at a level which seems to be lower than that of the late 1940s and early 1950s.

It has been able to extend its range in northern Scotland with the spread of plantations. It is widespread throughout the British Isles, even in mountain areas, but scarce and local in the Outer Hebrides and Orkney, and sporadic in Shetland. It tends to remain widespread in winter and there is also an influx of Scandinavian and continental birds. The population is estimated at about 7,000,000 pairs, and with the winter influx, this may reach about 30,000,000 birds.

Brambling *Fringilla montifringilla*

For anyone accustomed to the Chaffinch, the Brambling brings the surprise of the slightly unfamiliar. It looks like a Chaffinch but the sober greens, browns and slate of the plumage are replaced by bolder contrasts of orange, black and white. We rarely see it at its best, because the bold simple colouring of the male's plumage is obscured by buff tips to feathers that only fully fray away in spring. In winter the white rump between the black of wings and tail, and the deeper, harsher and more rapid *chucc-chucc-chucc* flight twitter identify it.

It is erratic. A flock of tens or hundreds may suddenly descend in a mantle of flickering colour on a good crop of beechmast, but subsequently not appear again for decades. It is a beechmast specialist, a slightly stouter bill making it more efficient than the Chaffinch in dealing with these. The vagaries of the crop from year to year force it to be nomadic and unpredictable, not just within the British Isles, but right across Europe. In wintering areas it disperses in flocks to feed, gathering at night to form larger communal roosts. As a breeding bird it is more scattered and strongly territorial. The male sings a short warbled song and uses a long-drawn *dweee* note that more often draws attention to it. Nesting is in general like that of the Chaffinch. As a breeder it is a bird of birch and mixed conifer woods, but usually towards the limits of tree growth, either in the far north or at higher altitudes. It rears its young on insects.

Unlike the Chaffinch it occurs right across Europe, and shows a wider range in the east, where it might perhaps have evolved as the Chaffinch's counterpart before spreading north of it. In Europe it is a bird of subartic to cool boreal zones. In winter it is wholly migrant to temperate zones. Its bones resemble those of the Chaffinch, and early occurrences that might refer to either are mentioned under that species. Its first mention in Britain is by Turner in 1544.

It might have bred in Britain in the cooler periods of the Pleistocene and at its end, if it were present in Europe as early on as that. In later times it would have been a migrant or winter visitor. It will feed on various seeds including grain and weed seeds, but could not have found extensive beechwoods in Britain until about 4,000–3,000 years ago. As a winter visitor it occurs through most of the British Isles, but less frequently in the west, and is scarce in Ireland and found mainly in the east. Distribution is local and varies from year to year. It tends to be absent where beech trees do not occur. Numbers in different years have been suggested to vary from about 50,000 to 2,000,000 birds.

In 1920 a pair nested in Sutherlandshire. In the 1970s singing males were noticed in various localities. In 1968–72 in Inverness, and again in 1978 in Hampshire, there was either hybridisation with Chaffinches or attendance at Chaffinch nests. Breeding was suspected in Scotland in 1972 and at two sites in 1977, but it was not until 1979 that a nesting was proved in the Grampians. Breeding has occurred from 1981 onwards, but although it was suspected at a maximum of 10 sites in 1982, no more than two nestings have been proved in any one year. In 1984 there was presumptive evidence for a locality in northern England. These territory occupations and breedings occur in typical types of habitat in birch or mixed woodland.

Twite *Carduelis flavirostris*

This is the northern arctic/alpine linnet, a finch of moorland and exposed shores with short vegetation. In Britain it is mainly a bird of north-west coasts, extending into upland moors in the Scottish mountains and the Pennines. It has a harsher, more nasal call note than the Linnet, and a more jangling and metallic tone to the song. The nest cup is virtually on the ground, tucked into heather, gorse or similar sites, or sometimes in small bushes or among rocks. It feeds on small plant seeds, but sometimes takes grain.

Its breeding range is in the north-west of the British Isles, and coastal Norway, the Caucasus region and the Sino-Tibetan region. It may be a cool upland bird with an original population west into south-west Europe, which became isolated and forced north by the increasing mildness of the Atlantic coastal regions in the Pleistocene past. It is a partial migrant to lower altitudes, with north-west European birds spreading around the southern North Sea and southern Baltic. According to James Fisher, it was first recognised as a British bird in 1562.

With its specialised habitat it may have been more widespread in Pleistocene and very early Holocene times. Subsequently it is likely to have been more restricted but to have experienced little change, and to have been affected only slightly by human activity; climatic variation has probably had the greatest effect on its distribution and population. It may have been at a relatively high level in the cooler fourteenth to nineteenth centuries.

Although it had a single breeding in Devon in 1904 and in north Wales in 1905, its range was reduced in the period of climatic amelioration from the late nineteenth century to about 1950. There has been evidence of some increase and limited spread in the southern Pennine and Peak region in the mid 1960s, and a nest on the north Wales coast; but in southern Scotland it seems to have largely disappeared in the 1950s to 1970s, and to have gone from the southern uplands and the Moray Firth region.

It now occurs through north-west Scotland and the islands, Orkney, Shetland, and a few coastal areas of south-west Scotland. In England it is in the Pennine and Peak regions; and in Ireland around the north and west coasts, with a few pairs in the south-east. The 1972 population was estimated at about 20,000–40,000 pairs. In winter some northern and western coastal populations remain, but there is a small shift of upland birds to nearer coasts, and a strong movement of birds to the east coast of England, with some continuing on to the continent.

Redpoll *Carduelis flammea*

This is a small finch of northern birch scrub, extending south into the British Isles in the cooler, higher parts of the north to produce an endemic population that appears more tolerant of milder conditions. It is a small dark bird, acrobatic in feeding, and usually identified by its undulating flight and loud, metallic *chi chi chi* flight call.

Its primary food for most of the year including the critical winter months is birch seed, which is not available in spring. Then, it turns to a variety of other

Twite

Redpoll

MALE

Siskin

MALE

Linnet

MALE

FEMALE

Brambling

WINTER MALE

SUMMER MALE

D.M.HENRY.

sources, including weed seeds, flower buds and also insects. When numbers are few it nests mainly in birch scrub, but when it is more numerous and disperses more widely, it uses other sites from willow and hawthorn thickets to gorse bushes and fruit bushes. Recently it has also taken to conifer plantations up to 6 metres high.

It breeds in boreal to subarctic zones around the northern hemisphere and in Europe extends to the British Isles, with isolated populations in the central European mountains. It is migrant from the northern half of its range, wintering south to temperate regions. Its earliest mention in Britain appears to be by Willughby and Ray in 1678. However, it is likely to have been numerous in many periods of the Pleistocene in Britain and in the earlier part of the Holocene. The British population has been isolated long enough to be recognised as a small, dark subspecies. With the greater spread of temperate broadleaf trees, it would have retreated further north or uphill. Since birch trees and scrub grow rapidly and are able to survive in the marginal areas of limited use to man, the Redpoll may have survived reasonably well through the historic period.

It showed an increase and dispersal into lowlands in about 1900–10, followed by a decrease and disappearance from many of the lowland areas by the 1920s. This may have been evidence in southern marginal areas of the kind of fluctuations mentioned below. In more recent increases, beginning with one from about 1950 onwards, it has been able to use the widely dispersed conifer plantations in southern areas from East Anglia to Devon and Wales for breeding.

Although winter movement is mainly linked with birch seed crops, the greater part of the population normally migrate into north-west Europe in winter. In some years, there have been large irruptive movements which have dispersed much further. These occurred in the autumns of 1959, 1964 and 1977. The period between may be marked by a large increase in numbers, making up the loss that follows such irruptions, and between 1965 and 1977 there was a four-fold rise in population. In 1978 numbers were very low again. Variations like these make it difficult to identify or evaluate long-terms trends. About 30–70% of the birds may migrate. In a more abundant period in 1972, it was widespread in the British Isles, but absent from most of the southern midlands of England, sparse in the extreme south, and mostly absent from the Outer Hebrides, Orkney and Shetland. The population was estimated then at about 300,000 pairs.

Siskin *Carduelis spinus*
This is the Goldfinch of the conifer woodlands. It is an acrobatic feeder in trees, with a tapering bill, but a little stouter and less long than that of the Goldfinch and better adapted for extracting seeds from small cones. It breeds in conifer woodland, often occurring in social groups, the male having a musical twittering Goldfinch-like song, often finishing with a long harsh note. The ordinary call is a plaintive *tsyzew*. The nest is usually high in a tree.

Its principal source of food is seeds extracted from tree cones, for which its bill and agility are suited, or taken from the ground below. Limited availability forces it to make some seasonal movements. Its main sequence of tree seeds is spruce or pine in spring, birch

in summer, and alder in winter. It has begun to take advantage of seeds of cypresses and other exotic conifers in gardens and parks, and probably moved from these to its more recent habit of feeding on peanuts at bird-tables.

Its range is discontinuous in western and eastern Eurasia. It occurs in boreal to temperate zones, where conifers or mixed woodland are present. In southern and western Europe it is in mountain regions, as it is in the northern British Isles. It migrates from the northern edge of its range and may occur through much of Europe in winter. In Britain its earliest reference is by Chaucer in 1369. It is likely to have been widespread in periods of the Pleistocene, and in the earlier millenia of the Holocene, when pines had a more southerly distribution. Subsequently its range is likely to have shrunk north with them. In recent centuries it would have decreased with the loss of woodland, becoming confined to Scotland and probably least numerous in the seventeenth century.

With the increasing planting of conifers, numbers must have increased from the early nineteenth century onwards; the nineteenth century use of newly-introduced species may have helped, since spruce rather than pine appears to have been its main food. Ireland lost its original conifers in about the sixteenth century, and Siskins may not have colonised or re-colonised it until the late nineteenth century. It recovered much ground generally by colonising maturing plantations, and suffered during periods of extensive felling.

It has spread very rapidly since the 1940s, and although this is attributed to more widespread conifer plantations, a cooler climate might also have been a factor. It spread at first to the larger plantings of East Anglia, the New Forest, Devon and north Wales, but is also present in many other areas. At present it occurs on higher grounds of mainland Scotland, patchily in Ireland in hill areas, in west Wales, and in England in the Pennines, Lakeland, East Anglia, and scattered sites elsewhere. The 1972 population was estimated at about 20,000–40,000 pairs. Linked with the spread, there has been widespread winter occurrence. There is also a big influx of continental birds, and it becomes widespread through the British Isles in winter, although it is sparse in Ireland. Numbers then might be in the order of 150,000–500,000 birds.

Linnet *Carduelis cannabina*
This is a small, stubby-billed finch of open places – commons, moors, stubbles, low hedgerows and dunes. It is sociable, tending to occur and to breed in small colonies. It is the male that usually draws attention to itself, perched on a bush-top and singing a subdued song of slow, varied phrases and notes: some musical, some twanging, and mixed with twitters and trills. Sometimes a number will sing at once, and much of the behaviour seems to take place against a background of small intermittent notes. It feeds on the ground in pairs and small parties, on a wide variety of small seeds. The nests are usually in low bushes. In winter it gathers into small flocks on arable fields, weedy areas and coastal marshes. They are easily disturbed, rising and circling in bouncy flight before settling again with a constant twitter.

It breeds across the western parts of Eurasia in warm boreal to warm-temperate zones, resident in the south of its range and in western Europe, and migrating into these regions in winter from the north-east. Its earliest British records are from towards the end of the Pleistocene, in the latter part of the last glaciation in Devon and Derbyshire. As a bird taking weed seeds in open areas, it is likely to have had a restricted distribution in much of the Holocene, and would have enjoyed an increase in habitat as land was cleared of woodland and cultivated, especially with the early medieval system of fallows.

In the nineteenth century it decreased, possibly because of a greater efficiency in farming and also, like the Goldfinch, from considerable trapping for sale as cage birds. There was some recovery in the earlier part of the present century. From the 1940s onwards, it has lost habitat and has been reduced in numbers through the increasing cultivation of marginal land. It is the first of the finches to be seriously hit by a new, more recent, problem. Most of its food, particularly in winter, consists of weed seeds from cultivated land. From about the 1970s onwards, there has been a greatly increased use throughout agriculture of selective weedkillers which destroy most of the weeds, and their seeds cease to become available.

It is thought to be this which has affected the population. The B.T.O. sample censuses showed that numbers fell, after hard winters, in the early 1960s and 1970s, but rose again. However, since 1975 they have fallen at an increasing rate, by about 45% in ten years. It still has a wide distribution through the British Isles; it is very sporadic in the Hebrides and Shetland, and absent on some mountain areas, and much of north-west Scotland. Its population might now be about 450,000–900,000 pairs.

In winter it tends to flock in low ground, and there is a move away from hilly areas. There is a small migration across to the continent, and possibly a small influx of Scandinavian birds. The winter population might be about 3,000,000 birds.

Serin *Serinus serinus*
NOT IN THE COLOUR PLATE

This small finch of Mediterranean origin is related to the Canary. It is small, slightly smaller than a Redpoll, with forked tail and stubby bill. It is streaky olive-green,

the male showing bright yellow on breast, forehead and around the ear-coverts. Like the Collared Dove, it has spread slowly across Europe and was a long-awaited arrival. In its southern range it has adapted to farmland, vineyards, orchards and gardens, feeding on weed seeds but also taking some buds and insects. It has a soft, rapid trilling flight call, and an exuberant if unmusical song, that is often uttered during a display flight, the male fluttering up and then gliding back to a perch. The nest is usually in a tree, out in a twig fork, but usually sheltered by thick foliage, and may be built in an evergreen.

The natural habitat is in the open woodland of the Mediterranean region. In the nineteenth century, it began to spread to parks, gardens and farm settlements with groves or scattered trees. It began extending its range and by 1875 was in central Europe. By 1925 it had spread through southern and central France and north-east to the southern Baltic. It was assumed that it would rapidly colonise the rest of Europe; but by 1960 it had moved only a little further north-west and still had not colonised the coastal regions of the Channel and North Sea. It is possible that the cooler and moister Atlantic climate does not wholly suit it. In the 1970s, it reached the coast from Cherbourg to southern Denmark and Sweden.

It has an early record in Britain in the warm penultimate interglacial, the Hoxnian, in Kent. In more recent times it would seem to have been a rare vagrant, first recorded in 1852, but with only 30 English records by 1940. There were another 155 by 1974. In 1967 a pair bred in Dorset, and in 1969 in Sussex. Between 1969 and 1977 there were only two suspected breedings in 1977. 1978 had three suspected and one proven in Devon, and one suspected in Worcestershire. There were none in 1979, but from 1980 onwards there was an increase.

By the mid 1980s they appeared to be usually present in Devon and Dorset, with birds occasionally seen from Kent to Suffolk and Norfolk, and in Shropshire. The south coast from Devon to Kent, and in East Anglia seem the most likely areas for long-term settlement. It is not clear at present whether these birds regularly winter, or are behaving as cross-channel migrants.

Studies of Serin

Crossbills

Loxia species

The crossbills have a history of Pleistocene isolation and speciation. The Common Crossbill is a bird of Spruce forest. Its main centre appears to have been further east in the boreal conifer zone of Eurasia. At some time in the past, it also extended into Europe. In a later period, presumably a glaciation, forest became fragmented and crossbill populations were isolated in areas dominated by other conifer species with stouter cones. They evolved larger bills to use in opening these. There is a group of heavy-billed forms on Mediterranean islands. Two past populations become isolated in areas of Scots pines. One, the Scottish Crossbills, were isolated in Britain, later in Scotland, and developed a slightly heavier bill. Another, the Parrot Crossbill of northern Scandinavia, developed one that was heavier still. In later times, the Common Crossbill moved westward into Europe and re-invaded to encounter both these forms, now regarded as separate species.

Common Crossbill *Loxia curvirostra*

Crossbills are the ultimate specialists in feeding among the finches. The horny bill-tips of upper and lower jaw, normal in nestlings, continue to elongate and cross over, producing a bill that appears to be a liability, but is designed to prize apart the overlapping scales of cones while the tongue extracts the seeds. Different bill-sizes are adapted to different cones, and this is a spruce cone specialist. It is a strong-footed acrobatic bird, and a cone is usually nipped off and held down in the foot while the seeds are extracted.

Feeding almost entirely on such seeds, its breeding season is synchronised with them, and nesting begins in late winter, the young being fed on the seeds. The nest is placed high in a pine tree, and young birds are a dark, streaky brown. It is nomadic in search of good crops, and in years of high population and poor seed crops, it disperses irruptively.

It occurs across Eurasia in conifer areas, limiting its distribution in Europe to Scandinavia and to montane areas of the European mainland. Its occurrence in Britain arises from its periodic irruptions. Several late Pleistocene records of crossbills might refer either to this species, or to the Scottish Crossbill that is probably a late Pleistocene derivative of the present species, and are listed under the Scottish Crossbill.

The Common Crossbill may have spread in Europe with the spruce. This shrunk back during the last glaciation, but appears to have had a westward spread about 6,000 years ago, and may not have been widely established in Norway or Sweden until about 3,000 years ago. Irruptions of Common Crossbills into the British Isles may date from this latter period. It may have found little suitable food in southern Britain in earlier times. The account by Matthew Paris of a crossbill invasion at St. Albans in the autumn of 1251 refers to them taking seeds from crab-apples.

With the planting of conifers from the late eighteenth and nineteenth centuries onwards, it was more likely to have found food. It has been recorded breeding in southern England after irruptions since 1815. Such breedings may occur for several years, but with birds diminishing and disappearing. There is some evidence of birds returning to the areas from which they irrupted after several years' absence.

However, after a very large invasion in 1910, breeding populations were established in the scots pine plantations and hedgerow belts of East Anglia, and on the heathlands of the New Forest and Dorset which seem to have persisted, probably reinforced by later irruptions. In recent decades, birds have also begun to appear regularly in the larger areas of planted conifers, mainly spruce, from Scotland and hill areas of northern England to Wales and Devon. In recent decades, there were four irruptions in the 1950s, three in the 1960s and subsequent occurrences in 1972, 1983, 1984 and 1985. The population may vary temporarily after a large irruption from less than 500 pairs to many times that number.

Scottish Crossbill *Loxia scotica*
NOT ILLUSTRATED

This is a slightly heavier-billed crossbill, adapted to scots pine as a source of seed, but not as large-billed as the Scandinavian Parrot Crossbill. It is limited largely to the stands of native scots pine, which remain in the highlands as relics of earlier forest. Like the Common Crossbill, it tends to stay up in the foliage of trees, except when it comes down to drink at a pool or puddle, and may be silent when feeding. Its most obvious character, unless one glimpses an orange or scarlet male, is the loud, incisive *chip* call used in flight and in moments of excitement.

It is likely to have been more widespread in pine woodlands in the early Holocene, probably through most of the British Isles. Since it was isolated for long enough to differentiate, it is possible that the late Pleistocene specimens in the end of the penultimate glaciation, the Wolstonian, in Devon, and the last glaciation, the Devensian, in Herefordshire, may be referred to this bird. It is now limited to an area of highland Scotland around the Spey Valley and Moray Firth, limited by mature scots pine distribution. Since recent conifer plantations are usually of spruce, they are more likely to be colonised by Common Crossbills. The population has been estimated at about 1,500 birds.

Parrot Crossbill *Loxia pytyopsittacus*
NOT IN THE COLOUR PLATE

This is a slightly larger version of the crossbill with a stouter and deeper bill, and a lower-pitched call note. It occurs in pine woodland from Norway to northern Russia, normally resident but nomadic and feeding on pine seeds, using the larger bill. The seed crop fluctuates less than that of spruce, and there are fewer irruptions, usually involving small numbers of birds. As with the Common Crossbill, birds may remain for a period – and breed – in a suitable locality in the area invaded.

After a larger irruption in autumn 1962, a pair are believed to have bred in Surrey in 1963. In 1982 about 120 birds were recorded in October, and some noted wintering in the Pennines. In 1983 and subsequently, two pairs nested on the north Norfolk coast in a belt of

Common Crossbill

MALE

FEMALE

Corn Bunting

Tree Sparrow

House Sparrow

FEMALE

MALE

D.M.HENRY.

Parrot Crossbill

Scarlet Rosefinch

pines. In theory there is a large amount of mature scots pine, not fully used by Common Crossbills in East Anglia and other parts of the south of Britain, which might sustain a small population of Parrot Crossbills.

Scarlet Rosefinch *Carpodacus erythrinus*
NOT IN THE COLOUR PLATE

This is an eastern finch, spreading west. In spite of its name, most birds seen are slim, sparrowy-looking, streaky-brown birds with spotty breasts. The breeding male has variable bright scarlet on head, breast and rump. It breeds in moist and swampy lowlands with willow, alder and poplar thickets, taking seeds, buds and insects. It is territorial, with a soft or hoarse *duwee* flight call, and a short *sti-fidyi-fidyuee* song phrase. The nest is usually in tall herbage at the base of a shrub.

It is a member of a genus with most species in southern or eastern Eurasia. It has a very wide range through most of Eurasia from Russia eastwards in warm boreal to warm-temperate zones, wintering from India to southern China. Its expansion into western Europe appears to be of fairly recent origin. It began to spread into eastern Europe at the beginning of the century, but its range subsequently contracted. Expansion began again in the early 1930s, extending around the southern Baltic to Finland, Poland, eastern Germany and southern Sweden by the 1950s. It was relatively slow, but by the early 1980s it was into Norway and Denmark and through the eastern half of mainland Europe.

It had been first recorded as a vagrant in Britain in 1869, and in Scotland in 1906. It was mainly an intermittent visitor to northern Scotland in autumn and by the 1960s was annual in small numbers. In theory it retains its old migration route south-east to India. In 1982, a pair bred in the Scottish highlands. In 1983 singing males were present at four localities, and in 1984 birds were present in Scotland and Devon. It may yet become established.

Sparrows
Passeridae

This is a small family of seed-eating birds, very closely related to the Weaverbirds, Ploceidae, and sometimes treated as a subfamily of the latter family. They build domed nests with a side entrance, but some species may tuck the nest into a cavity, when it tends to become a more sketchy structure. The young are fed on insects. Two widespread Eurasian species occur in the British Isles, the House Sparrow and Tree Sparrow.

Tree Sparrow *Passer montanus*
This is a smaller and quieter sparrow that can easily be overlooked, unless one notices the coppery-coloured crown and black patch on a white cheek that are common to both sexes. The call note also has a sharper and different tone. It is a hole-nesting bird that normally uses tree holes, occurring from woodland edge to parkland, and in scattered trees in farmland and similar areas. It will also use holes and crevices in quarries, rocks and buildings if it does not have to compete with the House Sparrow, and even hollow posts, nest-boxes and Sand Martins' holes.

The nests are usually grouped in loose colonies, which may be large and dense if sufficient cavities are available. The numbers locally and the occupation of colonies fluctuates inexplicably, independent of the main population variations. In winter it forms flocks and tends to wander further, often feeding and roosting with other seed-eating birds. It deserts many hill areas in the west, and in Ireland becomes mainly concentrated on the east coast.

It has a large breeding range across Eurasia from warm boreal to warm-temperate zones, and through south-east Asia to Indonesia. The first reference to it in Britain appears to be that of Ray in 1713. It is difficult to guess at its past history in Britain. It appears more temperature-tolerant than the House Sparrow, and considerably less reliant on man, but as a bird largely dependent on weed seeds and taking some grain, it tends to be associated with agricultural land. It would presumably have exploited woodland edge and rocky coastal sites during earlier periods, moving to cultivated areas in later periods as clearing progressed.

It shows the same ability to exploit human settlement that is so ably demonstrated by the House Sparrow in western Eurasia, and replaces it further east. As a slightly smaller and weaker species, it appears to be unable to compete with the House Sparrow in this respect in the west. As a result, it has been pushed into marginal habitats.

It appears to be liable to considerable, but unexplained, fluctuations in population and distribution. In Scotland it seems to have been widely if thinly distributed, and breeding towards the end of the nineteenth century, but to have declined significantly by the 1930s and 1940s. In Ireland it was present although scattered and scarce from 1852 onwards, but had disappeared by 1959–60. In the early part of this century it also seems to have disappeared from most of Wales, and decreased in England generally. It began to increase again from about 1958 onwards, re-colonising almost all of the lost areas in the 1960s.

It is now widely distributed in Britain north to the Scottish lowlands, but largely absent from the Hampshire Basin, most of Devon and Cornwall, the western edge of Wales, and high ground in northern England and Lakeland. It is also absent from most of northern Scotland, sparse up the east coast and on Islay, Skye, Lewis and St Kilda, but otherwise absent from the islands. In Ireland, it occurs in scattered localities around the coast and in the north-east. In a peak period in 1972 the population was estimated at about 250,000 pairs.

However, sample censuses indicate an increasing rate of decline from the 1970s onwards, with a loss of about two-thirds of the population. This is thought to be the result of weed-spraying and changes in farming practices, which have drastically reduced the seeds available to birds: a problem it shares with the Linnet and Corn Bunting, and probably the Goldfinch.

House Sparrow *Passer domesticus*
It is perhaps ironic that our successful urban bird should be a thuggish-looking entrepreneur with a dowdy wife. It appears to owe its success to a willingness to take a chance, combined with an inbuilt mistrust that never allows it to become too confident. Human beings appear to provide it with a secure nest-site and an assured basic food supply, and with them it has spread everywhere. Because of its persistent commensalism with humans in their settlements, it is difficult to envisage its status as an independent wild bird. It would presumably be a finch-like feeder on plant and tree seeds, taking insects when nesting, and living in scrub, woodland edge or rocky outcrops where nest-sites were available.

It sometimes builds well-constructed domed structures in twiggy trees, but more often uses a cavity or crevice on a building. Nests in trees may be well-spaced, but those on houses may be densely crammed into the niches available. It appears prepared to nest in tight colonies and is sociable in most of its behaviour, but fiercely aggressive in defending the possession of a nest-hole. The nest is kept lined and used as a roost throughout the year by resident birds. Young birds tend to form flocks from late summer onwards, often massing in favoured sites such as grain fields, and roosting communally. Local roosts in sheltered sites continue to be used through the winter months.

In addition to seeds it eats buds, flowers and berries of various kinds, and artificial foods such as bread. It has learned to take peanuts from variously constructed holders, and will use these to feed fledged young, without the need to go searching for food. Small young are fed on insects, and plants are assiduously searched for these in early summer.

Its original distribution appears to have been as a resident through western Eurasia, with another sub-species from Arabia to India. Although it has been suggested that it might have dispersed with man as a grain grower, its earliest British records are towards the latter end of the last glaciation in Derbyshire, Herefordshire and Devon. It may have used caves, and also cliffs and rock outcrops, as natural nesting-sites. It would appear to have been associated with human dwellings before the eighth century. It seems likely that at first it would have been a fairly scarce bird of small marginal areas, but would have increased considerably with the spread of farming and settlement.

It was already very common in England and Wales by the eighteenth century. Although also widespread in Scotland north to Shetland by the eighteenth century, it seems to have spread more widely, and increased greatly during the late eighteenth and nineteenth centuries. It spread though some of the western islands in the late nineteenth and early twentieth centuries. Similar increases seem to have occurred in Ireland. Its decrease in many urban areas with the disappearance of the horse seems to have been compensated for by a considerable increase in suburban areas. Most changes have been local. It has been suggested that there has been a steady if slight increase, levelling out by the 1970s, and it has possibly been decreasing slightly since.

It has a wide distribution throughout the British Isles, absent only from a few mountain areas of northern Scotland. Population estimates vary at around 3,500,000–7,000,000 pairs.

Buntings
Emberizidae

This is a large family of seed-eaters, superficially similar to finches and sparrows, but differing in the bill that has a more angled structure, with more slender, curved upper mandible, and stouter lower mandible; and it uses a slightly different seed-cracking technique. Eurasian species are birds of more open and more terrestrial habitats. They build cup nests in low sites. Young birds are fed mainly on insects. Most Eurasian species belong to the genus *Emberiza*, the species of which have diverged to occupy slightly different habitats. Others include two arctic birds: the Lapland Bunting, representative of a genus of terrestrial species with long hind-claws, and the arctic/alpine Snow Bunting. The Corn Bunting seems specialised for steppe-grassland.

Corn Bunting *Miliaria calandra*
This appears to be the dullest, largest and laziest of our buntings. It can fly rapidly and strongly, with an abrupt *quit* flight call, but on its territory tends to fly from one perch to another with a slow fluttering flight, and with its legs dangling as though it were too lazy to pull them up. In winter it feeds in flocks, mainly on arable areas.

Later, males take territories on open, rather bare areas, where they use a few posts, low bushes, or fence and telephone wires from which to sing a monotonous song, in which a few harsh chirps accelerate into a confused metallic jingle. The nest is on the ground in herbage or at the base of a small bush, and in some areas males are polygamous. In any case, they seem mainly to sing and to watch the females nesting.

It is basically a bird of drier, steppe-type grasslands. It occurs in the warm-temperate zone across western Eurasia, but in Europe extends north to the southern shores of the Baltic, to the southern North Sea, and the British Isles north to Shetland. It is mainly resident. In Britain there is evidence of it in the latter part of the last glaciation in Devon and Derbyshire. It might be relevant that drier steppe-type conditions were present in part of the Windermere Interstadial, just before the end of the glaciation.

It is difficult to see that there was much opportunity for it during the Holocene when natural woodland was extensive, but it could have found suitable habitat in cultivated areas, from the Neolithic and Bronze Ages onwards. The medieval and later periods of cultivation, with little woodland and extensive, open and hedgeless fields, would have suited it well. However, it has recently suffered from large fluctuations in population that cannot easily be associated with either climatic or farming factors, although both might be involved.

Widespread decline occurred in the northern and western parts of its range in the British Isles, apparently beginning in the 1930s. By the 1950s it had disappeared from most inland areas of Ireland, and was beginning to be scarce on the coast. By the 1960s it was confined to about half a dozen coastal regions. In Scotland, it began to decrease and disappear on western islands in the 1930s to 1950s. It disappeared from most of Wales between the 1910 and 1950s. In England the decreases were in the south-west, where it has largely disappeared from Devon, and in the west midlands.

By the end of the 1960s it was present in England, but absent from most of the south-west peninsula except the Cornish coast, absent from much of the home counties and inland East Anglia, the Welsh border, and the northern uplands. In Scotland it was present on coasts in the south, more numerous across the lowlands, through eastern coastal lowlands to the Moray Firth, and in the Outer Hebrides, with a few scattered sites on the west and north coasts, and in Orkney and Shetland. Ireland had it in a few coastal areas. The population was estimated at about 30,000 pairs.

Since then, it has suffered a further decline. This may be a combination of colder climate, insecticides on crops killing insects that are needed to feed young, and weedkillers destroying weeds and seeds. From the mid 1970s, its population in sample censuses showed a decrease of about 60% and is still falling. Its reliance on farming could be fatal.

PLATE FORTY-EIGHT

Lapland Bunting *Calcarius lapponicus*

In winter this is a drab, streaky bird of the shores. It calls with a flat, tuneless rattle, in a flight that is strong and swift to cope with the harsh environment, like that of the Snow Bunting but more undulating. On the ground it walks and runs easily and tends to have a crouching stance, hugging the ground and seeking small hollows in which to feed. It takes mainly small seeds. In winter it uses extensive areas of open saltmarsh and nearby rough pasture for feeding.

As a breeding bird in the Arctic it tends to use areas of shrub tundra, drier and with some bushy cover. The male develops the boldy-patterned spring plumage and a more upright swagger to go with it. He has a short but vigorous lark-like song, which he uses from vantage points in his territory, or in a display flight, in which he flies up strongly for about 14 metres and then glides down in a slow spiral, singing repetitions of his song. The nest is tucked into a hollow among ground vegetation and rocks.

It is a circumpolar breeder on the arctic tundra, extending down the mountain ridge of Norway and Sweden. It migrates to temperate areas, but in Europe some birds remain in north-west coastal Europe and around the southern North Sea. Although in theory Greenland birds migrate to North America, and Scandinavian birds south-east to steppe regions in Russia and Siberia, the population that reaches Britain in winter appears to include birds from both Greenland and Scandinavia.

There is an early British record from the latter part of the last glaciation in Devon; otherwise it does not appear to have been listed as a British bird until 1826. It could have nested in Britain in the cooler periods of the Pleistocene. Subsequently it would have occurred as a migrant. The Devon record is outside its present normal wintering area. It normally occurs along the east coast, from Northumberland to Kent, in small numbers on areas of saltmarsh. However, autumn movements may bring large numbers to the north and west of Scotland and Ireland, and the birds occurring in the British Isles appear to be an accidental result of drift, when winds carry migrants off-course. An average winter total of about 100–500 birds has been suggested.

During the late 1970s, a small breeding colony was temporarily established in the extreme north of Scotland. A single breeding was suspected in 1974, then nothing until 1977, when at six sites there were sixteen possible pairs and two proven breedings. In 1978 there were a possible six pairs at three sites, with two proven breedings; and in 1979 fourteen pairs at five sites, with eleven proven breedings. Females outnumbered males generally, and in 1979 one male was believed to have four mates. In 1980 there was only one pair, in 1981 only one bird seen. It is suspected that the birds might have originated from Greenland rather than Scandinavia. In at least one of these years there was also a breeding in the Faeroes.

Lapland Bunting

WINTER MALE

SUMMER MALE

Yellowhammer

MALE

FEMALE

Cirl Bunting

FEMALE

MALE

FEMALE

Reed Bunting

MALE

SUMMER FEMALE

Snow Bunting

SUMMER MALE

WINTER MALE

D.M.H.

Yellowhammer *Emberiza citrinella*

This is a bird whose song we learned as children, the rapid, tuneless repetition of a note, usually terminating in a high and low note: 'just a little bit of bread and no cheese'. An echo of the hungry past, its merits lie in its powers of evocation. I once heard a male Yellowhammer, temporarily incarcerated in a tiny show cage at a winter bird show, raise its head and give a quiet version of the song and its owner, a Welsh miner, said dreamily 'Man! can't you just smell the gorse?' In addition to gorse-grown commons and heaths, it is a bird of hedgerows and scrub, and bracken-covered hillsides. It seems to need fairly dry open space, some taller herbage and a few bushes, trees or just posts. It has soft *twitup* and *twick* flight calls.

In spring, males take up territory, singing from conspicuous perches, the bright head a canary-coloured signal from a distance. Birds will feed together outside the territories. It feeds on the ground, hopping and taking mainly weed seeds and fallen grain. The nest is placed low in a bush, or in the tall herbage bordering it.

It occurs across Eurasia to Lake Baikal, in boreal to temperate zones. It is a migrant from the colder boreal edge of its range to the warm-temperate zone, but is mainly resident. Its only British Pleistocene record is from the latter end of the last glaciation in Devon. As a bird of woodland edge and mixed scrub and open space, it would have found a rather restricted range during the greater part of the Holocene; but would have had increasingly suitable habitats, with woodland clearance and spread of farming. The later enclosure of fields by hedgerows provided suitable song posts and nest-sites; and populations may have been relatively high for the last few centuries. There was slight evidence of a decline at the periphery after the 1950s, in the extreme north of Scotland and north-west of Ireland.

In general, but more particularly in the south-east, there was a more marked decline in the late 1950s and early 1960s. This coincided with a similar decline in the Chaffinch, and presumably for the same reasons: the use of toxic chemicals for seed-dressing affecting birds that fed on fields and took grain, and the widespread use of insecticides affecting species that rear their young on insects often collected among crops, or on field edges. It has also suffered from the massive loss of hedgerows in arable regions of the south-east, and more generally from hard winters. Since a drop in the early 1960s, numbers have risen a little and appear stable, but subjective observation suggests that the population levels at present regarded as normal are considerably lower than those prior to the 1950s.

At present, it occurs throughout most of the British Isles, but is sparse or absent in some mountain areas, particularly in north-west Scotland, where it is also sporadic and local on north and west coasts and islands, and absent from Shetland. The population has been estimated at about 1,000,000 pairs.

Cirl Bunting *Emberiza cirlus*

This appears to be the Yellowhammer's replacement in the Mediterranean region, and has spread north to meet it. Unlike the Yellowhammer, it seems to need warmer slopes and sheltered places, and some trees seem to be essential. It usually feeds on short or sparse grassland or arable, taking mainly seeds or grain. Its soft *zit* call is a little higher-pitched than the Yellowhammer's, and in flight several may be run together to produce a sibilant twitter. The song is a repetitive flat note, a slightly metallic rattle like the latter part of a Lesser Whitethroat's song; or it is sometimes softer and more like a Yellowhammer's, without the two-note finale. Territories are relatively large, and pairs may be widely scattered. The song is usually sung from a high perch within it, sometimes from a tree. The nest is usually built into a tangle of vegetation in a bush or hedgerow, or on a bank.

Although a resident species, it may wander well away from the breeding area in winter, forming small parties and mixing with other seed-eating birds; where it is only present in small numbers, it may be difficult to verify its presence.

It is resident in Europe across the warm-temperate zone, extending north in western Europe to southern England. It was not recognised in Britain until 1830, by Montagu. It requires reasonably warm temperatures and is vulnerable to hard winters. We know nothing of its past history here, and it has even been suggested that it might not have been present until the end of the eighteenth century. One may surmise that numbers would have been low until the late nineteenth century.

It was certainly more widespread in the earlier part of the present century, when it occurred as a scarce breeder north to Cumbria and Yorkshire, and it bred more widely in Wales and the Midlands. From then onwards, it has steadily decreased. By the late 1930s, it was present but diminishing in parts of mid and south Wales, and in parts of Wiltshire and Buckinghamshire. However, at that time it still bred well in Denbigh and Carnarvonshire, western Pembrokeshire, and in more of Herefordshire and Worcestershire.

It suffers badly in hard winters and decreases were recorded after 1962–63, and 1970–71. By the end of the 1960s, there were a few pairs on the Malvern Hills. It was also on the south Chilterns, North and South Downs, Berkshire Downs and Hampshire Basin, Dorset coast and in the south-west, west of a line from Gloucester to Portland Bill. About 350–700 pairs were thought to be involved. By 1982 there were five pairs in Buckinghamshire, two each in Surrey and Hampshire, and more in Somerset and Cornwall, with the main stronghold in coastal south Devon. About 167 pairs were left, 130 of them in Devon. By the mid 1980s there is a continuing small decrease, with only single males noted outside the south-west. Decreases have also occurred in Belgium and north-east France, and the species seems to be contracting at the northern extremes of its range, as a response to gradual climatic change.

Reed Bunting *Emberiza schoeniclus*

This bunting always seems to have an air of quiet anxiety about it. Possibly because it inhabits rather more vegetated habitats than those of other buntings the tail has a contrasting pattern with bold white outer tail feathers; and it is frequently half-spread and flicked, creating a conspicuous signal in the drabness of reed-beds and marshes. This is also an identification mark in winter when, as in all these buntings, the male's conspicuous patterns are concealed by drab edges to the feathers, and the more uniform, brown-streaked plumages can be confusing. The rump colours that might aid species identification cannot always clearly be seen.

The striking head pattern of the male in spring is an

even more conspicuous mark, and he usually displays it by perching on a high stem, a little above the surrounding vegetation. The song is only three or four short, well-spaced notes with a final and more emphatic double note—*well, well, never*—and until one joins them up and detects the rhythm, they may pass unnoticed among other bird calls. The plaintive *tsweep* of alarm is less easily overlooked. The nest is usually well-hidden in low vegetation; often on a raised tussock or thicket.

It occurs as a breeding species across Eurasia, in subarctic to temperate zones. In western Europe it is resident north to south-west Norway and the British Isles, but east of the Adriatic it migrates from most of its northern range to enter in warm-temperate to subtropical regions. Its earliest records in Britain are from the latter part of the last glaciation in Devon and Derbyshire. As a bird of the taller herbage and shrubs of marshland, it is likely to have had an extensive habitat in the often extensive lowland marsh areas during much of the Holocene.

The widespread drainage that occurred from the seventeenth to mid nineteenth centuries, and the smaller-scale drainage occurring on farmland since, must have robbed it of a great deal of suitable habitat and reduced its numbers. It may have been at a relatively low level in the early part of the present century. However, from the 1930s onwards, it has shown an increasing tendency to move into drier habitats—overgrown ditches, hill scrub, hedgerows and young plantations. This has made an increase possible in spite of the loss of wetter areas.

It is mainly resident and is affected by hard winters. These create a periodic fluctuation in numbers. Even allowing for this, it appears to have reached a peak in the mid 1970s, but by 1984 the sample censuses show a halving of this peak figure, and there have been continuing small decreases since. Its 1972 population estimate was about 600,000 pairs, but this must have been considerably lowered.

Its distribution in Britain is still widespread throughout, but patchy in hilly and mountain areas. Although widespread, its actual abundance may only be local, and it is thinly distributed in most of Scotland. It did not colonise Shetland until 1948. In winter it tends to leave hill areas and to move to lowland farmland. Most birds are fairly sedentary, with about 1% migrating, and a small influx from the continent.

Snow Bunting *Plectrophenax nivalis*
Like the Ptarmigan with which it may share a habitat, the nesting Snow Bunting is a bird of late spring snowfields, and the bold black-and-white plumage pattern may be as much for camouflage as for advertisement. However, the bold white wing-patches of the males are important signals in flight, both in summer and winter plumage. In addition the male in territory sings while perched on a conspicuous rock or outcrop, and makes display flights in which it rises steeply and then glides down singing. The song is a variable repetition of short, loud and musical phrases. For most of the British Isles it is a winter bird, the bold pied plumage hidden by buffish feather tips.

The black-and-white wings of the male then become conspicuous, flickering as it rises in strong, fast undulating flight, with the trilled *tirrirrirrip* flight call; it circles over the feeding grounds, skimming in and around low before landing. On the ground it runs and walks easily, but like most birds of very open places tends to move in a half-crouching posture.

Dunes, saltmarsh and shorelines are important winter habitats, but in the north it occurs at many inland sites and on upland grass moors. It inhabits bare, windswept areas, taking small seeds, and on shores will also take sandhoppers and other small invertebrates. Some Scottish birds have learned to scavenge the crumbs and débris around the winter ski-runs. In summer it occurs on a few mountain-top areas of sparse vegetation that provide a tundra-type habitat. The nest is hidden in a rock crevice, and as with other buntings, the young are fed on insects.

Its breeding range is circumpolar in tundra areas, but it may extend south into boreal areas on mountains, as in central Norway and Sweden, and in the Scottish highlands. It winters in cool-temperate zones, and on temperate to boreal coasts. Its early British records are from the latter part of the last glaciation in Derbyshire, Kent, Somerset and Devon. It is likely to have bred widely in the British Isles in colder periods of the Pleistocene. With the advent of the warmer Holocene climate, it would have retreated to its present range.

As a breeding bird of Scottish mountains, its existence was known since the mid eighteenth century. It was more widespread in the cooler past, and evidence shows that up to the end of the nineteenth century and beginning of the present century, in addition to its presence as a breeding bird in the Grampians, there are records for the Shetlands in 1861–1907. It was suspected in Orkney in 1874, breeding on St Kilda in 1913, in Sutherlandshire in the 1880s to 1890s, and southwest to Breadalbane and possibly Cruachan, and even possibly in peaks of southwest Scotland. This is final evidence of something that might have been occurring for a much longer earlier period.

In the 1920s and until the 1950s, its range shrank to the presence of a few birds on the higher Cairngorm mountains. Here there had been a few regular pairs until 1912. Then breeding became sporadic. Between 1933 and 1945 there were three pairs breeding in 1934, but otherwise only odd males in four other years. Birds wintering in the British Isles appear to come from Greenland and Scandinavia, where males are mostly white-rumped, and more rarely from Iceland where the mainly resident males are black-rumped. The presence of both rump colours at different times in the Cairngorm birds suggests that the individuals that stay in summer may be accidental left-overs from winter flocks, rather than an endemic population.

From 1946 onwards, breeding in the Cairngorms was resumed, with several pairs and additional males. By the late 1960s breeding had spread back to Sutherland and Ross, with intermittent nestings on Ben Nevis. By the early 1980s, the main breeding area was still the Cairngorms, but with odd birds seen as far afield as Cumbria; and there was a general pattern for Scotland of about 5–15 pairs annually, and around 20 in 1975 and 1979.

In winter its main concentration is along the east coasts, from Shetland to Kent, with some around Lancashire in the west, in the Outer Hebrides, and scattered on the west Scottish coast. It is present at many inland sites in Scotland, and on some upland areas of northern England. In Ireland it is mainly in the north-east. Sites chosen seem to be mainly low sandy shores, or damp uplands where seeds of rushes or moorland grasses are available. There appears to be strong fidelity to certain favoured localities. Greenland and Iceland birds provide the majority of overwinterers, with a coastal passage of Scandinavian birds in the south-east. Numbers vary considerably with weather. What was regarded as a low estimate in the mid 1980s was in the order of 10,000–15,000 birds.

Selected bibliography

BAXTER, E. V. and RINTOUL, L. J., 1953, *The birds of Scotland.* 2 vols, 352 & 763pp. Oliver and Boyd: Edinburgh.

FISHER, J., 1966, *The Shell Bird Book.* 344pp. Ebury Press: London.

HARRISON, C., 1982, *Atlas of the birds of the Western Palaearctic.* 322pp. Collins: London.

LACK, P., 1986, *Ed. Atlas of wintering birds in Britain and Ireland.* 444pp. Poyser: Calton.

PARSLOW, J., 1973, *Breeding birds of Britain and Ireland; a historical survey.* 272pp. Poyser: Berkhamsted.

SHARROCK, J. T. R., 1976, *Ed. Atlas of breeding birds of Britain and Ireland.* 477pp. B.T.O. & I.W.C.: Tring.

SIMMS, E., 1971, *Woodland Birds.* 391pp. Collins: London.

SUTCLIFFE, A. J. 1985. *On the track of Ice Age mammals.* 224pp. B.M.(N.H.): London.

THOM, V. M. 1986. *Birds in Scotland.* 382pp. Poyser: Calton.

Index

Bold figures represent illustrations

221